DATE DUE

DEMCO 38-296

Vital Statistics
on American Politics

Vital Statistics on American Politics 1997–1998

Harold W. Stanley
University of Rochester

Richard G. Niemi
University of Rochester

Congressional Quarterly Inc.
Washington, D.C.

Printed in the United States of America.

Library of Congress Cataloging-in-Publication Data

Stanley, Harold W. (Harold Watkins)
    Vital statistics on American politics, 1997–1998 / Harold W.
Stanley, Richard G. Niemi -- [6th ed.]
        p.   cm.
    Includes bibliographical references and index.
    ISBN 1-56802-374-X
    1. United States--Politics and government--Statistics.   I. Niemi,
Richard G.   II. Title.
JK274.S74   1997
320.973'021--dc21
                                            97-38950

Contents

Tables and Figures

Chapter 3   Public Opinion and Voting

Chapter 6   Presidency and Executive Branch

Chapter 7   The Judiciary

Acknowledgments

In preparing the 1997–1998 edition of this book, we owe a great deal to those who have helped us in the past. Each edition presents its own problems and challenges, but it is clear that we continue to draw on the efforts of those who have worked on the earlier editions; they are thanked in the previous acknowledgments. For this edition, Alex Garnes, Kerri-Ann Kiniorski, Marc Romer, and Venkat Varadachary shared the workload—the library searches, phone calls, faxes, reminders, and other efforts that go into updating our many tables and figures.

Several individuals provided assistance with specific tables or figures. Special contributions to this edition were made by Sheldon Goldman, Bruce Jacobs, William Keech, and Tom Smith. At Rush Rhees library, Viki Burns, Catherine Hansen, and the entire reference department staff helped us out many times with respect to numerous tables and figures.

We thank a growing number of colleagues for reviewing the previous editions and for their helpful suggestions about specific tables, sets of tables, and entire chapters.

Our families provided understanding and encouragement on the many nights and weekends when we tracked down, validated, and proofed yet another table and figure.

Congressional Quarterly, as always, has been extremely helpful—especially Shana Wagger, who worked with us throughout the process of reworking the basic format of the book. Kerry Kern did her commendably fine job of copyediting, Talia Greenberg smoothly handled the production process, and Paul Pressau again adeptly handled the typesetting.

Vital Statistics
on American Politics

Introduction

The 1997–1998 volume represents a thoroughly revised edition of *Vital Statistics on American Politics*. We reorganized the chapters and reordered the tables so that the volume would be more useful to reference librarians and to political science researchers and students. That alone made preparation of this edition an adventure. But changes in data availability made it even more so. Surprisingly, in some ways, data are getting harder to come by. One might think that desktop publishing, and especially increased use of the Internet, would make data more readily available and more easily retrievable. Sometimes that happens. A good example is certain information collected by the Census Bureau. One can now "go on-line" and find up-to-the-minute estimates of the U.S. population—and watch those estimates change one minute after another. But it is not always easier.

For one thing, collection and dissemination of data seem to have been given a low priority when downsizing occurred. The effect is that some data are reported later than in the past or not reported at all. An example of a delay is the Census Bureau's biannual report on *Voting and Registration in the Election of 19xx*. As of September 1997, 1994 was the most recent year available from the census web site (see Table 1-1). In the past, this report was available in the summer after a presidential or congressional election; as of this writing, it appears as if the volume for the 1996 election will not appear until, perhaps, the end of 1997. An example of delay and some reduction in material reported is *Significant Features of Fiscal Federalism*. The group that had produced this volume was disbanded; a new volume has been promised for later but with some previous tables not appearing.

Appearance on the Internet is, in itself, a mixed blessing. In updating time series, one would ideally like to be able to find a duplicate of a previous source with an additional year or two newly appended. When material is moved to the Internet, however, the format is most often changed. It becomes impossible to "thumb through" a volume looking for familiar tables, explanatory notes, or elaborating commentary. Moreover, special software—readily available, but adding another step nonetheless—is sometimes required before one can access the information.

Despite these problems, we have persisted in our effort to provide readers intent on understanding and keeping up with American politics with an aid that is broad in coverage and committed to an over-time perspective. The text, along with the Guide to References for Political Statistics (which now contains suggestions for Internet use), can serve as a fundamental reference volume for those who wish to keep informed about the American political scene.

The volume covers a wide range of topics as we seek to provide numbers that count in American politics. In addition to such standard subjects as elections, Congress, the presidency, and the judiciary, the book provides information on the media; campaign finances; foreign, social, and economic policy; and a variety of issues related to state and local government. Coverage is not limited to "hard" data such as votes cast and offices won; rankings of public officials' reputations, content analyses of media coverage, and public opinion data about policy issues are included. The information ranges from simple lists to compilations of outcomes based on implicit analytical concerns. A historical perspective is maintained throughout; depending upon available data, the longest possible time periods are covered, even with public opinion data. The sources of material range from the findable to the fugitive: reference volumes, government publications, political science journals, monographs, the Internet, and press releases, among others.

The quantity and quality of statistical information have grown enormously in recent years, and this trend has yet to peak. The Internet potentially makes data overload just a click away. But statistics have a bad image. Even the numerically innocent can retort that "there're lies, damn lies, and statistics" and that "figures don't lie but liars can figure." But anyone seeking to understand politics—past, present, or future—would be ill-advised to take refuge in such skepticism. Increasingly, both public debates and political analyses contain points couched in or accompanied by statistics. Democracy turns in part on the ability of an informed public to follow such debates and analyses. Now more than ever, understanding politics requires an ability to comprehend numerical data and the assumptions behind them.

Although data are more essential and more readily available, the interpretive skills are all too often lacking. Unless one knows how to read them, tables and figures can be less than useful; they can be intimidating, incomprehensible, and boring. Yet properly understood, tables and figures can be a resource of considerable value and, surprisingly to many students, even intelligible and interesting.

This volume will not teach statistical methods, but it will foster a greater familiarity with the appropriate cautions about reading too much or too little into tables and figures. This introduction, the chapter introductions, and the guide are all intended to enhance the reader's understanding of how to make better use of tabular information. They are designed to help the reader to extract the maximum amount of information from tables, to understand the level of accuracy in tabular information as well as the various sources and kinds of inaccuracies, and to find additional information, including up-to-date information that must be found in serial publications rather than books.

Some readers, particularly students who are accustomed to working with numbers as they appear in textbooks, are sometimes frustrated, perhaps even mystified, when confronted with whole tables of numbers—not to mention a whole book of tables and figures. An important point of departure for these readers is to realize that this book is based principally on simple numerical data, not on the results of complicated statistical manipulations. The fanciest statistics presented are averages or medians. Regression coefficients, chi-squares, and the like can be revealing and useful, and increasingly political science has become methodologically sophisticated so that many journal articles are opaque to those without the ability to cope with advanced statistics. But this book fills a more fundamental need for a single volume encompassing a broad range of data about American politics and as such should be useful to the methodologically skilled and unskilled alike.

The figures and tables are easy to read. Many are merely lists, but useful lists. They are often lengthy because they may cover as many as two hundred years. Long historical stretches mean change, and that creates some complexities, as, for example, when the names of the dominant parties change so that going back in time introduces unfamiliar labels. Footnotes to the tables and figures contain the necessary explanations as well as important qualifications and details; they must be read to understand the table or figure content. Following conventional practice, large numbers are sometimes expressed in units of thousands or millions to enhance readability. This, too, can lead to minor problems for readers unaccustomed to reading tabular material, but with a bit of practice any such difficulties should be overcome. In general, a little care and caution in reading and interpreting numbers is all that is required.

The Accuracy of Published Data

Errors in Data

The material selected for this volume is intended to be the most accurate, up-to-date information possible from the most reputable sources available. But anyone who has used statistical information realizes that it is almost never completely error free. This is inevitably true here as well. Consider, for example, Tables 11-4 and 11-5. Both are taken from the same governmental publication, seventy pages apart. The figures reported for total outlays, which appear in both tables, typically match. For example, the $332.3 billion total outlays for 1975 noted in Table 11-4 appears identically in Table 11-5. Similarly, the total outlays for the other years match almost perfectly. Yet inexplicably, the figures for national defense never quite match, differing by as little as $.2 billion and as much as $1.1 billion.

Why do such discrepancies and other kinds of errors (or what appear to be errors) occur? The answer varies.

Rounding.   Sometimes what appears to be an error is simply a matter of rounding. For example, 20.2 plus 20.4 equals 41 if one adds and then rounds, but equals 40 if one rounds and then adds. Almost certainly this explains why the 1960 federal and state and local expenditures in Table 10-11 (24,957 and 27,337) do not add up exactly to the total shown (summing to 52,294 rather than 52,293). A similar sort of "error" occurs when percentages sum to 99.8 or 100.2 rather than to 100 plus or minus .1 percent.

Exact Date of Data Collection.   Accurate interpretation of data depends on knowing the precise date of collection and the period covered. Sometimes this is obvious. For example, the unemployment rate "at the end of the year" may differ if the phrase means the average of the November and December figures rather than the December figure alone. The time factor can be more subtle—for example, if a U.S. senator-elect dies and someone from the other party is appointed to fill the seat, the number of Democrats and Republicans elected will differ slightly from the number of Democrats and Republicans who actually take office a few months later. Even seemingly similar time spans sometimes conceal important differences. Dollar amounts for given years are likely to differ if one uses calendar years rather than fiscal years.

The date of data collection is important from another perspective as well. Data are often updated, and one needs to know whether one is dealing with the "original" or the "revised" figures. Sometimes data providers make it clear that initial figures are subject to change (as when the government reports preliminary economic statistics), and they will label revised statistics as such. But not always. We have found numerous instances in which data are revised—and not only for the most recent period. It is always a good idea to check the latest publication of a time series to see if there have been changes to previously reported information.

Handling of "Minor" Categories.   "Minor" categories may be uncounted, ignored, or dropped for analytical reasons. Often, for example, votes are given only for the candidates of the two major parties. The small number of votes for the Socialist, Libertarian, and Prohibition candidates, not to mention the stray ballots cast for Mickey Mouse or "none of the above," are unreported or lumped together under "other." Thus a vote may be correctly reported as 42.7 percent (of the total vote) and just as correctly reported as 42.9 percent (of the two-party vote). Occasionally minor categories create more complicated problems. For example, in New York State the same candidate may be nominated by two parties, such as the Democratic party and the Liberal party. The percentage of Democratic votes then differs from the percentage of votes received by the Democratic candidate.

A similar problem occurs in the reporting of survey data. In any large survey, in response to almost every question, there is a small number of respondents who give "odd-ball" responses, refuse to answer, say that they do not know, or from whom a response is simply not ascertained. Depending on how these responses are handled—often, but not always, they are eliminated before any further percentaging is done—simple distributions of responses can vary up to a few percentage points or more. "Don't know" responses are especially problematic. It is sometimes important to know how many individuals are uncertain of their response, so we include them in our tables (Table 3-14 through Table 3-22). Tabulations of the same items with these responses removed will differ by varying, unknown amounts.

Changes in Measurement Techniques.   Changes in the way measurements are made can produce different figures and can lead to time series that are not fully comparable. Though the two categories sometimes meld together, we might distinguish between: (a) changes in operationalization, and (b) changes in conceptualization.

A change in *operationalization* occurs when the underlying idea remains the same but there is a change in the precise way in which the measurement is carried out. A classic example occurs in survey research, in trying to measure concepts such as "political efficacy" and "political trust" or even such concepts as "support for gun control." Researchers at different times may define the concept in the same way but believe that they can "improve" on previous measures by changing the specific questions used to determine a person's efficacy, trust, or support. A consequence of doing so may be that we cannot measure change in public opinion because the new results are not truly comparable to those of earlier polls. Sometimes such changes are forced on reluctant researchers. For example, the "market basket" of items in the Consumer Price Index (Table 11-2) has changed over time. Fountain pens or carbon paper might have been reasonable items to include in the 1950s, but not in the 1990s; technological progress means some items could hardly have been included until recently.

A change in conceptualization occurs when researchers develop a new understanding of what is meant by some idea. A good example comes from the Current Population Survey (CPS), in which the Department of Labor tries to determine the status of "discouraged workers"—defined for many years as persons who are not employed, want a job, but are not looking for work because of perceived job market factors. Until recently, the measure of discouraged workers was based on the relatively subjective notion of "desire for work," whereas a new definition relied on more objective measures of recent efforts to search for a job. This altered conceptualization of what it means to be looking for work was one of many changes made in the CPS during the early

1990s. (These changes are described in the *Monthly Labor Review,* September 1993.)

Ad Hoc Problems. All sorts of small discrepancies can occur, with ad hoc explanations for each one. An example that nearly everyone is familiar with involves the counting of presidents. Bill Clinton is usually said to be the forty-second president, but he is only the forty-first individual to hold the office. Grover Cleveland is counted twice because his two terms were separated by four years. So, is the correct number forty-one or forty-two? It depends on precisely what one means. A less obvious problem occurs in counting Supreme Court nominations that failed. In 1987 Douglas Ginsburg was publicly announced as President Ronald Reagan's choice, but his name was withdrawn before it was formally submitted to the Senate. Technically, was he nominated? This kind of subtlety is exacerbated when we deal with events of the distant past. It would be easy, for example, to think that the two listings of the nomination of Edward King by President John Tyler are a typographical error. In fact, King was nominated twice, and the nomination was twice withdrawn in a fight between the president and Congress (Table 7-4).

Solutions to Errors in Data

Awareness that data may contain inaccuracies is no reason to ignore the data; nor is it an excuse to ignore the possible inaccuracies. A consideration of some "solutions" to data errors helps illustrate this point. The solutions, like the problems discussed above, are suggestive rather than exhaustive.

Sometimes errors are relatively obvious and can be easily corrected. Misprints occur, for example. One can encounter references to the 535 members of the House of Representatives when obviously the whole Congress is meant. Checking with alternative or more authoritative sources when mistakes are suspected can help remedy such problems.

Outlandish or illogical numbers should also be checked. A classic example of finding and explaining nonsensical results is the case of two researchers who were not willing to believe data from the 1950 census showing "a surprising number of widowed fourteen-year-old boys and, equally surprising, a decrease in the number of widowed teenage males at older ages."[1] They wrote a "detective story" about how they traced the problem to systematic errors in the way certain data were entered into the census records.

Another method—one that should always be used—is to check footnotes and accompanying text for exceptions and special comments. Recognize that the problem may not really be error, but misreading. Consider the table on U.S. casualties in Vietnam (Table 9-7). For 1973–1993 the bottom row shows there were no U.S. military forces in Vietnam but 1,118 battle deaths—surely an anomaly. But the note reveals that there were troops in Vietnam for nearly a month at the beginning of this period—the zero indicates the force count as of

December 31, 1973, and U.S. forces were withdrawn on January 27, 1973. In addition, forces dying of wounds incurred earlier or those who were missing and later classified as deceased are also considered battle deaths.

Another solution is what is formally called *sensitivity analysis*. When values are inexact or differ across sources, one needs to ask how sensitive the conclusion is to the precise values used. If the true values differed by some specified amount from the reported values, would the conclusion change? If not, one can be more confident about the conclusion. Similarly, if sources differ, consider the actual values from several sources. If the conclusion to be drawn does not vary with the different values, the discrepancies are only a minor problem. For example, almost any conclusion about social welfare expenditures would be the same whether 1973 expenditures were $213.3 billion (Table 10-10) or $212.3 billion (Table 10-12), even though the difference represents what in other contexts would be an astonishing one billion dollars.

In examining over-time data, one way to avoid possible errors is to be sure the data are truly comparable. For one thing, one should check for indications that the data were revised or updated. Preliminary reports sometimes are not directly comparable to initial reports. In addition, one must check that the data were collected uniformly or know what the differences are over time and their probable effects. Occasionally guesses about probable error can be confirmed by formal tests. An excellent example is a study in which both old and new survey questions were asked. Differences that had previously been attributed to changes in the electorate over time were shown to be methodological artifacts.[2]

Sometimes, when changes occur, one can develop new estimates, or incorporate ones that are supplied, for an entire existing time series. Recently, when the Bureau of Economic Analysis undertook a comprehensive revision of the National Income and Product Accounts (NIPA), it published new estimates of the gross domestic product back to 1929, which in turn, affect many other calculations. While frustrating in that older series might have to be replaced entirely by the new numbers, the new data provide a comparable time series for the entire period. Of course, in such situations, one also has to ask which figures should be used; the original calculations are arguably better if one is asking questions that depend on how people viewed the world at the time the original data were collected.

All data, perhaps especially data over time, should be examined for "outliers." If a series of values, say the percentages of votes for the Republican candidate in a given district, are 52, 56, 49, 85, and 50, the accuracy of the 85 percent must be checked. Is the 85 a transposition of 58? If 85 is the correct number, what is the reason for it? Was the candidate essentially unopposed that year? What conclusion should be drawn if the 85 were omitted?

One should always think carefully about what information is really wanted. There are instances when it is necessary to decide which of two or three sets of equally valid data are most appropriate to answer a given question. We noted, for example, that one might wish to employ only the two-party vote or the vote for all parties, include survey respondents who answer "don't know" or eliminate them, and use contemporary data rather than re-estimates made years later.

Finally, after taking all reasonable steps to be sure the data are as good as can be obtained and that they address the question at hand, one should indicate known errors. It is better to point out that there is some question about certain figures than to pretend that they are perfect. If a loftier reason does not come to mind, being straightforward about inaccuracies at least prevents readers from lobbing them back as if the author were too ignorant to notice the problems.

Obtaining Additional Material

This book provides essential figures and tables, but the coverage is far from exhaustive. Many readers may want data with a slightly different twist or of another sort altogether. The Guide to References for Political Statistics should help orient readers who seek information beyond that contained here. In addition, the sources given for the tables and figures in this book should also be considered in such searches.

Data on current events can be found in newspapers, weekly news magazines, the *Congressional Quarterly Weekly Report,* and the *National Journal.* Indexes for the *Weekly Report, National Journal,* and for major newspapers are a valuable guide. The *National Newspaper Index, Newsbank, Nexis,* and the *National Magazine Index* cover many sources.

Readers need to appreciate how useful reference librarians are in the quest for information. Librarians for government document collections are also invaluable resources. Interlibrary loans can help secure less readily available volumes, although principal reference works and current material seldom circulate in this fashion.

For some material, one may need to contact organizations that compile or disseminate the data. Various directories are available—of party organizations, interest groups, associations, research institutions, and state agencies. At the federal level, Congressional Quarterly's *Washington Information Directory* is a valuable guide to potential sources. The Council of State Governments, with directories such as *State Administrative Officials Classified by Functions* and *State Elective Officials and the Legislatures,* provides a similar service at the state level. (See also the references cited in the introduction to Chapter 8.)

Data and texts are becoming increasingly available in machine-readable form. Several commercial vendors offer on-line data services. *Nexis* provides newspaper and magazine articles in electronic form. Some government agencies also offer such access. The Internet has increasingly offered access to data holdings. For instance, recent census data in Table 12-1 were among several items obtained through the Internet. While this may make the information widely available, it can also restrict ready access to the computer literate. The Census Bureau seized publication on the Internet as a cost-savings opportunity—some previously published studies would no longer be published or available in conventional form. As personal computers and the Internet proliferate in the years ahead, such opportunities will undoubtedly expand.

For this volume, machine-readable data constituted a valuable source for several tables and figures. Descriptions of available machine-readable data would require another volume. The Inter-university Consortium for Political and Social Research (ICPSR) at the University of Michigan has the largest collection of such data and publishes an annual guide to resources. Most major research universities are members of the consortium. To learn how to obtain data, one should contact the official university representative of the ICPSR.

With recent changes in technology, the Internet warrants special mention. Because of the tremendous growth of sites on the world wide web, the appearance and disappearance of useful sites, and the availability of powerful search engines, it would be pointless (and probably impossible) to try to develop anything like a comprehensive list. Nonetheless, the Guide to References lists a number of sites that may be of special interest in searching for political statistics.

These hints are merely starting suggestions for those who wish to go beyond this volume to track down particular pieces of information. We hope the reader will find the extensive coverage in this obviously nonexhaustive volume to be convenient and valuable.

Notes

1. Ansley J. Coale and Frederick F. Stephan, "The Case of the Indians and the Teen-Age Widows," *Journal of American Statistical Association* 57 (1962): 338.
2. John L. Sullivan, James E. Pierson, and George E. Marcus, "Ideological Constraint in the Mass Public: A Methodological Critique and Some New Findings," *American Journal of Political Science* 22 (1978): 233–249.

1

Elections and Political Parties

- **Turnout**
- **Political Parties**
- **Election Results (president, Congress, and state)**
- **Minority Elected Officials**
- **Presidential Nominations**
- **Districting**
- **Voting Rights**
- **Term Limits**

Elections and campaigns provide an abundance of numbers. Indeed, if asked for examples of political statistics, most people would think first of election results. Not only are there a great many electoral statistics, but they extend back to the early years of the country. Here, for example, data are provided on voter turnout (Figures 1-1 and 1-2 and Table 1-1) and on presidential (Table 1-6) and congressional (Table 1-9) election results going back to 1788. Results abound, as well, because of the federal system in the United States and because of the nature of our party system. Thus, the most recent results for elections to the governorships and to the state legislatures (Table 1-5) are provided, as well as information on primaries (Tables 1-22 through 1-25 and 1-28).

In part because there are so many results, some form of summarization is needed. Typically, such summaries are in partisan terms, as in the contrast between a party's share of the vote won and the share of House seats gained (Table 1-11). Wins by the major parties are presented in a variety of ways, but sometimes such results need to be broken down further. Reporting results by region (Table 1-3) or by state (Tables 1-2, 1-4, and 1-8) is frequently informative. In addition, historians and political scientists often report election results by so-called party systems separated by periods of "realignment"—fundamental shifts in support for parties and the coalitions supporting them. Scholarly consensus holds that such realignments occurred in the 1850s, 1890s, between 1928 and 1932, and probably in the 1960s;[1] these categories are freely utilized in the reporting for this analysis (Tables 1-3, 1-7, and 1-10).

There is particular interest in the current period. Available data document recent trends in campaigns and elections: the decline in presidential voter turnout after 1960 (Figure 1-1), the electoral advantages of incumbency (Table 1-17), the increasingly long quests (until 1992) for the presidential nomination (Figure 1-4), the greater emphasis on primaries (Tables 1-22 and 1-23), the growing contributions from political action committees (Table 2-16), and the expense of political campaigns (Tables 2-4 through 2-6 and 2-7).

Besides the arsenal of statistics reporting and summarizing election results by party, other characteristics concerning the individuals elected to office are of interest. Information is included on the election of African Americans, Hispanics, and women (Tables 1-19 through 1-21) and on the districts they come from (Table 1-18). Political scientists and others also find it useful to tabulate numbers of districts in which the vote for president and Congress goes to different parties (Table 1-12), to determine individual and partisan turnover rates for members of Congress (Tables 1-13, 1-14, 1-16, and 1-17), and to document the regular pattern of losses by the president's party at midterm elections (Table 1-15).

To interpret these election results, it is often useful to have auxiliary information. One helpful item is a list of political parties that have competed in elections at various times in our history (Figure 1-3). The location and size of presidential nominating conventions (Table 1-26) are also provided, as well as information about the types of delegates who have attended them (Table 1-27). Relevant to the election of minorities is information on legislative districts (Table 1-29) and application of the Voting Rights Act (Table 1-30). Of recent interest is information on which states have passed term limits and the length of the limits they have imposed (Table 1-31).

Despite this volume of data there are some gaps, which impose limits on what is known about campaigns, elections, and parties. The lack of survey data on realignments prior to the 1930s, for example, is troublesome because it robs researchers of helpful historical comparisons. Only recently has much data become available on campaign finances (see Chapter 2). Nonetheless, in the area of campaigns and elections, more than anywhere, there is almost an embarrassment of riches.

Notes

1. John Aldrich and Richard G. Niemi, "The Sixth American Party System: Electoral Change, 1952–1992," in *Broken Contract? Changing Relationships Between Americans and Their Government,* ed. Stephen Craig (Boulder, Colo.: Westview, 1996).

Figure 1-1   Voter Turnout, Presidential and Midterm Elections, 1789–1996

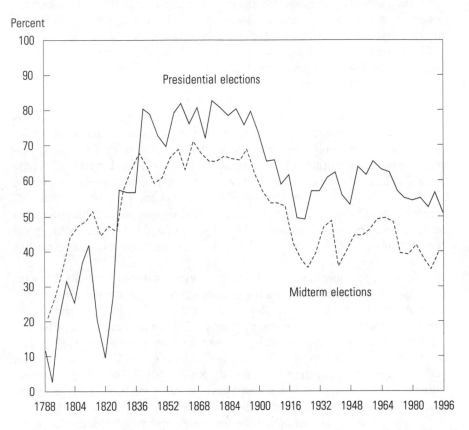

Note: Turnout calculations based on citizen voting-age population in 1924 and later; prior to 1924 the eligible voting-age population reflects various state restrictions as to citizenship, race, and sex.

Sources: 1790–1986: Walter Dean Burnham, "The Turnout Problem," in *Elections American Style,* ed. A. James Reichley (Washington, D.C.: Brookings, 1987), 113–114; 1988–1996: Walter Dean Burnham, personal communication.

Figure 1-2   Voter Turnout, Presidential Elections, South and Nonsouth, 1800–1996

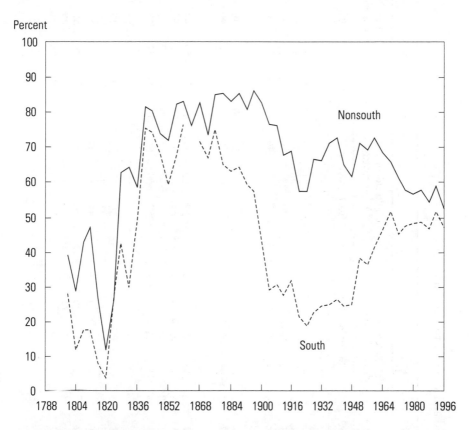

Percent

Note: Turnout calculations based on citizen voting-age population in 1924 and later; prior to 1924 the eligible voting-age population reflects various state restrictions as to citizenship, race, and sex.

Sources: 1800–1984: Walter Dean Burnham, "The Turnout Problem," in *Elections American Style,* ed. A. James Reichley (Washington, D.C.: Brookings, 1987), 113–114; 1988–1996: Walter Dean Burnham, personal communication.

Table 1-1 Voting-Age Population Registered and Voting, Cross-Sections, 1976–1994 (percent)

| | Percentage reporting they registered | | | | | | | | | | Percentage reporting they voted | | | | | | | | | |
| | Presidential election years | | | | | Congressional election years | | | | | Presidential election years | | | | | Congressional election years | | | | |
	1976	1980	1984	1988	1992	1978	1982	1986	1990	1994	1976	1980	1984	1988	1992	1978	1982	1986	1990	1994
Race/ethnicity																				
White	68	68	70	68	70	64	66	65	64	64	61	61	61	59	64	47	50	47	47	47
Black	59	60	66	65	64	57	59	64	59	58	49	51	56	52	54	37	43	43	39	37
Hispanic origin[a]	38	36	40	36	35	33	35	36	32	30	32	30	33	29	29	24	25	24	21	19
Hispanic citizen[a]	51	54	59	57	59	48	52	54	52	53	43	44	48	46	48	34	37	36	34	34
Sex																				
Male	67	67	67	65	67	63	64	63	61	61	60	59	59	56	60	47	49	46	45	44
Female	66	67	69	68	69	63	64	65	63	63	59	59	61	58	62	45	48	46	45	45
Region[b]																				
Northeast	66	65	67	65	67	62	63	62	61	61	60	59	60	57	61	48	50	44	45	45
Midwest	72	74	75	73	75	68	71	71	68	69	65	66	66	63	67	51	55	50	49	49
South	68	64	64	66	67	60	62	63	61	61	55	56	57	55	59	40	42	43	42	41
West	63	63	65	63	64	59	61	61	58	58	58	57	59	56	59	48	51	48	45	46
Age																				
18–20	47	45	47	45	48	35	35	35	35	37	38	36	37	33	38	20	20	19	18	17
21–24	55	53	54	51	55	45	48	47	43	46	46	43	44	38	46	26	28	24	22	22
25–34	62	62	63	58	61	56	57	56	52	52	55	55	55	48	53	38	40	35	34	32
35–44	70	71	71	69	69	67	68	68	66	63	63	64	64	61	64	50	52	49	48	46
45–64	76	76	77	76	75	74	76	75	71	71	69	69	70	68	70	59	62	59	56	56
65 and older	71	75	77	78	78	73	75	77	80	76	62	65	68	69	70	56	60	61	66	61

Employment																				
Employed	69	69	69	67	70	63	66	64	63	63	62	62	62	58	64	47	50	46	45	45
Unemployed	52	50	54	50	54	44	50	49	45	46	44	41	44	39	46	27	34	30	28	28
Not in labor force	65	66	68	67	67	63	64	66	63	62	57	57	59	57	59	46	49	48	47	45
Education (years)																				
8 or less	54	53	53	48	44	53	52	51	44	40	44	43	43	37	35	35	36	33	28	23
1–3 of high school	56	55	55	53	50	53	53	52	48	45	47	46	44	41	41	35	38	34	31	27
4 of high school	67	66	67	65	65	62	63	63	60	59	59	59	59	55	58	45	47	44	42	40
1–3 of college	75	74	76	74	75	69	70	70	69	68	68	67	68	65	69	52	53	50	50	49
4 or more college	84	84	84	83	85	77	78	78	77	76	80	80	79	78	81	64	67	63	63	63
Total	67	67	68	67	68	62	64	64	62	62	59	59	60	57	61	46	49	46	45	45

Note: Figures for 1996 should be published in late 1997 and may be available at *http://www.census.gov.* Data for earlier years can be found in previous editions of *Vital Statistics on American Politics.*

[a] Persons of Hispanic origin may be of any race.
[b] For composition of regions, see Table A-1.

Sources: U.S. Bureau of the Census, Current Population Reports, *Voting and Registration in the Election of November 1976* (Washington, D.C.: U.S. Government Printing Office, 1993), Series P-20, no. 322, 11–12, 14–21, 57, 61; *November 1978*, no. 344, 8, 11–19, 60, 65; *November 1980*, no. 370, 10–20, 50, 56; *November 1982*, no. 383, 1–12, 46, 49; *November 1984*, no. 405, 13–24, 59; *November 1986*, no. 414, 11–22, 29, 31; *November 1988*, no. 440, 13–24, 48, 50; *November 1990*, no. 453, 1–2, 4, 13–14, 17; *November 1992*, no. 466, v–vii, 1, 5; "Voter Turnout in November 1994 Election," press release, 8 June 1995, from the November 1994 Current Population Survey on Internet (*http://www.census.gov/org/pop*).

Figure 1-3   American Political Parties Since 1789

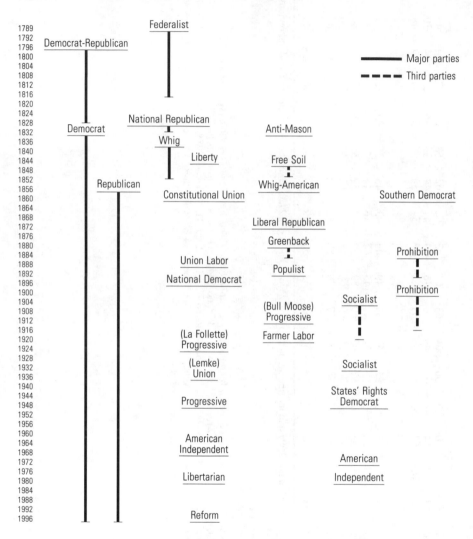

Note: The chart indicates the years in which the presidential candidate of a political party received 1.0 percent or more of the popular vote. Minor parties are not included if the minor party candidate is also the candidate of one of the two major parties (as happened in 1896 when the Populists endorsed Bryan, the Democratic candidate). Party candidates sometimes run under different designations in different states (in 1968 George C. Wallace ran for president under at least ten party labels). In such cases the vote totals for the candidate were aggregated under a single party designation. Sometimes candidates run under no party label as H. Ross Perot did in 1992. (In 1996, Perot ran under the Reform Party label.)

Sources: 1789–1984: Congressional Quarterly, *Congressional Quarterly's Guide to U.S. Elections*, 2d ed. (Washington, D.C.: Congressional Quarterly, 1985), 329–377; 1988–1992: *Congressional Quarterly Weekly Report* (1989), 139; (1993), 191; (1997), 444.

Table 1-2 Party Competition: The Presidency, 1968–1996

				Number of times Republican presidential candidate carried the state			
0-1[a]	2	3	4	5	6	7	8
District of Columbia (3)	Hawaii (4)	Maryland (10)	Arkansas (6)	Connecticut (8)	Alabama (9)	Arizona (8)	Alaska (3)
Minnesota (10)	Massachusetts (12)	New York (33)	Georgia (13)	Delaware (3)	California (54)	Colorado (8)	Idaho (4)
	Rhode Island (4)		Louisiana (9)	Iowa (7)	Florida (25)	Montana (3)	Indiana (12)
	West Virginia (5)		Pennsylvania (23)	Kentucky (8)	Illinois (22)	North Carolina (14)	Kansas (6)
			Washington (11)	Maine (4)	Mississippi (7)	South Carolina (8)	Nebraska (5)
			Wisconsin (11)	Michigan (18)	Nevada (4)		North Dakota (3)
				Missouri (11)	New Hampshire (4)		Oklahoma (8)
				Ohio (21)	New Jersey(15)		South Dakota (3)
				Oregon (7)	New Mexico (5)		Utah (5)
				Tennessee (11)	Texas (32)		Virginia (13)
					Vermont (3)		Wyoming (3)

Note: Number of electoral votes for 1992, 1996, and 2000 are shown in parentheses.

[a] District of Columbia, 0 times; Minnesota, 1 time.

Sources: Compiled by the editors from Richard M. Scammon and Alice V. McGillivray, comps. and eds., *America Votes 16: A Handbook of Contemporary American Election Statistics* (Washington, D.C.: Elections Research Center, Congressional Quarterly, 1985), 31, 33, 35, 37, 41; *Congressional Quarterly Weekly Report* (1988), 3245; (1992), 3552; (1996), 3192.

Table 1-3   Party Competition, by Region, 1860–1996 (percent)

Region/office	1860–1895	1896–1931	1932–1965	1966–1996
New England				
President	85.2	85.5	53.7	54.2
Governor	74.3	85.5	63.1	50.0
U.S. representative	86.8	82.8	60.6	34.6
U.S. senator	a	83.3	65.1	48.3
Middle Atlantic				
President	38.9	88.9	47.2	53.1
Governor	34.9	66.7	51.4	50.0
U.S. representative	59.3	68.9	52.9	41.8
U.S. senator	a	76.9	57.7	56.1
Midwest				
President	77.8	84.4	44.4	70.0
Governor	78.8	78.9	46.9	73.2
U.S. representative	61.1	74.5	57.8	49.5
U.S. senator	a	83.3	50.8	37.0
Plains				
President	88.9	77.8	57.4	83.3
Governor	94.4	71.3	70.4	48.9
U.S. representative	88.6	84.2	76.4	59.7
U.S. senator	a	83.9	79.7	51.8
South				
President	18.4	6.1	15.8	70.5
Governor	21.2	4.2	0.0	42.6
U.S. representative	25.0	7.5	7.2	33.5
U.S. senator	a	0.0	1.5	56.7
Border South				
President	8.6	56.8	22.2	50.0
Governor	22.2	38.6	16.7	33.3
U.S. representative	19.4	36.5	18.7	30.4
U.S. senator	a	42.4	23.4	42.6
Rocky Mountain				
President	73.3	57.8	35.2	85.9
Governor	58.3	51.1	38.5	43.2
U.S. representative	70.0	67.6	30.3	60.4
U.S. senator	a	32.4	20.6	58.6
Pacific Coast				
President	75.0	75.0	37.5	62.5
Governor	47.4	70.8	59.4	43.6
U.S. representative	64.4	85.6	49.0	40.0
U.S. senator	a	73.7	44.4	51.8

Note: Table entries are the percentages of all elections won by Republicans. For composition of regions, see Table 12-3.

[a] Direct election of U.S. senators began after passage of the Seventeenth Amendment in 1913.

Sources: Congressional Quarterly's Guide to U.S. Elections, 3d ed. (Washington, D.C.: Congressional Quarterly, 1994), 1344; *Congressional Quarterly Weekly Report* (1996), 3192, 3226, 3238, 3242.

Table 1-4   Party Competition in the States, 1968–1996

Percentage of Republican wins[a]				
0–20	21–40	41–60	61–80	81–100
Alabama	California	Alaska	Arizona	Idaho
Arkansas	Connecticut	Delaware	Colorado	New
Florida	Maine	Illinois	Indiana	Hampshire
Georgia	Nebraska[b]	Iowa	Kansas	South Dakota
Hawaii	Nevada	Michigan	North Dakota	Wyoming
Kentucky	New Jersey	Montana	Utah	
Louisiana	Oregon	New York		
Maryland	South	Ohio		
Massachusetts	Carolina	Pennsylvania		
Minnesota	Washington	Vermont		
Mississippi	Wisconsin			
Missouri				
New Mexico				
North				
Carolina				
Oklahoma				
Rhode Island				
Tennessee				
Texas				
Virginia				
West Virginia				

[a] The governorship, control of the lower chamber, and control of the upper chamber are figured separately. That is, if in a given year the Republicans won the governorship and control of one chamber, they had 66.7 percent of the wins.
[b] Results are for the governorship only because the legislature is nonpartisan.

Sources: Calculated by the editors. 1968–1986: Republican National Committee, *Republican Almanac, 1987: State Political Profiles* (Washington, D.C.: Republican National Committee, 1987); 1987–1996: *Congressional Quarterly Weekly Report* (1988), 3298; (1990), 3840; (1992), 3599; (1994), 3250; (1996), 3242; National Conference of State Legislatures, unpublished data.

Table 1-5 Partisan Division of Governors and State Legislatures

	Governor			Legislature				
				Upper House		Lower House		
State	Name	Party	Next up for election	Democrats	Republicans	Democrats	Republicans	Next up for election[a]
Alabama	Fob James Jr.	R[b]	1998	22	12	72	33	1998
Alaska	Tony Knowles	D[b]	1998	7	13	16	24	1998
Arizona	Jane Dee Hull	R[b]	1998	12	16	22	38	1998
Arkansas	Mike Huckabee	R[b]	1998	28	6	86	13	1998
California	Pete Wilson	R	1998	24	15[c]	43	37	1998
Colorado	Roy Romer	D	1998	15	20	24	41	1998
Connecticut	John G. Rowland	R[b]	1998	19	17	97	54	1998
Delaware	Thomas R. Carper	D	2000	13	8	14	27	1998
Florida	Lawton Chiles	D	1998	17	23	59	61	1998
Georgia	Zell Miller	D	1998	34	22	106	74	1998
Hawaii	Benjamin J. Cayetano	D	1998	23	2	39	12	1998
Idaho	Phil Batt	R[b]	1998	5	30	11	59	1998
Illinois	Jim Edgar	R	1998	28	31	60	58	1998
Indiana	Frank L. O'Bannon	D	2000	19	31	50	50	1998
Iowa	Terry E. Branstad	R[b]	1998	21	29	48	54	1998
Kansas	Bill Graves	R[b]	1998	13	27	48	77	1998
Kentucky	Paul E. Patton	D[b]	1999	20	18	64	38	1998
Louisiana	Mike Foster	R[b]	1999	25	14	76	28	1999
Maine	Angus King	I[b]	1998	19	15[c]	81	69[c]	1998
Maryland	Parris Glendening	D	1998	32	15	100	41	1998
Massachusetts	William F. Weld	R	1998	34	6	134	25[c]	1998
Michigan	John Engler	R	1998	16	22	58	52	1998

State	Governor	Party	Year					Year
Minnesota	Arne Carlson	R	1998	42	24[c]	70	64	1998
Mississippi	Kirk Fordice	R	1999	34	18	86	33[d]	1999
Missouri	Mel Carnahan	D	2000	19	15	88	75	1998
Montana	Marc Racicot	R	2000	16[e]	34[e]	35[e]	65[e]	1998
Nebraska	Ben Nelson	D	1998					1998
Nevada	Bob Miller	D[b]	1998	9	12	25	17	1998
New Hampshire	Jeanne Shaheen	D[b]	1998	9	15	143	255[f]	1998
New Jersey	Christine Todd Whitman	R[b]	2001	16	24	31	49	1999
New Mexico	Gary E. Johnson	R[b]	1998	25	17	42	28	1998
New York	George E. Pataki	R[b]	1998	26	35	96	52	1998
North Carolina	James B. Hunt Jr.	D	2000	30	20	59	61	1998
North Dakota	Edward T. Schafer	R	2000	19	30	26	72	1998
Ohio	George V. Voinovich	R[b]	1998	12	21	39	60	1998
Oklahoma	Frank Keating	R[b]	1998	33	15	65	36	1998
Oregon	John Kitzhaber	D	1998	10	20	29	31	1998
Pennsylvania	Tom Ridge	R[b]	1998	20	30	99	104	1998
Rhode Island	Lincoln C. Almond	R[b]	1998	41	9	84	16	1998
South Carolina	David Beasley	R	1998	26	20	53	70[c]	1998
South Dakota	William J. Janklow	R[b]	1998	13	22	23	47	1998
Tennessee	Don Sundquist	R[b]	1998	18	15	61	38	1998
Texas	George W. Bush	R	1998	15	16	82	68	1998
Utah	Michael O. Leavitt	R	2000	9	20	20	55	1998
Vermont	Howard Dean	D	1998	17	13	88	58[c]	1998
Virginia	Jim Gilmore	R	2001	19	20	51	48[c]	1999
Washington	Gary Locke	D[b]	2000	23	26	45	53	1998
West Virginia	Cecil H. Underwood	R[b]	2000	25	9	74	26	1998
Wisconsin	Tommy G. Thompson	R[b]	1998	17	16	47	52	1998
Wyoming	Jim Geringer	R[b]	1998	9	21	17	43	1998
Total				999	929	2,887	2,540	

(Notes continue)

Table 1-5 *(Continued)*

Note: Legislatures as of December 18, 1996. Legislative divisions in New Jersey and Virginia reflect the results of 1997 elections. Legislative divisions reflect seated members; some vacancies exist.

a Only some members may be up for reelection.
b Change in party control from previous election.
c One independent.
d Three independents.
e Nebraska's forty-nine member state legislature is nonpartisan and unicameral.
f Two independents.

Sources: Governors: *Congressional Quarterly Weekly Report* (1996), 3242; state legislative divisions: National Conference of State Legislatures; next up for reelection: Council of State Governments, *Book of the States, 1996–1997* (Lexington, Ky: Council of State Governments, 1996), 149–150, 153–154.

Table 1-6 Popular and Electoral Votes for President, 1789–1996

Year	Number of states	Candidates	Electoral vote (number and percent) — (Democrat-Republican)	Electoral vote (number and percent) — (Federalist)	Popular vote (number and percent)
1789[a]	10	*(Federalist)* Washington		69 / 100%	
1792[a]	15	Washington		132 / 98%	
1796[a]	16	*(Federalist)* Adams		71 / 51%	
		(Democrat-Republican) Jefferson	68 / 49%		
1800[a]	16	Adams		65 / 47%	
		Jefferson	73 / 53%		
1804	17	Pinckney		14 / 8%	
		King			
		Jefferson	162 / 92%		
		Clinton			
1808	17	Pinckney		47 / 27%	
		King			
		Madison	122 / 69%		
		Clinton			
1812	18	Clinton (Fusionist)		89 / 41%	
		Ingersoll			
		Madison	128 / 59%		
		Gerry			
1816	19	King		34 / 15%	
		Howard			
		Monroe	183 / 83%		
		Tompkins			
1820	24	*(Independent Democrat-Republican)* Adams		1 / 0%	
		Stockton			
		(Democrat-Republican) Monroe	231 / 98%		
		Tompkins			
1824[b]	24	Adams		84 / 32%	
		Sanford			
		Jackson	99 / 38%		
		Calhoun			

(Table continues)

Table 1-6 (Continued)

Year	Number of states	Candidates (Democrat-Republican)	Candidates (National Republican)	Electoral vote (number and percent) (Democrat-Republican)	Electoral vote (National Republican)	Popular vote (number and percent) (Democrat-Republican)	Popular vote (National Republican)
1828	24	Jackson / Calhoun	Adams / Rush	178 / 68%	83 / 32%	642,553 / 56.1%	500,897 / 43.6%
1832	24	Jackson / Van Buren	Clay / Sergeant	219 / 76%	49 / 17%	701,780 / 54.2%	484,205 / 37.4%
1836	26	*(Democrat)* Van Buren / Johnson	*(Whig)* Harrison / Granger	170 / 58%	73ᶜ / 25%	764,176 / 50.8%	550,816 / 36.6%
1840	26	Van Buren / Johnson	Harrison / Tyler	60 / 20%	234 / 80%	1,128,854 / 46.8%	1,275,390 / 52.9%
1844	26	Polk / Dallas	*(Whig)* Clay / Frelinghuysen	170 / 62%	105 / 38%	1,339,494 / 49.5%	1,300,004 / 48.1%
1848	30	Cass / Butler	Taylor / Fillmore	127 / 44%	163 / 56%	1,223,460 / 42.5%	1,361,393 / 47.3%
1852	31	Pierce / King	Scott / Graham	254 / 86%	42 / 14%	1,607,510 / 50.8%	1,386,942 / 43.9%
1856	31	*(Democrat)* Buchanan / Breckinridge	*(Republican)* Fremont / Dayton	174 / 59%	114 / 39%	1,836,072 / 45.3%	1,342,345 / 33.1%
1860	33	Douglas / Johnson	Lincoln / Hamlin	12 / 4%	180 / 59%	1,380,202 / 29.5%	1,865,908 / 39.8%
1864	36	McClellan / Pendleton	Lincoln / Johnson	21 / 9%	212 / 91%	1,812,807 / 45.0%	2,218,388 / 55.0%
1868	37	Seymour / Blair	Grant / Colfax	80 / 27%	214 / 73%	2,708,744 / 47.3%	3,013,650 / 52.7%

Year	No.	Democratic ticket	Electoral	%	Republican ticket	Electoral	%	Dem. popular	%	Rep. popular	%
1872	37	Greeley, Brown	d		Grant, Wilson	286	78%	2,834,761	43.8%	3,598,235	55.6%
1876	38	Tilden, Hendricks	184	50%	Hayes, Wheeler	185	50%	4,288,546	51.0%	4,034,311	47.9%
1880	38	Hancock, English	155	42%	Garfield, Arthur	214	58%	4,444,260	48.2%	4,446,158	48.3%
1884	38	Cleveland, Hendricks	219	55%	Blaine, Logan	182	45%	4,874,621	48.5%	4,848,936	48.2%
1888	38	Cleveland, Thurman	168	42%	Harrison, Morton	233	58%	5,534,488	48.6%	5,443,892	47.8%
1892	44	Cleveland, Stevenson	277	62%	Harrison, Reid	145	33%	5,551,883	46.1%	5,179,244	43.0%
1896	45	Bryan, Sewall	176	39%	McKinley, Hobart	271	61%	6,511,495	46.7%	7,108,480	51.0%
1900	45	Bryan, Stevenson	155	35%	McKinley, Roosevelt	292	65%	6,358,345	45.5%	7,218,039	51.7%
1904	45	Parker, Davis	140	29%	Roosevelt, Fairbanks	336	71%	5,028,898	37.6%	7,626,593	56.4%
1908	46	Bryan, Kern	162	34%	Taft, Sherman	321	66%	6,406,801	43.0%	7,676,258	51.6%
1912	48	Wilson, Marshall	435	82%	Taft, Sherman	8	2%	6,293,152	41.8%	3,486,333	23.2%
1916	48	Wilson, Marshall	277	52%	Hughes, Fairbanks	254	48%	9,126,300	49.2%	8,546,789	46.1%
1920	48	Cox, Roosevelt	127	24%	Harding, Coolidge	404	76%	9,140,884	34.2%	16,133,314	60.3%
1924	48	Davis, Bryant	136	26%	Coolidge, Dawes	382	72%	8,386,169	28.8%	15,717,553	54.1%
1928	48	Smith, Robinson	87	16%	Hoover, Curtis	444	84%	15,000,185	40.8%	21,411,991	58.2%

(Table continues)

Table 1-6 *(Continued)*

Year	Number of states	Candidates	Electoral vote (number and percent)		Popular vote (number and percent)	
1932	48	Roosevelt	472	89%	22,825,016	57.4%
		Garner				
		Hoover	59	11%	15,758,397	39.6%
		Curtis				
1936	48	Roosevelt	523	90%	27,747,636	60.8%
		Garner				
		Landon	8	2%	16,679,543	36.5%
		Knox				
1940	48	Roosevelt	449	85%	27,263,448	54.7%
		Wallace				
		Willkie	82	15%	22,336,260	44.8%
		McNary				
1944	48	Roosevelt	432	81%	25,611,936	53.4%
		Truman				
		Dewey	99	19%	22,013,372	45.9%
		Bricker				
1948	48	Truman	303	57%	24,105,587	49.5%
		Barkley				
		Dewey	189	36%	21,970,017	45.1%
		Warren				
1952	48	Stevenson	89	17%	27,314,649	44.4%
		Sparkman				
		Eisenhower	442	83%	33,936,137	55.1%
		Nixon				
1956	48	Stevenson	73	14%	26,030,172	42.0%
		Kefauver				
		Eisenhower	457	86%	35,585,245	57.4%
		Nixon				
1960	50	Kennedy	303	56%	34,221,344	49.7%
		Johnson				
		Nixon	219	41%	34,106,671	49.5%
		Lodge				
1964	50	Johnson	486	90%	43,126,584	61.1%
		Humphrey				
		Goldwater	52	10%	27,177,838	38.5%
		Miller				
1968	50	Humphrey	191	36%	31,274,503	42.7%
		Muskie				
		Nixon	301	56%	31,785,148	43.4%
		Agnew				
1972	50	McGovern	17	3%	29,171,791	37.5%
		Shriver				
		Nixon	520	97%	47,170,179	60.7%
		Agnew				
1976	50	Carter	297	55%	40,830,763	50.1%
		Mondale				
		Ford	240	45%	39,147,793	48.0%
		Dole				
1980	50	Carter	49	9%	35,483,883	41.0%
		Mondale				
		Reagan	489	91%	43,904,153	50.7%
		Bush				

Year	States	Candidates	Electoral vote	%	Popular vote	%
1984	50	Mondale / Ferraro	13	2%	37,577,185	40.6%
		Reagan / Bush	525	98%	54,455,075	58.8%
1988	50	Dukakis / Bentsen	111	21%	41,809,074	45.6%
		Bush / Quayle	426	79%	48,886,097	53.4%
1992	50	Clinton / Gore	370	69%	44,909,326	43.0%
		Bush / Quayle	168	31%	39,103,882	37.4%
1996	50	Clinton / Gore	379	70%	47,401,054	49.2%
		Dole / Kemp	159	30%	39,197,350	40.7%

Note: For details of the electoral system as well as popular and electoral votes polled by minor candidates, see source. Popular vote returns are shown since 1824 because of availability and because by that time most electors were chosen by popular vote.

[a] The elections of 1789–1800 were held under different rules, which did not include separate voting for president and vice president. Scattered electoral votes are not shown.

[b] All candidates in 1824 represented factions of the Democratic-Republican party. Figures are for the two candidates with the highest electoral votes. The two other candidates were Crawford and Clay with 41 and 37 electoral votes, respectively.

[c] Three Whig candidates ran in 1836. Their electoral votes totalled 113.

[d] The Democratic presidential nominee, Horace Greeley, died between the popular vote and the meeting of presidential electors. Democratic electors split 63 votes among several candidates, Congress refused to count the three Georgians who insisted on casting their votes for Greeley, and an additional 14 electoral votes were not cast.

Sources: Congressional Quarterly's Guide to U.S. Elections, 3d ed. (Washington, D.C.: Congressional Quarterly, 1994), 358–410, 429–468; *Congressional Quarterly Weekly Report* (1997) 444; Table 1-8, this volume.

Table 1-7 Party Winning Presidential Election, by State, 1789–1996

State	1789–1824			1828–1856			1860–1892			1896–1928			1932–1964			1968–1996		
	D	F	O	D	R	O	D	R	O	D	R	O	D	R	O	D	R	O
Alabama	2	0	0	8	0	0	6	2	0	9	0	0	7	1	1	1	6	1
Alaska	—	—	—	—	—	—	—	—	—	—	—	—	1	1	0	0	8	0
Arizona	—	—	—	—	—	—	—	—	—	2	3	0	5	4	0	1	7	0
Arkansas	—	—	—	6	0	0	6	1	1	9	0	0	9	0	0	3	4	1
California	—	—	—	2	0	0	2	7	0	1	7	1	6	3	0	2	6	0
Colorado	—	—	—	—	—	—	0	4	1	5	4	0	4	5	0	1	7	0
Connecticut	2	8	0	2	6	0	4	5	0	1	8	0	5	4	0	3	5	0
Delaware	2	8	0	2	6	0	7	1	1	1	8	0	5	4	0	3	5	0
District of Columbia[a]	—	—	—	—	—	—	—	—	—	—	—	—	1	0	0	8	0	0
Florida	—	—	—	2	1	0	4	3	1	8	1	0	6	3	0	2	6	0
Georgia	8	2	0	5	3	0	7	0	1	9	0	0	8	1	0	3	4	1
Hawaii	—	—	—	—	—	—	—	—	—	—	—	—	2	0	0	6	2	0
Idaho	—	—	—	—	—	—	0	0	1	4	5	0	6	3	0	0	8	0
Illinois	2	0	0	8	0	0	1	8	0	1	8	0	7	2	0	2	6	0
Indiana	3	0	0	6	2	0	3	6	0	1	8	0	3	6	0	0	8	0
Iowa	—	—	—	2	1	0	0	9	0	1	8	0	4	5	0	3	5	0
Kansas	—	—	—	—	—	—	0	7	1	3	6	0	3	6	0	0	8	0
Kentucky	8	1	0	2	6	0	8	0	1	6	3	0	7	2	0	3	5	0
Louisiana	4	0	0	6	2	0	5	1	1	9	0	0	6	2	1	3	4	1
Maine	2	0	0	5	3	0	0	9	0	1	8	0	1	8	0	3	5	0
Maryland	4	6	0	1	6	1	7	1	1	4	5	0	6	3	0	5	3	0
Massachusetts	3	7	0	0	8	0	0	9	0	2	7	0	7	2	0	6	2	0
Michigan	—	—	—	4	2	0	0	9	0	0	8	1	5	4	0	6	2	0
Minnesota	—	—	—	—	—	—	0	9	0	0	8	1	7	2	0	7	1	0
Mississippi	2	0	0	7	1	0	5	1	1	9	0	0	6	1	2	1	6	1
Missouri	—	—	—	8	0	0	7	2	0	4	5	0	8	1	0	3	5	0
Montana	—	—	—	—	—	—	0	1	0	4	5	0	6	3	0	1	7	0

Nebraska	—	—	—	—	—	—	0	7	0	4	5	0	3	6	0	0	8	0
Nevada	—	—	—	—	—	—	1	6	1	5	4	0	7	2	0	2	6	0
New Hampshire	4	6	0	6	2	0	0	9	0	2	7	0	4	5	0	2	6	0
New Jersey	5	5	0	3	5	0	7	2	0	1	8	0	6	3	0	2	6	0
New Mexico	—	—	—	—	—	—	—	—	—	2	3	0	7	3	0	2	6	0
New York	6	3	0	5	3	0	4	5	0	1	8	0	6	0	0	5	3	0
North Carolina	8	1	0	5	3	0	5	2	1	8	1	0	9	6	0	1	7	0
North Dakota	—	—	—	—	—	—	—	—	—	2	7	0	3	4	0	0	8	0
Ohio	6	0	0	4	4	0	0	9	0	2	7	0	5	3	0	3	5	0
Oklahoma	—	—	—	—	—	—	—	—	—	4	2	0	5	4	0	0	8	0
Oregon	—	—	—	—	—	—	1	8	0	1	8	1	5	4	0	3	5	0
Pennsylvania	8	2	0	6	2	0	0	9	0	0	8	0	7	2	1	4	4	0
Rhode Island	4	5	0	2	6	0	0	9	0	2	7	0	7	6	0	6	2	0
South Carolina	8	2	0	6	0	2	4	3	1	9	0	0	7	3	0	1	7	0
South Dakota	—	—	—	—	—	—	0	1	0	1	7	1	3	2	0	0	8	0
Tennessee	8	0	0	3	5	0	6	1	1	7	2	0	6	3	0	3	5	0
Texas	—	—	—	3	0	0	7	0	0	8	1	0	7	8	0	2	6	0
Utah	—	—	—	—	—	—	—	—	—	2	7	0	6	3	0	2	8	0
Vermont	6	3	0	7	1	0	0	9	0	0	9	0	1	3	0	2	8	0
Virginia	8	2	0	8	0	0	5	1	1	8	1	1	6	1	1	4	4	0
Washington	—	—	—	—	—	—	—	—	—	2	8	0	8	4	0	4	4	0
West Virginia	—	—	—	—	—	—	5	3	0	1	7	0	5	4	1	6	2	0
Wisconsin	—	—	—	2	1	0	1	8	0	1	7	1	5	4	0	4	4	0
Wyoming	—	—	—	—	—	—	0	1	0	3	6	0	5	4	0	0	8	0
Total[b]	113	61	0	136	79	3	118	189	15	170	244	7	274	158	5	128	275	5

Note: "D" indicates the Democratic-Republican party from 1796 to 1820 and in 1828, the Jackson faction in 1824, and the Democratic party in 1832 and later; "F" indicates the Federalists from 1792 to 1816, Independent Democrat-Republicans in 1820, and the Adams faction in 1824; "R" indicates the National Republicans in 1828 and 1832, Whigs from 1836 to 1852, and the Republican party in 1856 and later. The "O" column refers to other (third-party) parties. Southern Democrats in 1860 are counted as Democratic. "—" indicates that the state was not yet admitted to the Union.

[a] Residents of the District of Columbia received the presidential vote in 1961.

[b] Fewer total votes for a given state within a party system indicate admission of the state during the party system or nonvoting in certain southern states in 1864, 1868, and 1872.

Sources: Compiled by the editors from *Congressional Quarterly's Guide to U.S. Elections*, 3d ed. (Washington, D.C.: Congressional Quarterly, 1994), 359ff, 423; *Congressional Quarterly Weekly Report* (1996), 3192.

Table 1-8 Presidential General Election Returns, by State, 1996

| | Popular vote | | | | | | | | | | | Electoral vote | |
| State | Clinton (Democrat) | | Dole (Republican) | | Perot (Independent) | | Other | | | Plurality[a] | | | |
	Vote	%	Vote	%	Vote	%	Vote	%	Total Vote	Vote	%	D	R
Alabama	662,165	43.2	769,044	50.1	92,149	6.0	10,991	0.7	1,534,349	106,879	7.0		9
Alaska	80,380	33.3	122,746	50.8	26,333	10.9	12,161	5.0	241,620	42,366	17.5		3
Arizona	653,288	46.5	622,073	44.3	112,072	8.0	16,972	1.2	1,404,405	31,215	2.2	8	
Arkansas	475,171	53.7	325,416	36.8	69,884	7.9	13,791	1.6	884,262	149,755	16.9	6	
California	5,119,835	51.1	3,828,380	38.2	697,847	7.0	373,422	3.7	10,019,484	1,291,455	12.9	54	
Colorado	671,152	44.4	691,848	45.8	99,629	6.6	48,075	3.2	1,510,704	20,696	1.4		8
Connecticut	735,740	52.8	483,109	34.7	139,523	10.0	34,242	2.5	1,392,614	252,631	18.1	8	
Delaware	140,355	51.8	99,062	36.6	28,719	10.6	2,674	1.0	270,810	41,293	15.2	3	
District of Columbia	158,220	85.2	17,339	9.3	3,611	1.9	6,556	3.5	185,726	140,881	75.9	3	
Florida	2,545,968	48.0	2,243,324	42.3	483,776	9.1	27,859	0.5	5,300,927	302,644	5.7	25	
Georgia	1,053,849	45.8	1,080,843	47.0	146,337	6.4	17,870	0.8	2,298,8x99	26,994	1.2		13
Hawaii	205,012	56.9	113,943	31.6	27,358	7.6	13,807	3.8	360,120	91,069	25.3	4	
Idaho	165,443	33.6	256,595	52.2	62,518	12.7	7,155	1.5	491,711	91,152	18.5		4
Illinois	2,341,744	54.3	1,587,021	36.8	346,408	8.0	36,218	0.8	4,311,391	754,723	17.5	22	
Indiana	887,424	41.6	1,006,693	47.1	224,299	10.5	17,015	0.8	2,135,431	119,269	5.6		12
Iowa	620,258	50.3	492,644	39.9	105,159	8.5	16,014	1.3	1,234,075	127,614	10.3	7	
Kansas	387,659	36.1	583,245	54.3	92,639	8.6	10,757	1.0	1,074,300	195,586	18.2		6
Kentucky	636,614	45.8	623,283	44.9	120,396	8.7	8,414	0.6	1,388,707	13,331	1.0	8	
Louisiana	927,837	52.0	712,586	39.9	123,293	6.9	20,243	1.1	1,783,959	215,251	12.0	9	
Maine	312,788	51.6	186,378	30.8	85,970	14.2	20,761	3.4	605,897	126,410	20.8	4	
Maryland	966,207	54.3	681,530	38.3	115,812	6.5	17,321	1.0	1,780,870	284,677	16.0	10	
Massachusetts	1,571,509	61.5	718,058	28.1	227,206	8.9	39,686	1.6	2,556,459	853,451	33.4	12	
Michigan	1,989,653	51.7	1,481,212	38.5	336,670	8.7	41,309	1.1	3,848,844	508,441	13.2	18	
Minnesota	1,120,438	51.1	766,476	35.0	257,704	11.8	48,022	2.2	2,192,640	353,962	16.1	10	

	Dem. vote	%	Rep. vote	%	Perot vote	%	Other	%	Total	Plurality %	Dem. EV	Rep. EV
Mississippi	394,022	44.1	439,838	49.2	52,222	5.8	7,775	0.9	893,857	5.1		7
Missouri	1,025,935	47.5	890,016	41.2	217,188	10.1	24,926	1.2	2,158,065	6.3	11	
Montana	167,922	41.3	179,652	44.1	55,229	13.6	4,280	1.1	407,083	2.9		3
Nebraska	236,761	35.0	363,467	53.7	71,278	10.5	5,909	0.9	677,415	18.7		5
Nevada	203,974	43.9	199,244	42.9	43,986	9.5	17,075	3.7	464,279	1.0	4	
New Hampshire	246,166	49.3	196,486	39.4	48,387	9.7	8,014	1.6	499,053	10.0	4	
New Jersey	1,652,361	53.7	1,103,099	35.9	262,134	8.5	58,266	1.9	3,075,860	17.9	15	
New Mexico	273,495	49.2	232,751	41.9	32,257	5.8	17,571	3.2	556,074	7.3	5	
New York	3,756,177	59.5	1,933,492	30.6	503,458	8.0	123,002	1.9	6,316,129	28.9	33	
North Carolina	1,107,849	44.0	1,225,938	48.7	168,059	6.7	13,961	0.6	2,515,807	4.7		14
North Dakota	106,905	40.1	125,050	46.9	32,515	12.2	1,941	0.7	266,411	6.8		3
Ohio	2,148,222	47.4	1,859,883	41.0	483,207	10.7	43,122	1.0	4,534,434	6.4	21	
Oklahoma	488,105	40.4	582,315	48.3	130,788	10.8	5,505	0.5	1,206,713	7.8		8
Oregon	649,641	47.2	538,152	39.1	121,221	8.8	68,746	5.0	1,377,760	8.1	7	
Pennsylvania	2,215,819	49.2	1,801,169	40.0	430,984	9.6	58,146	1.3	4,506,118	9.2	23	
Rhode Island	233,050	59.7	104,683	26.8	43,723	11.2	8,791	2.3	390,247	32.9	4	
South Carolina	506,152	44.0	573,339	49.8	64,377	5.6	7,554	0.7	1,151,422	5.8		8
South Dakota	139,333	43.0	150,543	46.5	31,250	9.7	2,700	0.8	323,826	3.4		3
Tennessee	909,146	48.0	863,530	45.6	105,918	5.6	15,511	0.8	1,894,105	2.4	11	
Texas	2,459,683	43.8	2,736,167	48.8	378,537	6.7	37,257	0.7	5,611,644	4.9		32
Utah	221,633	33.3	361,911	54.4	66,461	10.0	15,624	2.3	665,629	21.1		5
Vermont	137,894	53.4	80,352	31.1	31,024	12.0	9,179	3.6	258,449	22.3	3	
Virginia	1,091,060	45.1	1,138,350	47.1	159,861	6.6	27,371	1.1	2,416,642	2.0		13
Washington	1,123,323	49.8	840,712	37.3	201,003	8.9	88,799	3.9	2,253,837	12.5	11	
West Virginia	327,812	51.5	233,946	36.8	71,639	11.3	3,062	0.5	636,459	14.7	5	
Wisconsin	1,071,971	48.8	845,029	38.5	227,339	10.4	51,830	2.4	2,196,169	10.3	11	
Wyoming	77,934	36.8	105,388	49.8	25,928	12.3	2,321	1.1	211,571	13.0		3
Total	47,401,054	49.2	39,197,350	40.7	8,085,285	8.4	1,589,573	1.7	96,273,262	8.5	379	159

[a] "Plurality" indicates the vote margin between the leader and the second-place finisher.

Source: Congressional Quarterly Weekly Report (1997), 188.

Table 1-9 House and Senate Election Results, by Congress, 1788–1996

| | | House | | | Gains/losses[c] | | Senate | | | Gains/losses[c] | | |
| | | Dem.[a] | Rep.[b] | Other | Dem. | Rep. | Dem.[a] | Rep.[b] | Other | Dem. | Rep. | |
Year	Congress											President[d]
1788	1st	26	38				9	17				Washington (F)
1790	2d	33	37				13	16				
1792	3d	57	48				13	17				Washington (F)
1794	4th	52	54				13	19				
1796	5th	48	58				12	20				John Adams (F)
1798	6th	42	64				13	19				
1800	7th	69	36				18	13				Jefferson (DR)
1802	8th	102	39				25	9				
1804	9th	116	25				27	7				Jefferson (DR)
1806	10th	118	24				28	6				
1808	11th	94	48				28	6				Madison (DR)
1810	12th	108	36				30	6				
1812	13th	112	68				27	9				Madison (DR)
1814	14th	117	65				25	11				
1816	15th	141	42				34	10				Monroe (DR)
1818	16th	156	27				35	7				
1820	17th	158	25				44	4				Monroe (DR)
1822	18th	187	26				44	4				
1824	19th	105	97				26	20				John Q. Adams (DR)
1826	20th	94	119				20	28				
1828	21st	139	74				26	22				Jackson (D)
1830	22d	141	58				25	21				
1832	23d	147	53				20	20				Jackson (D)
1834	24th	145	98				27	25				

1836	25th	108	107	24			30	18	4			Van Buren (D)
1838	26th	124	118				28	22				
1840	27th	102	133	6			28	22				Harrison (W)
1842	28th	142	79	1			25	28	1			Tyler (W)
1844	29th	143	77	6			31	25	2			Polk (D)
1846	30th	108	115	4			36	21	3			
1848	31st	112	109	9			35	25	2			Taylor (W)
1850	32d	140	88	5			35	24				Fillmore (W)
1852	33d	159	71	4			38	22	5			Pierce (D)
1854	34th	83	108	43			42	15	5			
1856	35th	131	92	14	+48	−16	39	20	2	+5	−3	Buchanan (D)
1858	36th	101	113	23	−30	+21	38	26		+6	−1	
1860	37th	42	106	28	−59	−7	11	31	7	+5	−27	Lincoln (R)
1862	38th	80	103		+38	−3	12	39		+8	+1	
1864	39th	46	145		−34	+42	10	42		+3	−2	Lincoln (R)
1866	40th	49	143		+3	−2	11	42		0	+1	A. Johnson (R)
1868	41st	73	170		+24	+27	11	61		+19	0	Grant (R)
1870	42d	104	139		+31	−31	17	57		−4	+6	
1872	43d	88	203		−16	+64	19	54		−3	+2	Grant (R)
1874	44th	181	107	3	+93	−96	29	46		−8	+10	
1876	45th	156	137		−25	+30	36	39	1	−7	+7	Hayes (R)
1878	46th	150	128	14	−6	−9	43	33		−6	+7	
1880	47th	130	152	11	−20	+24	37	37	2	+4	−6	Garfield (R)
1882	48th	200	119	6	+70	−33	36	40		+3	−1	Arthur (R)
1884	49th	182	140	2	−18	+21	34	41		+2	−2	Cleveland (D)
1886	50th	170	151	4	−12	+11	37	39		−2	+3	
1888	51st	156	173	1	−14	+22	37	47		+8	0	Harrison (R)
1890	52d	231	88	14	+75	−85	39	47	2	0	+2	
1892	53d	220	126	8	−11	+38	44	38	3	−9	+5	Cleveland (D)
1894	54th	104	246	7	−116	+120	39	44	5	+6	−5	
1896	55th	134	206	16	+30	−40	34	46	10	+2	−5	McKinley (R)

(Table continues)

Table 1-9 *(Continued)*

Year	Congress	House					Senate					President[d]
		Dem.[a]	Rep.[b]	Other	Gains/losses[c]		Dem.[a]	Rep.[b]	Other	Gains/losses[c]		
					Dem.	Rep.				Dem.	Rep.	
1898	56th	163	185	9	+29	−21	26	53	11	−8	+7	McKinley (R)
1900	57th	153	198	5	−10	+13	29	56	3	+3	+3	Roosevelt (R)
1902	58th	178	207		+25	+9	32	58		+3	+2	Roosevelt (R)
1904	59th	136	250		−42	+43	32	58		0	0	
1906	60th	164	222		+28	−28	29	61		−3	−3	
1908	61st	172	219		+8	−3	32	59		+3	−2	Taft (R)
1910	62d	228	162	1	+56	−57	42	49		+10	−10	
1912	63d	290	127	18	+62	−35	51	44	1	+9	−5	Wilson (D)
1914	64th	231	193	8	−59	+66	56	39	1	+5	−5	
1916	65th	210	216	9	−21	+23	53	42	1	−3	+3	Wilson (D)
1918	66th	191	237	7	−19	+21	47	48	1	−6	+6	
1920	67th	132	300	1	−59	+63	37	59		−10	+11	Harding (R)
1922	68th	207	225	3	+75	−75	43	51	2	+6	−8	
1924	69th	183	247	5	−24	+22	40	54	1	−3	+3	Coolidge (R)
1926	70th	195	237	3	+12	−10	47	48	1	+7	−6	
1928	71st	163	267	1	−32	+30	39	56	1	−8	+8	Hoover (R)
1930	72d	216	218	1	+53	−49	47	48	1	+8	−8	
1932	73d	313	117	5	+97	−101	59	36	1	+12	−12	Roosevelt (D)
1934	74th	322	103	10	+9	−14	69	25	2	+10	−11	Roosevelt (D)
1936	75th	333	89	13	+11	−14	75	17	4	+6	−8	Roosevelt (D)
1938	76th	262	169	4	−71	+80	69	23	4	−6	+6	
1940	77th	267	162	6	+5	−7	66	28	2	−3	+5	Roosevelt (D)
1942	78th	222	209	4	−45	+47	57	38	1	−9	+10	
1944	79th	243	190	2	+21	−19	57	38	1	0	0	Roosevelt (D)

1946	80th	188	246	1	−55	+56	45	51		−12	+13	Truman (D)
1948	81st	263	171	1	+75	−75	54	42		+9	−9	Truman (D)
1950	82d	234	199	2	−29	+28	48	47		−6	+5	
1952	83d	213	221	1	−21	+22	47	48	1	−1	+1	Eisenhower (R)
1954	84th	232	203		+19	−18	48	47	1	+1	−1	
1956	85th	234	201		+2	−2	49	47	1	+1	0	Eisenhower (R)
1958	86th	283	154		+49	−47	64	34		+17	−13	
1960	87th	263	174		−20	+20	64	36		−2	+2	Kennedy (D)
1962	88th	258	176		−4	+2	67	33		+4	−4	
1964	89th	295	140	1	+38	−38	68	32		+2	−2	L. Johnson (D)
1966	90th	248	187		−47	+47	64	36		−3	+3	
1968	91st	243	192		−4	+4	58	42		−5	+5	Nixon (R)
1970	92d	255	180		+12	−12	55	45		−4	+2	
1972	93d	243	192		−12	+12	57	43		+2	−2	Nixon (R)
1974	94th	291	144		+43	−43	61	38		+3	−3	Ford (R)
1976	95th	292	143		+1	−1	62	38		0	0	Carter (D)
1978	96th	277	158		−11	+11	59	41		−3	+3	0
1980	97th	243	192		−33	+33	47	53		−12	+12	Reagan (R)
1982	98th	269	166		+26	−26	46	54		0	0	
1984	99th	253	182		−14	+14	47	53		+2	−2	Reagan (R)
1986	100th	258	177		+5	−5	55	45		+8	−8	
1988	101st	260	175		+3	−3	55	45		+1	−1	Bush (R)
1990	102d	267	165	1	+9	−8	56	44		+1	−1	
1992	103d	258	176	1	−10	+10	57	43		0	0	Clinton (D)
1994	104th	203	231	1	−53	+53	48[e]	52[e]		−7[e]	+7[e]	
1996	105th	207	227	1	+9	−9	45	55		−2	+2	Clinton (D)

[a] "Democratic" column indicates Democratic partisans in 1828 and later, "Administration" in 1824 and 1826, "Democratic Republicans" from 1790 to 1822, and "Opposition" in 1788.

[b] The "Republican" column indicates Republican partisans in 1854 and later, "Whigs" from 1834 to 1852, "Anti-Masons" in 1832, "National Republicans" in 1828 and 1830, "Jacksonians" in 1824 and 1826, "Federalists" from 1790 to 1822, and "Administration" in 1788.

(Notes continue)

Table 1-9 *(Continued)*

---

[c] Because of changes in the overall number of seats in the Senate and House, in the number of seats won by third parties, and in the number of vacancies, a Republican loss is not always matched precisely by a Democratic gain, or vice versa. Gains/losses reflect preelection/postelection changes. Deaths, resignations, and special elections can cause further changes in party make-up. In the 1930 election, for example, Republicans won majority control, but when Congress organized, special elections held to fill fourteen vacancies resulted in a Democratic majority.

[d] President elected in the year indicated or, if a midterm election year, nonelected president in office at the time of the midterm election.

[e] In 1994 Senator Richard Shelby switched from Democrat to Republican the day after the election. With his switch the partisan balance became 53–47 and the Republicans gained 8 seats.

Sources: 1788–1852: Bureau of the Census, *Historical Statistics of the United States, Colonial Times to 1970* (Washington, D.C.: U.S. Government Printing Office, 1975), 1083–1084; 1854: Congressional Quarterly, *Elections '84* (Washington, D.C.: Congressional Quarterly, 1984), 106; 1856–1992: *Congressional Quarterly's Guide to U.S. Elections*, 3d ed. (Washington, D.C.: Congressional Quarterly, 1994), 1344; 1994–1996: *Congressional Quarterly Weekly Report* (1994), 3232, 3240; (1996), 3233, 3402.

Table 1-10 Party Victories in U.S. House Elections, by State, 1860–1996

State	Total 1860–1895			Total 1896–1931			Total 1932–1965			Total 1966–1996		
	Dem.	Rep.	Other	Dem.	Rep.	Other	Dem.	Rep.	Other	Dem.	Rep.	Other
Alabama	92	19	8	170	0	8	146	5	0	70	45	0
Alaska	—	—	—	—	—	—	4	0	0	2	15	0
Arizona	—	—	—	11	0	0	26	7	0	23	49	0
Arkansas	54	5	6	124	0	0	109	0	0	42	21	0
California[a]	29	46	8	30	133	15	234	212	0	412	304	0
Colorado	1	9	3	21	34	6	43	26	0	42	43	0
Connecticut	33	36	5	11	77	0	58	44	0	59	37	0
Delaware	15	3	2	5	14	0	9	8	0	5	11	0
Florida	18	8	1	57	4	1	111	8	0	163	112	0
Georgia	111	11	12	207	0	1	170	1	0	129	35	1
Hawaii	—	—	—	0	0	1	6	0	0	30	2	0
Idaho	0	4	0	5	42	2	20	14	0	6	26	0
Illinois	118	191	20	136	333	1	220	221	0	194	172	0
Indiana	104	105	17	97	139	0	85	108	0	84	75	0
Iowa	16	131	11	10	193	0	35	105	0	37	62	0
Kansas	0	62	12	30	114	0	16	90	0	19	58	0
Kentucky	133	20	38	151	54	0	122	25	0	64	46	0
Louisiana	69	20	2	136	0	2	139	0	0	90	37	0
Maine	3	76	7	4	71	0	8	41	0	14	18	0
Maryland	74	15	18	63	49	0	87	25	0	84	47	0
Massachusetts	31	165	17	60	211	2	103	136	0	148	34	0
Michigan	33	118	13	12	214	2	112	187	0	166	125	0
Minnesota	11	51	5	8	146	12	44	91	16	75	53	1
Mississippi	70	17	3	142	0	0	110	1	0	61	20	0
Missouri	143	43	38	202	88	0	157	49	0	111	41	0
Montana	1	3	0	13	14	1	23	12	0	17	13	0

(Table continues)

Table 1-10 *(Continued)*

State	Total 1860–1895			Total 1896–1931			Total 1932–1965			Total 1966–1996		
	Dem.	Rep.	Other	Dem.	Rep.	Other	Dem.	Rep.	Other	Dem.	Rep.	Other
Nebraska	3	28	5	36	63	9	21	50	0	5	43	0
Nevada	4	9	4	5	10	4	14	3	0	13	10	0
New Hampshire	11	33	3	3	33	0	3	31	0	7	25	0
New Jersey	53	58	5	66	137	0	84	158	0	136	94	0
New Mexico	—	—	—	7	5	0	29	0	1	15	25	0
New York	236	312	66	328	397	6	387	368	1	357	226	0
North Carolina	78	32	19	157	11	9	189	9	0	119	60	0
North Dakota	0	4	0	0	44	9	2	33	0	10	9	0
Ohio	146	186	39	123	264	0	163	238	0	142	208	0
Oklahoma	—	—	—	70	27	0	112	14	0	65	31	0
Oregon	7	13	2	2	44	0	22	41	0	50	22	0
Pennsylvania	158	300	38	83	522	17	255	291	0	208	178	0
Rhode Island	8	32	2	13	34	0	32	2	0	25	8	0
South Carolina	62	30	6	127	0	0	97	2	0	61	36	0
South Dakota	6	11	0	3	42	2	7	27	0	12	12	0
Tennessee	83	52	13	139	39	4	121	37	1	81	57	0
Texas	110	1	3	295	7	0	365	8	0	309	106	0
Utah	—	—	—	7	23	0	23	11	0	14	26	0
Vermont	0	42	5	0	36	0	1	16	0	0	12	4
Virginia	81	23	23	167	15	0	147	15	0	81	79	0
Washington	0	6	0	8	61	2	54	55	0	83	41	0
West Virginia	37	15	6	23	75	0	84	16	0	61	3	0
Wisconsin	40	94	9	18	176	4	46	105	21	78	71	0
Wyoming	1	2	0	1	17	0	3	14	0	4	12	0

Note: "—" indicates that the state was not yet admitted to the Union. The 1966–1992 period does not include special elections; candidates endorsed by both major and minor parties are counted as major party candidates.

[a] When it could be determined, candidates who ran as both Republican and Democrat were classified by their usual party affiliation.

Sources: Congressional Quarterly's Guide to U.S. Elections, 2d ed. (Washington, D.C.: Congressional Quarterly, 1985), 1118–1119; 1986–1996: *Congressional Quarterly Weekly Report* (1986), 2843, (1988), 3269, (1990), 3802, (1992), 3571, (1994), 3236, (1997), 3226.

Table 1-11 Popular Vote and Seats in House Elections, by Party, 1896-1996

	Democratic candidates		Republican candidates		Change from last election[a]		Difference between Democratic percentage of all seats and all votes[a]
Year	Percentage of all votes	Percentage of all seats	Percentage of all votes	Percentage of all seats	Percentage of major party votes	Percentage of major party seats	
1896	43.3	37.6	46.7	57.9	—	—	-5.6
1898	46.7	45.7	45.7	51.8	2.5D	7.4D	-1.0
1900	44.7	43.0	51.2	55.6	3.9R	3.2R	-1.7
1902	46.7	46.2	49.3	53.8	2.1D	2.6D	-0.5
1904	41.7	35.2	53.8	64.8	5.0R	11.0R	-6.5
1906	44.2	42.5	50.7	57.5	2.9D	7.3D	-1.7
1908	46.1	44.0	49.7	56.0	1.6D	1.5D	-2.1
1910	47.4	58.3	46.5	41.4	2.4D	14.5D	10.9
1912	45.3	66.7	34.0	29.2	6.6D	11.1D	21.3
1914	43.1	53.5	42.6	44.7	6.8R	15.1R	10.3
1916	46.3	48.3	48.4	49.7	1.5R	5.2R	2.0
1918	43.1	43.9	52.5	54.5	3.8R	4.7R	0.8
1920	35.8	30.5	58.6	69.3	7.1R	14.1R	-5.4
1922	44.7	47.6	51.7	51.7	8.4D	17.4D	2.8
1924	40.4	42.1	55.5	56.8	4.3R	5.4R	1.7
1926	40.5	44.8	57.0	54.5	0.5R	2.6D	4.3
1928	42.4	37.8	56.5	61.9	1.3D	7.2R	-4.5
1930	44.6	49.7	52.6	50.1	3.0D	11.9D	5.1
1932	54.5	72.0	41.4	26.9	11.0D	23.0D	17.4
1934	53.9	74.0	42.0	23.7	0.7R	3.0D	20.1
1936	55.8	76.6	39.6	20.5	2.3D	3.1D	20.7
1938	48.6	60.2	47.0	38.9	7.7R	18.1R	11.6
1940	51.3	61.4	45.6	37.2	2.2D	1.4D	10.1

(Table continues)

Table 1-11 (*Continued*)

Year	Democratic candidates		Republican candidates		Change from last election[a]		Difference between Democratic percentage of all seats and all votes[a]
	Percentage of all votes	Percentage of all seats	Percentage of all votes	Percentage of all seats	Percentage of major party votes	Percentage of major party seats	
1942	46.1	51.0	50.6	48.0	5.3R	10.7R	5.0
1944	50.6	55.9	47.2	43.7	4.0D	4.6D	5.3
1946	44.2	43.2	53.5	56.6	6.4R	12.8R	-1.0
1948	51.9	60.5	45.5	39.3	8.0D	17.3D	8.6
1950	49.0	53.8	49.0	45.7	3.2R	6.6R	4.7
1952	49.7	49.0	49.3	50.8	0.2D	5.0R	-0.8
1954	52.5	53.3	47.0	46.7	2.6D	4.3D	0.8
1956	51.1	53.8	48.7	46.2	1.6R	0.5D	2.7
1958	56.3	64.8	43.5	35.2	5.2D	11.0D	8.5
1960	54.2	60.2	45.4	39.8	1.9R	4.6R	6.0
1962	52.3	59.3	47.4	40.5	2.0R	0.7R	7.0
1964	57.4	67.8	42.1	32.2	5.3D	8.4D	10.4
1966	50.9	57.0	48.2	43.0	6.3R	10.8R	6.1
1968	50.2	55.9	48.5	44.1	0.5R	1.1R	5.7
1970	53.4	58.6	45.1	41.4	3.4D	2.8D	5.2
1972	51.7	55.9	46.4	44.1	1.5R	2.7R	4.2
1974	57.6	66.9	40.6	33.1	5.9D	11.0D	9.9
1976	56.2	67.1	42.1	32.9	1.4R	0.2D	10.9
1978	53.4	63.7	44.7	36.3	2.8R	3.4R	10.3
1980	50.4	55.9	48.0	44.1	3.2R	7.8R	5.5
1982	55.6	61.8	42.9	38.2	5.3D	5.9D	6.2
1984	52.1	58.2	47.0	41.8	3.9R	3.6R	6.0
1986	54.5	59.3	44.6	40.7	2.4D	1.1D	4.8
1988	53.3	59.8	45.5	40.2	1.0R	0.5D	6.5

1990	52.9	61.4	45.0	38.4	0.1D	1.8D	8.5
1992	50.8	59.3	45.6	40.5	1.4R	2.1R	8.5
1994	45.4	46.7	52.4	53.1	6.3R	12.7R	1.2
1996	48.5	47.6	48.9	52.2	4.4D	0.9D	−1.0

Note: "—" indicates not available.

[a] Calculated before rounding.

Source: Votes, 1896-1970: U.S. Bureau of the Census, *Historical Statistics of the United States, Colonial Times to 1970*, Bicentennial ed. (Washington, D.C.: U.S. Government Printing Office, 1975), Part 2, 1084; votes, 1972–1974: U.S. Bureau of the Census, *Statistical Abstract of the United States, 1976* (Washington, D.C.: U.S. Government Printing Office, 1976), 460; votes, 1976-1994: *Congressional Quarterly Weekly Report* (1977), 488; (1979), 571; (1981), 713; (1983), 387; (1985), 687; (1987), 484; (1989) 1063; (1991), 487; (1993), 965; (1995), 1079; (1997), 444; seats: this volume, Table 1-9.

Table 1-12   Split District Outcomes: Presidential and House Voting, 1900–1996

Year	Total number of districts[a]	Number of districts with split results[b]	Percentage of total
1900	295	10	3.4
1904	310	5	1.6
1908	314	21	6.7
1912	333	84	25.2
1916	333	35	10.5
1920	344	11	3.2
1924	356	42	11.8
1928	359	68	18.9
1932	355	50	14.1
1936	361	51	14.1
1940	362	53	14.6
1944	367	41	11.2
1948	422	90	21.3
1952	435	84	19.3
1956	435	130	29.9
1960	437	114	26.1
1964	435	145	33.3
1968	435	139	32.0
1972	435	192	44.1
1976	435	124	28.5
1980	435	143	32.8
1984	435	196	45.0
1988	435	148	34.0
1992	435	100	23.0
1996	435	111	25.5

[a] Before 1952 complete data are not available on every congressional district.
[b] Congressional districts carried by a presidential candidate of one party and a House candidate of another party.

Source: Norman J. Ornstein et al., eds., *Vital Statistics on Congress, 1993–1994* (Washington, D.C.: Congressional Quarterly, 1994), 64; *Congressional Quarterly Weekly Report* (1997), 862.

Table 1-13 Turnover in the House of Representatives, by Decade and Party System, 1789–1996

	Total turnover	Deaths	Retired/ resigned[a]	Denied renom- ination	General election defeat	Unknown/ other[b]
Decade						
1790s	.387	.015	.169	.002	.028	.173
1800s	.358	.016	.145	.001	.034	.161
1810s	.491	.020	.178	.009	.067	.218
1820s	.390	.014	.134	.002	.080	.161
1830s	.485	.023	.176	.005	.122	.159
1840s	.584	.023	.250	.010	.099	.203
1850s	.577	.014	.248	.014	.143	.157
1860s	.488	.020	.229	.027	.121	.090
1870s	.476	.018	.214	.035	.148	.061
1880s	.436	.016	.189	.047	.128	.055
1890s	.386	.017	.169	.044	.128	.028
1900s	.269	.025	.110	.033	.087	.014
1910s	.287	.028	.111	.028	.115	.006
1920s	.216	.029	.073	.026	.087	.000
1930s	.280	.037	.078	.047	.117	.000
1940s	.247	.026	.083	.032	.106	.000
1950s	.170	.025	.074	.014	.056	.000
1960s	.167	.016	.072	.022	.058	.000
1970s	.188	.010	.112	.014	.052	.000
1980s	.122	.010	.072	.006	.032	.000
1990s	.219	.005	.134	.019	.060	.000
Overall, 1789–1996	.347	.020	.144	.021	.089	.073
Party system						
First, 1789–1824	.408	.017	.161	.003	.045	.182
Second, 1825–1854	.518	.020	.201	.007	.113	.176
Third, 1855–1896	.475	.017	.214	.035	.136	.073
Fourth, 1897–1932	.270	.027	.101	.034	.099	.009
Fifth, 1933–1964	.219	.028	.078	.027	.085	.000
Sixth, 1965–1996	.165	.009	.095	.013	.046	.000

Note: Figures are proportions of the original House membership for each Congress failing to return to the following Congress, averaged across all Congresses within a decade (or a party system). Decades are defined by the first year of a Congress (e.g., the 1980s includes 1981–1982 through 1989–1990); each decade mean is based on five Congresses, except for the 1790s (six) and the 1990s (three). Results reflect the final disposition of challenged elections. Data are current through January 27, 1997.

[a] Includes retirements from public office, retirements to seek or accept other elective office (including the Senate), retirements to accept federal executive branch appointments, and resignations.

[b] "Unknown" are cases in which the member was not a candidate in the next general election but it could not be determined whether he or she was denied renomination or deliberately chose not to seek re-election. "Other" refers mainly to expulsions (almost all of which were connected with disloyalty in the Civil War).

Source: Revised from John W. Swain, Stephen A. Borrelli, Brian C. Reed, and Sean F. Evans, "U.S. House Turnover, 1789–1995: Toward a 'Systemic' Perspective," paper presented at the annual meeting of the American Political Science Association, 1996.

Table 1-14   House and Senate Seats That Changed Party, 1954–1996

Chamber/ year	Total changes	Incumbent defeated		Open seat	
		Democrat to Republican	Republican to Democrat	Democrat to Republican	Republican to Democrat
House					
1954	26	3	18	2	3
1956	20	7	7	2	4
1958	50	1	35	0	14
1960	37	23	2	6	6
1962	19	9	5	2	3
1964	57	5	39	5	8
1966	47	39	1	4	3
1968	11	5	0	2	4
1970	25	2	9	6	8
1972	23	6	3	9	5
1974	55	4	36	2	13
1976	22	7	5	3	7
1978	33	14	5	8	6
1980	41	27	3	10	1
1982	31	1	22	3	5
1984	22	13	3	5	1
1986	21	1	5	7	8
1988	9	2	4	1	2
1990	21	6	9	0	6
1992	43	16	8	11	8
1994	61	35	0	22	4
1996	35	3	18	10	4
Senate					
1954	8	2	4	1	1
1956	8	1	3	3	1
1958	13	0	11	0	2
1960	2	1	0	1	0
1962	8	2	3	0	3
1964	4	1	3	0	0
1966	3	1	0	2	0
1968	9	4	0	3	2
1970	6	3	2	1	0
1972	10	1	4	3	2
1974	6	0	2	1	3
1976	14	5	4	2	3
1978	13	5	2	3	3
1980	12	9	0	3	0
1982	4	1	1	1	1
1984	4	1	2	0	1
1986	10	0	7	1	2
1988	7	1	3	2	1
1990	1	0	1	0	0

Table 1-14   *(Continued)*

Chamber/ year	Total changes	Incumbent defeated		Open seat	
		Democrat to Republican	Republican to Democrat	Democrat to Republican	Republican to Democrat
1992	4	2	2	0	0
1994	8	2	0	6	0
1996	4	0	1	3	0

Note: This table reflects shifts in party control from before to after the November elections. It does not include shifts from the creation of districts or the reduction of two districts to one.

Sources: 1954–1992: Norman J. Ornstein et al., eds., *Vital Statistics on Congress, 1993–1994* (Washington, D.C.: Congressional Quarterly, 1994), 54, 56; 1994: *Congressional Quarterly Weekly Report* (1994), 3232–3233, 3240; (1996), 3228, 3238, 3402.

Table 1-15   Losses by President's Party in Midterm Elections, 1862–1994

Year	Party holding presidency	President's party: gain/loss of seats in House	President's party: gain/loss of seats in Senate
1862	R	−3	8
1866	R	−2	0
1870	R	−31	−4
1874	R	−96	−8
1878	R	−9	−6
1882	R	−33	3
1886	D	−12	3
1890	R	−85	0
1894	D	−116	−5
1898	R	−21	7
1902	R	9[a]	2
1906	R	−28	3
1910	R	−57	−10
1914	D	−59	5
1918	D	−19	−6
1922	R	−75	−8
1926	R	−10	−6
1930	R	−49	−8
1934	D	9	10
1938	D	−71	−6
1942	D	−55	−9
1946	D	−55	−12
1950	D	−29	−6
1954	R	−18	−1
1958	R	−48	−13
1962	D	−4	3
1966	D	−47	−4
1970	R	−12	2
1974	R	−48	−5
1978	D	−15	−3
1982	R	−26	1
1986	R	−5	−8
1990	R	−8	−1
1994	D	−53	−8

Note: Each entry is the difference between the number of seats won by the president's party in that midterm election and the number of seats won by that party in the preceding general election. Because of changes in the overall number of seats in the Senate and House, in the number of seats won by third parties, and in the number of vacancies, a Republican loss is not always matched precisely by a Democratic gain, or vice versa

[a] Although the Republicans gained nine seats in the 1902 elections, they actually lost ground to the Democrats, who gained twenty-five seats after the increase in the overall number of representatives after the 1900 census.

Sources: 1862–1990: Norman J. Ornstein et al., eds., *Vital Statistics on Congress, 1993–1994* (Washington, D.C.: Congressional Quarterly, 1994), 53; 1994: *Congressional Quarterly Weekly Report* (1994), 3232, 3240, and this volume, Table 1-9.

Table 1-16 House and Senate Incumbents Reelected, Defeated, or Retired, 1946–1996

Chamber/ years	Retired[a]	Number seeking reelection	Defeated Primaries	Defeated General election	Reelected Total	Reelected Percentage of those seeking reelection
House						
1946	32	398	18	52	328	82.4
1948	29	400	15	68	317	79.3
1950	29	400	6	32	362	90.5
1952	42	389	9	26	354	91.0
1954	24	407	6	22	379	93.1
1956	21	411	6	16	389	94.6
1958	33	396	3	37	356	89.9
1960	26	405	5	25	375	92.6
1962	24	402	12	22	368	91.5
1964	33	397	8	45	344	86.6
1966	22	411	8	41	362	88.1
1968	23	409	4	9	396	96.8
1970	29	401	10	12	379	94.5
1972	40	390	12	13	365	93.6
1974	43	391	8	40	343	87.7
1976	47	384	3	13	368	95.8
1978	49	382	5	19	358	93.7
1980	34	398	6	31	361	90.7
1982	40	393	10	29	354	90.1
1984	22	411	3	16	392	95.4
1986	40	394	3	6	385	97.7
1988	23	409	1	6	402	98.3
1990	27	406	1	15	390	96.0
1992	65	368	19	24	325	88.3
1994	48	382	4	35	347	90.8
1996	45	379	2	21	358	94.5
Senate						
1946	9	30	6	7	17	56.7
1948	8	25	2	8	15	60.0
1950	4	32	5	5	22	68.8
1952	4	31	2	9	20	64.5
1954	6	32	2	6	24	75.0
1956	6	29	0	4	25	86.2
1958	6	28	0	10	18	64.3
1960	5	29	0	1	28	96.6
1962	4	35	1	5	29	82.9
1964	2	33	1	4	28	84.8
1966	3	32	3	1	28	87.5
1968	6	28	4	4	20	71.4

(Table continues)

Table 1-16   *(Continued)*

Chamber/ years	Retired[a]	Number seeking reelection	Defeated		Reelected	
			Primaries	General election	Total	Percentage of those seeking reelection
1970	4	31	1	6	24	77.4
1972	6	27	2	5	20	74.1
1974	7	27	2	2	23	85.2
1976	8	25	0	9	16	64.0
1978	10	25	3	7	15	60.0
1980	5	29	4	9	16	55.2
1982	3	30	0	2	28	93.3
1984	4	29	0	3	26	89.6
1986	6	28	0	7	21	75.0
1988	6	27	0	4	23	85.2
1990	3	32	0	1	31	96.9
1992	7	28	1	4	23	82.1
1994	8	26	0	2	24	92.2
1996	13	20	1	1	19	92.3

[a] Does not include persons who died or resigned from office before the election.

Sources: 1946–1992: Norman J. Ornstein et al., eds., *Vital Statistics on Congress, 1993–1994* (Washington, D.C.: Congressional Quarterly, 1994), 58, 59; *Congressional Quarterly Weekly Report* (1994), 2995, 3232, 3240; (1996), 3225, 3232, 3233.

Table 1-17   Incumbent Reelection Rates: Representatives, Senators, and Governors, General Elections, 1960–1996

Year/office	Number of incumbents			Incumbents winning election	Incumbents reelected with 60+ percent of the major-party vote
	Ran	Won	Lost		
1960					
House	400	374	26	93.5%	58.9%
Senate	29	28	1	96.6	41.3
Governor	13	7	6	53.8	15.4
1962					
House	396	381	15	94.3	63.6
Senate	34	29	5	85.3	26.4
Governor	24	15	9	62.5	12.5
1964					
House	389	344	45	88.4	58.5
Senate	32	28	4	87.5	46.8
Governor	14	12	2	85.7	42.9
1966					
House	402	362	40	90.1	67.7
Senate	29	28	1	96.6	41.3
Governor	21	14	7	66.7	23.8
1968					
House	401	396	5	98.8	72.2
Senate	24	20	4	83.3	37.5
Governor	13	9	4	69.2	15.4
1970					
House	391	379	12	96.9	77.3
Senate	29	23	6	79.3	31.0
Governor	24	17	7	70.8	4.2
1972					
House	380	367	13	95.6	77.8
Senate	25	20	5	80.0	52.0
Governor	9	7	2	77.8	44.5
1974					
House	383	343	40	89.6	66.4
Senate	25	23	2	92.0	40.0
Governor	22	17	5	77.3	36.4
1976					
House	381	368	13	96.6	69.2
Senate	25	16	9	64.0	40.0
Governor	7	5	2	71.4	28.6
1978					
House	378	359	19	95.0	76.6
Senate	22	15	7	68.1	31.8
Governor	21	16	5	76.2	28.6

(Table continues)

Table 1-17   *(Continued)*

Year/office	Number of incumbents			Incumbents winning election	Incumbents reelected with 60+ percent of the major-party vote
	Ran	Won	Lost		
1980					
House	392	361	31	90.7	72.9
Senate	25	16	9	55.2	40.0
Governor	10	7	3	70.0	30.0
1982					
House	381	352	29	92.4	68.9
Senate	30	28	2	93.3	56.7
Governor	24	19	5	79.2	41.7
1984					
House	407	391	16	96.1	78.9
Senate	29	26	3	89.7	65.5
Governor	6	4	2	66.7	50.0
1986					
House	391	385	6	98.5	84.5
Senate	28	21	7	75.0	50.0
Governor	17	15	2	88.2	52.9
1988					
House	409	402	6	98.3	87.3
Senate	27	23	4	85.0	60.9
Governor	9	8	1	89.0	37.5
1990					
House	406	391	15	96.3	79.5
Senate	32	31	1	96.9	66.7
Governor	23	17	6	73.9	64.7
1992					
House	349	325	24	93.1	65.0
Senate	28	24	4	85.7	46.4
Governor	4	4	0	100.0	100.0
1994					
House	384	349	35	90.9	63.0
Senate	25	23	2	92.0	48.0
Governor	4	4	0	100.0	100.0
1996					
House	382	361	21	94.5	59.9
Senate	20	19	1	95.0	30.0
Governor	7	7	0	100.0	71.4

Note: Percentage gaining more than 60 percent of the vote is calculated on the basis of the vote for the two major parties. "Off-off" year gubernatorial elections, held in Kentucky, Louisiana, Mississippi, New Jersey, and Virginia, are not included in the above totals. For these gubernatorial election outcomes, see *Congressional Quarterly's Guide to U.S. Elections.*

Table 1-17 *(Continued)*

Sources: House and Senate, 1960–1978: Congressional Quarterly, *Elections '80* (Washington, D.C.: Congressional Quarterly, 1980), 14; House and Senate, 1980–1982, and governor, 1960–1966: Richard M. Scammon and Alice V. McGillivray, comps. and eds., *America Votes 16: A Handbook of Contemporary American Election Statistics* (Washington, D.C.: Elections Research Center, Congressional Quarterly, 1985); 1984: *Congressional Quarterly Almanac 1984* (Washington, D.C.: Congressional Quarterly, 1985), B7, B13, B19; House and Senate, 1986–1996, and governor, 1968–1996: *Congressional Quarterly Weekly Report* (1988), 3249, 3266, 3296–3298, 3301–3307; (1989), 1074–1080, 1149; (1990), 3797, 3801, 3838, 3847–3854; (1991), 493–500; (1992), 3557, 3570, 3579, 3596, 3719, 3821; (1993), 973–980; (1995), 1090–1097, (1997), 447–455.

Table 1-18   Congressional Districts with a "Majority-Minority" Population, 1996

State	District number	Percentage of district total population				Representative elected in 1996	Party	Race or ethnicity
		White	Black	His-panic	Other			
Alabama	7	32.0	67.4	0.3	0.3	Hilliard	D	Black
Arizona	2	38.2	6.4	50.5	5.0	Pastor	D	Hispanic
California	8	44.3	12.4	15.7	27.6	Pelosi	D	White
California	9	44.1	31.0	12.0	15.9	Dellums	D	Black
California	16	37.5	4.8	36.8	20.8	Lofgren	D	White
California	20	32.6	6.0	55.4	6.0	Dooley	D	White
California	26	34.2	5.7	52.7	7.4	Berman	D	White
California	30	15.2	3.0	61.5	20.4	Becerra	D	Hispanic
California	31	17.5	1.4	58.5	22.5	Martinez	D	Hispanic
California	32	23.6	38.2	30.2	8.0	Dixon	D	Black
California	33	8.1	3.8	83.7	4.4	Roybal-Allard	D	Hispanic
California	34	26.7	1.7	62.3	9.2	Torres	D	Hispanic
California	35	10.4	40.4	43.1	6.1	Waters	D	Black
California	37	12.0	32.2	45.2	10.7	Millender-McDonald	D	Black
California	46	35.6	2.2	50.0	12.2	Sanchez	D	Hispanic
California	50	31.5	13.6	40.6	14.3	Filner	D	White
Florida	17	19.8	55.7	23.0	1.5	Meek	D	Black
Florida	18	29.2	2.9	66.7	1.2	Ros-Lehtinen	R	Hispanic
Florida	21	25.6	3.3	69.6	1.6	Diaz-Balart	R	Hispanic
Florida	23	39.3	50.2	9.4	1.2	Hastings	D	Black
Georgia	5	—	—	—		Lewis	D	Black
Hawaii	1	27.6	2.4	5.5	64.5	Abercrombie	D	White
Hawaii	2	35.1	2.3	9.2	53.4	Mink	D	Asian
Illinois	1	25.9	69.3	3.6	1.2	Rush	D	Black
Illinois	2	24.6	68.0	6.6	0.7	Jackson	D	Black
Illinois	4	26.8	5.5	65.0	2.7	Gutierrez	D	Hispanic
Illinois	7	27.2	65.2	4.3	3.3	Davis	D	Black
Louisiana	2	—	—	—		Jefferson	D	Black
Maryland	4	31.1	57.7	6.4	4.9	Wynn	D	Black
Maryland	7	26.9	70.6	0.9	1.6	Cummings	D	Black
Michigan	14	28.8	68.8	1.0	1.3	Conyers	D	Black
Michigan	15	24.9	69.7	4.3	1.2	Kilpatrick	D	Black
Mississippi	2	36.5	62.6	0.5	0.3	Thompson	D	Black
Missouri	1	45.8	52.2	0.9	1.2	Clay	D	Black
New Jersey	10	26.4	58.6	12.3	2.7	Payne	D	Black
New Jersey	13	42.3	11.4	41.5	4.8	Menendez	D	Hispanic
New Mexico	3	44.0	1.1	34.6	20.4	Richardson	D	Hispanic
New York	6	22.8	53.3	16.9	7.0	Flake	D	Black
New York	10	21.0	56.6	19.7	2.8	Towns	D	Black
New York	11	15.8	69.4	11.6	3.2	Owens	D	Black
New York	12	14.0	8.7	57.9	19.4	Velázquez	D	Hispanic
New York	15	14.0	36.8	46.4	2.8	Rangel	D	Black

Table 1-18   *(Continued)*

State	District number	Percentage of district total population				Representative elected in 1996	Party	Race or ethnicity
		White	Black	His- panic	Other			
New York	16	4.2	33.2	60.2	2.4	Serrano	D	Hispanic
New York	17	29.1	37.8	29.1	4.0	Engel	D	White
North Carolina	1	41.4	57.0	0.7	0.8	Clayton	D	Black
North Carolina	12	41.4	56.4	0.9	1.3	Watt	D	Black
Ohio	11	39.3	58.3	1.1	1.3	Stokes	D	Black
Pennsylvania	1	36.0	51.4	9.9	2.6	Foglietta	D	White
Pennsylvania	2	34.1	61.8	1.6	2.5	Fattah	D	Black
South Carolina	6	37.1	62.0	0.6	0.4	Clyburn	D	Black
Tennessee	9	39.3	59.0	0.7	0.9	Ford	D	Black
Texas	15	23.9	1.0	74.5	0.6	Hinojosa	D	Hispanic
Texas	16	25.0	3.3	70.4	1.3	Reyes	D	Hispanic
Texas	18	—	—	—		Jackson-Lee	D	Black
Texas	20	32.3	5.5	60.7	1.6	Gonzalez	D	Hispanic
Texas	23	33.6	2.8	62.6	1.1	Bonilla	R	Hispanic
Texas	27	30.7	2.2	66.2	0.9	Ortiz	D	Hispanic
Texas	28	30.4	8.2	60.4	1.6	Rodriguez	D	Hispanic
Texas	29	—	—	—		Green	D	White
Texas	30	—	—	—		Johnson	D	Black
Virginia	3	33.4	63.7	1.4	1.5	Scott	D	Black

Note: "—" indicates districts newly drawn for the 1996 elections for which the Census Bureau had not (as of July 15, 1997) recalculated population data, racial and ethnic breakdowns, and age statistics. Districts listed are those in which the non-Hispanic white population does not constitute a majority. Blacks elected from majority-white districts: Brown (D-Fla.); McKinney (D-Ga.); Bishop (D-Ga.); Carson (D-Ind.); Watts (R-Okla.). Asians elected from majority-white districts: Matsui (D-Calif.); Kim (R-Calif.). Population values are based on the 1990 Census. New districts created by court-ordered redistricting for 1996 are Fla. (3), Ga. (5), La. (2), and Texas (18, 29, 30). In 1999, court-ordered redistricting will go into effect for N.Y. (10, 11, 12).

Sources: District population composition: Election Data Services, Inc.; *Congressional Quarterly Weekly Report* (1996), 3229, (1997), 28, 52.

Table 1-19   Black Elected Officials, by Category of Office, 1970–1993

Year	Federal	State	Substate regional	County	Muni- cipal	Judicial, law en- forcement	Educa- tion	Total
1970	10	169	—	92	623	213	362	1,469
1971	14	202	—	120	785	274	465	1,860
1972	14	210	—	176	932	263	669	2,264
1973	16	240	—	211	1,053	334	767	2,621
1974	17	239	—	242	1,360	340	793	2,991
1975	18	281	—	305	1,573	387	939	3,503
1976	18	281	30	355	1,889	412	994	3,979
1977	17	299	33	381	2,083	447	1,051	4,311
1978	17	299	26	410	2,159	454	1,138	4,503
1979	17	313	25	398	2,224	486	1,144	4,607
1980	17	323	25	451	2,356	526	1,214	4,912
1981	18	341	30	449	2,384	549	1,267	5,038
1982	18	336	35	465	2,477	563	1,266	5,160
1983	21	379	29	496	2,697	607	1,377	5,606
1984[a]	21	389	30	518	2,735	636	1,371	5,700
1985	20	396	32	611	2,898	661	1,438	6,056
1986	20	400	31	681	3,112	676	1,504	6,424
1987	23	417	23	724	3,219	728	1,547	6,681
1988	23	413	22	742	3,341	738	1,550	6,829
1989	24	424	18	793	3,595	760	1,612	7,226
1990	24	423	18	810	3,671	769	1,655	7,370
1991	26	458	15	810	3,683	847	1,638	7,480
1992	26	484	15	857	3,697	847	1,623	7,552
1993	39	533	13	913	3,903	922	1,689	8,015

Note: "—" indicates not available. Figures are for January of the year indicated. In 1992 and 1993 the total includes two shadow senators and one shadow representative from the District of Columbia. As of July 1997 the Joint Center for Political and Economic Studies was preparing a new edition of *National Roster of Black Elected Officials,* which will give information through the 1996 elections.

[a] The 1984 figures reflect blacks who took office during the seven-month period between July 1, 1983, and January 30, 1984.

Source: Black Elected Officials: A National Roster (Washington, D.C.: Joint Center for Political and Economic Studies Press, 1994), xxii.

Table 1-20   Black Elected Officials and Black Voting-Age Population (VAP), by State, 1993

State	Number of black elected officials	Total number of elected officials	Percentage of blacks among elected officials	Percentage black VAP	Ratio of percent black elected officials to percent black VAP[a]
Alabama	699	4,315	16.2	22.9	.707
Alaska	3	1,757	.2	3.8	.053
Arizona	15	3,183	.5	2.8	.179
Arkansas	380	8,331	4.6	13.7	.336
California	273	19,236	1.4	7.4	.189
Colorado	20	8,035	.2	3.9	.051
Connecticut	62	8,489	.7	7.8	.090
Delaware	23	1,227	1.9	16.4	.116
District of Columbia	198	325	60.9	64.3	.947
Florida	200	5,256	3.8	11.8	.322
Georgia	545	6,556	8.3	24.6	.338
Hawaii	0	160	.0	2.1	.000
Idaho	0	4,678	.0	.4	.000
Illinois	465	38,936	1.2	13.9	.086
Indiana	72	11,355	.6	7.3	.082
Iowa	11	17,044	.1	1.5	.067
Kansas	21	16,410	.1	5.4	.019
Kentucky	63	7,388	.9	6.7	.134
Louisiana	636	4,966	12.8	28.5	.449
Maine	1	6,978	.0	.3	.000
Maryland	140	1,943	7.2	24.4	.295
Massachusetts	30	13,631	.2	4.9	.041
Michigan	333	19,923	1.7	13.2	.129
Minnesota	16	18,887	.1	1.9	.053
Mississippi	751	4,944	15.2	32.0	.475
Missouri	185	17,115	1.1	9.8	.112
Montana	0	5,646	.0	.2	.000
Nebraska	6	15,064	.0	3.3	.000
Nevada	10	1,174	.9	5.9	.153
New Hampshire	2	6,721	.0	.6	.000
New Jersey	211	9,345	2.3	13.1	.176
New Mexico	3	2,096	.1	1.8	.056
New York	299	25,999	1.2	16.1	.075
North Carolina	468	5,531	8.5	20.2	.421
North Dakota	0	15,141	.0	.4	.000
Ohio	219	19,750	1.1	10.0	.110
Oklahoma	123	9,290	1.3	6.7	.194
Oregon	10	8,367	.1	1.5	.067
Pennsylvania	158	29,586	.5	8.7	.057
Rhode Island	12	1,120	1.1	3.7	.297
South Carolina	450	3,692	12.2	27.1	.450

(Table continues)

Table 1-20   *(Continued)*

State	Number of black elected officials	Total number of elected officials	Percentage of blacks among elected officials	Percentage black VAP	Ratio of percent black elected officials to percent black VAP[a]
South Dakota	3	9,249	.0	.2	.000
Tennessee	168	6,841	2.5	14.6	.171
Texas	472	26,932	1.8	11.5	.157
Utah	0	2,588	.0	.7	.000
Vermont	2	8,021	.0	.2	.000
Virginia	155	3,112	5.0	17.8	.281
Washington	19	8,032	.2	2.8	.071
West Virginia	21	2,838	.7	2.9	.241
Wisconsin	30	18,242	.2	4.3	.047
Wyoming	1	2,340	.0	.6	.000
Total	7,984	497,785	1.6	11.0	.146

Note: Numbers of black elected officials are as of January 1993. As of July 1997 the Joint Center for Political and Economic Studies was preparing a new edition of *National Roster of Black Elected Officials*, which will give information through the 1996 elections.

[a] Ratios calculated before rounding.

Sources: Number of black elected officials and total number of elected officials: Joint Center for Political and Economic Studies, *Black Elected Officials: A National Roster* (Washington, D.C.: Joint Center for Political and Economic Studies, 1993), xxiii; voting-age population: U.S. Bureau of the Census, Current Population Reports, "Projections of the Population of Voting Age for States: November 1992" (Washington, D.C.: U.S. Government Printing Office, 1992), Series P-25, no. 1085, 5–10.

Table 1-21 Blacks, Hispanics, and Women as a Percentage of State Legislators and State Voting-Age Population

State	Total number of legislators	Blacks				Hispanics				Women			
		Legislators	Percentage	Percentage VAP	Ratio[a]	Legislators	Percentage	Percentage VAP	Ratio[a]	Legislators	Percentage	Percentage VAP	Ratio[a]
Alabama	140	35	25.0	23.0	1.087	0	.0	.6	.000	5	3.6	52.6	.068
Alaska	60	1	1.7	3.7	.450	1	1.7	3.3	.506	8	13.3	48.0	.278
Arizona	90	4	4.4	2.7	1.646	8	8.9	19.5	.457	33	36.7	52.2	.702
Arkansas	135	13	9.6	13.6	.708	1	.7	1.0	.765	23	17.0	53.0	.322
California	120	9	7.5	7.3	1.027	18	15.0	27.3	.549	26	21.7	50.9	.426
Colorado	100	3	3.0	3.9	.769	8	8.0	12.3	.648	34	34.0	51.3	.663
Connecticut	187	13	7.0	7.9	.880	11	5.9	7.0	.839	52	27.8	52.2	.533
Delaware	62	3	4.8	16.5	.293	0	.0	2.7	.000	15	24.2	52.3	.463
Florida	160	20	12.5	12.1	1.033	14	8.8	12.8	.686	37	23.1	53.5	.432
Georgia	236	42	17.8	25.0	.712	0	.0	1.9	.000	39	16.5	51.7	.319
Hawaii	76	0	.0	.2	.000	1	1.3	7.8	.168	12	15.8	51.6	.306
Idaho	105	0	.0	.2	.000	1	1.0	5.8	.164	24	22.9	51.7	.442
Illinois	177	22	12.4	14.0	.888	6	3.4	8.3	.408	46	26.0	51.9	.501
Indiana	150	12	8.0	7.4	1.081	1	.7	1.9	.360	28	18.7	52.0	.359
Iowa	150	1	.7	1.8	.370	0	.0	1.4	.000	31	20.7	52.2	.396
Kansas	165	7	4.2	5.6	.758	3	1.8	4.0	.460	49	29.7	51.7	.575
Kentucky	138	5	3.6	6.8	.533	0	.0	.5	.000	13	9.4	52.2	.181
Louisiana	144	30	20.8	28.5	.731	3	.7	2.4	.290	16	11.1	52.7	.211
Maine	186	0	.0	.2	.000	0	.0	.6	.000	48	25.8	52.1	.496
Maryland	188	36	19.1	25.1	.763	0	.0	2.9	.000	55	29.3	52.1	.561
Massachusetts	200	8	4.0	5.0	.800	0	.0	5.0	.000	45	22.5	52.2	.431
Michigan	148	16	10.8	13.5	.801	0	.0	2.2	.000	34	23.0	52.3	.440
Minnesota	201	1	.5	1.9	.262	2	1.0	1.3	.772	61	30.3	51.7	.587
Mississippi	174	47	27.0	32.0	.844	0	.0	.6	.000	19	10.9	52.8	.207
Missouri	197	16	8.1	9.9	.820	0	.0	1.2	.000	44	22.3	52.4	.426

(Table continues)

Table 1-21 (Continued)

State	Total number of legislators	Blacks				Hispanics				Women			
		Legis-lators	Percent-age	Percent-age VAP	Ratio[a]	Legis-lators	Percent-age	Percent-age VAP	Ratio[a]	Legis-lators	Percent-age	Percent-age VAP	Ratio[a]
Montana	150	0	.0	.2	.000	0	.0	1.4	.000	35	23.3	51.9	.449
Nebraska	49	1	2.0	3.4	.600	0	.0	2.9	.000	13	26.5	52.2	.509
Nevada	63	6	9.5	6.1	1.561	3	4.8	12.3	.388	20	31.7	50.8	.624
New Hampshire	424	1	.2	.4	.590	0	.0	1.0	.000	132	31.1	51.6	.603
New Jersey	120	11	9.2	13.3	.689	3	2.5	10.5	.238	18	15.0	52.3	.287
New Mexico	112	2	1.8	1.8	.992	38	33.9	41.7	.813	30	26.8	52.2	.513
New York	211	26	12.3	16.5	.747	12	5.7	11.9	.478	39	18.5	52.5	.352
North Carolina	170	24	14.1	20.3	.695	1	.6	1.3	.469	29	17.1	51.8	.329
North Dakota	147	0	.0	.4	.000	0	.0	.6	.000	25	17.0	51.6	.330
Ohio	132	16	12.1	10.2	1.188	1	.8	1.3	.565	29	22.0	52.4	.419
Oklahoma	149	5	3.4	6.7	.501	0	.0	2.9	.000	15	10.1	52.1	.193
Oregon	90	3	3.3	1.5	2.222	0	.0	4.2	.000	23	25.6	52.0	.491
Pennsylvania	253	18	7.1	8.7	.818	1	.4	2.1	.185	31	12.3	52.5	.233
Rhode Island	150	8	5.3	3.8	1.404	1	.7	5.2	.128	39	26.0	52.3	.497
South Carolina	170	31	18.2	27.5	.663	0	.0	1.0	.000	23	13.5	52.3	.259
South Dakota	105	1	1.0	.4	2.381	0	.0	.8	.000	19	18.1	52.3	.346
Tennessee	132	16	12.1	14.5	.836	1	.8	.7	1.050	18	13.6	52.3	.261
Texas	181	15	8.3	11.4	.727	35	19.3	27.4	.706	34	18.8	51.5	.365
Utah	104	0	.0	.7	.000	2	1.9	5.2	.369	16	15.4	51.8	.297
Vermont	180	1	.6	.2	2.778	0	.0	.7	.000	58	32.2	51.7	.623
Virginia	140	13	9.3	17.9	.519	0	.0	2.6	.000	21	15.0	51.5	.291
Washington	147	2	1.4	2.7	.504	1	.7	4.7	.145	57	38.8	51.4	.754
West Virginia	134	3	2.2	2.7	.829	0	.0	.5	.000	21	15.7	52.5	.298
Wisconsin	132	8	6.1	4.6	1.318	0	.0	2.0	.000	31	23.5	51.9	.452
Wyoming	90	0	.0	.6	.000	2	2.2	5.7	.391	17	18.9	51.1	.369
United States	7,424	555	7.5	11.4	.656	179	2.4	9.5	.255	1,590	21.4	52.0	.412

Note: Hispanics may be of any race. The counts of black legislators are as of January 1995; Hispanic and female legislators are as of January 1997. Black voting-age population percentage is for November 1994; Hispanic and female voting-age population percentages are for November 1996. As of July 1997 the Joint Center for Political and Economic Studies was preparing a new edition of *National Roster of Black Elected Officials*, which will give information through the 1996 elections.

[a]The ratio between the group's indicated percentage of state legislators and the group's percentage of the state voting-age population. Calculated before rounding.

Sources: Total number of legislators and women legislators: National Conference of State Legislators, "Women in State Legislatures," *http://ncsl.org/programs/legman/about/women.htm* (as of April 16, 1997); black legislators: Joint Center for Political and Economic Studies; Hispanic legislators: National Association of Latino Elected and Appointed Officials Educational Fund, unpublished data; black voting-age population percentage calculated by editors from U.S. Bureau of the Census, Current Population Reports, "Projections of the Voting Age Population for States: November 1994" (Washington, D.C.: U.S. Government Printing Office, 1994), Series P-25, no. 1117, 8–16; Hispanic and female voting-age population percentage calculated by editors from U.S. Bureau of the Census, "Projections of the Population of Voting Age, for States, by Sex, Race, and Selected Ages," *http://www.census.gov/population/www/socdemo/voting/tabcon.html* (as of July 25, 1997).

Table 1-22   Presidential Primaries, 1912–1996

	Democratic party			Republican party		
Year	Number of primaries	Votes cast	Percentage of delegates from primary "states"[a]	Number of primaries	Votes cast	Percentage of delegates from primary "states"[a]
1912	12	974,775	32.9	13	2,261,240	41.7
1916	20	1,187,691	53.5	20	1,923,374	58.9
1920	16	571,671	44.6	20	3,186,248	57.8
1924	14	763,858	35.5	17	3,525,185	45.3
1928	17	1,264,220	42.2	16	4,110,288	44.9
1932	16	2,952,933	40.0	14	2,346,996	37.7
1936	14	5,181,808	36.5	12	3,319,810	37.5
1940	13	4,468,631	35.8	13	3,227,875	38.8
1944	14	1,867,609	36.7	13	2,271,605	38.7
1948	14	2,151,865	36.3	12	2,635,255	36.0
1952	16	4,928,006	39.2	13	7,801,413	39.0
1956	19	5,832,592	41.3	19	5,828,272	43.5
1960	16	5,686,664	38.4	15	5,537,967	38.6
1964	16	6,247,435	41.4	17	5,935,339	45.6
1968	17	7,535,069	48.7	17	4,473,551	47.0
1972	23	15,993,965	66.5	22	6,188,281	58.2
1976	30	16,052,652	76.1	29	10,374,125	70.4
1980	35	18,747,825	81.1	36	12,690,451	78.0
1984	30	18,009,217	67.1	29	6,575,651	66.6
1988	37	23,230,525	81.4	38	12,169,003	80.7
1992	40	20,179,973	88.0	39	13,025,824	85.4
1996	35	10,813,135	70.9	43	14,115,048	85.9

Note: Primaries include binding and nonbinding presidential preference primaries as well as primaries selecting national convention delegates only without indication of presidential preference. Prior to 1980, votes cast in the delegate-only primaries are not included in the total votes cast.

[a] "States" include all jurisdictions having delegates.

Sources: 1936 Democratic delegates: Democratic National Committee; 1964 Democratic delegates: *Congressional Quarterly Weekly Report* (1964), 1140; votes cast, number of primaries, and remaining delegates: *Congressional Quarterly's Guide to U.S. Elections*, 2d ed. (Washington, D.C.: Congressional Quarterly, 1985), 188–221, 387–441; 1988: *Congressional Quarterly Weekly Report* (1987), 1988, (1988), 1892, 1894–1897, 2033, 2254–2255; 1992: Congressional Quarterly, *Guide to the 1992 Democratic National Convention* (Washington, D.C.: Congressional Quarterly, 1992), 69–71, 82, and *Guide to the 1992 Republican National Convention* (Washington, D.C.: Congressional Quarterly, 1992), 63, 67, 78; 1996: *Congressional Quarterly Weekly Report* (1996), 63–64, 79–80.

Figure 1-4 Democratic and Republican Presidential Nominations, Campaign Lengths, 1968–1996

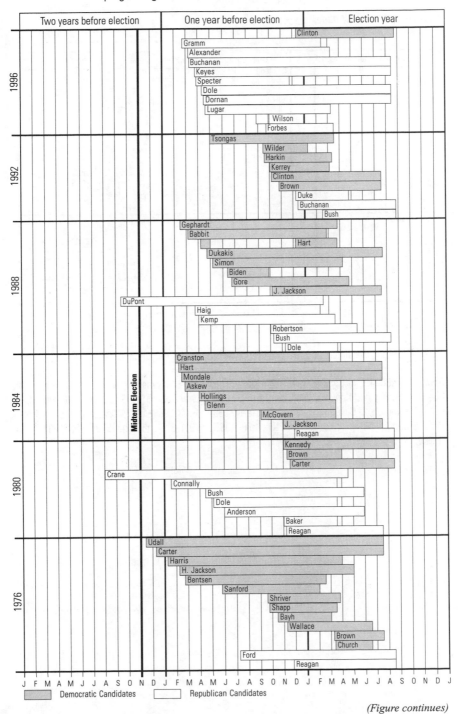

(Figure continues)

Figure 1-4   *(Continued)*

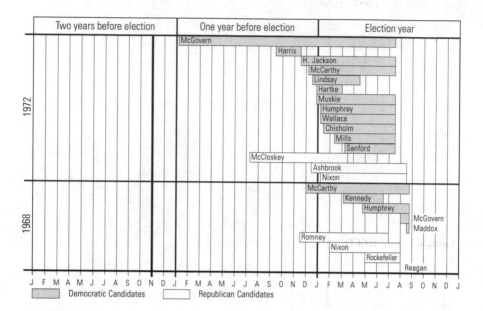

Note: Beginning of campaigns is determined by date of the formal announcement.

Sources: 1968–1984: Congressional Quarterly, *Elections '80* (Washington, D.C.: Congressional Quarterly, 1980), and Congressional Quarterly, *Congressional Quarterly's Guide to U.S. Elections,* 2d ed. (Washington, D.C.: Congressional Quarterly, 1985), 387; 1988–1996: *Congressional Quarterly Weekly Report* (1987), 2732, (1988), 1894, 1896, 1899, (1991), 3735, (1992), 66, 361, 556, 633, 1086, (1995), 2, 13, 15, 3025, 3606, (1996), 641, 716.

Table 1-23 State Methods for Choosing National Convention Delegates, 1968–1996

State	1968	1972	1976	1980	1984	1988	1992	1996
Alabama	DP	DP	OP	OP	CPI	CPI	CPI	CPI
Alaska	CC	CC	CC	CC	CC	CC	CC	CC
Arizona	(D)CO (R)CC	CC	CC	CC	CC	CC	CC	CC
Arkansas	CO	CC	OP	(D)OP (R)CC	CC	OP	OP	OP
California	CP	CP	CP	CP	CP	CP	CP	CP
Colorado	CC	CC	CC	CC	CC	CC	OP	OP
Connecticut	CC	CC	CC	CP	(D)CP (R)CC	CP	CP	CP
Delaware	CC	CC	CC	CC	CC	CC	CC	(D)CC (R)CO
District of Columbia	CP	CP	CP	CP	CP	CP	CP	CP
Florida	CP	CP	CP	CP	CP	CP	CP	CP
Georgia	(D)CO (R)CC	CC	OP	OP	CPI	CPI	CPI	CPI
Hawaii	CC	CC	CC	CC	CC	CC	CC	CC
Idaho	CC	CC	OP	(D)CC (R)OP	(D)CPI	(D)X (R)OP	(D)X (R)OP	(D)X (R)OP
Illinois	DP,CC	CP	OP	OP	DP	DP	DP	DP
Indiana	OP	OP	OP	OP	CPI	CPI	CPI	CPI
Iowa	CC	CC	CC	CC	CC	CC	CC	CC
Kansas	CC	CC	CC	CPI	CC	CC	CPI	CPI
Kentucky	C	CC	CP	CP	CC	CP	CP	CP
Louisiana	CO	CC	CC	CP	CP	CP	CP	(D)CP (R)CC
Maine	CC	CC	CC	CC	CC	CC	CC	CC
Maryland	(D)CO (R)CC	CP	CP	CP	DP	CP	CP	CP
Massachusetts	CPI	CPI	CPI	CPI	CPI	CPI	CPI	CPI
Michigan	CC	OP	OP	(D)CC (R)OP	CC	(D)CC (R)X	CP	(D)CC (R)OP
Minnesota	CC	CC	CC	CC	CC	CC	CC	CC
Mississippi	CC	CC	CC	(D)CC (R)DP	CC	CPI	CPI	CPI
Missouri	(D)CC,CO (R)CC	CC	CC	CC	CC	CPI	CC	CC
Montana	CC	CC	OP	OP	DP	(D)CPI (R)X	(D)OP (R)X	(D)OP (R)X
Nebraska	OP	OP	OP	OP	CP	CP	CP	CPI
Nevada	CC	CC	CP	CP	CC	CC	CC	CC
New Hampshire	CPI	CPI	CPI	CPI	CPI	CPI	CPI	CPI
New Jersey	CPI	CPI	CPI	CPI	DP	DP	DP	(D)CPI (R)DP
New Mexico	CC	CP	CC	CP (R)CP	CP	CP	CP	CP
New York	DP,CO	DP,CO	DP	(D)CP	DP	CP	CP	CP

(Table continues)

Table 1-23   *(Continued)*

State	1968	1972	1976	1980	1984	1988	1992	1996
North Carolina	CC	CP	CP	CP	CP	CP	(D)C (R)O	(D)CP (R)CPI
North Dakota	CC	CC	CC	CC	DP	(D)X (R)OP	(D)X (R)OP	(D)X (R)OP
Ohio	OP	OP	OP	OP	CPI	CPI	CPI	CPI
Oklahoma	CC	CC	CC	CC	CC	CP	CP	CP
Oregon	CP	CP	CP	CP	CP	CP	CP	CP
Pennsylvania	CP,CO	CP	CP	CP	DP	DP	DP	DP
Rhode Island	(D)CO (R)CC	CPI	CPI	CPI	CPI	CPI	CPI	CPI
South Carolina	CC	CC	CC (R)OP	(D)CC	CC (R)OP	(D)CC (R)CC	OP	(D)CC (R)OP
South Dakota	CP	CP	CP	CP	CP	CP	CP	CP
Tennessee	CC	OP	OP	OP	CPI	CPI	CPI	CPI
Texas	CC	CC	OP	CP	(D)CC (R)OP	CPI	CPI	CPI
Utah	CC	CC	CC	CC	CC	CC	CC	CC
Vermont	CC	CC	X	X	X	X	X	OP
Virginia	CC	CC	CC	CC	CC	(D)CPI (R)X	CC	CC
Washington	(D)CC,CO (R)CC (R)OP,CC	CC CP	CC CP	CC CP	CC	CC	CP	(D)CC
West Virginia	CP	CP	CP	CP	CP	CP	(D)CP (R)CPI	(D)CP (R)CPI
Wisconsin	OP	OP	OP	OP	(D)X (R)OP	(D)CPI (R)OP	(D)CPI (R)OP	OP
Wyoming	CC	CC	CC	CC	CC	CC	CC	CC
(Puerto Rico)	(D)C	CC	CC	OP	(D)CPI (R)CC	CPI	CPI	CPI

Note: "CC" indicates delegates chosen by state and local caucuses and conventions; "CO" indicates delegates chosen by state party committee; "CP" indicates delegates chosen or bound by presidential preference primaries open only to voters preregistered as members of the particular parties; "CPI" indicates delegates chosen or bound by presidential preference primaries open only to voters preregistered or considered as members of the particular parties or as independents; "(D)" indicates Democrats; "DP" indicates delegates chosen directly by voters in primaries-no binding presidential preference poll; "OP" indicates delegates chosen or bound by presidential preference primaries open to all registered voters without regard to party preregistration; "(R)" indicates Republicans; "X" indicates having nonbinding presidential preference primaries, but delegates are chosen by party caucuses and conventions.

Sources: 1968–1984: Austin Ranney, ed., *The American Elections of 1984* (Durham, N.C.: Duke University Press, 1985), 330–332 (copyright © American Enterprise Institute for Public Policy Research, reprinted by permission); 1988: derived by the editors from Kevin Coleman, "A Summary of National and State Party Rules and State Laws Concerning the Election of Delegates to the 1988 Democratic and Republican National Conventions" (Washington, D.C.: Congressional Research Service, 1988), Report no. 88-102 GOV; 1992: derived by the editors from *The First Hurrah: A 1992 Guide to the Nomination of the President* (Washington, D.C.: Congressional Quarterly, 1991); *Congressional Quarterly Weekly Report* (1991), 3478; and Thomas M. Durbin and L. Paige Whitaker, *Nomination and Election of the President and Vice President of the United States, 1992: Including the Manner of Selecting Delegates to National Party Conventions* (Washington, D.C.: U.S. Government Printing Office, 1992); 1996: *Congressional Quarterly Weekly Report* (1995), 2485–2599.

Table 1-24 Republican Presidential Primary Returns, 1996

State (date)	Turnout	Alexander	Buchanan	Dole	Forbes	Keyes	Uncommitted
New Hampshire (2/20)	208,993	22.6%[a]	27.2%	26.2%	12.2%	2.7%	9.1%
Delaware (2/24)	32,773	13.3	18.7	27.2	32.7	5.3	2.8
Arizona (2/27)	347,482	7.1	27.6	29.6	33.4	0.8	1.5
North Dakota (2/27)	63,734	6.3	18.3	42.1	19.5	3.2	10.6
South Dakota (2/27)	69,170	8.7	28.6	44.7	12.8	3.4	1.8
South Carolina (3/2)	276,741	10.4	29.2	45.1	12.7	2.1	0.6
Puerto Rico (3/3)	238,748	0.5	0.4	97.9	0.5	0.0	0.7
Colorado (3/5)	247,752	9.8	21.5	43.6	20.8	3.7	0.6
Connecticut (3/5)	130,418	5.4	15.1	54.4	20.1	1.7	3.3
Georgia (3/5)	559,067	13.6	29.1	40.6	12.7	3.1	0.9
Maine (3/5)	67,280	6.6	24.5	46.3	14.8	1.8	5.9
Maryland (3/5)	254,246	5.5	21.1	53.3	12.7	5.4	2.0
Massachusetts (3/5)	284,833	7.5	25.2	47.7	13.9	1.8	3.8
Rhode Island (3/5)	15,009	19.0[b]	2.6[a]	64.4	0.9[a]	0.2[a]	12.9
Vermont (3/5)	58,113	10.6[b]	16.7	40.3	15.6	—	16.8
Florida (3/12)	898,070	1.6	18.1	56.9	20.2	1.9	1.3
Louisiana (3/12)	77,789	2.1	33.1	47.8	13.2	3.2	0.6
Mississippi (3/12)	151,925	1.8	25.9	60.3	8.0	1.9	2.1
Oklahoma (3/12)	264,542	1.3	21.5	59.3	14.1	2.4	1.4
Oregon (3/12)	407,514	7.0	21.3	50.8	13.3	3.5	4.1
Tennessee (3/12)	289,043	11.3	25.2	51.2	7.7	2.7	1.9
Texas (3/12)	1,019,803	1.8	21.4	55.6	12.8[b]	4.1	4.2
Illinois (3/19)	818,364	1.5	22.7	65.1	4.9	3.7	2.1
Michigan (3/19)	524,161	1.5	33.9	50.6	5.1	3.1	5.9
Ohio (3/19)	955,017	2.0	21.5	66.4	6.0	2.9	1.1
Wisconsin (3/19)	576,575	1.9	33.8	52.3	5.6	3.1	3.3
California (3/26)	2,452,312	1.8	18.4	66.1	7.5	3.8	2.5

(Table continues)

Table 1-24 *(Continued)*

State (date)	Turnout	Alexander	Buchanan	Dole	Forbes	Keyes	Uncommitted
Nevada (3/26)	140,637	2.3	15.2	51.9	19.2	1.4	10.0
Washington (3/26)	120,684	1.3	20.9	63.1	8.6	4.6	1.4
Pennsylvania (4/23)	684,204	—	18.0	63.6	8.0	5.8	4.5
District of Columbia (5/7)	2,941	—	9.5	75.5	—	—	15.0
Indiana (5/7)	498,444	—	19.4	70.6	9.9	—	—
North Carolina (5/7)	283,213	2.7	13.0	71.5	4.1	4.1	4.5
Nebraska (5/14)	170,591	2.6	10.4	75.7	6.2	3.0	2.1
West Virginia (5/14)	125,413	2.9	16.3	68.8	4.9	3.8	3.3
Arkansas (5/21)	42,648	—	23.5	76.5	—	—	—
Idaho (5/28)	118,715	—	22.3	62.3	—	5.0	10.4
Kentucky (5/28)	103,206	3.2	8.1	73.8	3.3	3.7	7.8
Alabama (6/4)	143,295	—	15.7	74.9	—	3.6	5.8
Montana (6/4)	114,463	—	24.4	61.3	7.2	—	7.1
New Jersey (6/4)	209,998	—	11.0	82.3	—	6.7	—
New Mexico (6/4)	67,122	3.9	8.2	75.4	5.7	3.2	3.7
Total	14,115,048	3.5	21.3	59.1	10.1	3.2	2.8

Note: "___" indicates that the candidate or the uncommitted line was not listed on the ballot. Results are based on official returns for the primaries held through April except for Ohio, and on nearly complete but unofficial returns for the primaries held in May and June, except for Idaho and Nebraska, where official returns were available. The New York primary March 7, not listed above, was for election of delegates only; Dole won all 93 at stake.

[a] Votes won by Buchanan, Forbes, and Keyes in Rhode Island were write-ins.

[b] Alexander withdrew from the race March 6. Forbes withdrew from the race March 14.

Source: Congressional Quarterly Weekly Report, March 9, 1996, 646; Congressional Quarterly, *Guide to the Republican National Convention* (Washington, D.C.: Congressional Quarterly, 1996), supplement to vol. 54, no. 31, 63–64.

Table 1-25 Republican Presidential Caucus Results, 1996

State (date)	Turnout	Alexander	Buchanan	Dole	Forbes	Keyes	Uncommitted
Alaska (1/27-29)	9,172	0.6%	32.6%	17.1%	30.7%	9.8%	9.2%
Louisiana (2/6)	22,846	—	44.4	—	—	4.0	51.6
Iowa (2/12)	96,451	17.6	23.3	26.3	10.2	7.4	15.1
Wyoming (3/2)	915	7.2	19.8	40.4	17.6	6.7	8.3
Minnesota (3/5)	28,256	4.6	33.1	41.2	10.3	9.5	1.4
Washington (3/5)	26,158	2.1	28.1	36.4	21.8	7.9	3.8
Missouri (3/9)	10,000	—	36.5	28.5	0.9	9.2	25.0

Note: "—" indicates the candidate was not listed on the caucus ballot or his votes were not tabulated separately. In most cases, results are based on straw votes of caucus participants at first-round caucus events. However, in Louisiana, voters balloted directly for national convention delegates; in Missouri, the results reflected the preferences of delegates elected to the next stage of the caucus process. Turnout is estimated for Missouri. Percentages do not always add to 100 percent due to rounding.

Source: Congressional Quarterly, Guide to the Republican National Convention (Washington, D.C.: Congressional Quarterly, 1996), supplement to vol. 54, no. 31, 62.

Table 1-26   Location and Size of National Party Conventions, 1932–1996

Year	Democrats Location	Delegate votes	Republicans Location	Delegate votes
1932	Chicago	1,154	Chicago	1,154
1936	Philadelphia	1,100	Cleveland	1,003
1940	Chicago	1,100	Philadelphia	1,000
1944	Chicago	1,176	Chicago	1,056
1948	Philadelphia	1,234	Philadelphia	1,094
1952	Chicago	1,230	Chicago	1,206
1956	Chicago	1,372	San Francisco	1,323
1960	Los Angeles	1,521	Chicago	1,331
1964	Atlantic City	2,316	San Francisco	1,308
1968	Chicago	2,622	Miami Beach	1,333
1972	Miami Beach	3,016	Miami Beach	1,348
1976	New York	3,008	Kansas City	2,259
1980	New York	3,331	Detroit	1,994
1984	San Francisco	3,933	Dallas	2,235
1988	Atlanta	4,161	New Orleans	2,277
1992	New York	4,288	Houston	2,210
1996	Chicago	4,289	San Diego	1,990

Note: The number of delegates (persons attending) may be larger because of fractional votes.

Sources: 1932–1992: *Congressional Quarterly's Guide to U.S. Elections*, 3d ed. (Washington, D.C.: Congressional Quarterly, 1994), 14–15; 1996: *Congressional Quarterly Weekly Report* (1996, supplement to no. 33), 74, 90.

Table 1-27 Profile of National Convention Delegates, 1944–1996 (percent)

	1944 D	1944 R	1968 D	1968 R	1972 D	1972 R	1976 D	1976 R	1980 D	1980 R	1984 D	1984 R	1988 D	1988 R	1992 D	1992 R	1996 D	1996 R
Women	11	9	13	16	40	29	33	31	49	29	49	44	48	33	50	43	53	36
Black	—	—	5	2	15	4	11	3	15	3	18	4	23	4	18	5	17	3
Under thirty	—	—	3	4	22	8	15	7	11	5	8	4	4	3	5	—	6	2
Lawyer	38	37	28	22	12	—	16	15	13	15	17	14	16	17	12	—	10	11
Teacher	—	—	8	2	11	—	12	4	15	4	16	6	14	5	9	—	9	2
Union member	—	—	—	—	16	—	21	3	27	4	25	4	25	3	28	—	24	4
Attending first convention	63	63	67	66	83	78	80	78	87	84	78	69	65	68	62	—	61	56
Protestant	—	—	—	—	42	—	47	73	47	72	49	71	50	69	49	—	47	62
Catholic	—	—	—	—	26	—	34	18	37	22	29	22	30	22	31	—	30	25
Jewish	—	—	—	—	9	—	9	3	8	3	8	2	7	2	9	—	6	3
Liberal	—	—	—	—	—	—	40	3	46	2	48	1	43	0	47	1	43	0
Moderate	—	—	—	—	—	—	47	45	42	36	42	35	43	35	44	32	48	27
Conservative	—	—	—	—	—	—	8	48	6	58	4	60	5	58	5	63	5	70
Median age	—	—	49	49	42	—	43	48	44	49	43	51	46	51	46	—	—	—

Note: "D" indicates Democrat; "R" indicates Republican; "—" indicates not available.

Sources: 1944: Barbara Farah, "Delegate Polls: 1944–1984," *Public Opinion* (August/September 1984): 43–45; 1968–1988: Martin Plissner and Warren J. Mitofsky, "The Making of the Delegates, 1968–1988," *Public Opinion* (September/October 1988): 47 (reprinted with permission of the American Enterprise Institute for Public Policy Research); 1992 (ideology, Democratic): *"The New York Times* Democratic Delegate Poll"; 1992 (other Democratic): "New York *Newsday* Democratic Delegate Survey"; 1992 (Republican): Martin Plissner, "The 1992 Republican Convention Delegates," CBS News; 1996: *New York Times*/CBS News Poll, 1996 Democratic Delegate Survey and 1996 Republican Delegate Survey.

Table 1-28   Convention Votes Presidential Candidates Received from Caucus State Delegates and Primary State Delegates, 1964–1992

Year/candidate	Caucus states	Primary states	Number of convention votes	Percentage of convention
1964 Republican convention				
Goldwater	74.5%	60.5%	883	67.5
Scranton	10.7	22.1	214	16.4
Rockefeller	0.6	16.8	114	8.7
Others	14.2	0.6	97	7.4
Total	N=655	N=653	1,308	100.0
1968 Democratic convention				
Humphrey	80.2	53.4	1,760.25	67.1
McCarthy	12.1	34.4	601	22.9
McGovern	3.8	7.5	146.5	5.6
Others	4.0	4.7	114.25	4.4
Total	N=1,346	N=1,276	2,622	100.0
1968 Republican convention				
Nixon	59.6	43.2	692	51.9
Rockefeller	14.4	27.9	277	20.8
Reagan	11.2	16.4	182	13.7
Others	14.7	12.4	182	13.7
Total	N=706	N=627	1,333	100.0
1972 Democratic convention				
McGovern	41.0	64.9	1,715.4	56.9
Jackson	30.0	11.5	534	17.7
Wallace	7.3	15.5	385.7	12.8
Others	21.7	8.1	380.9	12.6
Total	N=1,009	N=2,007	3,016	100.0
1976 Republican convention				
Ford	44.9	55.9	1,187	52.5
Reagan	55.1	43.9	1,070	47.4
Others	0.0	0.1	2	0.1
Total	N=693	N=1,566	2,259	100.0
1980 Democratic convention				
Carter	71.0	60.8	2,123	63.7
Kennedy	24.3	38.6	1,150.5	34.5
Others	4.7	0.5	57.5	1.7
Total	N=953	N=2,378	3,331	100.0

Table 1-28   *(Continued)*

Year/candidate	Caucus states	Primary states	Number of convention votes	Percentage of convention
1984 Democratic convention				
Mondale	56.3%	55.6%	2,191	55.9
Hart	29.6	31.2	1,200.5	30.6
Jackson	11.9	11.9	465.5	11.9
Others	2.3	1.3	66	1.7
Total	N=1,460	N=2,463	3,923	100.0
1988 Democratic convention				
Dukakis	62.6	71.5	2,876.25	69.9
Jackson	36.2	28.1	1,218.50	29.6
Others	1.2	0.4	23	0.6
Total	N=766.75	N=3,351.00	4,117.75	100.0
1992 Democratic convention				
Brown	10.9	14.2	596	13.9
Clinton	84.4	77.8	3,372	78.6
Tsongas	3.7	5.5	209	4.9
Others	1.0	2.5	111	2.6
Total	N=514	N=3,774	4,288	100.0

Note: Shown are major presidential candidates with substantial opposition. In 1996, neither the Republican candidate (Dole) nor the Democratic candidate (Clinton) had substantial opposition at the nominating convention. The table is based on first-ballot votes before switches. For 1984–1992, votes of Democratic superdelegates not chosen through caucuses or primaries are counted as if they were chosen by the delegate selection method in their state. States holding both primaries and caucuses are counted among primary states in these calculations. ("States" include all jurisdictions having delegates.)

Sources: 1964–1980: Congressional Quarterly, *Elections '84* (Washington, D.C.: Congressional Quarterly, 1984), 50; 1984: compiled by the editors from *Congressional Quarterly Almanac 1984* (Washington, D.C.: Congressional Quarterly, 1985), B68; 1988: *Congressional Quarterly Weekly Report* (1988), 2033, 1872–1892, 1894–1895, (1992), 2220.

Table 1-29 Legislative Districting: Deviations from Equality in Congressional and State Legislative Districts (percent)

| | Congressional districts | | | State legislative districts | | | | | |
| | | | | Senate | | | House | | |
State	1960s	1980s	1990s	1960s	1980s	1990s	1960s	1980s	1990s
Alabama	38.6	2.45	[a]	665.4	8.50	9.22	317.7	9.80	10.20
Alaska	AL	AL	AL	467.3	9.77	11.70	75.6	9.99	15.50
Arizona	107.2	.08	[a]	704.7	8.40	9.85	151.4	8.40	9.85
Arkansas	54.2	.73	.73	88.4	9.15	9.27	150.9	9.15	9.52
California	451.4	.08	.49	1,528.4	4.60	1.60	118.9	3.60	1.80
Colorado	104.5	[a]	[a]	117.6	3.98	4.90	107.6	4.94	4.96
Connecticut	87.7	.46	.05	200.6	3.92	7.98	937.8	8.35	8.78
Delaware	AL	AL	AL	251.0	9.78	10.18	444.3	25.10	9.58
Florida	102.5	.13	[a]	710.7	1.05	0.86	592.5	0.46	4.99
Georgia	139.9	—	.93	746.1	9.99	9.95	954.9	9.94	9.95
Hawaii	AL	[a]	[a]	217.3	18.60	9.86	151.5	8.60	9.78
Idaho	45.8	.04	[a]	611.0	5.35	9.88[a]	139.2	5.35	9.88[a]
Illinois	65.2	.03	[a]	295.2	1.75	[a]	220.7	2.80	[a]
Indiana	96.0	2.96	[a]	130.9	4.04	2.19	162.2	4.45	3.36
Iowa	22.7	.05	.05	419.2	0.71	1.45	490.7	1.78	1.97
Kansas	38.2	.34	.01	599.5	6.50	6.89	381.8	9.90	9.72
Kentucky	60.0	1.39	[a]	208.6	7.52	6.13	185.9	13.47	9.91
Louisiana	66.8	.42	.04	259.6	8.40	9.78	364.2	9.69	9.97
Maine	8.6	[a]	[a]	114.0	10.18	4.16	167.8	10.94	43.74[b]
Maryland	123.6	.35	[a]	443.5	9.80	9.84	258.0	15.70	10.67
Massachusetts	23.9	1.09	[a]	88.6	—	4.75	213.9	—	9.92
Michigan	156.7	[a]	[a]	306.1	16.24	15.83	142.4	16.34	16.13
Minnesota	25.2	.01	[a]	143.0	4.61	3.42	348.6	3.93	5.90
Mississippi	72.2	—	.02	251.9	4.61	8.96	359.8	4.90	9.97
Missouri	29.7	.18	.20	46.1	6.10	8.42	184.8	9.30	8.96

State									
Montana	37.4	—	AL	648.6	—	9.51	161.6	—	9.97
Nebraska	26.8	.23	.20[a]	99.5	9.43	3.81	c	c	c
Nevada	AL	.60	a	754.6	8.20	2.28	730.9	9.70	4.55
New Hampshire	18.6	.24	.07	101.3	7.60	12.36	383.7	13.74	14.53
New Jersey	81.7	.69	a	305.2	7.70	4.60	93.2	7.70	4.60
New Mexico	AL	.87	.16[a]	876.7	9.83	9.58	189.7	9.87	9.89
New York	29.5	1.64	a	81.6	5.29	4.29	120.6	8.17	9.43
North Carolina	55.6	1.76	a	249.6	9.46	9.94	204.7	9.66	9.97
North Dakota	10.8	AL	AL[a]	288.6	9.93	8.71	103.7	9.93	8.71
Ohio	121.1	.68	a	72.8	8.88	13.60	122.6	9.67	13.60
Oklahoma	83.8	.58	a	629.2	5.60	3.93	293.9	10.98	6.13
Oregon	58.2	.15	a	74.3	3.73	1.69	69.7	5.34	1.89
Pennsylvania	59.6	.24	.01	222.1	1.93	1.86	249.8	2.82	4.94
Rhode Island	14.0	.02	.02	248.9	—	13.00	215.4	10.47	14.70
South Carolina	65.3	.28	a	400.6	—	1.00	108.1	9.88	5.20
South Dakota	92.6	AL	AL[a]	170.9	12.90	9.47	145.2	12.40	9.47
Tennessee	101.8	2.40	a	183.2	10.22	13.92	211.8	1.66	9.96
Texas	167.0	.28	a	355.8	1.82	9.98	111.9	9.95	9.99
Utah	57.2	.43	.02	154.9	7.80	7.60	224.4	5.41	7.94
Vermont	AL	AL	AL[a]	120.3	16.18	16.36	2,088.4	19.33	17.62
Virginia	57.1	1.81	a	235.9	10.65	8.53	308.8	5.11	9.67
Washington	41.2	.06	a	217.5	5.40	a	158.4	5.70	a
West Virginia	32.0	.50	.09[a]	372.4	8.96	9.98	188.9	9.94	9.96
Wisconsin	74.3	.14	a	110.7	1.23	0.52	171.7	1.74	0.92
Wyoming	AL	AL	AL	221.4	63.70	9.60	120.6	89.40	9.97

Note: "AL" indicates at-large district (only one congressional representative). "—" indicates not available. Figures represent the absolute sum of the maximum percentage deviations (positive and negative) from the average district population. 1960s data are from 1962; 1980s data are as of April 1983; 1990s data are as of August 1994. The 1980 state house plans for Delaware and Rhode Island contained errors that increased total deviation, but had not been corrected.

[a] Less than .01 percent.
[b] Apart from two districts, the deviation is 8.15.
[c] Nebraska's state legislature is unicameral.

Sources: 1960s: Robert G. Dixon Jr., Democratic Representation: Reapportionment in Law and Politics (New York: Oxford University Press, 1968), Appendices A–B (copyright 1985, Regents of the University of California, all rights reserved); 1980s: Election Data Services, Inc.; 1990s: Supreme Judicial Court of Maine, In re Apportionment of 1993 (Docket #IC-93-229) and unpublished data from the National Conference of State Legislators, the Illinois State Board of Elections, the

Table 1-30   Jurisdictions Subject to Federal Preclearance of Election Law
Changes and to Minority Language Provisions of the Voting
Rights Act

Coverage under preclearance provisions	Coverage under minority language provisions	
Alabama	Alaska (16)[a]	Nevada (2)
Alaska	Arizona	New Jersey (5)
Arizona	California (21)	New Mexico (26)
California (4)	Colorado (11)	New York (7)
Florida (5)	Connecticut (4)[a]	North Carolina (1)
Georgia	Florida (9)	North Dakota (3)
Louisiana	Hawaii (3)	Oklahoma (1)
Michigan (2)[a]	Idaho (4)	Oregon (1)
Mississippi	Illinois (1)	Pennsylvania (1)
New Hampshire (10)[a]	Iowa (1)	Rhode Island (1)[a]
New York (3)	Louisiana (1)	South Dakota (8)
North Carolina (40)	Massachusetts (5)[a]	Texas
South Carolina	Michigan (4)[a]	Utah (2)
South Dakota (2)	Mississippi (6)	Wisconsin (1)
Texas		
Virginia		

Note: "Preclearance" means that changes in elections laws must be approved by the U.S. Justice Department. "Language provisions" require covered jurisdictions to provide bilingual voting materials to members of specified minority language groups. Numbers in parentheses indicate the number of counties in the state affected by the provisions. If there are no parentheses, coverage is statewide.

[a] Number of towns, townships, cities, boroughs, or areas.

Sources: Preclearance: 28 *Code of Federal Regulations* Ch. 1 (7-1-89 Edition), 577–578; language: 28 *Code of Federal Regulations*, Pt. 55, Appendix, 611–615. *Federal Register*, vol. 57, no. 182, September 18, 1992, 43214–43217.

Table 1-31 Term Limits on State Legislators

State[a]	Lower house (years)[b]	Upper house (years)[b]	Year adopted	Percent support	Effective as of[c]	Mechanism[d]	Break in service[e]
Arizona	8	8	1992	74	2000	L	2 years
Arkansas	6	8	1992	60	1998 & 2000	L	lifetime
California[f]	6	8	1990	52	1996 & 1998[g]	L	lifetime
Colorado	8	8	1990	71	1998	L	4 years
Florida	8	8	1992	77	2000	B	2 years
Idaho	8/15	8/15	1994	59	2002	B	contingent
Louisiana	12	12	1995	76	2007	L	4 years
Maine	8	8	1993	68	1996	L	2 years
Massachusetts[h]	8	8	1994	52	2002	B	2 years
Michigan	6	8	1992	59	1998 & 2000	L	lifetime
Missouri	8	8	1992	75	2000	L	lifetime
Montana	8/16	8/16	1992	67	2000	B	contingent
Nebraska[i]	Unicameral	8	1994	68	2002	L	4 years
Nevada	12	12	1994	70	1998	L	lifetime
Ohio	8	8	1992	66	2000	L	4 years
Oklahoma	12 years total in legislature		1990	67	2002	L	lifetime
Oregon	6[j]	8[j]	1992	70	1998 & 2000	L	lifetime
South Dakota	8	8	1992	64[k]	2000	L	2 years
Utah	12	12	1994		2006	L	2 years
Washington	6/12[l]	8/14[l]	1992	52	1998 & 2000	B	contingent
Wyoming	6/12	12/24	1992	77	1998 & 2004	L	contingent

Note: States have varying provisions for counting partial terms due to appointment or special election. In many states, limits are defined in terms of times elected rather than years served or contain a clause such as "or, but for resignation, would have served."

(Notes continue)

Table 1-31 *(Continued)*

[a] Twenty-two states enacted term limits for members of Congress between 1992 and 1994—20 of those listed here, plus Alaska and North Dakota. (In addition, a federal as well as a state limitation was scheduled to be on the ballot in 1995 in Mississippi, and New Hampshire was about to enact term limits for members of Congress.) On May 23, 1995, the Supreme Court ruled 5–4 in *U.S. Term Limits v. Thornton* that these provisions were unconstitutional. In Florida, Michigan, Missouri, and Oregon, the term limits provision stated that, should any part of the law be declared unconstitutional, it is the wish of the voters that the expressed limits be respected voluntarily.

[b] Number of years an individual may serve before limits are applied. A pair of numbers indicates that an individual may not serve more than a certain number of years over a longer period—e.g., six of the previous 12 years—whether or not those years are consecutive.

[c] The year in which incumbent legislators will first be excluded from ballots or prevented from serving.

[d] Strict term limits (L) prohibit service in the legislature. Ballot access restrictions (B) prevent a candidate's name from being placed on the ballot but do not prevent a candidate from being elected on write-in votes.

[e] Length of time an individual must "sit out" before serving (or having ballot access) again. The time may vary when the term limit law specifies that an individual may serve no more than a certain number of years over a longer period.

[f] In October 1997, the U.S. Court of Appeals struck down the California term limits law on the grounds that voters had not been informed that individuals would be barred for their lifetimes from serving more than the stated limits. It is unknown whether the case will be heard by the Supreme Court.

[g] Senators in office on November 6, 1990, whose office was not on the ballot on that date may serve only one additional term.

[h] On July 11, 1997, the Massachusetts Supreme Court struck down the state term limit statute on constitutional grounds.

[i] Nebraska voters have twice approved state term limits. However, the law has been voided both times on technical grounds.

[j] No more than 12 years total in the legislature.

[k] Passed by the legislature in early 1994. In November 1994, voters rejected an initiative that included additional term limit and other electoral reforms.

[l] No more than 14 our of 20 years combined in both houses of the legislature.

Sources: Texts of state measures. Percent of support: "21 States with Term Limits" (Washington, D.C.: U.S. Term Limits, April 28, 1997).

2

Campaign Finance and Political Action Committees (PACs)

- **Contribution Limits**
- **Presidential and Congressional Campaign Financing**
- **Party Expenditures**
- **Political Action Committees (PACs)**

One of the most important aspects of election campaigns and political activities more generally is money: who gives it, who spends it, who regulates it, and what effect it has. Surprisingly, there is a huge quantity of information available on the subject. This is chiefly owing to the large number of elections in the United States and the effort in the past two decades to collect data about them and make these data available to the public. This chapter presents information on the amounts of money spent by individual presidential candidates (Table 2-4), along with more aggregated information about expenditures by the political parties (Tables 2-8 through 2-10) and congressional candidates (Tables 2-6 and 2-7). The most recent campaign expenditures for all 435 representatives and 100 senators can be found in the section on Congress (Tables 5-10 and 5-11).

One could, in fact, easily be inundated by numbers relating to campaign finance. The publications of the Federal Election Commission (FEC) alone run to multiple volumes every two years, with detailed accountings of receipts and expenditures of candidates in federal elections. More volumes are produced, though inconsistently and much less systematically, by various state agencies. Because such information is so voluminous, it is often summarized as it is here: how much money was contributed to incumbents versus challengers in congressional campaigns (Table 2-6), how much was spent by various types of political action committees (Table 2-13), which PACs are the biggest contributors (Table 2-15), and so on.

This wealth of information has now been collected since the mid-1970s, when the FEC was established. Although there were studies of campaign costs before then, present time series are often limited to this span of twenty years.

Laws regulating campaign contributions, expenditures, and interest groups' activities change so frequently that longer time series are often unobtainable and would be misleading if they could be compiled. For example, the growth of PACs dates from 1974 because changes in the laws at that time allowed their establishment (Table 2-11). Similarly, data on public funding of presidential campaigns date from 1976 (Table 2-5). More recently, vastly increased reliance on so-called soft money has led to new compilations (Table 2-10).

Concern about money is not limited strictly to candidate spending. Indeed, there is probably more concern over interest group spending and about where candidates' funds come from and what, if anything, that money buys. Fortunately, data are increasingly available on interest group finances and on candidates' fund raising as well as expenditures. Much of the data concern PACs, the dominant organizations through which interest groups raise and spend money (Table 2-12). The primary information is about general categories of PACs (Tables 2-11, 2-13, 2-14, and 2-16); the list of the largest PAC contributors illustrates the variety of organizations that fall into these categories (Table 2-15).

Because money is at the heart of interest group activities, matters of campaign finance law are directly relevant in this chapter. At the federal level these regulations consist mainly of fairly straightforward contribution limits (Table 2-1). At the state level, there is a myriad of contribution and expenditure limits (Tables 2-2 and 2-3).

Of course, not all questions about efforts to influence the electoral or the political process involve money (directly anyway). Other aspects of interest group activity that can be quantified are reflected elsewhere in this volume, such as the growth and decline of labor unions (Table 11-8) and interest group ratings of members of Congress on how favorable their votes were to the groups' interests (Tables 5-10 and 5-11).

For obvious reasons no one is able to collect systematically what would surely be the most captivating data on the activities of organized interests, that is, bribes, threats, blackmail, and so forth. While political analysts now have a larger body of material on campaign finances and related matters than ever before, much of this information is buried in hard-to-digest volumes or in seemingly bland lists showing what interests are represented. Yet such data provide more knowledge and more research capabilities than ever before about the scope and potential influence of organized interests.

Table 2-1   Contribution Limits Under Federal Election Commission Act

	Recipient			
Source	Candidate or his/her authorized committee	National party committee[a]	Any other committee	*Total contributions*
Individual	$1,000 per election[b]	$20,000	$5,000	$25,000
Multicandidate committee[c]	$5,000 per election	$15,000	$5,000	NL
Party committee	$1,000–5,000 per election[d]	NL	$5,000	NL
Republican or Democratic Senatorial Campaign Committee,[e] or the National Party Committee, or a combination of both	$17,500 to Senate candidate per calendar year in which candidate seeks election	NA	NA	NA
Any other committee or group[f]	$1,000 per election	$20,000	$5,000	NL

Note: "NL" indicates no limit; "NA" indicates not applicable. Limits on contributions to national party committees and other committees and on total contributions are per calendar year. Contribution limits have been unchanged since the passage of FECA amendments in 1974 (i.e., they have not been raised to take account of inflation). While these limits have decreased the reliance of presidential campaign committees on large contributions and increased the number of contributors (see Clifford W. Brown Jr., Lynda W. Powell, and Clyde Wilcox, *Serious Money*, New York: Cambridge University Press, 1995, chap. 2), the limits have been regularly circumvented, especially in the 1996 election. So-called "soft money" contributions, mostly to the political parties, and which nominally are not coordinated with a candidate's campaign committee, are sometimes very large.

[a] The following are considered national party committees: a party's national committee, the Senate campaign committees, and the national congressional committees, provided they are not authorized by any candidate. Individual contributions made or earmarked to influence a specific election of a clearly identified candidate are counted as if made during the year in which the election is held.
[b] The following are considered separate elections: primary election, general election, runoff election, special election, and party caucus or convention that has authority to select the nominee.
[c] A multicandidate committee is any committee with more than fifty contributors that has been registered for at least six months and, with the exception of state party committees, has made contributions to five or more federal candidates. Most PACs qualify as a multicandidate committee.
[d] Limit depends on whether party committee is a multicandidate committee.
[e] Republican and Democratic Senatorial Campaign committees are subject to all other limits applicable to a multicandidate committee.
[f] Group includes an organization, partnership, or group of persons.

Source: Federal Election Commission.

Table 2-2 Contribution Limits for Funding of State Election Campaigns

State	Individual	Candidate	Candidate's family members	Corporations	Labor unions	PACs	Regulated industries	Parties
Alabama	no	no	no	yes	no	no	yes	no
Alaska	yes	no	yes	yes	yes	yes	yes	no
Arizona	yes	no	no	prohibited	prohibited	yes	prohibited	—
Arkansas	yes	no	yes	yes	yes	yes	yes	yes
California	yes	no	yes	yes	yes	yes	yes	yes
Colorado	no	no	no	no	no	no	no	no
Connecticut	yes	no	yes	prohibited	prohibited	yes	prohibited	no
Delaware	yes	yes	yes	yes	yes	yes	yes	yes
District of Columbia	yes	yes	yes	yes	yes	yes	yes	—[a, c]
Florida	yes	yes	yes	yes	yes	yes	yes	yes
Georgia	yes	no	no	yes	yes	yes	yes	yes
Hawaii	yes	yes	yes	yes	yes	yes	yes	yes
Idaho	no[a]	no[a]	no	no	no	no	no	no
Illinois	no[a]	no[a]	no	no	no	no	no	no
Indiana	no	no	no	yes	yes	yes	yes	no
Iowa	no	no	no	prohibited	no	no	prohibited	no
Kansas	yes	no	yes	yes	yes	yes	yes	no
Kentucky	yes	no	yes	prohibited	yes	yes	prohibited	yes
Louisiana	yes	no	yes	yes	yes	yes	—	no
Maine	yes	no	unlimited for spouse	yes	yes	yes	yes	yes
Maryland	yes	no	unlimited for spouse	yes	yes	yes	yes	no
Massachusetts	yes	no[b]	yes[b]	prohibited	yes	yes	prohibited	yes
Michigan	yes	no[b]	no[b]	prohibited	yes	yes	prohibited	yes
Minnesota	yes	no	yes	prohibited	yes	yes	prohibited	yes
Mississippi	no	no	no	yes	no	no	prohibited	no
Missouri	no	no	yes	no	no	yes	no	yes
Montana	yes	no	yes	prohibited	yes	yes	prohibited	yes

State							
Nebraska	no	no	no	yes	yes	yes	yes
Nevada	yes	yes	yes	yes	yes	yes	no
New Hampshire	yes	no[b]	yes[b]	prohibited	yes	prohibited	yes
New Jersey	yes	no	no[b]	yes	yes	prohibited	yes
New Mexico	no	no	no	no	no	no	no[c]
New York	yes	no	unlimited for spouse	yes	yes	yes	no[c]
North Carolina	yes	no	no	prohibited	yes	prohibited	no
North Dakota	no	no	no	prohibited	no[d]	prohibited	no
Ohio	no	no	no	prohibited	no[d]	prohibited	no
Oklahoma	yes	no	yes	yes	yes	prohibited	yes
Oregon	yes	no	yes	yes	yes	yes	yes
Pennsylvania	no	no[e]	no	prohibited	no	prohibited	no
Rhode Island	yes	no[e]	yes	prohibited	yes	prohibited	yes
South Carolina	yes	no	yes	yes	yes	prohibited	yes
South Dakota	yes	no	no	prohibited	no	prohibited	no
Tennessee	yes	yes	yes	yes	yes	prohibited	yes
Texas	no	no	no	no	no	yes	no
Utah	no	no	no	no	no	yes	no
Vermont	yes	yes	no	yes	yes	yes	no
Virginia	no	no	no	no	no	no	no
Washington	yes	yes	yes	yes	yes	yes	yes
West Virginia	yes	yes	yes	prohibited	yes	prohibited	yes
Wisconsin	yes	no[e]	no[e]	prohibited	yes	prohibited	yes
Wyoming	yes	no	no	prohibited	no	prohibited	no[c]

Note: "—" indicates not available. Limits on sizes of contributions and other restrictions (e.g., from government employees, regulated industries) vary widely across states. For details see source.

[a] Prohibited for judges.
[b] Limited for governor only.
[c] Prohibited in primaries.
[d] Limited for judicial candidates only.
[e] Limited if candidate receives public funds.

Source: Campaign Finance Law 96 (Washington, D.C.: National Clearinghouse Election Administration, Federal Election Commission, 1996), Charts 2A–2B.

Table 2-3   State Campaign Finance: Tax Provisions, Public Funding, and Expenditure Limits

State	Tax provisions[a]	Public funding Source of funds	Public funding Distribution of funds[b]	Expenditure limits[c]
Alabama	surcharge	surcharge	parties	no
Arizona	deduction, surcharge	surcharge, donations	parties	no
California	surcharge	surcharge, direct appropriation	parties	no
District of Columbia	credit	—	—	no
Florida	surcharge	direct appropriation	candidates	yes
Hawaii	deduction, checkoff	checkoff, direct appropriation	candidates	voluntary
Idaho	checkoff	checkoff	parties	no
Indiana	none	revenues from personalized license plates	parties	no
Iowa	checkoff	checkoff	parties	no
Kentucky	checkoff	checkoff	parties	yes
Maine	surcharge	surcharge	parties	yes
Maryland	surcharge	direct appropriation	candidates	yes
Massachusetts	checkoff	checkoff	candidates	no
Michigan	checkoff	checkoff	candidates	yes
Minnesota	checkoff, credit	checkoff, contributions	candidates	yes
Montana	deduction	—	—	no
Nebraska	surcharge	direct appropriation	candidates	no
New Hampshire	—	—	—	voluntary
New Jersey	checkoff	checkoff, direct appropriation	candidates	yes
New Mexico	checkoff	checkoff	parties	no

Table 2-3   *(Continued)*

| State | Tax provisions[a] | Public funding | | Expenditure limits[c] |
		Source of funds	Distribution of funds[b]	
North Carolina	deduction, checkoff, surcharge	checkoff, surcharge	parties, candidates	yes
Ohio	checkoff, credit	checkoff	parties	no
Oklahoma	deduction	—	—	no
Oregon	credit	—	—	voluntary
Rhode Island	checkoff	checkoff	parties, candidates	yes
Utah	checkoff	checkoff	parties	no
Virginia	surcharge	surcharge	parties	no
Wisconsin	checkoff	checkoff	candidates	yes[d]

Note: "—" indicates no such provision. Omitted states have no tax provisions or public funding for campaign finance.

[a] Credits and deductions reduce the taxes paid by an individual; checkoffs neither raise nor lower an individual's taxes; surcharges add to an individual's taxes. Checkoffs and surcharges are usually limited to $1.00–$5.00; deductions and credits are for larger amounts. For details, see source.

[b] Funds distributed to parties are usually given to a party designated by the taxpayer, often for party activities and distribution to candidates. Funds distributed to candidates are given to nonfederal candidates; states vary as to which candidates and whether for primary or general election. For details, see source.

[c] "Yes" indicates a limit on total expenditures. (Only states that provide public funding of candidates or political parties are permitted expenditure limits. See *Buckley v. Valeo*, 424 U.S. 1 [1976].) Most states have some provisions governing the use of campaign funds (e.g., who may make expenditures, how postelection surpluses are handled). For details, see source.

[d] Unless opponents who have not accepted public financing exceed limits.

Source: Campaign Finance Law 96 (Washington, D.C.: National Clearinghouse on Election Administration, Federal Election Commission, 1996), Charts 3A, 4.

Table 2-4 Presidential Prenomination Campaign Finance, 1996

Party/candidate	Federal matching funds	Individual contributions minus refunds	Candidate contributions	Candidate loans minus repayments	Transfers from prior races	Other receipts[a]	Adjusted total receipts	Adjusted total disbursements
Democrats								
Bill Clinton[a]	$13,412,197	$28,285,108	$0	0	$250,000	$542,243	$42,489,548	$38,105,490
Lyndon Larouche	624,691	3,058,562	0	0	0	1,000	3,684,253	3,706,949
Total Democrats	14,036,888	31,343,670	0	0	250,000	543,243	46,173,801	41,812,439
Republicans								
Lamar Alexander	4,573,442	12,635,615	9,583	0	0	396,338	17,614,978	16,353,539
Pat Buchanan	9,812,517	14,659,228	0	0	0	29,431	24,501,176	24,489,005
Bob Dole	13,545,770	29,555,502	0	0	242,169	1,260,651	44,604,092	42,173,706
Bob Dornan	0	297,511	0	44,000	0	5,374	346,885	341,718
Steve Forbes	0	4,203,792	1,000	37,456,000	0	32,689	41,693,481	41,657,444
Phil Gramm	7,356,218	15,880,676	0	0	4,782,085	772,523	28,791,502	28,038,313
Alan Keyes	892,436	3,442,056	2,500	5,000	0	6,173	4,348,165	4,252,471
Richard Lugar[b]	2,643,477	4,803,612	0	0	85,000	237,294	7,769,383	7,631,213
Arlen Specter[b]	1,010,455	2,284,901	0	0	17,000	177,939	3,490,295	3,391,843
Morry Taylor	0	37,854	3,342	6,471,754	0	3,900	6,516,850	6,504,966
Pete Wilson	1,724,254	5,285,889	0	0	2,000	351,072	7,363,215	7,219,912
Total Republicans	41,558,569	93,086,636	16,425	43,976,754	5,128,254	3,273,384	187,040,022	182,054,130
Other party								
Harry Browne (Libertarian)	0	1,112,482	34,271	0	0	1,244	1,147,997	1,073,600
John Hagelin (Natural Law Party)	358,883	700,085	15,250	50,000	0	100	1,124,318	1,117,266

Ross Perot (Reform)	0	82,781	8,215,746	0		0	8,298,527	8,031,229
Dick Lamm[b] (Reform)	0	140,281	5,000	25,000		0	170,281	39,364
Total other parties	358,883	2,035,629	8,270,267	75,000		1,344	10,741,123	10,261,459
Grand total	55,954,340	126,465,935	8,286,692	44,051,754	5,378,254	3,817,971	243,954,946	234,128,028

Note: Figures are from inception through August 31, 1996.

[a] "Other receipts" include party contributions minus refunds, other committee contributions minus refunds, and other loans minus repayment.

[b] Reports covering August 1996 not yet received.

Source: Federal Election Commission, "Financing the 1996 Presidential Campaign," *http://www.fec.gov/pres96/presmstr.htm.*

Table 2-5 Public Funding of Presidential Elections, 1976–1996 (millions)

Year	Spending Limits Primary[a]	Spending Limits Primary plus 20%[a]	Maximum entitlement, primary matching funds[b]	Public funds for each major party convention[c]	Public funds for each major party nominee for general election[d]	Coordinated party spending limit[e]
1976	$10.9	$13.1	$5.5	$2.2	$21.8	$3.2
1980	14.7	17.7	7.4	4.4	29.4	4.6
1984	20.2	24.2	10.1	8.1	40.4	6.9
1988	23.1	27.7	11.5	9.2	46.1	8.3
1992	27.6	33.1	13.8	11.0	55.2	10.3
1996	30.9	37.1	15.5	12.4	61.8	12.0

Note: Amounts in current dollars. John B. Anderson, Independent, received $4.194 million for the 1980 presidential election. Ross Perot received $29.055 million for the 1996 general election.

[a] $10 million + *COLA*. (*COLA* is the cost-of-living adjustment over the base year of 1974.) Campaigns are also allowed to exempt 20 percent of fundraising costs from the overall limit, which, in effect, raises their total spending limit by 20 percent. Legal and accounting costs incurred to comply with the law are exempt from the limit.

[b] Eligible candidates in the presidential primaries may receive public funds to match the individual contributions they raise. Contributions from PACs and party committees are not matchable. Although an individual may give up to $1,000 to a primary candidate, only the first $250 of that contribution is matchable. Presidential candidates become eligible for matching funds by raising more than $5,000 in matchable contributions in each of 20 different states. Candidates must agree to use these public funds only for campaign expenses and they must comply with spending limits.

[c] $4 million + *COLA*. Originally, the limit was $2 million + *COLA*. The base was raised to $3 million for the 1980 convention, then to $4 million for the 1984 convention.

[d] $20 million + *COLA*. Legal and accounting costs incurred to comply with the law are exempt from the limit and may be defrayed from private monies raised in separate compliance funds (subject to contribution limitations and prohibitions).The Republican and Democratic candidates who win their parties' nominations for president are each eligible to receive a grant to cover all the expenses of their general election campaigns. Nominees who accept the funds must agree not to raise private contributions (from individuals, PACs, or party committees) and to limit their campaign expenditures to the amount of public funds they receive. They may use the funds only for campaign expenses. A third-party presidential candidate may qualify for some public funds after the general election if he or she receives at least 5 percent of the popular vote.

[e] $.02 X voting-age population of U.S. + *COLA*. This is the amount that the national party may spend on behalf of its nominee. The party may work in conjunction with the campaign, but the money is raised, spent, and reported by the national party committee. This limit only applies to the general election.

Source: Federal Election Commission Press Office.

Table 2-6 Congressional Campaign Costs, by Party and Incumbency Status, 1987–1996

Year/party/ status	House					Senate				
	Number of candidates	Receipts[a]	Percentage individual contributions	Percentage committee contributions[b]	Expenditures[a]	Number of candidates	Receipts[a]	Percentage individual contributions	Percentage committee contributions[b]	Expenditures[a]
1987–1988										
Democrats	429	137.38	40.88	47.57	123.06	33	96.52	61.84	24.04	96.97
Incumbents	248	102.53	39.46	52.04	88.85	15	51.00	63.84	29.94	51.86
Challengers	154	22.50	47.96	32.62	22.14	12	26.18	73.87	17.38	25.93
Open seats	27	12.35	39.76	37.65	12.07	6	19.34	40.28	17.48	19.18
Republicans	384	105.08	54.43	32.12	99.19	33	86.09	68.15	24.63	88.01
Incumbents	164	72.46	52.40	39.58	67.11	12	47.25	66.94	28.40	49.34
Challengers	194	19.83	59.61	10.94	19.48	15	23.13	75.53	13.49	23.21
Open seats	26	12.79	57.94	22.67	12.60	6	15.71	60.92	29.66	15.45
Other	188	0.81	85.84	0.11	0.81	42	0.24	77.70	1.35	0.23
Total	1,001	243.28	46.88	40.73	223.07	108	182.86	64.83	24.28	185.21
1989–1990										
Democrats	413	142.83	39.61	48.33	130.70	34	85.67	66.49	23.74	83.78
Incumbents	249	111.35	37.98	52.63	99.70	17	63.58	67.82	26.74	61.51
Challengers	132	14.61	47.78	30.25	14.35	14	19.26	63.76	14.54	19.47
Open seats	32	16.87	43.27	35.63	16.65	3	2.83	55.12	18.73	2.81
Republicans	394	105.95	52.43	32.87	98.70	33	92.65	63.69	21.89	88.73
Incumbents	159	70.00	50.86	41.14	63.22	15	55.18	69.50	22.07	52.01
Challengers	206	22.95	56.38	11.29	22.62	15	30.04	57.36	17.44	29.93
Open seats	26	13.00	53.92	26.46	12.86	3	7.42	46.09[c]	38.54[c]	6.80[c]
Other	164	0.96	61.39	8.72	0.97	11	[c]			
Total	971	249.74	45.13	41.62	230.37	78	178.33	65.03	22.78	172.52

(Table continues)

Table 2-6 *(Continued)*

	House					Senate				
Year/party/status	Number of candidates	Receipts[a]	Percentage individual contributions	Percentage committee[b] contributions	Expenditures[a]	Number of candidates	Receipts[a]	Percentage individual contributions	Percentage committee[b] contributions	Expenditures[a]
1991–1992										
Democrats	426	178.57	44.19	44.36	186.53	35	97.65	67.13	25.47	98.63
Incumbents	213	119.35	41.12	51.57	128.44	15	41.43	55.35	37.82	42.71
Challengers	139	22.80	52.73	28.49	22.39	13	37.45	78.82	13.70	37.29
Open seats	74	36.42	48.86	30.69	35.70	7	18.76	69.82	21.70	18.63
Republicans	417	139.55	52.95	28.29	140.30	34	91.87	64.19	21.88	96.70
Incumbents	137	73.06	52.57	40.20	74.59	12	51.90	66.55	27.20	57.37
Challengers	210	41.06	51.03	10.19	40.56	15	19.38	67.63	11.97	19.20
Open seats	70	25.42	57.13	23.28	25.15	7	20.59	54.68	17.79	20.13
Other	294	3.29	58.40	9.17	3.23	43	1.27	31.34	0.75	1.27
Total	1,137	321.40	48.14	37.02	330.05	112	190.79	65.44	23.58	196.60
1993–1994										
Democrats	832	216.87	46.26	40.61	213.23	106	133.51	60.21	17.75	135.87
Incumbents	232	140.62	43.62	50.54	138.79	16	79.94	58.78	19.85	82.46
Challengers	379	29.17	53.88	21.22	28.71	50	15.74	53.97	15.69	15.56
Open Seats	221	47.08	49.41	22.98	45.73	40	37.84	65.84	14.17	37.86
Republicans	871	201.83	56.76	21.66	190.47	118	183.52	57.11	12.52	180.53
Incumbents	159	82.15	59.18	36.37	72.77	10	33.39	63.39	31.31	32.63
Challengers	498	69.77	55.57	9.25	68.62	70	102.30	48.38	30.93	101.60
Open seats	214	49.91	54.45	14.79	49.08	38	47.82	71.40	19.58	46.30
Other	342	2.82	41.34	10.01	1.95	109	2.03	63.31	1.33	1.99
Total	2,045	421.53	51.26	31.33	405.7	333	319.06	58.45	14.64	318.39

1995–1996									
Democrats	827	233.07	50.43	33.18	221.15	96	126.49	62.55	13.13	127.42
Incumbents	172	107.52	47.70	46.36	97.89	7	35.11	76.43	13.88	36.44
Challengers	427	73.07	54.11	22.65	71.72	42	40.52	52.95	6.59	40.39
Open Seats	228	52.48	50.90	20.83	51.55	47	50.86	60.61	17.82	50.59
Republicans	853	266.94	58.20	29.11	251.38	114	157.74	55.64	18.41	159.13
Incumbents	214	172.28	57.43	37.06	158.25	14	46.74	62.22	30.99	49.09
Challengers	414	45.98	63.34	10.27	45.47	32	38.00	61.88	11.25	37.78
Open seats	225	48.67	56.10	18.77	47.66	68	73.00	48.18	14.07	72.26
Other	609	5.38	66.82	14.48	5.30	106	0.93	69.13	0.33	0.92
Total	2,289	505.38	54.71	30.83	477.84	316	285.15	58.75	16.01	287.47

Note: Figures are for general election candidates (primary and general election activity included) for the calendar years indicated. Numbers of candidates are determined from election ballots in the states; financial activity determined from reports filed with the Federal Election Commission. Federal candidates raising or spending less than $5,000 are not required to file with the Federal Election Commission. Data for earlier years can be found in previous editions of *Vital Statistics on American Politics.*

[a] In millions of current dollars.
[b] Prior to 1993–1994, "Committee" refers to contributions received mostly from PACs but also from other candidates' committees and some bodies not registered with the Federal Election Commission. In 1993–1994 "Committee" refers to PACs.
[c] Neither receipts nor expenditures exceeded $5,000.

Sources: 1987–1988 (Other and Total): Federal Election Commission, "FEC Final Report on 1988 Campaign Shows $459 Million Spent," press release, October 31, 1989, 7–8; 1987–1988 (all except Other and Total) and 1989–1990: "1990 Congressional Election Spending Drops to Low Point," press release, February 22, 1991, 7–9; 1991–1992: Federal Election Commission, "1992 Congressional Election Spending Jumps 52% to $678 Million," press release, March 4, 1993, 7; 1993–1994: "1994 Congressional Fundraising Climbs to New High," press release, April 28, 1995, 4–5; 1995–1996: Federal Election Commission, "1995–96 Financial Activity of All Senate and House Campaigns," *http://www.fec.gov/finance/allsum.htm* (as of July 28, 1997).

Table 2-7   Campaign Spending for Winning Congressional Candidates, 1975–1996

Chamber/years	Receipts[a]	Expenditures[a]	Political action committee contributions	
			Total[a]	Percentage of receipts
House				
1975–1976	$42.5	$38.0	$10.9	25.6
1977–1978	60.0	55.6	17.0	28.3
1979–1980	86.0	78.0	27.0	31.4
1981–1982	123.1	114.7	42.7	34.7
1983–1984	144.8	127.0	59.5	41.1
1985–1986	172.7	154.9	72.8	42.2
1987–1988	191.0	171.0	86.4	45.2
1989–1990	198.3	179.1	91.5	46.1
1991–1992	235.9	243.6	97.7	41.4
1993–1994	245.8	230.6	97.6	39.7
1995–1996	321.9	297.2	122.8	38.1
Senate				
1975–1976	21.0	20.1	3.1	14.8
1977–1978	43.0	42.3	6.0	14.0
1979–1980	41.7	40.0	10.2	24.5
1981–1982	70.7	68.2	15.6	22.1
1983–1984	100.9	97.5	20.0	19.8
1985–1986	106.8	104.3	28.4	26.6
1987–1988	121.7	123.6	31.8	26.1
1989–1990	121.5	115.4	31.1	25.6
1991–1992	118.5	123.7	32.2	27.2
1993–1994	151.0	150.7	32.7	21.7
1995–1996	124.9	128.0	29.6	23.7

[a] In millions of current dollars.

Sources: 1975–1980: Federal Election Commission, "1994 Congressional Fundraising Climbs to New High," press release, April 28, 1995, 2; 1981–1996: "Congressional Fundraising and Spending Up Again in 1996," press release, April 14, 1997, 2; percentages calculated by the editors.

Table 2-8 Financial Activity of the National Political Parties, 1983–1996 (millions)

Party/activity	1983–1984	1985–1986	1987–1988	1989–1990	1991–1992	1993–1994	1995–1996
Democrat							
Raised	$98.5	$64.8	$127.9	$85.7	$177.7	$139.1	$221.6
Spent	97.4	65.9	121.9	90.9	171.9	137.8	214.3
Contributions	2.6	1.7	1.7	1.5	1.9	2.2	2.2
Coordinated expenditures[a]	9.0	9.0	17.9	8.7	28.0	21.1	22.6
Independent expenditures[b]	—	—	—	—	—	—	1.5
Republican							
Raised	297.9	255.2	263.3	206.3	267.3	245.6	416.5
Spent	300.8	258.9	257.0	213.5	256.1	234.7	408.5
Contributions	4.9	3.4	3.4	2.9	3.0	2.8	3.7
Coordinated expenditures[a]	20.1	14.3	22.7	10.7	33.8	20.4	31.0
Independent expenditures[b]	—	—	—	—	—	—	10.0

Note: Amounts are in current dollars. Building funds and state and local election spending are not reported to the Federal Election Commission. Data for earlier years can be found in previous editions of *Vital Statistics on American Politics*.

[a] Party committees are also allowed to spend money on behalf of federal candidates, in addition to the money party committees may contribute directly. This spending may be coordinated with a candidate.
[b] The 1996 election cycle was the first in which party committees were permitted to make independent expenditures.

Source: Federal Election Commission, "FEC Reports Major Increase in Party Activity for 1995–96," March 19, 1997, 1.

Table 2-9   Party Contributions and Coordinated Expenditures, by Office and Party, 1975–1996

	Senate		House	
Year/party	Contributions	Expenditures	Contributions	Expenditures
1975–1976				
Democrats	$468,795	$4,359	$1,465,629	$500
Republicans	930,034	113,976	3,658,310	329,583
1977–1978				
Democrats	466,683	229,218	1,262,298	72,892
Republicans	703,204	2,723,880	3,621,104	1,297,079
1979–1980				
Democrats	480,464	1,132,912	1,025,989	256,346
Republicans	677,004	5,434,758	3,498,323	2,203,748
1981–1982				
Democrats	579,337	2,265,197	1,052,286	694,321
Republicans	600,221	8,715,761	4,720,959	5,293,260
1983–1984				
Democrats	441,467	3,947,731	1,280,672	1,774,452
Republicans	590,922	6,518,415	4,060,120	6,190,309
1985–1986				
Democrats	583,305	6,066,372	610,840	1,545,376
Republicans	629,472	9,959,330	1,655,250	4,098,389
1987–1988				
Democrats	488,899	6,592,264	1,197,537	2,880,301
Republicans	721,237	10,260,600	2,650,569	4,162,644
1989–1990				
Democrats	515,332	5,210,002	943,135	3,401,579
Republicans	862,621	7,725,853	2,019,279	3,012,313
1991–1992				
Democrats	689,953	11,915,878	1,234,593	5,883,678
Republicans	807,397	16,509,940	2,197,611	6,906,729
1993–1994				
Democrats	664,700	13,220,395	1,499,943	8,519,892
Republicans	753,551	11,549,856	2,198,148	9,063,415
1995–1996				
Democrats	531,054	8,717,875	1,525,150	6,783,902
Republicans	1,016,699	11,014,061	2,627,868	8,240,158

Note: Includes direct contributions made by party committees to congressional candidates and coordinated expenditures made on their behalf. In current dollars.

Sources: 1975–1984: Norman J. Ornstein et al., eds., *Vital Statistics on Congress, 1987–1988* (Washington, D.C.: Congressional Quarterly, 1987), 102; 1985–1996: Federal Election Commission, press releases.

Table 2-10   National Party Nonfederal Receipts ("Soft Money"),
1991–1996 (millions)

Party	1991–1992	1993–1994	1995–1996
Democrat			
Raised	$36.3	$49.1	$123.9
Spent	32.9	50.4	121.8
Cash on hand	3.8	1.1	3.1
Republican			
Raised	49.8	52.5	138.2
Spent	46.2	48.4	149.7
Cash on hand	4.2	3.7	2.0

Note: Amounts are in current dollars. Totals do not include transfers among national party committees. Prior to the 1991–1992 election cycle, nonfederal receipts of national party committees were not reported. Party committees may, without affecting their other contribution and expenditure limits, spend unlimited amounts ("soft money") on certain grassroots activities specified in the law (for example, voter drives by volunteers in support of the party's presidential nominees and the production of campaign materials for volunteer distribution). "Soft money" can be used to pay a portion of the overhead expenses of party organizations, as well as other shared expenses that benefit candidates in both federal and nonfederal elections. It can be used for issue advocacy, as well as generic party advertising. A portion is transferred from national committees to state and local party committees, while some is contributed directly to candidates in nonfederal races. "Soft money" can also support construction and maintenance of party headquarters.

Source: Federal Election Commission, "FEC Reports Major Increase in Party Activity for 1995–96," March 19, 1997, 2, 9.

Table 2-11   Number of Political Action Committees (PACs), 1974–1996

	Connected[a]						
Date	Corpor-ate	Labor	Trade/member-ship/health	Cooper-ative	Corpor-ation without stock	Noncon-nected[b]	Total
December 31, 1974	89	201	318	—	—	—	608
November 24, 1975	139	226	357	—	—	—	722
December 31, 1976	433	224	489	—	—	—	1,146
December 31, 1977	550	234	438	8	20	110	1,360
December 31, 1978	785	217	453	12	24	162	1,653
December 31, 1979	950	240	514	17	32	247	2,000
December 31, 1980	1,206	297	576	42	56	374	2,551
December 31, 1981	1,329	318	614	41	68	531	2,901
December 31, 1982	1,469	380	649	47	103	723	3,371
December 31, 1983	1,538	378	643	51	122	793	3,525
December 31, 1984	1,682	394	698	52	130	1,053	4,009
July 1, 1985	1,687	393	694	54	133	1,039	4,000
December 31, 1985	1,710	388	695	54	142	1,003	3,992
July 1, 1986	1,734	386	707	56	146	1,063	4,092
December 31, 1986	1,744	384	745	56	151	1,077	4,157
July 1, 1987	1,762	377	795	56	152	967	4,109
December 31, 1987	1,775	364	865	59	145	957	4,165
July 1, 1988	1,806	355	766	60	143	1,066	4,196
December 31, 1988	1,816	354	786	59	138	1,115	4,268
July 1, 1989	1,802	349	831	58	143	1,051	4,234
December 31, 1989	1,796	349	777	59	137	1,060	4,178
July 1, 1990	1,782	346	753	58	139	1,115	4,192
December 31, 1990	1,795	346	774	59	136	1,062	4,172
July 1, 1991	1,745	339	749	57	137	1,096	4,123
December 31, 1991	1,738	338	742	57	136	1,083	4,094
July 1, 1992	1,731	344	759	56	144	1,091	4,125
December 31, 1992	1,735	347	770	56	142	1,145	4,195
July 1, 1993	1,715	338	767	55	139	1,011	4,025
December 31, 1993	1,789	337	761	56	146	1,121	4,210
July 1, 1994	1,666	336	777	53	138	963	3,933
December 31, 1994	1,660	333	792	53	136	980	3,954
July 1, 1995	1,670	334	804	43	129	1,002	3,982
December 31, 1995	1,674	334	815	44	129	1,020	4,016
July 1, 1996	1,645	332	829	43	126	1,058	4,033
December 31, 1996	1,642	332	838	41	123	1,103	4,079

Note: "—" indicates not available. The counts above reflect federally registered PACs. Registration does not necessarily imply financial activity. Trade/membership/health category for 1974–1976 includes all PACs except corporate and labor; no further breakdown available. Midyear counts for additional years can be found in earlier editions of *Vital Statistics on American Politics*.

Table 2-11   *(Continued)*

[a] Connected PACs are associated with a sponsoring organization that may pay operating and fund-raising expenses. They are typically subdivided by the type of sponsor: corporate (with stockholders), labor (unions), membership/trade/health (professional groups and associations of corporations), cooperatives (primarily agricultural), and corporations without stock.
[b] Nonconnected PACs do not have a sponsoring organization.

Source: Federal Election Commission, "FEC Releases Semi-Annual Federal PAC Count," press release, January 24, 1997.

Table 2-12   PACs: Receipts, Expenditures, and Contributions, 1975–1996

Election cycle[a]	Receipts[b] (millions)	Expenditures[b] (millions)	Contributions to congressional candidates[c] (millions)	Percentage contributed to congressional candidates
1975–1976	$54.0	$52.9	$22.6	42
1977–1978	80.0	77.4	34.1	43
1979–1980	137.7	131.2	60.2	44
1981–1982	199.5	190.2	87.6	44
1983–1984	288.7	266.8	113.0	39
1985–1986	353.4	340.0	139.8	40
1987–1988	384.6	364.2	159.2	41
1989–1990	372.1	357.6	159.1	43
1991–1992	385.5	394.9	188.9	49
1993–1994	391.8	388.1	189.6	48
1995–1996	437.4	429.9	217.8	50

Note: Figures are in current dollars.

[a] Data cover January 1 of the odd-numbered year to December 31 of the even-numbered year.
[b] Receipts and expenditures for 1975–1984 exclude funds transferred between affiliated committees.
[c] Contributions to candidates for election in the even-numbered year, made during the two-year election cycle.

Sources: 1975–1976: Joseph E. Cantor, "Political Action Committees: Their Evolution and Growth and Their Implications for the Political System" (Washington, D.C.: Congressional Research Service, 1982), report no. 83, 87–88; 1977–1978: Federal Election Commission, "FEC Releases First PAC Figures for 1985–86," press release, May 21, 1987, 1; 1979–1984: "PAC Activity in 1994 Elections Remains at 1992 Levels," press release, March 31, 1995, 12; 1985–1996: "Summary of PAC Financial Activitiy, 1986–1996," *http://www.fec.gov/finance/paclngye.htm* (as of June 26, 1997).

Table 2-13   Spending, by Type of PAC, 1977–1996 (millions)

Election cycle	Corporate	Labor	Trade membership/ health	Non- connected	Other connected[a]	Total
1977–1978	$15.2	$18.6	$23.8	$17.4	$2.4	$77.4
1979–1980	31.4	25.1	32.0	38.6	4.0	131.2
1981–1982	43.3	34.8	41.9	64.3	5.8	190.2
1983–1984	59.2	47.5	54.0	97.4	8.7	266.8
1985–1986	79.3	57.9	73.3	118.4	11.1	340.0
1987–1988	89.9	74.1	83.7	104.9	11.7	364.2
1989–1990	101.1	84.6	88.1	71.4	12.5	357.6
1991–1992	112.4	94.6	97.5	76.2	14.1	394.8
1993–1994	116.8	88.4	94.1	75.1	13.7	388.1
1995–1996	130.6	99.8	105.4	81.3	12.9	429.9

Note: Figures are in current dollars. Expenditures exclude transfers of funds between affiliated committees for 1975–1984. Detail may not add to totals because of rounding.

[a] This category combines the FEC categories of cooperatives and corporations without stock.

Sources: 1977–1978: Norman J. Ornstein et al., eds., *Vital Statistics on Congress*, 1987–1988 (Washington, D.C.: Congressional Quarterly, 1987), 105; 1979–1984: Federal Election Commission, "PAC Activity in 1994 Elections Remains at 1992 Levels," press release, March 31, 1995, 12; 1985–1996: *http://www.fec.gov/finance/paclngye.htm* (as of June 25, 1997).

Table 2-14 Contributions and Independent Expenditures, by Type of PAC, 1991–1996

Type of PAC	Number[a]	Receipts[b]	Contributed to candidates[c]		Independent expenditures[d]	
			Amount	Percentage	Amount	Percentage
1991–1992						
Corporate	1,501	$112,359,989	$68,442,883	61	$47,883	0.0
Labor	254	89,863,124	41,339,090	46	298,497	0.3
Trade/membership/health	625	95,729,703	53,746,146	56	3,422,300	3.6
Cooperative	48	4,798,441	2,981,390	62	0	0.0
Corporations without stock	112	8,713,184	3,983,452	46	385,300	4.4
Nonconnected	531	73,851,846	18,183,052	25	6,276,696	8.5
Total	3,071	385,316,287	188,676,013	49	10,430,676	2.7
1993–1994						
Corporate	1,461	114,978,803	69,581,799	61	31,214	0.0
Labor	255	89,898,089	41,825,927	47	103,743	0.1
Trade/membership/health	628	96,370,335	52,799,649	55	1,767,450	1.8
Cooperative	50	4,377,763	3,042,328	69	0	0.0
Corporations without stock	112	8,848,760	4,071,108	46	509,901	5.8
Nonconnected	500	76,535,445	18,049,730	24	2,307,490	3.0
Total	3,006	391,009,195	189,370,541	48	4,719,848	1.2
1995–1996						
Corporate	1,470	133,793,654	78,194,723	58	387,797	0.3
Labor	236	104,059,450	47,980,492	46	663,400	0.6
Trade/membership/health	650	105,956,146	60,153,725	57	4,633,414	4.4
Cooperative	41	3,897,164	3,006,471	77	4,916	0.1

(Table continues)

97

Table 2-14 (*Continued*)

Type of PAC	Number[a]	Receipts[b]	Contributed to candidates[c]		Independent expenditures[d]	
			Amount	Percentage	Amount	Percentage
Corporations without stock	109	8,500,508	4,535,098	53	386,888	4.6
Nonconnected	529	81,165,399	23,960,110	30	4,542,952	5.6
Total	3,035	437,372,321	217,830,619	50	10,619,367	2.4

Note: Figures are in current dollars. Data for earlier years can be found in previous editions of *Vital Statistics on American Politics.*

[a] The numbers shown are those PACs that actually made contributions.
[b] Not adjusted for money transferred between affiliated committees.
[c] Figures include contributions to all federal candidates, including those who did not run for office during the years indicated.
[d] Independent expenditures include money spent on behalf of candidates and against candidates.

Sources: Federal Election Commission, "PAC Activity Rebounds in 1991–1992 Election Cycle," press release, April 29, 1993, 3, 8–9, "PAC Activity in 1994 Elections Remains at 1992 Levels," press release, March 31, 1995, 3, 11–12; "PAC Financial Activity 1995–96," as reported at *http://www.fec.gov/finance/pacsumye.htm* (as of June 30, 1997).

Table 2-15   Top Twenty PACs in Overall Spending and in Contributions to
Federal Candidates, 1995–1996

Rank	PAC name	Overall spending
1. Emily's List		$12,494,230
2. Democratic Republican Independent Voter Education Committee		9,931,244
3. NRA Political Victory Fund		6,642,888
4. Association of Trial Lawyers of America Political Action Committee		5,084,785
5. National Education Association Political Action Committee		5,031,657
6. Campaign America		4,491,926
7. American Federation of State County & Municipal Employees-PEOPLE, Qualified		4,307,967
8. American Medical Association Political Action Committee		4,133,528
9. UAW-V-CAP (UAW Voluntary Community Action Program)		3,955,068
10. Machinists Non-Partisan Political League		3,615,292
11. International Brotherhood of Electrical Workers Committee on Political Education		3,413,113
12. Dealers Election Action Committee of the National Automobile Dealers Association (NADA)		3,247,206
13. Active Ballot Club, A Department of United Food & Commercial Workers International Union		3,167,640
14. United Parcel Service of America Inc. Political Action Committee (UPSPAC)		2,957,935
15. Voice of Teachers for Education/Committee on Political Education of NY State United Teachers (VOTE/COPE) of NYSUT		2,904,037
16. American Telephone & Telegraph Company Political Action Committee (AT&T PAC)		2,746,738
17. American Federation of Teachers Committee on Political Education		2,655,527
18. Transportation Political Education League		2,507,028
19. Women's Campaign Fund Inc.		2,450,019
20. Laborers' Political League		2,392,101

Rank	PAC name	Contributions to federal candidates
1. Democratic Republican Independent Voter Education Committee		$2,611,140
2. American Federation of State County & Municipal Employees-PEOPLE, Qualified		2,505,021
3. UAW-V-CAP (UAW Voluntary Community Action Program)		2,467,319
4. Association of Trial Lawyers of America Political Action Committee		2,362,938
5. Dealers Election Action Committee of the National Automobile Dealers Association (NADA)		2,351,925
6. National Education Association Political Action Committee		2,326,830
7. American Medical Association Political Action Committee		2,319,197
8. Realtors Political Action Committee		2,099,683

(Table continues)

Table 2-15   *(Continued)*

Rank	PAC name	Overall spending
9.	International Brotherhood of Electrical Workers Committee on Political Education	$2,080,587
10.	Active Ballot Club, a Dept of United Food & Commercial Workers International Union	2,030,795
11.	Machinists Non-Partisan Political League	1,999,675
12.	Laborers' Political League	1,933,300
13.	United Parcel Service of America Inc. Political Action Committee (UPSPAC)	1,788,147
14.	Committee on Letter Carriers Political Education (Letter Carriers Political Action Fund)	1,715,064
15.	American Institute of Certified Public Accountants Effective Legislation Committee (AICPA)	1,690,925
16.	American Federation of Teachers Committee on Political Education	1,614,833
17.	NRA Political Victory Fund	1,565,821
18.	United Steelworkers of America Political Action Fund	1,524,650
19.	Build Political Action Committee of the National Association of Home Builders	1,472,849
20.	Carpenters Legislative Improvement Committee, United Brotherhood of Carpenters & Joiners of America	1,470,106

Note: Figures are in current dollars. Information for earlier years can be found in previous editions of *Vital Statistics on American Politics*.

Sources: Federal Election Commission, spending: *http://www.fec.gov/finance/pacdisye.htm*; contributions: *http://www.fec.gov/finance/paccnye.htm* (as of June 26, 1997).

Table 2-16 Political Action Committee (PAC) Congressional Campaign Contributions, by Type of PAC and Incumbency Status of Candidate, 1981–1996 (millions)

Election cycle/ PAC type	House						Senate					
	Dem.	Rep.	Incum-bent	Chal-lenger	Open seat[a]	Total	Dem.	Rep.	Incum-bent	Chal-lenger	Open seat[a]	Total
1981–1982												
Corporate	7.0	12.0	14.4	2.0	2.6	18.9	2.4	6.2	5.5	1.7	1.4	8.6
Trade/membership/health	7.2	9.7	12.4	2.1	2.3	16.8	2.2	2.8	3.7	0.8	0.5	5.0
Labor	14.7	0.7	8.5	4.3	2.6	15.4	4.5	0.4	3.0	1.3	0.5	4.9
Nonconnected[b]	3.9	3.5	3.4	2.5	1.6	7.4	1.6	1.7	1.5	1.3	0.5	3.3
Total[b]	34.2	26.8	40.8	10.9	9.4	61.1	11.2	11.4	14.3	5.2	3.0	22.6
1983–1984												
Corporate	10.4	13.1	18.8	2.6	2.0	23.4	3.2	8.8	8.8	1.1	2.2	12.0
Trade/membership/health	10.5	9.9	16.5	2.1	1.7	20.4	2.7	3.7	4.5	0.9	1.0	6.3
Labor	18.8	1.0	14.3	3.5	2.0	19.8	4.7	0.3	1.6	2.3	1.2	5.0
Nonconnected[b]	4.7	4.4	4.9	2.9	1.3	9.1	3.0	2.4	2.4	2.0	1.0	5.4
Total[b]	46.3	29.3	57.2	11.3	7.2	75.7	14.0	15.6	17.9	6.3	5.4	29.7
1985–1986												
Corporate	12.9	14.0	22.9	1.0	3.0	26.9	4.8	14.4	11.7	2.7	4.9	19.2
Trade/membership/health	12.3	11.2	19.3	1.3	2.8	23.4	3.8	5.7	5.7	1.6	2.1	9.5
Labor	21.1	1.6	14.7	4.3	3.6	22.6	6.6	0.6	2.2	3.2	1.9	7.2
Nonconnected[b]	6.6	4.5	6.1	2.4	2.6	11.1	4.2	3.4	3.1	2.4	2.2	7.7
Total[b]	54.7	32.6	65.9	9.1	12.4	87.4	20.2	25.1	23.7	10.2	11.4	45.3

(Table continues)

Table 2-16 (*Continued*)

Election cycle/ PAC type	House						Senate					
	Dem.	Rep.	Incumbent	Challenger	Open seat[a]	Total	Dem.	Rep.	Incumbent	Challenger	Open seat[a]	Total
1987–1988												
Corporate	16.3	15.3	28.7	1.1	1.9	31.7	7.2	11.6	12.9	2.4	3.7	18.8
Trade/membership/health	16.6	12.0	24.6	1.5	2.5	28.6	4.8	5.6	7.1	1.2	2.0	10.3
Labor	24.9	2.0	18.4	5.1	3.4	26.9	6.5	0.5	3.6	2.2	1.3	7.1
Nonconnected	7.4	3.9	7.3	2.1	1.9	11.3	4.8	3.0	4.2	2.0	1.6	7.7
Total[b]	67.6	34.6	82.4	10.0	9.9	102.3	24.1	21.5	28.7	8.0	8.9	45.6
1989–1990												
Corporate	19.1	17.1	31.4	1.5	3.2	36.2	8.4	13.5	16.8	3.6	1.5	22.0
Trade/membership/health	19.3	13.4	27.7	1.4	3.6	32.7	5.2	6.5	9.0	1.8	0.9	11.7
Labor	26.1	1.8	20.1	3.3	4.5	28.0	6.2	0.6	4.6	1.7	0.4	6.8
Nonconnected	6.0	3.1	5.8	1.2	2.0	9.1	4.0	2.5	4.9	1.0	0.5	6.5
Total[b]	73.4	36.9	89.0	7.7	13.6	110.4	24.9	23.9	36.9	8.4	3.4	48.8
1991–1992												
Corporate	24.3	20.5	36.9	2.9	5.0	44.9	9.9	13.5	16.8	2.4	4.2	23.4
Trade/membership/health	23.9	16.2	30.5	3.0	6.5	40.2	7.1	6.3	9.3	1.7	2.4	13.5
Labor	29.8	1.7	20.7	4.5	6.2	31.7	8.9	0.4	4.2	2.9	2.2	9.3
Nonconnected	6.9	3.7	6.5	1.6	2.4	10.6	4.6	2.9	4.4	1.5	1.5	7.4
Total[b]	88.1	43.7	98.7	12.4	20.7	132.2	31.8	23.9	36.3	8.7	10.7	55.7

1993–1994												
Corporate	24.8	20.4	37.9	3.1	4.3	45.3	9.2	15.1	15.2	2.0	7.1	24.2
Trade/membership/health	22.7	17.1	31.0	3.4	5.4	39.9	5.6	7.4	8.3	1.1	3.5	12.9
Labor	32.5	1.4	24.2	4.2	5.6	34.1	7.4	0.3	4.0	1.7	1.9	7.7
Nonconnected[b]	7.5	4.4	7.6	1.9	2.4	11.9	3.3	2.8	3.6	0.8	1.7	6.1
Total[b]	90.9	45.0	104.9	13.0	18.2	136.2	26.6	26.5	32.6	5.8	14.7	53.1
1995–1996												
Corporate	16.2	36.8	45.8	2.0	5.3	53.2	4.9	18.5	13.7	2.6	7.1	23.4
Trade/membership/health	16.8	28.4	35.5	3.8	6.1	45.4	4.1	10.3	7.7	1.7	5.1	14.5
Labor	37.3	2.7	22.2	11.9	6.0	40.2	7.0	0.7	2.4	1.5	3.8	7.7
Nonconnected[b]	6.8	8.7	9.6	3.6	2.5	15.7	2.7	5.2	3.8	1.3	2.8	7.9
Total[b]	79.4	79.7	117.7	21.7	20.5	159.9	19.4	36.1	28.7	7.4	19.3	55.5

Note: Figures are current dollar amounts given during the two-year calendar period indicated to candidates in primary, general, runoff, and special elections. Data for earlier years can be found in previous editions of *Vital Statistics on American Politics*.

[a] "Open seat" refers to candidates in elections ir which an incumbent did not seek reelection.
[b] Includes PACs classified by the Federal Election Commission as cooperatives and corporations without stock.

Sources: 1979–1984: *Statistical Abstract of the United States, 1987* (Washington, D.C.: U.S. Government Printing Office, 1986), 246; 1985–1988: *Statistical Abstract of the United States, 1990,* 269; 1989–1990: Federal Election Commission, "PAC Activity Falls in 1990 Elections," press release, March 31, 1991, 3; 1991–1992: "PAC Activity Rebounds in 1991–1992 Election Cycle," press release, April 29, 1993, 4–5; 1993–1994: "PAC Activity in 1994 Elections Remains at 1992 Levels," press release, March 31, 1995, 4, 5, 1995–1996: "PAC Contributions to Federal Candidates January 1, 1995–December 31, 1996," *http://www.fec.gov/finance/pacconye.htm* (as of July 28, 1997).

3

Public Opinion and Voting

- **Partisanship**
- **Ideology**
- **Voting by Groups**
- **Presidential and Congressional Approval**
- **Confidence in Government and the Economy**
- **Most Important Problem**
- **Parties' Handling of Peace and Prosperity**
- **Specific Issues**

Public opinion data are everywhere. They are perhaps most prominent in pre-election polls showing who is ahead and who is behind, but they are more important and more often used as guides by candidates and officeholders about what the public thinks and how it would react to changes in public policies. Surveys are also used, in a more partisan way, by politicians, journalists, and interest groups to support their positions. And, in a slightly different form, they are even more widely used by advertisers and manufacturers to gauge consumer reactions to new products and services. Reflecting this frequent and varied use, this chapter contains broad-gauged measures of public opinion as well as opinions on numerous specific issues.

In addition, information is included on the way groups of individuals voted. Overall election results (presented in Chapter 1) determine which party or individual won an election, but it is also useful to see how specific groups of individuals voted. Votes are shown by region, gender, race, religion, and so on, as well as for groups of ideologues, such as liberals and conservatives, partisan groups, and sometimes special groups such as first-time voters. Because these data are analogous to public opinion data in that they come from sample surveys and indicate group opinions rather than overall election outcomes, they are included in this chapter.

Figures 3-1 through 3-3 and Tables 3-1 through 3-3 cover two of the most frequently cited components of public opinion—partisanship and political ideology. These characteristics merit emphasis due to their practical political significance. They are of interest not only to those who wish to understand scientifically why people behave as they do. They also attract the attention of those who analyze long-term political and social trends and are of intense interest to those who track day-to-day politics.

From another perspective, these results are important because they illustrate the reliability and validity of public opinion polling, as well as the hazards of gauging personal opinions. Figures 3-1 and 3-2, showing self-proclaimed party identification, are reasonably similar for the period they jointly cover. If public opinion data were totally unreliable, as some contend, such similarity would be unlikely. Moreover, these figures illustrate two aspects of reliability and validity. First, polling as few as fifteen hundred people tells something very real about the entire population; two separate organizations, as represented in Figures 3-1 and 3-2, would not obtain such similarity over several decades of interviewing if the results represented only those actually interviewed. (Of course, one must choose the fifteen hundred respondents according to scientific sampling procedures, as do all the major polling organizations.) Second, poll results are not completely dependent on exact question wording. The Gallup question focuses on the immediate situation ("In politics, as of today. . . ."), while the National Election Studies question is broader ("Generally speaking. . . ."), suggesting that the Gallup question might pick up more short-term fluctuations in partisanship. Yet the results are quite similar.

At the same time, differences between the two series indicate that we cannot consider one a mere clone of the other. The National Election Studies surveys probe those who claim to be independents to determine whether they lean toward one party or the other. The responses to this probe as well as other evidence (Table 3-9) raise the question of whether independents are really closet partisans. How we answer that question, as the contrast between the two plots in Figure 3-1 shows, has major implications for conclusions about the relative strengths of the parties. As has been emphasized in earlier introductions, even simple data descriptions involve interpretation.

Because surveys are not exact counts of the whole population, "sampling error" is often reported to convey the range within which the true population result lies. For example, results are said to be accurate to within plus or minus 3 percent. Yet even with greater precision (achieved by increasing the size of the sample), survey results still require interpretation. Suppose one could ask every American adult simultaneously whether he or she was a Democrat, an independent, or a Republican. There would then be no sampling error; because everyone was asked, the information would describe the entire U.S. population at that particular time. But that returns us to an equally vexing question: What does it mean to be an independent?

The "don't know" and "no opinion" responses to the ideology question about liberal or conservative self-identification in Table 3-3—and in the other public opinion tables—illustrate a similar point. Whether pollsters ask about a general position or a specific issue, some proportion of the sample—often as many as 15 percent and sometimes many more—respond "don't know." It is not immediately apparent how to interpret such responses; some people have information about the subject matter but no opinion, some have no information and no opinion, and a few have no information but have an opinion anyway—and the pollster's decision about how to treat such responses can make a large difference. For example, in a preelection poll, should a pollster assume that those who have not yet chosen whom to support will eventually (1) split votes between candidates in similar proportions as those who have already decided, (2) not vote, (3) divide evenly between the candidates, or (4) overwhelmingly support a particular candidate?

For public officials seeking guidance on public sentiment, no simple reading suffices because they must assess intensity as well as direction. Those seeking a theoretical understanding of politics face the same problem. For example, although more than public opinion accounted for the outcome, consider the Senate rejection of Judge Robert Bork's nomination to the Supreme Court in 1987 (Table 7-4). Polls showed the public almost evenly divided on the matter, with a slight edge to those opposing the nomination. Such a close balance was misleading. Deeper political meaning turned on the intensity of those views. One senator said, "If you vote against Bork, those in favor of him will be mad at you for a week. But if you vote for him, those who don't like him will be mad at you for the rest of their lives." Understanding the importance of public opinion in politics requires more than a simple nose count. The salience of an opinion to the person holding it also counts.

In addition, a particular survey result usually tells little in isolation. The soundest interpretations depend upon several surveys stretching over time, often over a period of years. Consider the decline and partial recovery in public confidence in government (Figure 3-7). The confidence level at a particular time is a mere point, difficult or impossible to interpret. Yet that point, when viewed with comparable points from similar surveys over the years, indicates a trend—decline, upsurge, constancy, whatever. Consequently, reports of public opinion increasingly emphasize long time series, as we do here (Figures 3-10 through 3-15, Tables 3-6, 3-13 through 3-22). Such time series data can be usefully supplemented by cross-sections (Table 3-2); such within-survey contrasts convey whether and how groups differ in attitudes.

What issues are most salient in the public's mind varies across time. This fact itself has been measured, by asking people what they regard as the nation's most important problem (Figures 3-10 and 3-11). Yet many issues are of perennial interest, and over-time assessments often date back to the 1940s or 1950s (Tables 3-13 and 3-14, 3-17 through 3-19, 3-21), in one case even to the 1930s (Table 3-15). From the point of view of elections, the significance of public opinion lies chiefly in how the public translates its feelings into summary judgments of the president (Figures 3-4 and 3-5), Congress (Figure 3-6), and government and society as a whole (Figures 3-7 and 3-8). Yet another set consists of judgments of which party is better able to handle the "most important problem" and two long-standing issues, peace and prosperity (Figures 3-12 through 3-14). Finally, public satisfaction with the status quo and consumer confidence in the economy are summary judgments that are perennial concerns in politics (Figures 3-8 and 3-9).

Of course, the most direct and important judgments about political leaders, candidates, and parties occur in elections. As previously noted, data about the behavior of individual voters necessarily come from surveys. Here it is shown how various groups voted for president, both in the general election (Tables 3-4 and 3-5) and in presidential primaries (Tables 3-7 and 3-8), and for Congress (Table 3-10). These data also answer questions of great theoretical and practical interest, such as the extent to which individuals vote in accordance with their general party preference and in straight- or split-tickets (Tables 3-9, 3-11, and 3-12).

A final note. Even a firm understanding of public opinion can be contradicted by events, as one cannot blindly equate opinion with behavior. The growth of racial tolerance in the South, such as it is, is a telling counterpoint to a political atmosphere formerly committed to white supremacy. As one respondent, a segregationist, told a pollster in the mid-1960s: "You asked me what I favored, not what I will accept graciously, not what I thought was right."[1]

Note

1. Donald R. Matthews and James W. Prothro, *Negroes and the New Southern Politics* (New York: Harcourt, Brace & World, 1966), 363.

Table 3-1 Partisan Identification, National Election Studies, 1952–1996
(percent)

	Democrat			Inde-pen-dent	Republican			Apo-litical	Total	Number of inter-views
Year	Strong	Weak	Inde-pendent		Inde-pendent	Weak	Strong			
1952	22	25	10	6	7	14	14	3	101	1,784
1954	22	25	9	7	6	14	13	4	100	1,130
1956	21	23	6	9	8	14	15	4	100	1,757
1958	27	22	7	7	5	17	11	4	100	1,808
1960	20	25	6	10	7	14	16	2	100	1,911
1962	23	23	7	8	6	16	12	4	99	1,287
1964	27	25	9	8	6	14	11	1	101	1,550
1966	18	28	9	12	7	15	10	1	100	1,278
1968	20	25	10	11	9	15	10	1	101	1,553
1970	20	24	10	13	8	15	9	1	100	1,501
1972	15	26	11	13	10	13	10	1	99	2,694
1974	17	21	13	15	9	14	8	3	100	2,505
1976	15	25	12	15	10	14	9	1	101	2,850
1978	15	24	14	14	10	13	8	3	101	2,283
1980	18	23	11	13	10	14	9	2	100	1,613
1982	20	24	11	11	8	14	10	2	100	1,418
1984	17	20	11	11	12	15	12	2	100	2,236
1986	18	22	10	12	11	15	10	2	100	2,166
1988	17	18	12	11	13	14	14	2	101	2,032
1990	20	19	12	11	12	15	10	2	101	1,991
1992	17	18	14	12	13	15	11	1	101	2,487
1994	15	19	13	10	12	15	16	1	101	1,795
1996	19	20	14	9	11	15	13	0	101	1,695

Note: Question: "Generally speaking, do you consider yourself a Republican, a Democrat, an Independent, or what?" If Republican or Democrat: "Would you call yourself a strong (R/D) or a not very strong (R/D)?" If Independent or other: "Do you think of yourself as closer to the Republican or Democratic party?"

Source: Calculated by the editors from National Election Studies data (Ann Arbor, Mich.: Center for Political Studies, University of Michigan).

Figure 3-1 Partisan Identification, National Election Studies. 1952–1996

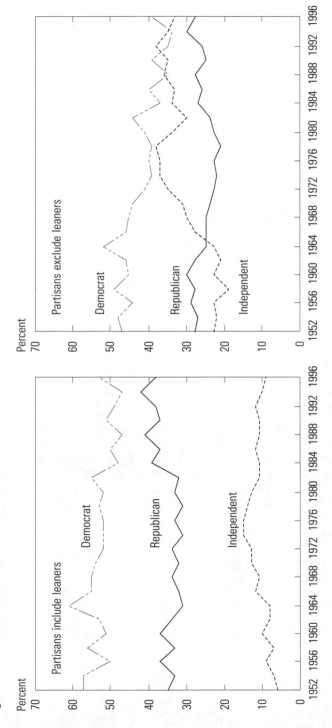

Note: See Table 3-1 for question. "Leaners" are independents who consider themselves closer to one party.

Source: Calculated by the editors from National Election Studies codebooks and data sets.

Figure 3-2   Partisan Identification, Gallup Poll, 1937–1997

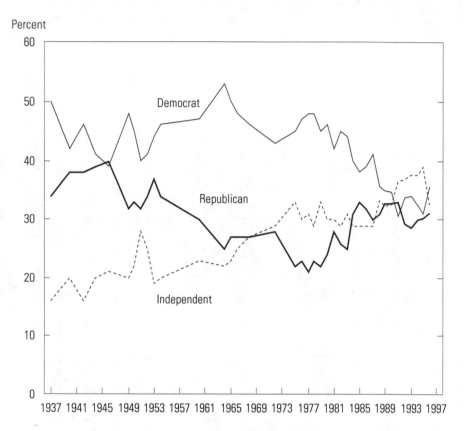

Note: Respondents who gave replies other than Democrat, Republican, or Independent are excluded. Question: "In politics, as of today, do you consider yourself a Republican, a Democrat, or an Independent?" Data from 1988 and later are from telephone surveys, which tend to report more Republican and fewer Democratic partisans than in-person interviews. See Larry Hugick, "Party Identification: The Disparity between Gallup's In-person and Telephone Interview Findings," *Public Perspective,* September/October 1991, 23–24.

Sources: The Gallup Organization, "The Gallup Poll Party ID Trend to 1937," no date; and unpublished data from the Gallup Poll.

Table 3-2   Partisan Identification, Gallup Poll, Cross-Section, 1996 (percent)

	Republican	Independent	Democrat
Gender			
Men	33	35	32
Women	29	30	40
Age			
18–29	27	40	33
30–49	31	34	35
50–64	35	29	36
65 and over	31	23	46
Race			
White	35	33	32
Black	3	24	73
Education			
No college	26	32	43
College incomplete	33	33	34
College graduate	41	29	30
Post graduate	34	35	31
Household income			
Under $20,000	19	34	47
$20,000–29,999	27	28	45
$30,000–49,999	34	34	33
$50,000 and over	41	30	29
Ideology			
Conservative	51	25	25
Moderate	23	36	41
Liberal	6	34	59
Region[a]			
East	24	31	45
Midwest	32	34	34
South	32	35	33
West	35	30	35
National	31	33	37

Note: Question: "In politics, as of today, do you consider yourself a Republican, a Democrat, or an Independent?" Percentages are based on the 2,416 total respondents in a general election tracking poll, November 3–4, 1996.

[a] For composition of regions, see Table 12-2.

Sources: Unpublished data from the Gallup Poll.

Table 3-3 Liberal or Conservative Self-Identification, 1973–1996 (percent)

Date	Extremely liberal	Liberal	Slightly liberal	Moderate	Slightly conservative	Conservative	Extremely conservative	Don't know	Number of interviews
March 1973	4	14	13	36	13	13	3	6	1,484
March 1974	1	14	14	38	15	11	2	5	1,480
March 1975	3	12	13	38	16	10	2	5	1,478
March 1976	2	13	12	37	15	13	2	6	1,494
March 1977	2	11	14	37	16	12	3	5	1,524
March 1978	1	9	16	36	17	12	2	5	1,505
March 1980	2	8	14	40	18	12	3	2	1,451
March 1982	2	9	15	39	14	13	4	4	1,495
March 1983	2	8	12	40	18	13	2	4	801
March 1984	2	9	12	39	19	13	3	4	1,462
March 1985	2	11	11	37	18	14	3	4	1,525
March 1986	2	9	12	39	16	14	3	5	1,468
March 1987	2	12	13	37	16	12	2	4	1,437
March 1988	2	12	13	35	17	15	2	4	1,472
March 1989	3	12	12	37	16	13	2	6	1,530
March 1990	3	10	13	35	18	14	4	4	1,368
March 1991	2	10	14	39	14	14	3	4	1,513
March 1993	2	11	13	36	17	16	3	3	1,597
March 1994	2	11	13	35	16	16	3	3	2,980
March 1996	2	10	12	36	16	16	3	5	2,898

Note: Question: "We hear a lot of talk these days about liberals and conservatives. I'm going to show you a seven-point scale on which the political views that people might hold are arranged from extremely liberal—point 1—to extremely conservative—point 7. Where would you place yourself on this scale?"

Source: General Social Survey, National Opinion Research Center, University of Chicago.

Figure 3-3   Ideological Self-Identification of College Freshmen, 1970–1996

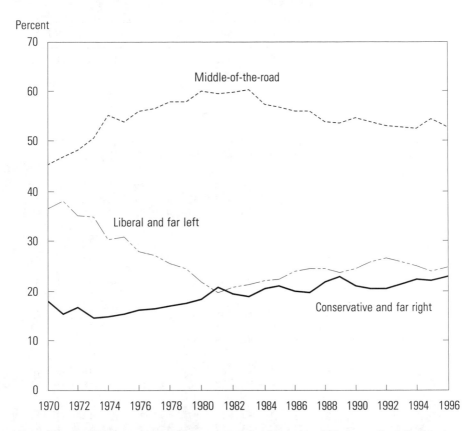

Note: Question: "How would you characterize your political views? Mark one: Far left, liberal, middle-of-the-road, conservative, far right."

Sources: Eric Dey, Alexander Astin, and William Korn, *The American Freshman: Twenty-five Year Trends* (Los Angeles: Higher Education Research Institute, University of California, Los Angeles, 1991); *The American Freshman: National Norms for Fall 1991* (Los Angeles: Higher Education Research Institute, University of California, Los Angeles, 1991); *Fall 1992* (1992); *Fall 1993* (1993); *Fall 1994* (1994); *Fall 1995* (1995); *Fall 1996* (1996).

Table 3-4 Presidential Vote in General Elections, by Groups, Gallup Poll, 1952–1996 (percent)

	1952		1956		1960		1964		1968			1972	
	D	R	D	R	D	R	D	R	D	R	I[a]	D	R
Sex													
Male	47	53	45	55	52	48	60	40	41	43	16	37	63
Female	42	58	39	61	49	51	62	38	45	43	12	38	62
Race/ethnicity													
White	43	57	41	59	49	51	59	41	38	47	15	32	68
Nonwhite	79	21	61	39	68	32	94	6	85	12	3	87	13
Education													
Grade school	52	48	50	50	55	45	66	34	52	33	15	49	51
High school	45	55	42	58	52	48	62	38	42	43	15	34	66
College	34	66	31	69	39	61	52	48	37	54	9	37	63
Employment													
Manual	55	45	50	50	60	40	71	29	50	35	15	43	57
White collar	40	60	37	63	48	52	57	43	41	47	12	36	64
Professional and business	36	64	32	68	42	58	54	46	34	56	10	31	69
Age													
Under 30	51	49	43	57	54	45	64	36	47	38	15	48	52
30–49	47	53	45	55	54	46	63	37	44	41	15	33	67
50 and older	39	61	39	61	46	54	59	41	41	47	12	36	64
Religion													
Protestant	37	63	37	63	38	62	55	45	35	49	16	30	70
Catholic	56	44	51	49	78	22	76	24	59	33	8	48	52
Political affiliation													
Democrat	77	23	85	15	84	16	87	13	74	12	14	67	33
Independent	35	65	30	70	43	57	56	44	31	44	25	31	69
Republican	8	92	4	96	5	95	20	80	9	86	5	5	95
Region[b]													
East	45	55	40	60	53	47	68	32	50	43	7	42	58
Midwest	42	58	41	59	48	52	61	39	44	47	9	40	60
South	51	49	49	51	51	49	52	48	31	36	33	29	71
West	42	58	43	57	49	51	60	40	44	49	7	41	59
Union family	61	39	57	43	65	35	73	27	56	29	15	46	54
Total	45	55	42	58	50	50	61	39	43	43	14	38	62

Note: "D" indicates Democrat; "R" indicates Republican; "-" indicates less than 0.5 percent; "—" indicates not available.

[a] "I" indicates the vote for George Wallace in 1968, for Eugene McCarthy in 1976, for John Anderson in 1980, and for Ross Perot in 1992. Table does not include votes for minor-party candidates other than those shown for 1968, 1976, 1980, and 1992.
[b] For composition of regions, see Appendix Table A-2.

Sources: 1952–1988: *The Gallup Report,* November 1988, 6–7; 1992: unpublished data from the Gallup Poll.

Table 3-4   *(Continued)*

1976			1980			1984		1988		1992			1996		
D	R	I[a]	D	R	I[a]	D	R	D	R	D	R	I[a]	D	R	I[a]
53	45	1	38	53	7	36	64	44	56	41	37	22	45	44	11
48	51	-	44	49	6	45	55	48	52	46	38	16	54	39	7
46	52	1	36	56	7	34	66	41	59	39	41	20	46	45	9
85	15	-	86	10	2	87	13	82	18	77	11	12	82	12	6
58	41	1	54	42	3	51	49	55	45	56	28	16	58	27	15
54	46	-	43	51	5	43	57	46	54	40	38	22	52	34	14
42	55	2	35	53	10	39	61	42	58	43	40	17	49	45	6
58	41	1	48	48	5	46	54	—	—	—	—	—	—	—	—
50	48	2	40	51	9	47	53	—	—	—	—	—	—	—	—
42	56	1	33	55	10	34	66	—	—	—	—	—	—	—	—
53	45	1	47	41	11	40	60	37	63	40	37	23	54	30	16
48	49	2	38	52	8	40	60	45	55	42	37	21	49	41	10
52	48	-	41	54	4	41	59	49	51	46	39	15	50	45	5
46	53	-	39	54	6	39	61	42	58	41	41	18	45	46	9
57	41	1	46	47	6	39	61	51	49	47	35	18	54	33	13
82	18	-	69	26	4	79	21	85	15	82	8	10	90	6	4
38	57	4	29	55	14	33	67	43	57	39	30	31	48	33	19
9	91	-	8	86	5	4	96	7	93	7	77	16	10	85	5
51	47	1	43	47	9	46	54	51	49	47	35	18	60	31	9
48	50	1	41	51	7	42	58	47	53	44	34	22	46	45	9
54	45	-	44	52	3	37	63	40	60	38	45	17	44	46	10
46	51	1	35	54	9	40	60	46	54	45	35	20	51	43	6
63	36	1	50	43	5	52	48	63	37	—	—	—	—	—	—
50	48	1	41	51	7	41	59	46	54	43	38	19	50	41	9

Table 3-5 Presidential Vote in General Elections, by Groups, Network Exit Polls, 1976–1996 (percent)

	Percentage of voters					1976		1980			1984		1988		1992			1996		
	1980	1984	1988	1992	1996	D	R	D	R	I	D	R	D	R	D	R	I	D	R	I
Sex																				
Men	51	47	48	46	48	50	48	36	55	7	37	62	41	54	41	38	21	43	44	10
Women	49	53	52	54	52	50	48	45	47	7	44	56	49	50	45	37	17	54	38	7
Race/ethnicity																				
White	88	86	85	87	83	47	52	36	55	7	35	64	40	59	39	40	20	43	46	9
Black	10	10	10	8	10	83	16	85	11	3	89	9	86	12	83	10	7	84	12	4
Hispanic	2	3	3	3	5	76	24	56	35	8	61	37	69	30	61	25	14	72	21	6
Age																				
Under 30	23	24	20	22	17	51	47	44	43	11	40	59	47	52	43	34	22	53	34	10
30–44	31	34	35	38	33	49	49	36	54	8	42	57	45	54	41	38	21	48	41	9
45–59	23	23	22	24	26	47	52	39	55	5	39	59	42	57	41	40	19	48	41	9
60 and older	18	19	22	16	24	47	52	41	54	4	39	60	49	50	50	38	12	48	44	7
Education																				
Not high school graduate	—	8	8	6	6	—	—	51	46	2	50	49	56	43	54	28	18	59	28	11
High school graduate	—	30	27	25	24	—	—	43	51	4	39	60	49	50	43	36	21	51	35	13
College incomplete	28	30	30	29	27	—	—	35	55	8	37	61	42	57	41	37	21	48	40	10
College graduate	27	29	35	40	43	—	—	35	52	11	41	58	43	56	44	39	17	47	44	7
Religion																				
White Protestant	46	51	48	49	46	41	58	31	63	6	27	72	33	66	33	47	21	36	53	10
Catholic	25	26	28	27	29	54	44	42	49	7	45	54	47	52	44	35	20	53	37	9
Jewish	5	3	4	4	3	64	34	45	39	15	67	31	64	35	80	11	9	78	16	3
White fundamentalist	17	15	9	17	—	—	—	33	63	3	22	78	18	81	23	61	15	—	—	—

Region																				
East	32	24	25	24	23	51	47	42	47	9	47	52	49	50	47	35	18	55	34	9
Midwest	20	28	28	27	26	48	50	40	51	7	40	58	47	52	42	37	21	48	41	10
South	27	29	28	30	30	54	45	44	52	3	36	64	41	58	41	43	16	46	46	7
West	11	18	19	20	20	48	51	34	53	10	38	61	46	52	43	34	23	48	40	8
Union household	26	26	25	19	23	59	39	48	43	6	53	46	57	42	55	24	21	59	30	9
Family income																				
Lowest category	13	15	12	14	11	58	40	51	42	6	54	45	62	37	58	23	19	59	28	11
Second lowest category	14	27	20	24	23	55	43	46	44	7	42	57	50	49	45	35	20	53	36	9
Middle category	30	21	20	30	27	48	50	39	52	7	40	59	44	56	41	38	21	48	40	10
Second highest category	24	18	20	20	39	36	63	32	59	8	33	66	42	56	39	44	17	44	48	7
Highest category	—	13	24	13	18	—	—	26	63	9	30	69	37	62	36	48	16	41	51	7
Party																				
Republican	28	35	35	35	35	9	90	8	86	4	6	93	8	91	10	73	17	13	80	6
Independent	23	26	26	27	26	43	54	30	55	12	35	63	43	55	38	32	30	43	35	17
Democrat	43	38	37	38	39	77	22	67	26	6	75	24	82	17	77	10	13	84	10	5
Ideology																				
Liberal	17	17	18	21	20	71	28	60	25	11	70	28	81	18	68	14	18	78	11	7
Moderate	46	44	45	49	47	51	48	42	48	8	47	53	50	49	47	31	21	57	33	9
Conservative	28	35	33	29	33	29	70	23	72	4	17	82	19	80	18	64	18	20	71	8
1984 vote																				
Reagan voter	—	56	56	—	—	—	—	9	75	2	0	100	19	80	—	—	—	—	—	—
Democrat for Reagan	—	9	9	—	—	—	—	23	57	2	0	100	51	48	—	—	—	—	—	—
Mondale voter	—	28	28	—	—	—	—	63	14	8	100	0	92	7	—	—	—	—	—	—

(Table continues)

Table 3-5 (*Continued*)

	Percentage of voters					1976		1980			1984			1988			1992			1996		
	1980	1984	1988	1992	1996	D	R	D	R	I	D	R	I	D	R	I	D	R	I	D	R	I
Previous presidential vote																						
Republican	—	50	56	53	35	18	79	11	83	6	11	88	—	19	80	—	21	59	20	13	82	4
Independent/third party	—	5	—	—	12	—	—	—	—	—	27	69	—	—	—	—	—	—	—	22	44	33
Democrat	—	31	28	27	43	73	26	63	29	6	82	18	—	92	7	—	83	5	12	85	9	4
First time voter	—	8	7	11	9	—	—	—	—	—	38	61	—	47	51	—	46	32	22	54	34	11
Total	100	100	100	100	100	50	48	41	51	7	40	59	—	45	53	—	43	38	19	49	41	8

Note: "D" indicates Democrat; "R" indicates Republican; "I" indicates Independent; "—" indicates not available. The number of respondents in 1976 was 15,300; in 1980, 15,201; in 1984, 9,174; in 1988, 11,645; in 1992, 15,490; and in 1996, 16,627.

[a] Income categories in 1976 were: less than $8,000, $8,000–11,999, $12,000–19,999, and $20,000 and over; in 1980: less than $10,000, $10,000–14,999, $15,000–24,999, $25,000–49,999, and $50,000 and over; in 1984 and 1988: under $12,500, $12,500–24,999, $25,000–34,999, $35,000–49,999, $50,000 and over; in 1992: under $15,000, $15,000–29,999, $30,000–49,999, $50,000–74,999, $75,000 and over; and in 1996: under $15,000, $15,000–29,999, $30,000–49,999, $50,000 and over, and $75,000 and over.

Sources: 1988 percentage of the vote for previous presidential vote: *National Journal* (1992), 2543; other: *New York Times*, November 8, 1984, A19; November 10, 1988, B6; November 5, 1992, B9; November 10, 1996, 16 (copyright © 1984, 1988, 1992, and 1996 by the New York Times Company, reprinted by permission); 1992 data collected by Voter Research and Surveys; 1996 data collected by Voter News Service.

Table 3-6   Presidential Preferences Throughout the Election Year,
1948–1996

Year/candidate	First poll of year	First poll after conventions	Early October	Final survey	Election results
1948					
Truman (D)[a]	46 (+5)	37	40	45	50 (+5)
Dewey (R)	41	48 (+11)	46 (+6)	50 (+5)	45
1952					
Eisenhower (R)	59 (+28)	50 (+7)	53 (+12)	51 (+2)	55 (+11)
Stevenson (D)	31	43	41	49	44
1956					
Eisenhower (R)[a]	61 (+26)	52 (+11)	51 (+10)	60 (+19)	57 (+15)
Stevenson (D)	35	41	41	41	42
1960					
Kennedy (D)	43	44	49 (+3)	51 (+2)	50 (+0.2)
Nixon (R)	48 (+5)	50 (+6)	46	49	50
1964					
Johnson (D)[a]	75 (+57)	65 (+36)	64 (+35)	64 (+28)	61 (+23)
Goldwater (R)	18	29	29	36	38
1968					
Nixon (R)	43 (+9)	43 (+12)	43 (+12)	43 (+1)	43 (+0.7)
Humphrey (D)	34	31	31	42	43
Wallace (AIP)[b]	9	19	20	15	14
1972					
Nixon (R)[a]	53 (+19)	64 (+34)	60 (+26)	62 (+24)	61 (+23)
McGovern (D)	34	30	34	38	38
1976					
Carter (D)	47 (+5)	51 (+15)	47 (+2)	48	50 (+2)
Ford (R)[a]	42	36	45	49 (+1)	48
1980					
Reagan (R)	33	38	40	47 (+3)	51 (+10)
Carter (D)[a]	62 (+29)	39 (+1)	44 (+4)	44	41
Anderson (I)		13	9	8	7
1984					
Reagan (R)[a]	48 (+1)	55 (+15)	56 (+17)	59 (+18)	59 (+18)
Mondale (D)	47	40	39	41	41
1988					
Bush (R)	52 (+12)	48 (+4)	49 (+6)	53 (+11)	54 (+8)
Dukakis (D)	40	44	43	42	46
1992					
Bush (R)[a]	53 (+15)	42	35	37	37
Clinton (D)	38	52 (+10)	52 (+17)	49 (+12)	43 (+6)
Perot	—	—	7	14	19

(Table continues)

Table 3-6   *(Continued)*

Year/candidate	First poll of year	First poll after conventions	Early October	Final survey	Election results
1996					
Dole (R)	39	34	34	41	41
Clinton (D)[a]	43(+4)	55(+21)	55(+21)	52(+11)	49(+8)
Perot	16	6	6	7	9

Note: "—" indicates not included in survey question.

[a] Incumbent.
[b] American Independent Party.

Sources: Congressional Quarterly Weekly Report (1984), 2648, (1988), 3245; 1984 final survey: *The Gallup Report*, November 1984, 31; 1988–1996: Gallup Poll, various press releases.

Table 3-7 Vote in Democratic Presidential Primaries, by Groups, 1984–1992 (percent)

Group	1984				1988				1992			
	Percentage of primary voters	Mondale	Hart	Jackson	Percentage of primary voters	Dukakis	Jackson	Others	Percentage of primary voters	Clinton	Brown	Tsongas
Sex												
Men	46	38	36	17	47	41	29	30	47	50	21	20
Women	54	39	35	20	53	43	30	26	53	51	20	21
Race/ethnicity												
White	78	42	43	5	75	54	12	35	80	47	23	25
Black	18	19	3	77	21	4	92	4	14	70	15	8
Hispanic	—	—	—	—	3	48	30	20	4	51	30	15
Age												
Under 30	17	26	39	26	14	35	38	27	12	47	24	19
30–44	30	30	38	23	31	37	36	26	33	45	26	22
45–59	24	41	34	18	25	42	30	28	25	51	19	20
60 and older	28	52	31	10	30	53	19	29	30	59	15	18
Religion												
Catholic	—	—	—	—	30	60	18	22	50	55	14	21
White Protestant	—	—	—	—	36	43	10	47	30	44	24	24
Jewish	—	—	—	—	7	75	8	17	6	75	15	33
Party												
Democrat	74	42	33	20	72	43	33	24	67	57	19	17
Independent	20	28	44	16	20	44	20	34	29	36	25	27

(Table continues)

Table 3-7 *(Continued)*

Group	1984 Percentage of primary voters	Mondale	Hart	Jackson	1988 Percentage of primary voters	Dukakis	Jackson	Others	1992 Percentage of primary voters	Clinton	Brown	Tsongas
Ideology												
Liberal	27	34	36	25	27	41	41	19	35	47	26	20
Moderate	47	41	37	15	47	47	25	28	45	54	18	19
Conservative	21	37	34	16	22	38	23	38	20	48	17	23
Union household	33	45	31	19	—	—	—	—	—	—	—	—
Total	100	38	36	19	100	43	29	28	100	50	21	20

Note: "—" indicates not available. Entries are derived from exit poll data in twenty-four contested delegate selection primaries in 1984, thirty-three in 1988, and twenty-nine in 1992. No exit poll in Louisiana in 1984 or in Montana, Oregon, or Washington, D.C., in 1988.

Sources: Adam Clymer, "The 1984 National Primary," *Public Opinion* (August/September 1984): 52–53 (reprinted with permission of the American Enterprise Institute for Public Policy Research); *New York Times*, June 13, 1988, B7, July 12, 1992, section 1, 18 (copyright © 1988, 1992 by the New York Times Company, reprinted by permission).

Table 3-8   Vote in Republican Presidential Primaries, by Groups, 1996 (percent)

Group	Percent of voters	Buchanan	Dole	Forbes	Other
Age					
Under 30	10	25	52	12	11
30-44	30	25	50	12	11
45-59	28	24	52	13	11
60 or older	32	18	65	10	7
Education					
Not a high school graduate	3	24	49	8	19
High school graduate	20	27	57	9	7
Some college	30	24	54	11	11
College graduate	27	20	55	13	12
Post-graduate	19	12	39	10	39
In 1992 voted for					
Bill Clinton	12	24	40	16	20
George Bush	66	20	63	9	6
Ross Perot	13	29	38	20	13
Party affiliation					
Republican	75	21	61	10	8
Independent	21	28	41	15	16
Democrat	4	29	29	11	31
Ideology					
Very liberal	2	19	45	10	26
Somewhat liberal	7	19	53	14	14
Moderate	33	16	59	13	12
Somewhat conservative	37	20	59	11	10
Very conservative	21	38	44	9	9
Constitutional ban on abortion in Republican Party platform					
Favor	38	35	49	7	9
Do not favor	57	18	58	15	12
U.S. trade					
Creates more jobs in own state	43	14	61	11	14
Costs more jobs in own state	39	34	49	8	9
Pat Buchanan					
Too extreme	56	5	71	13	11
Not too extreme	41	47	35	10	8
Percent of 11.9 million total vote		22.7	55.5	12.6	9.2

Note: Based on combined vote totals and results from exit polls conducted in twenty-eight states by Voter News Service. Some questions were not asked in each state. There was no exit poll in Nevada.

Source: Richard L. Berke, "Polls Find Far Right Doesn't Define G.O.P. Vote," *New York Times,* March 31, 1996, section 1, 24 (copyright © 1996 by the New York Times Company, reprinted by permission).

Table 3-9 Strength of Party Identification and the Presidential Vote, 1952–1996 (percent)

Year/candidate	Strong Democrat	Weak Democrat	Independent Democrat	Independent	Independent Republican	Weak Republican	Strong Republican	Total
1952								
Stevenson (D)	84	62	61	20	7	6	2	42
Eisenhower (R)	16	38	39	80	93	94	98	58
1956								
Stevenson (D)	85	63	67	17	6	7	0	40
Eisenhower (R)	15	37	33	83	94	93	100	60
1960								
Kennedy (D)	91	72	90	46	12	13	2	49
Nixon (R)	9	28	10	54	88	87	98	51
1964								
Johnson (D)	95	82	90	77	25	43	10	68
Goldwater (R)	5	18	10	23	75	57	90	32
1968								
Humphrey (D)	92	68	64	30	5	11	3	46
Nixon (R)	8	32	36	70	95	89	97	54
1972								
McGovern (D)	73	48	61	30	13	9	3	36
Nixon (R)	27	52	39	70	87	91	97	64
1976								
Carter (D)	92	75	76	44	14	22	3	51
Ford (R)	8	25	24	56	86	78	97	49
1980								
Carter (D)	89	65	60	26	13	5	5	44
Reagan (R)	11	35	40	74	87	95	95	56

1984								
Mondale (D)	89	68	79	28	7	6	3	42
Reagan (R)	11	32	21	72	93	94	97	58
1988								
Dukakis (D)	94	72	88	35	15	17	2	47
Bush (R)	6	28	12	65	85	83	98	53
1992								
Clinton (D)	97	84	92	65	15	20	3	58
Bush (R)	3	16	8	35	85	80	98	42
1996								
Clinton (D)	98	91	93	49	23	23	5	58
Dole (R)	2	9	7	51	77	77	95	42

Note: "D" indicates Democrat; "R" indicates Republican. Results are from surveys in which voters are asked which party they identify with and who they voted for. The exact question is as follows: "Generally speaking, do you consider yourself a Republican, a Democrat, an Independent, or what?" If Republican or Democrat: "Would you consider yourself a strong (R/D) or a not very strong (R/D)?" If Independent or other: "Do you think of yourself as closer to the Republican or Democratic party?" Votes for candidates other than the Democrat or Republican were excluded.

Source: Calculated by the editors from National Election Studies data (Ann Arbor, Mich. Center for Political Studies, University of Michigan).

Table 3-10 Congressional Vote in General Elections, by Groups, 1980–1996 (percent)

Group	1982 D	1982 R	1984 D	1984 R	1986 D	1986 R	1988 D	1988 R	1990 D	1990 R	1992 D	1992 R	1994 D	1994 R	1996 D	1996 R
Gender																
Men	55	45	48	52	51	49	52	48	51	49	52	48	42	58	46	54
Women	58	42	54	46	54	46	57	43	54	46	55	45	53	47	55	45
Race/ethnicity																
Whites	54	46	46	54	49	51	50	50	50	50	50	50	42	58	45	55
Blacks	89	11	92	8	86	14	85	15	79	21	89	11	92	8	82	18
Hispanics	75	25	69	31	75	25	76	24	72	28	72	28	61	39	73	27
Asian	—	—	—	—	—	—	—	—	—	—	—	—	54	46	43	57
Age																
Under 30	59	41	51	49	51	49	54	46	52	48	55	45	49	51	55	45
30–44	54	46	54	46	52	48	54	46	53	47	53	47	46	54	50	50
45–59	56	44	50	50	54	46	54	46	51	49	52	48	47	53	50	50
60 and over	58	42	48	52	52	48	55	45	53	47	56	44	49	51	49	51
Education																
Not a high school graduae	—	—	60	40	57	43	63	37	60	40	67	33	58	42	65	35
High school graduate	—	—	51	49	55	45	57	43	56	44	58	42	47	53	55	45
Some college	—	—	49	51	50	50	53	47	52	48	53	47	41	59	50	50
College graduate or more	—	—	50	50	51	49	50	50	51	49	50	50	50	50	46	54
Region																
East	65	35	54	46	52	48	54	46	54	46	55	45	50	50	56	44
Midwest	49	51	50	50	53	47	55	45	49	51	52	48	45	55	51	49
South	59	41	52	48	56	44	54	46	54	46	53	47	47	53	45	55
West	53	47	48	52	51	49	53	47	54	46	56	44	47	53	51	49
Religion																
Catholic	63	37	58	42	55	45	55	45	54	46	57	43	47	53	54	46
Jewish	82	18	70	30	70	30	68	32	73	27	79	21	77	23	74	26

White Protestant	62	38	63	34	57	43	55	45	56	44	57	43	62	38	57
White born-again[a]	73	27	63	37	66	34	66	34	66	34	69	31	65	35	54
Union household	37	63	40	60	33	67	—	—	37	63	37	63	36	64	32
Family income[b]															
Under $15,000	37	63	38	62	31	69	37	63	33	67	44	56	37	63	27
$15,000 to 29,999	44	56	49	51	43	57	45	55	43	57	47	53	46	54	40
$30,000 to 49,999	50	50	55	45	48	52	48	52	47	53	47	53	51	49	48
Over $50,000	56	44	58	42	53	47	51	49	55	45	53	47	61	39	63
Party															
Democrat	14	86	11	89	11	89	21	79	17	83	19	81	15	85	10
Independent	51	49	57	43	56	54	48	52	46	54	48	52	51	49	49
Republican	90	10	92	8	85	15	77	23	79	21	80	20	86	14	88
Ideology															
Liberal	18	82	19	81	19	81	27	73	20	80	29	71	24	76	20
Moderate	43	57	43	57	43	57	44	56	43	57	42	58	43	57	40
Conservative	79	21	81	19	72	28	63	37	66	34	65	35	69	31	65
Vote history															
Reagan, Bush, or Dole	91	9	89	11	85	15	63	37	72	28	65	35	79	21	69
Carter, Mondale, Dukakis or Clinton	15	85	16	84	11	89	19	81	16	84	17	83	7	93	11
Total	50	50	53	51	46	54	48	52	46	54	48	52	49	51	43

Note: "D" indicates Democrat; "R" Republican; "—" indicates not available. Data based on questionnaires completed by voters leaving polling places around the nation on election day. Those who gave no answer are excluded in the above percentages. Data for 1990 collected by Voter Research and Surveys, other years collected by the *New York Times*/CBS News Poll. The number of respondents in 1982 was 7,855; in 1984, 9,174; in 1986, 8,994; in 1988, 11,645; in 1990, 19,888. Data for earlier years can be found in previous editions of *Vital Statistics on American Politics*.

[a] Christians only. Born-again/Evangelical (1994); Born-again/Fundamentalist (1992); Fundamentalist/Evangelical (1990, 1988, 1986); Born-again (1984, 1982, 1980).

[b] Family income categories in 1980: under $15,000, $15,000–$24,999, $25,000–$50,000 and over $50,000; 1982: under $10,000, $10,000–19,999, $20,000–29,999, $30,000–50,000, and over $50,000; 1984, 1986, and 1988: under $12,500, $12,500–24,999, $25,000–34,999, $35,000–49,999, and over $50,000; 1990–1996: under $15,000, $15,000–29,000 $30,000–49,000, and over $50,000.

Source: 1990–1992 New York Times, "Portrait of the Electorate: Who Voted for Whom in the House," press release; March 1, 1995; 1994–1996: "Who Voted for Whom in the House," November 7, 1996 (copyright © 1995, 1996 by the New York Times Company, reprinted by permission).

Table 3-11 Party-Line Voting in Presidential and Congressional Elections, 1952–1996 (percent)

Year	Presidential elections			U.S. Senate elections			U.S. House elections		
	Party-line voters[a]	Defectors[b]	Independents	Party-line voters[a]	Defectors[b]	Independents	Party-line voters[a]	Defectors[b]	Independents
1952	77	18	5	79	16	5	80	15	5
1956	76	15	9	80	12	8	82	9	9
1958				84	11	5	84	11	5
1960	79	13	8	79	12	9	80	11	8
1962					—		83	11	6
1964	79	15	5	78	16	6	79	15	6
1966				76	17	7	76	17	5
1968	69	24	7	73	20	7	74	19	7
1970				77	13	10	76	16	7
1972	67	25	8	69	22	9	74	17	9
1974				74	18	8	74	18	8
1976	73	16	11	69	19	12	72	19	9
1978				71	20	9	67	23	10
1980	68	24	8	71	21	8	69	23	8
1982				77	17	6	76	17	6
1984	79	13	8	72	20	9	70	23	7
1986				76	20	4	72	22	6
1988	81	12	7	72	20	7	74	19	7
1990				73	23	6	76	19	5
1992	68	24	9	74	20	7	71	21	7
1994				77	17	6	77	17	6
1996	78	16	5	77	16	7	77	17	5

Note: "—" indicates not available. In presidential elections the base for percentages is all voters. In Senate and House elections the base for percentages is all voters supporting Democratic or Republican candidates.

[a] Democratic or Republican identifiers who vote for the candidate of their party. Party identification is based on surveys in which voters are asked which party they identify with. See Table 3-8 for question. "Independent partisans," or "leaners," are included here as party-line voters or defectors.

[b] Democratic or Republican identifiers who do not vote for the candidate of their party.

Source: Calculated by the editors from National Election Studies data (Ann Arbor, Mich.: Center for Political Studies, University of Michigan).

Table 3-12   Split-Ticket Voting, 1952–1996 (percent)

Year	President-House	Senate-House	State-local
1952	13	9	26
1956	16	10	29
1958		10	31
1960	14	9	27
1962		—	42
1964	14	18	41
1966		21	50
1968	17	21	47
1970		20	51
1972	30	22	58
1974		24	61
1976	25	23	—
1978		35	—
1980	28	31	59
1982		24	55
1984	25	20	52
1986		28	—
1988	25	27	—
1990		25	—
1992	22	25	—
1994		24	—
1996	18	19	—

Note: "—" indicates not available. Entries are the percentages of voters who "split" their ticket by supporting candidates of different parties for the offices indicated. Those who cast ballots for other than Democratic and Republican candidates are excluded in presidential and congressional calculations. The state-local figure is based on a general question: "Did you vote for other state and local offices? Did you vote a straight ticket, or did you vote for candidates from different parties?"

Source: Calculated by the editors from National Election Studies data (Ann Arbor, Mich.: Center for Political Studies, University of Michigan).

Figure 3-4   Presidential Approval, Gallup Poll, 1938–1997

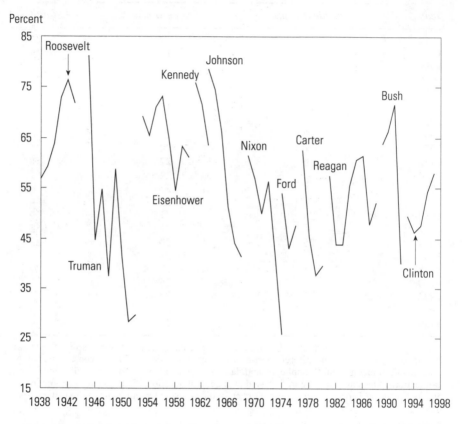

Note: Averaged by year. Question: "Do you approve or disapprove of the way _____ (last name of president) is handling his job as president?"

Sources: Calculated by the editors; 1938–1980: *The Gallup Opinion Index,* October–November 1980, 13–38; 1981–1995: *The Gallup Report,* July 1988, 19–20; The Gallup Poll, "Reagan Regaining Public Confidence," press release, October 9, 1988; the Gallup organization home page (*http://www.gallup.com/*); and unpublished data from the Gallup Poll.

Figure 3-5 Presidential Approval, 1977–1997

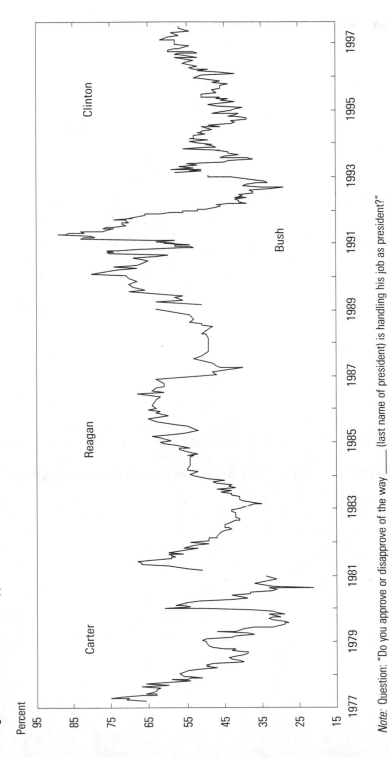

Note: Question: "Do you approve or disapprove of the way _____ (last name of president) is handling his job as president?"

Sources: 1977–1980: *The Gallup Opinion Index,* October–November 1980, 13–14; 1981–1995: *The Gallup Report,* July 1988, 19–20: The Gallup Poll, "Reagan Regaining Public Confidence," press release, October 9, 1988; the Gallup organization home page (*http://www.gallup.com/*); and unpublished data from the Gallup Poll.

Figure 3-6   Approval of Congress, 1974–1997

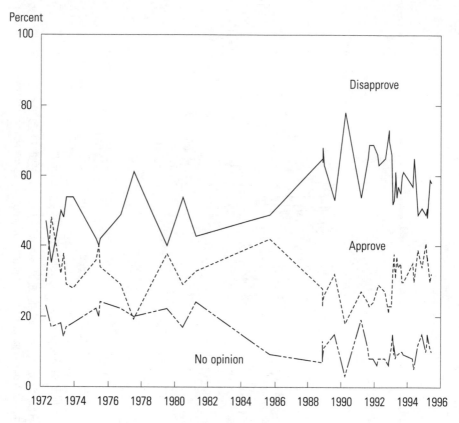

Note: Question: "Do you approve or disapprove of the way the U.S. Congress is handling its job?"

Source: Gallup Poll Monthly, July 1994, 48; and unpublished data from the Gallup Poll.

Figure 3-7   Individual Confidence in Government, 1952–1996

Percentage difference index

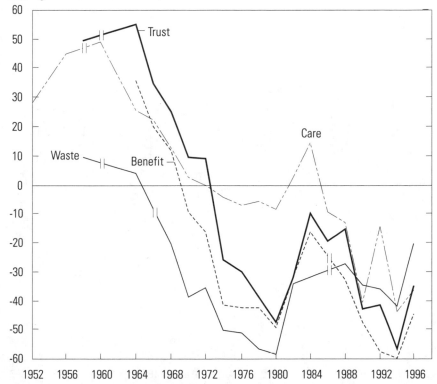

Note: Broken line indicates question not asked that year in the biennial National Election Study. Questions: (Care) "I don't think public officials care much about what people like me think." (Trust) "How much of the time do you think you can trust the government in Washington to do what is right—just about always, most of the time, or only some of the time?" (Benefit) "Would you say the government is pretty much run by a few big interests looking out for themselves or that it is run for the benefit of all people?" (Waste) "Do you think that people in the government waste a lot of money we pay in taxes, waste some of it, or don't waste very much of it?" The percentage difference index is calculated by subtracting the percentage giving a cynical response from the percentage giving a trusting response.

Source: Calculated by the editors from National Election Studies codebooks and data sets.

Figure 3-8   Satisfaction with "The Way Things Are," 1979–1997

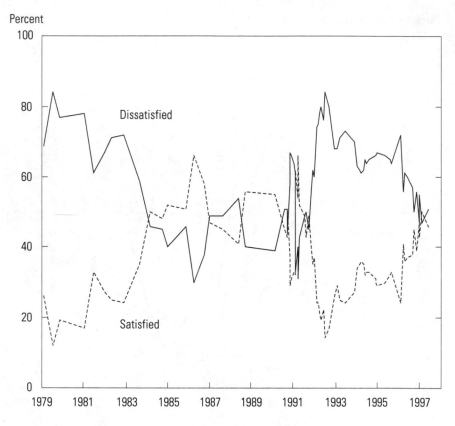

Note: Question: "In general, are you satisfied or dissatisfied with the way things are going in the United States at this time?"

Sources: The Gallup Poll News Service, vol. 55, no. 12, July 25, 1990, 3; and unpublished data from the Gallup Poll.

135

Figure 3-9 Consumer Confidence, 1952–1997

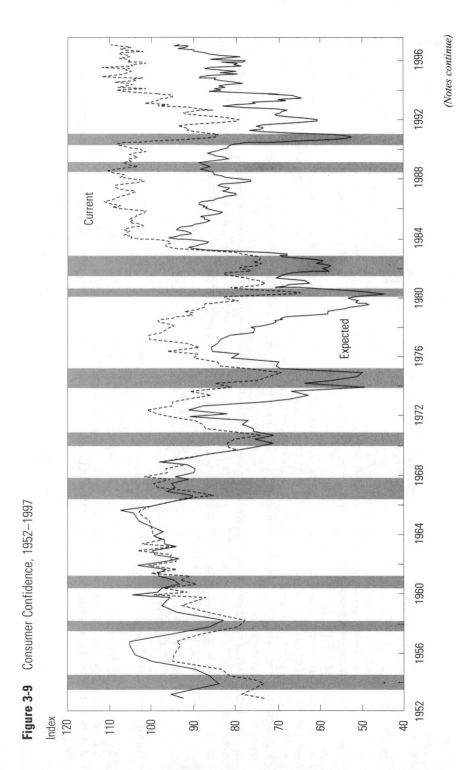

(Notes continue)

Figure 3-9 *(Continued)*

Note: Shaded areas indicate periods of economic recession, as determined by the National Bureau of Economic Research. Figures above reflect data from surveys conducted two or three times a year before 1960, quarterly from 1960 through 1977, and as a three-month moving average since 1978 based on monthly survey data. "Current" indicates the Index of Current Economic Conditions (ICC) and "Expected" the Index of Consumer Expectations (ICE).

The current index includes the following survey questions: (X1) "We are interested in how people are getting along financially these days. Would you say that you (and your family living there) are better off or worse off financially than you were a year ago?" (X5) "About the big things people buy for their homes—such as furniture, a refrigerator, stove, television, and things like that. Generally speaking, do you think now is a good or a bad time for people to buy major household items?"

The expected index includes the following survey questions: (X2) "Now looking ahead—do you think that a year from now you (and your family living there) will be better off financially, or worse off, or just about the same as now?" (X3) "Now turning to business conditions in the country as a whole—do you think that during the next twelve months we'll have good times financially, or bad times, or what?" (X4) "Looking ahead, which would you say is more likely—that in the country as a whole we'll have continuous good times during the next five years or so, or that we will have periods of widespread unemployment or depression?"

As a first step in calculating each index, a relative score is calculated from the percent giving favorable replies minus the percent giving unfavorable replies, plus 100 percent, for each question used. Each relative score is rounded to the nearest whole number. Using the following equation for each index, the relative scores of the appropriate survey questions are summed, divided by the 1966 base period constant for the index, and 2 is added (a constant to correct for sample design changes from the 1950s).

$$ICC = ((X1+X5)/2.6424)+2.0$$
$$ICE = ((X2+X3+X4)/4.1134)+2.0$$

The Index of Consumer Sentiment is a weighted average of the current and expected indexes.

Sources: 1952–1990: Surveys of Consumers, *Historical Data* (Ann Arbor: Institute for Social Research, University of Michigan, 1991), 10–14; 1991–1995: Survey of Consumers, unpublished data; questions and equations from Surveys of Consumers, "Index Calculations" (Ann Arbor: Institute for Social Research, University of Michigan, n.d.); recession periods determined by the National Bureau of Economic Research and listed (through 1990) in Surveys of Consumers, *December 1990* (Ann Arbor: Institute for Social Research, University of Michigan, 1991).

Figure 3-10 The Most Important Problem: Domestic or Foreign, 1947–1997

Percent

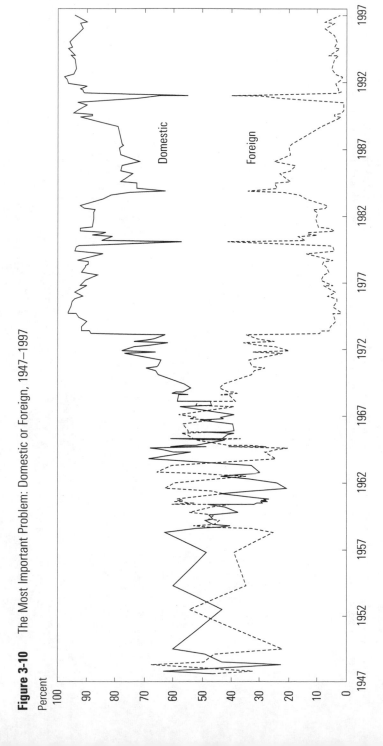

(Notes continue)

Figure 3-10 (Continued)

Note: Typical question: "What do you think is the most important problem facing this country today?"

Sources: Gallup polls as reported in Tom W. Smith, "The Polls: America's Most Important Problems," *Public Opinion Quarterly* 49 (1985): 268–274; data updated by the editors from *The Gallup Report,* July 1984, 17, December 1985, 13, September 1986, 29, May 1987, 7; The Gallup Poll, "Republicans Gain on Issue Barometers," press release, September 28, 1988, 1; *The Gallup Poll News Service,* July 25, 1990; *The Gallup Poll Monthly,* May 1996, 37; and unpublished data from the Gallup Poll.

Figure 3-11 The Most Important Problem: Civil Rights, Drugs, Economics, and Vietnam, 1947–1997

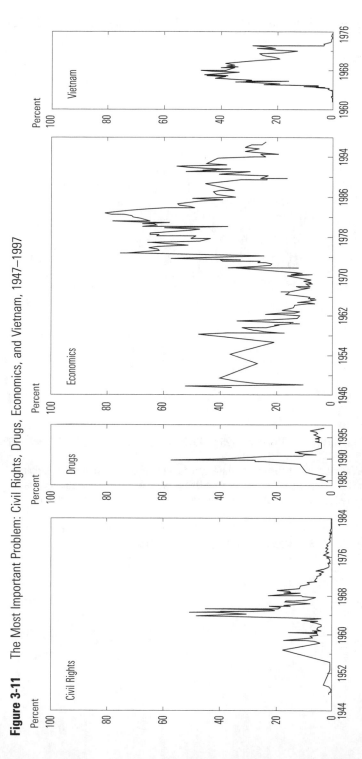

Note: Typical question: "What do you think is the most important problem facing this country today?"

Sources: Gallup polls as reported in Tom W. Smith, "The Polls: America's Most Important Problems," *Public Opinion Quarterly* 49 (1985): 268–274; data calculated by the editors from *The Gallup Report,* July 1984, 17, December 1985, 13, September 1986, 29, May 1987, 7; The Gallup Poll, "Republicans Gain on Issue Barometers," press release, September 28, 1988, 1; *The Gallup Poll Newsletter,* July 25, 1990, 2; The Gallup Poll Monthly, May 1996, 37; and unpublished data from the Gallup Poll.

Figure 3-12   The Party Better Able to Handle the Most Important Problem, 1945–1997

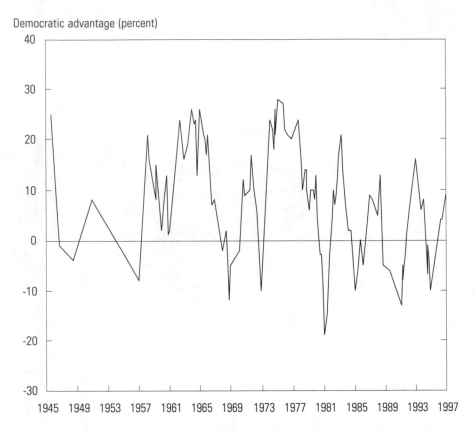

Democratic advantage (percent)

Note: Question: "Which political party do you think can do a better job of handling the problems you have just mentioned—the Republican party or the Democratic party?" "Democratic advantage" is the percentage responding Democratic minus the percentage responding Republican.

Sources: The Gallup Report, May 1987, 9; The Gallup Poll, "Republicans Gain on Issue Barometers," press release, September 28, 1988; and unpublished data from the Gallup Poll.

Figure 3-13   The Party More Likely to Keep the United States Out of War, 1951–1996

Democratic advantage (percent)

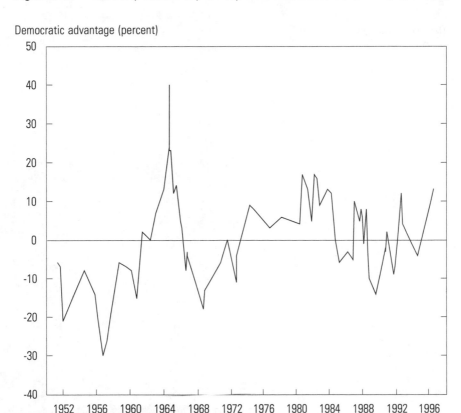

Note: Question: "Looking ahead for the next few years, which political party would be more likely to keep the United States out of World War III—the Republican or the Democratic party?" In 1992 and subsequent years the question phrasing was "keep the country out of war." "Democratic advantage" is the percentage responding Democratic minus the percentage responding Republican.

Sources: The Gallup Report, October 1988, 5; *The Gallup Poll News Service,* vol. 55, no. 18, September 12, 1990, 2; *The Gallup Poll Monthly,* July 1992, 47; and unpublished data from the Gallup Poll.

Figure 3-14   The Party Better Able to Keep the United States Prosperous, 1951–1996

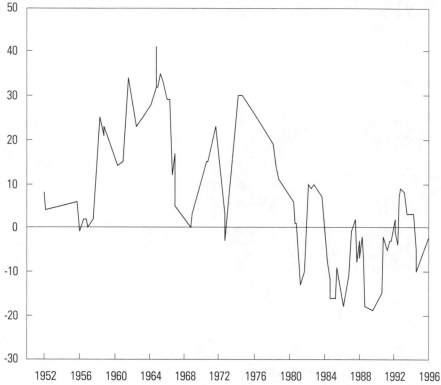

Democratic advantage (percent)

Note: Question: "Which political party—the Republican or the Democratic party—would do a better job of keeping the country prosperous?" "Democratic advantage" is the percentage responding Democratic minus the percentage responding Republican.

Sources: The Gallup Report, October 1988, 5; *The Gallup Poll News Service,* vol. 55, no. 18, September 12, 1990, 1; and unpublished data from the Gallup Poll.

Table 3-13   Public Opinion on Issues Relating to Proposed Constitutional
Amendments, 1963–1996 (percent)

Proposed amendment/year	Favor	Oppose	Don't know or no opinion
Abortion amendment			
1985 (January)	38	58	4
1985 (September)	37	55	8
1987	25	69	6
1988	34	60	6
1989 (January)	29	68	3
1989 (March)	28	63	9
1989 (April)	27	65	8
1989 (June)	31	60	9
1989 (July)	27	62	11
1989 (October)	29	62	2
1990	21	73	6
1992	25	67	8
1996 (June)	24	75	1
1996 (August)	26	72	2
Supreme Court decision in *Roe v. Wade*			
1974	47	44	9
1981	45	46	9
1983	50	43	7
1986	45	45	10
1988	58	37	5
1989	61	33	6
1991 (June)	52	42	6
1991 (July)	56	37	7
1991 (September)	57	36	7
1991 (December)	64	30	6
Balanced budget amendment[a]			
1976	78	13	9
1981 (April)	70	22	8
1981 (September)	73	19	8
1982 (May)	74	17	9
1982 (August)	63	23	14
1983	71	21	8
1985	49	27	24
1987	53	23	24
1989	59	24	17
1994	80	12	8
1995	76	18	6

(Table continues)

Table 3-13   *(Continued)*

Proposed amendment/year	Favor	Oppose	Don't know or no opinion
Equal rights amendment[a]			
1975	58	24	18
1976	57	24	19
1978	58	31	11
1980	58	31	11
1981	63	32	5
1982	56	34	10
1984	63	31	6
Flag burning amendment			
1989 (June)	71	24	5
1989 (June)	67	29	4
1989 (July)	67	28	5
1990 (June)	68	25	5
1990 (June)	57	42	1
Supreme Court decision banning school prayer			
1963	24	70	6
1971	28	67	6
1974	31	66	3
1975	35	62	3
1977	33	64	2
1981	31	66	3
1982	37	60	3
1983	40	57	4
1985 (March)	43	54	3
1985 (September)	37	62	1
1986	37	61	2
1988	37	59	4
1989	41	56	3
1990	40	56	5
1991	38	58	4
1993	39	58	4
1994	37	58	4
Supreme Court one-person, one-vote decision			
1964	47	30	23
1969	52	23	25

Note: All results are based on national, adult samples. Questions: Abortion amendment—"Do you favor or oppose a constitutional amendment to ban abortions?," or very similar wording. *Roe v. Wade*, 1974–1986—"The U.S. Supreme Court has ruled that a woman may go to a doctor to end her pregnancy at any time during the first three months of pregnancy. Do you favor or oppose this ruling?" *Roe v. Wade*, 1988–1989—"The Supreme Court's 1973 *Roe versus Wade* decision established a woman's constitutional right to an abortion at least in the first three months

Table 3-13   *(Continued)*

of pregnancy. Would you like to see the Supreme Court completely overturn its *Roe versus Wade* decision, or not?" (Question did not include "completely" in 1988.) Balanced budget—"Have you heard (or read) about the proposal for a constitutional amendment which would require the federal government to balance the national budget each year? A proposed amendment to the Constitution would require Congress to approve a balanced federal budget each year. Government spending would have to be limited to no more than expected revenues, unless a three-fifths majority of Congress voted to spend more than expected revenues. Would you favor or oppose this amendment to the Constitution?" (Slightly different wording in 1976 and 1989.) Equal rights— "Have you heard or read about the Equal Rights Amendment to the U.S. Constitution which would prohibit discrimination on the basis of sex? Do you favor or oppose this amendment?" Flag burning—"Do you favor or oppose a constitutional amendment which would make it illegal to burn the American flag?," or very similar wording. School prayer—"The U.S. Supreme Court has ruled that no state or local government may require the reading of the Lord's Prayer or Bible verses in public schools. What are your views on this—do you approve or disapprove of the court ruling?" One-person, one-vote, decision, 1964—"As you know, the U.S. Supreme Court has ruled that the number of representatives of both the lower house and the Senate in all state legislatures must be in proportion to population. In most states, this means reducing the number of legislators from the rural areas and increasing the number from urban areas. Do you approve or disapprove of this ruling?" One-person, one-vote decision, 1969—"The U.S. Supreme Court has required states to change their legislative districts so that each member of the upper house represents the same number of people. Some people would like to return to the earlier method of electing members of the upper house according to counties or other units regardless of population. Would you favor continuing the present equal districting plan or returning to the earlier plan?"

[a] Of those who were aware of the proposed amendment (except 1984 for equal rights, 1976 and 1987–1995 for balanced budget). Between 88 and 91 percent of those asked were aware of the equal rights amendment. Between 48 and 66 percent of those asked were aware of the proposed balanced budget amendment.

Sources: Abortion: (1985, January 1989) Harris surveys; (1987) CBS/*New York Times* survey; (1988, October 1989, 1992, 1996) ABC/*Washington Post* surveys; (March 1989) *Los Angeles Times* survey; (April, June, July, 1989, 1990) Yankelovich, Clancy, Shulman surveys; *Roe v. Wade*: *The Gallup Poll* (Wilmington, Del.: Scholarly Resources, Inc., 1983), 140, *The Gallup Report*, January/February 1986, 17–18, October 1990, 17, *Los Angeles Times* survey, *The Gallup Poll* (New York: Random House, 1972), 1897, 2205–2206, Gallup Poll Surveys; school prayer: (1963, 1971) *The Gallup Poll* (1972), 1837; 1981, 1985 (September) ABC News/*Washington Post* survey; (1974–1977, 1982–1985 (June), 1986–1994) General Social Survey, National Opinion Research Center, University of Chicago; equal rights: *The Gallup Poll* (1982), 140, (1984), 242; balanced budget: (1976–1989) *The Gallup Poll* (1972), 679, (1982), 125, 231, (1983), 127, *The Gallup Report*, September 1985, 10–11, July 1987, 8, February 1989, 3 (1994–1995) CBS News Poll; flag burning: (1989 June, first; 1990, June, first) *Gallup Poll Monthly*, June 1990, 3–4; (1989, June, second) Yankelovich, Clancy, Shulman survey; (1989 July) *Los Angeles Times* survey; 1990 (June, second) Harris survey.

Table 3-14   Public Opinion on Civil Liberties, 1940–1996 (percent)

Issue/year	Allow[a]	Don't forbid[b]
Public speeches against democracy		
1940	25	46
1974	56	72
1976a	55	80
1976b	52	79

Issue/year	Allow to speak	Allow to teach college	Keep book in library
Atheist[c]			
1954	37	12	35
1964[d]	—	—	61
1972	65	40	61
1973a	65	41	61
1973b	62	39	57
1974	62	42	60
1976	64	41	60
1977	62	39	59
1978	63	—	60
1980	66	45	62
1982	64	46	61
1984	68	46	64
1985	65	45	61
1987	69	47	66
1988	70	45	64
1989	72	51	67
1990	73	50	67
1991	72	52	69
1993	71	52	67
1994	73	52	70
1996	73	55	68
Admitted communist[c]			
1954	27	6	27
1972	52	32	53
1973a	60	39	58
1973b	53	30	54
1974	58	42	59
1976	55	41	56
1977	55	39	55
1978	60	—	61
1980	55	41	57
1982	56	43	57
1984	59	46	60
1985	57	44	57
1987	60	46	61
1988	60	48	59

Table 3-14   *(Continued)*

Issue/year	Allow to speak	Allow to teach college	Keep book in library
1989	64	50	62
1990	64	52	64
1991	67	54	67
1993	69	56	67
1994	67	55	66
1996	64	57	65
Racist[c]			
1943[e]	17	—	—
1976	61	41	60
1977	59	41	61
1978	62	—	65
1980	62	43	64
1982	59	43	60
1984	57	41	63
1985	55	42	60
1987	61	44	64
1988	61	42	62
1989	62	46	65
1990	63	45	64
1991	62	42	66
1993	61	43	64
1994	61	42	66
1996	61	46	64
Admitted homosexual[c]			
1973	61	47	53
1974	62	50	55
1976	62	52	55
1977	62	49	55
1980	66	55	58
1982	65	55	56
1984	68	59	59
1985	67	58	55
1987	67	56	57
1988	70	56	60
1989	76	63	64
1990	74	63	64
1991	76	63	68
1993	78	69	67
1994	79	71	69
1996	81	75	69

(Notes continue)

Table 3-14   *(Continued)*

Note: "—" indicates not available.

[a] Question: "Do you think the United States should allow public speeches against democracy?"
[b] Question: "Do you think the United States should forbid public speeches against democracy?"
[c] Question: "There are always some people whose ideas are considered bad or dangerous by other people. For instance, somebody who (is against all churches and religion/admits he is a communist/believes that blacks are genetically inferior/admits that he is a homosexual). If such a person wanted to make a speech in your (city/town/community), should he be allowed to speak or not? Should such a person be allowed to teach in a college or university, or not? If some people in your community suggested that a book he wrote (against churches and religion/promoting communism/which said blacks are inferior/in favor of homosexuality) should be taken out of your public library, would you favor removing this book or not?" (Slight variations in wording across groups.)
[d] In 1964 the question was as follows: "Suppose a man admitted in public that he did not believe in God. Do you think a book he wrote should be removed from a public library?"
[e] In 1943 the question was as follows: "In peacetime, do you think anyone in the United States should be allowed to make speeches against certain races in this country?"

Sources: Public speeches against democracy: Howard Schuman and Stanley Presser, *Questions and Answers in Attitude Surveys* (New York: Academic Press, 1981), 277; 1943, 1964, and 1973b: National Opinion Research Center surveys; 1954: Samuel A. Stouffer, *Communism, Conformity, and Civil Liberties* (Garden City, N.Y.: Doubleday, 1955), 32–34, 40–43; 1973a: Clyde Z. Nunn et al., *Tolerance for Nonconformity* (San Francisco: Jossey-Bass, 1978), 40–43; data for all other years from General Social Survey.

Table 3-15   Public Opinion on the Death Penalty, 1936–1996 (percent)

Date	Favor	Oppose	Don't know
April 1936	62	33	5
December 1936	59	38	3
November 1937	61	33	7
October 1953[a]	68	26	6
April 1956	53	34	13
September 1957	47	34	18
March 1960	53	36	11
February 1965	45	43	12
July 1966	42	47	11
June 1967	54	38	8
January 1969	51	40	9
October 1971	48	41	11
February 1972	51	41	8
March 1972	53	39	8
November 1972	60	30	10
March 1973	60	35	5
March 1974	63	32	5
March 1975	60	33	7
March 1976	66	30	5
April 1976	67	27	7
March 1977	67	26	6
March 1978	66	28	6

Table 3-15   *(Continued)*

Date	Favor	Oppose	Don't know
July 1979	65	27	8
March 1980	67	27	6
March 1981	66	25	9
March 1982	74	21	6
June 1982	71	20	9
March 1983	73	22	5
March 1984	70	24	6
January 1985	72	20	8
March 1985	76	19	5
November 1985	75	17	8
January 1986	70	22	8
March 1986	71	23	5
March 1987	70	24	6
March 1988	71	22	7
September 1988	79	16	5
March 1989	74	20	6
March 1990	75	19	6
March 1991	72	22	6
March 1993	72	21	7
March 1994	74	19	6
September 1994	80	16	4
May 1995[a]	85	13	2
March 1996	71	22	7

Note: Questions: 1936–1937—"Are you in favor of the death penalty for murder?" 1953-February 1972, November 1972, April 1976, January 1981, January 1985, November 1985, September 1994, May 1995—"Are you in favor of the death penalty for persons [or: "a person"] convicted of murder?" All others—"Do you favor or oppose the death penalty for persons [or: "people"] convicted of murder?"

[a] "Favor" includes those responding with a qualified yes or qualified no.

Sources: 1936 through February 1972, November 1972, April 1976, January 1981, January 1985, November 1985, September 1988, September 1994, and May 1995: Gallup surveys; others: General Social Survey.

Table 3-16   Public Opinion on Abortion, 1962–1996 (percent)

	Abortion should be legal under these circumstances						
Year	Mother's health	Rape	Birth defect	Low income	Single mother	As form of birth control	Any reason
1962	77	—	55	15	—	—	—
1965	70	56	55	21	17	15	—
1969	80	—	63	23	—	—	—
1972	83	75	75	46	41	38	—
1973	91	81	82	52	47	46	—
1974	90	83	83	52	48	45	—
1975	88	80	80	51	46	44	—
1976	89	81	82	51	48	45	—
1977	89	81	83	52	48	45	37
1978	88	81	80	46	40	39	32
1980	88	80	80	50	46	45	39
1982	90	83	81	50	47	46	39
1983	87	80	76	42	38	38	33
1984	88	77	78	45	43	41	37
1985	87	78	76	42	40	39	36
1987	86	78	77	44	40	40	38
1988	86	77	76	40	38	39	35
1989	88	80	78	46	43	43	39
1990	89	81	78	46	43	43	42
1991	88	82	79	46	42	45	41
1993	86	79	79	47	46	45	43
1994	88	81	79	49	46	47	45
1996	88	81	79	45	43	45	43

Note: "—" indicates not available. Question: "Please tell me whether or not you think it should be possible for a pregnant woman to obtain a legal abortion [in the order asked in the survey] if there is a strong chance of serious defect in the baby? If she is married and does not want any more children? If the woman's own health is seriously endangered by the pregnancy? If the family has a very low income and cannot afford any more children? If she became pregnant as a result of rape? If she is not married and does not want to marry the man? The woman wants it for any reason?"

Sources: 1962 and 1969: Gallup surveys; 1965: National Opinion Research Center surveys; 1972–1996: General Social Survey.

Table 3-17   Public Opinion of Whites on School and Neighborhood
Integration, 1942–1997 (percent)

| Date | Blacks and whites should attend | | |
	Same schools	Separate schools	Don't know
June 1942	30	66	4
September 1956	48	49	3
December 1963	65	29	6
June 1964	62	32	5
October 1965	68	28	4
April 1970	74	24	3
March 1972	85	14	2
November 1972	80	15	5
March 1976	83	15	3
March 1977	85	14	2
March 1980	86	12	2
March 1982	88	9	2
March 1984	90	8	2
March 1985	92	7	1

| Date | If blacks lived next door | | | |
	Would definitely move	Might move	Would not move	Don't know
1958	21	23	56	—
1963	20	25	55	—
1965	13	22	65	—
1966	13	21	66	—
1967	12	23	65	—
1978	4	9	84	3
1990	1	4	93	2
1997	a	1	98	1

| Date | If many blacks lived in neighborhood | | | |
	Would definitely move	Might move	Would not move	Don't know
1958	50	30	21	—
1963	49	29	22	—
1965	40	29	31	—
1966	39	31	30	—
1967	40	31	29	—
1978	20	31	45	4
1990	8	18	68	6
1997	a	18	75	7

(Notes continue)

Table 3-17   *(Continued)*

Note: "—" indicates not available. School questions: "Do you think white students and (Negro/black) students should go to the same schools or to separate schools?" Asked of whites only. Neighborhood questions: "If (colored/black) people came to live next door, would you move?" "Would you move if (colored/black) people came to live in great numbers in your neighborhood?" Asked of nonblacks only.

[a] For 1997, the "definitely" and "might move" responses were not separately available.

Sources: Schools (1942–1970): November 1972, National Opinion Research Center; (March 1972, 1976–1985): General Social Survey, National Opinion Research Center, University of Chicago; neighborhood integration: *Gallup Poll Monthly*, June 1990, 27; and unpublished data from the Gallup Poll.

Table 3-18   Public Opinion of Whites on School Integration, by Racial Composition of School, 1958–1997 (percent)

| | Object to own children attending school with | | |
Date	A few blacks	Half blacks	More than half blacks
September 1958	25	53	70
February 1959	20	47	71
May 1963	25	52	75
April 1965	16	42	67
June 1965	20	44	68
May 1966	11	41	67
July 1969	11	38	66
March 1970	8	32	66
April 1970	10	34	63
March 1972	6	25	55
August 1973	9	36	67
March 1974	4	33	67
March 1975	6	38	66
September 1975	7	35	62
March 1977	7	26	64
March 1978	4	24	61
July 1978	7	36	67
December 1980	6	28	62
March 1982	4	21	54
March 1983	3	25	65
March 1985	4	22	60
March 1986	4	24	64
March 1988	3	21	62
March 1989	4	23	58
March 1990	2	20	59
March 1991	4	26	62
March 1993	2	19	54
March 1994	4	21	54
March 1996	4	18	50
May 1997	4	14	42

Note: Question: "Would you, yourself, have any objection to sending your children to a school where a few of the children are (Negroes/blacks)?" If no: "Where half of the children are (Negroes/blacks)?" If no: "Where more than half of the children are (Negroes/blacks)?" Those saying "don't know" were assumed to have expressed some objection. Question asked of nonblacks with school-age children only.

Sources: 1958–1970, 1973, September 1975, July 1978, 1980, 1997: Gallup surveys; other years: General Social Survey.

Table 3-19   Public Opinion on Gun Control, 1959–1996 (percent)

Date	Favor	Oppose	Don't know
July 1959	75	21	4
December 1963	79	17	4
January 1965	73	23	4
September 1965	70	25	5
August 1966	67	29	3
August 1967	73	24	4
October 1971	72	24	4
March 1972	70	27	3
May 1972	72	24	4
March 1973	74	25	2
March 1974	75	23	1
February 1975	71	28	1
March 1975	74	24	3
February 1976	73	24	4
March 1976	72	27	1
March 1977	72	27	2
March 1980	69	29	2
March 1982	72	26	2
March 1984	70	27	3
March 1985	72	27	1
March 1987	70	28	2
March 1988	74	24	3
March 1989	78	21	2
March 1990	79	20	2
March 1991	81	18	1
March 1993	81	17	2
March 1994	78	20	2
March 1996	80	18	2

Note: Question: "Would you favor or oppose a law which would require a person to obtain a police permit before he or she could buy a gun?"

Sources: 1959–1971: Gallup surveys; February 1975, February 1976: Survey Research Center, University of Michigan; others: General Social Survey.

Table 3-20 Public Opinion on the Courts, 1965–1996 (percent)

Date	Too harsh	About right	Not harsh enough	Don't know
April 1965	2	34	48	16
August 1965	2	27	60	12
February 1968	2	19	63	16
January 1969	2	13	74	10
March 1972	7	16	66	11
December 1972	4	13	74	8
March 1973	5	13	73	9
March 1974[a]	5	6	60	29
March 1974	6	10	78	7
March 1975	4	10	79	7
March 1976	3	10	81	6
March 1977	3	8	83	6
March 1978	3	7	85	5
March 1980	3	8	83	6
January 1981	3	13	77	7
March 1982[a]	4	5	76	14
March 1982	3	8	86	4
March 1983	4	6	85	4
March 1984	3	11	82	4
March 1985	3	9	84	3
March 1986	3	8	85	4
March 1987	3	12	79	6
March 1988	4	10	82	5
March 1989	3	9	84	4
March 1990	3	9	83	5
March 1991	4	11	80	5
March 1993	3	10	81	6
March 1994	3	8	85	5
March 1996	5	11	78	7

Note: Question: "In general, do you think the courts in this area deal too harshly or not harshly enough with criminals?"

[a] In 1974 and 1982 half of the General Social Survey sample was asked the question as noted above and half the sample was asked the same question but with the phrase "or don't you have enough information about the courts to say" added at the end. The "don't know" column for these rows includes those saying "not enough information."

Sources: 1965–1969, December 1972: Gallup survey; 1981: *Los Angeles Times* survey; others: General Social Survey.

Table 3-21   Public Opinion on U.S. Involvement in World Affairs,
1945–1994 (percent)

Date	Active part	Stay out	No opinion
October 1945	70	19	11
September 1947	65	26	9
September 1949	67	25	8
November 1950	64	25	11
December 1950	66	25	9
October 1952	68	23	9
February 1953	73	22	5
September 1953	71	21	8
April 1954	69	25	6
March 1955	72	21	7
November 1956	71	25	4
June 1965	79	16	5
March 1973	66	31	3
March 1975	61	36	4
March 1976	63	32	5
March 1978	64	32	4
December 1978	59	29	12
March 1982	61	34	5
November 1982	53	35	12
March 1983	65	31	4
March 1984	65	29	6
March 1985	70	27	2
March 1986	65	32	4
March 1988	65	32	4
March 1989	68	28	4
March 1990	69	27	4
March 1991	73	24	2
March 1993	67	28	5
March 1994	65	32	4
October 1994	65	29	6

Note: Question: "Do you think it would be best for the future of this country if we take an active part in world affairs, or if we stay out of world affairs?"

Sources: 1945, 1947, November 1950, December 1978, November 1982, October 1994: Gallup surveys; 1949, December 1950, 1952–1965: National Opinion Research Center; all others: General Social Survey, National Opinion Research Center, University of Chicago.

Table 3-22 Public Opinion on U.S. Defense Spending, 1960–1993
(percent)

Year	Too much	About right	Too little	No opinion
1960	18	45	21	16
1969	52	31	8	9
1971	50	31	11	8
1973	46	30	13	11
1974	44	32	12	12
1976	36	32	22	10
1977	23	40	27	10
1979	21	33	34	12
1980	14	24	49	13
1981	15	22	51	12
1982	41	31	16	12
1983	37	36	21	6
1985	46	36	11	7
1986	47	36	13	4
1987	44	36	14	6
1990 Jan.	50	35	10	5
1990 Aug.	41	40	15	4
1991 Mar.	26	60	10	4
1991 Aug.	47	38	10	5
1991 Oct.	50	36	10	4
1993 Mar.	42	38	17	3

Note: Question: "There is much discussion as to the amount of money the government in Washington should spend for national defense and military purposes. How do you feel about this? Do you think we are spending too little, too much, or about the right amount?"

Sources: *Gallup Opinion Index*, February 1980, 10; *The Gallup Report*, March 1985, 4; *The Gallup Poll* (Wilmington, Del.: Scholarly Resources, Inc., 1992), 202; *The Gallup Poll Monthly*, April 1993, 45.

158

Figure 3-15 Public Opinion on U.S. Military Involvement: Vietnam, Persian Gulf, and Haiti

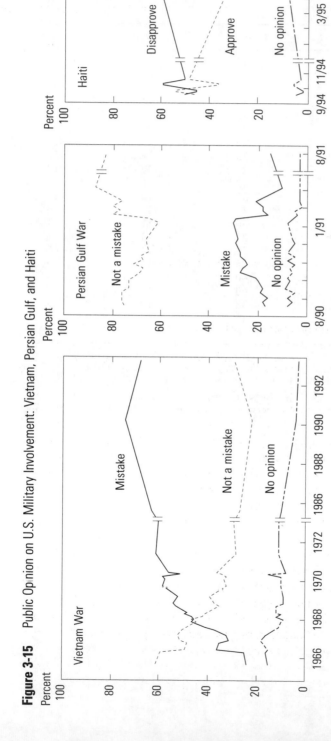

Note: Question for Vietnam War: "In view of the developments since we entered the fighting in Vietnam, do you think the United States made a mistake sending troops to fight in Vietnam?" In 1985, 1990, and 1993, the question was, "Looking back, do you think. . .?" The question was not asked between 1974 and 1984. Question for Persian Gulf War: "In view of the developments since we first sent our troops to the Persian Gulf region, do you think the United States made a mistake in sending troops to the Persian Gulf region, or not?" Prior to January 17–20, 1991, "Saudi Arabia" was used instead of the "Persian Gulf region." Results are plotted using the midpoint of the survey dates. The last two surveys were early March and mid-July 1991. The Gulf War began on January 15, 1991; a cease-fire was declared on February 28, 1991, with the surrender of all Iraqi troops occurring over the next several days. Question for Haiti: "Concerning Haiti. . . Do you approve or disapprove of the presence of U.S. troops in Haiti?"

Sources: Vietnam War: Gallup polls cited in John Mueller, *War, Presidents and Public Opinion* (New York: Wiley, 1973), 54–55 (reprinted in 1985 by University Press of America, Lanham, Md.); *The Gallup Poll, 1972–1975,* vol. I (Wilmington, Del.: Scholarly Resources, 1977), 87; *Gallup Poll Monthly,* January 1993, 37. Persian Gulf War: *Gallup Poll Monthly,* July 1991, 36. Haiti: *Gallup Poll Monthly,* October 1994, 31, and Gallup Poll Surveys.

4

Media

- **National Reach**
- **Presence in Washington**
- **Public Use**
- **Coverage and Viewership of Presidential Campaigns, Conventions, and Debates**
- **Newspaper Endorsements**

The mass media thrive on numbers. Nearly every American adult has heard of audience ratings games—serious games with millions of dollars and many individual careers at stake—played by television, newspapers, radio, and magazines. Will the top-ranked television show remain first in the ratings, and how much will it help the show that follows it? Can a new magazine, such as John Kennedy's *George,* be profitable? Will a radio station increase its audience ratings—and what kind of audience will it attract—by playing more hard rock? How many extra copies and how much more advertising will a weekly news magazine sell with excerpts of soon-to-be-published political memoirs—and how much can the publisher afford to pay for those excerpts? So much money is at stake that media organizations annually spend millions of dollars to find the answers to such questions.

Politics, as it relates to the media, also involves numbers. Some questions simply involve market share and audience, much like the questions noted above: How many and what kinds of individuals follow the media generally (Table 4-1, 4-2, and 4-4)? What is the availability of information about specific parts of government, and how has it changed over time (Figure 4-1 and Table 4-3)? How much attention do people pay to political news stories, candidate advertisements, campaign debates, and so on (Tables 4-4, 4-6, 4-14)? Somewhat more analytical is the question of how much trust people have of various media (Table 4-5). Of course, all of these matters, while important, are relatively straightforward. More complicated and controversial are other matters that involve numbers. Some critics charge, for example, that television emphasizes only the "horse race" aspect of political campaigns (who is ahead and by how much) to the exclusion of issues (Table 4-8) and that both print and electronic media give too much emphasis to the early presidential primaries and caucuses (Table 4-7).

Though data specifically about politics and the media are not as plentiful as one might think (e.g., because some information, such as candidates' private surveys, are propriety), more is now available than in the past. Television coverage extends over a forty-year period (with extended coverage since the 1960s), and congressional proceedings have been televised for nearly two decades (from 1979 in the House and 1986 in the Senate). This means that researchers should now be in a position to do more extensive studies of the media and politics than heretofore. Predictably, there has been a spurt in such studies. Perhaps as a consequence of the closer attention, there is an increasingly strong sense of media influence on individual voters and on the political system generally.

Increasing amounts of data are available about media coverage of the presidential campaign. This includes detailed content analyses of various campaign periods (Tables 4-8 through 4-12), information on both generic type of coverage and coverage of specific issues (Tables 4-8 and 4-9), and assessments of the coverage of specific candidates and parties (Tables 4-10 through 4-12). It also includes information about the electorate's viewing of the nominating conventions (Table 4-13) and presidential and vice-presidential debates (Table 4-14). Some of this material is now available for up to five elections (Table 4-7), and long-standing tabulations are available of newspaper endorsements of presidential candidates (Table 4-15 and Figure 4-2).

Media themselves are increasingly well preserved and documented in ways that make them highly accessible. Magazines are saved and are well indexed. Major newspapers are widely available and well indexed; small newspapers—though often kept only locally—combine to give widespread coverage of politics as practiced and perceived throughout the country. CBS News has published transcripts and indexes of its news programs since 1975 to facilitate research. Network television news programs since 1968 have been stored at Vanderbilt University; the archives are indexed and available to researchers. These efforts at preservation mean that studies can be made of past as well as contemporary events. Indeed, some of the most interesting studies of politics and the media are yet to come because they will be able to cover long expanses of time.

As in all areas of research, data about the media are rarely self-interpreting. One specific problem here is that the media both shape the news and reflect it. The shift in emphasis from parties to candidates (see, for example, Tables 1-12 and 3-12 on split-ticket voting) is a case in point. To some degree this shift simply reflects the weakening hold of political parties over American voters, a process that began as long ago as the turn of the century, well before the advent of television. On the other hand, the power of television to bring individual candidates directly into one's living room has accelerated the declining influence of party organizations in particular and of party affiliation more generally.

Problems of interpretation—especially whether the media cause or simply reflect events—thus make inferences about media influence difficult. The usual response to such problems of inference is to bring additional data to bear on the subject. With more data now available, researchers can safely anticipate better answers to questions about media audiences, coverage, emphasis, and influence as they relate to the political process.

Table 4-1   Growth and Reach of Selected Media, 1950–1996

Year	Percentage of households with			Percentage of TV households with		Average TV viewing per day (hours)[e]
	Telephone service[a]	Radio sets[b]	Television sets[c]	Cable TV[d]	VCRs[d]	
1950	—	92.6	9	—	—	4.6
1960	78.5	96.3	87	—	—	5.1
1970	87.0	98.6	95	6.7	—	5.9
1975	—	98.6	97	12.6	—	6.1
1980	93.0	99.0	98	19.9	1.1	6.6
1981	—	99.0	98	25.2	1.8	6.8
1982	—	99.0	98	29.8	3.1	6.8
1983	—	99.0	98	34.0	5.5	7.0
1984	91.8	99.0	98	39.3	10.6	7.1
1985	91.8	99.0	98	42.8	20.8	7.2
1986	92.2	99.0	98	45.6	36.0	7.1
1987	92.5	99.0	98	47.7	48.7	7.0
1988	92.9	99.0	98	49.4	58.0	7.1
1989	93.0	99.0	98	52.8	64.6	7.0
1990	93.3	99.0	98	56.4	68.6	6.9
1991	93.6	99.0	98	58.9	71.9	7.0
1992	93.9	99.0	98	60.2	75.0	7.1
1993	94.2	99.0	98	61.4	77.1	7.2
1994	93.9	99.0	98	62.4	79.0	7.3
1995	—	99.0	98	63.4	81.0	7.3
1996	—	99.0	98	65.3	82.2	—

Note: "—" indicates not available.

[a] For occupied housing units. 1950 through 1980, as of April 1; thereafter, as of March.
[b] As of December 31. Estimated after 1987.
[c] 1970–1975, as of September of prior year; all other years as of January of year shown.
[d] Cable as of January; VCR as of February. Excludes Alaska and Hawaii prior to 1989.
[e] Calendar year data.

Sources: Telephone service: U.S. Bureau of the Census, *Statistical Abstract of the United States, 1996* (Washington, D.C.: U.S. Government Printing Office, 1996), 561; radios: Radio Advertising Bureau; television, 1950–1960: National Broadcasting Company, Inc.; television, 1970–1994, cable, VCR, and viewing: Television Bureau of Advertising, *Trends in Television* (New York: Television Bureau of Advertising, 1996), 3, 5, 7.

Table 4-2   Newspaper Circulation, Daily Papers, 1850–1996

Year	Number	Circulation (thousands)	Circulation as a percentage of population
1850	254	758	3.3
1860	387	1,478	4.7
1870	574	2,602	6.5
1880	971	3,566	7.1
1890	1,610	8,387	13.3
1900	2,226	15,102	19.8
1904	2,452	19,633	23.4
1909	2,600	24,212	26.2
1914	2,580	28,777	28.6
1919	2,441	33,029	31.0
1921	2,334	33,742	31.7
1923	2,271	35,471	30.6
1925	2,116	37,407	32.3
1927	2,091	41,368	35.7
1929	2,086	42,015	34.1
1931	2,044	41,294	33.6
1933	1,903	37,630	29.6
1935	2,037	40,871	32.1
1937	2,065	43,345	34.1
1939	2,040	42,966	32.4
1947	1,854	53,287	37.0
1950	1,772	53,800	35.3
1954	1,820	56,410	34.6
1958	1,778	58,713	33.6
1960	1,763	58,900	32.6
1963	1,766	63,831	33.7
1965	1,751	60,400	31.1
1967	—	66,527	33.5
1970	1,748	62,100	30.3
1975	1,756	60,700	28.1
1978	1,756	62,000	27.9
1979	1,763	62,200	27.6
1980	1,745	62,200	27.3
1981	1,730	61,400	26.7
1982	1,711	62,500	26.9
1983	1,701	62,600	26.7
1984	1,688	63,300	26.8
1985	1,676	62,800	26.3
1986	1,657	62,500	26.0
1987	1,645	62,826	25.9
1988	1,642	62,695	25.6
1989	1,626	62,649	25.3
1990	1,611	62,328	24.9
1991	1,586	60,687	23.9
1992	1,570	60,164	23.1

(Table continues)

Table 4-2   *(Continued)*

Year	Number	Circulation (thousands)	Circulation as a percentage of population
1993	1,556	59,812	22.6
1994	1,548	59,305	22.2
1995	1,533	58,193	21.9
1996	1,520	56,983	21.1

Note: "—" indicates not available. Data are for English language newspapers only. In 1900 and earlier, figures include a small number of periodicals. In 1970 and later, the number of newspapers is for February of the following year and circulation figures are as of September 30 of the year indicated.

Sources: Daily papers, 1850–1967: U.S. Bureau of the Census, *Historical Statistics of the United States* (Washington, D.C.: U.S. Government Printing Office, 1975), 810; 1970–1996: *Editor & Publisher International Yearbook* (New York: Editor & Publisher), annual; population: U.S. Bureau of the Census, *Statistical Abstract of the United States, 1991* (Washington, D.C.: U.S. Government Printing Office, 1991), 7; 1991: U.S. Bureau of the Census, *Current Population Reports* (Washington, D.C.: U.S. Government Printing Office, 1992), Series P-25, no. 1087; 1992–1996: estimated by *Editor & Publisher.*

Figure 4-1   Growth of Congressional Press Corps, 1864–1995

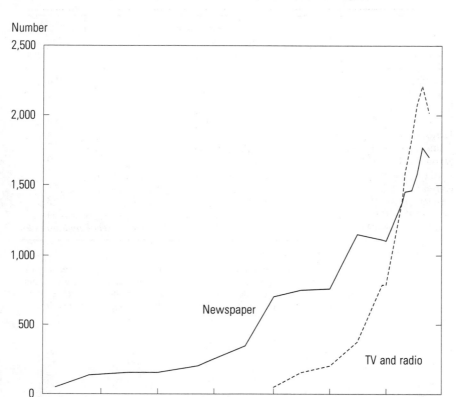

Note: Press corps members are those correspondents entitled to admission to the Senate and House press galleries and radio and television galleries. Prior to 1986, the number of press corps members was recorded approximately every ten years.

Sources: Samuel Kernell, *Going Public: New Strategies of Presidential Leadership* (Washington, D.C.: CQ Press, 1986), 57; updated by the editors from successive volumes of U.S. Congress Joint Committee on Printing, *Official Congressional Directory* (Washington, D.C.: U.S. Government Printing Office).

Table 4-3   Presidential News Conferences with White House
Correspondents, 1929–1996

President	Average number of press conferences per month	Total number of press conferences
Hoover (1929–1933)	5.6	268
Roosevelt (1933–1945)	6.9	998
Truman (1945–1953)	3.6	334
Eisenhower (1953–1961)	2.0	193
Kennedy (1961–1963)	1.9	65
Johnson (1963–1969)	2.2	135
Nixon (1969–1974)	0.6	39
Ford (1974–1977)	1.3	39
Carter (1977–1981)	1.2	59
Reagan (1981–1989)	0.6	53
Bush (1989–1993)	1.3	64
Clinton (1993–1996)[a]	0.7	34

[a] As of December 31, 1996.

Sources: Hoover and Truman through Carter: compiled by the editors from *Public Papers of the President* (Washington, D.C.: U.S. Government Printing Office); Roosevelt: Elizabeth Denier, comp., "List of FDR Press Conferences" (Hyde Park, N.Y.: Franklin Delano Roosevelt Library, n.d. [1991]); Reagan through Clinton: compiled by the editors from *Congressional Quarterly Weekly Report.*

Table 4-4 Use of Television, Radio, and Newspapers, Cross-Section, 1996

	Total adult population (thousands)	Television watchers								Magazines / Newspapers					
		Network news		Documen-tary, prime	News specials	Sunday interviews	Sports		Newsweek	New York Times daily	Time	US News & World Report	USA Today	Wall Street Journal
		Early eve.[a]	Late night[b]				Pro Bas-ketball	Pro Football						
Age														
18–24	24,848	7.3	0.8	4.5	2.8	1.4	19.1	18.7	11.5	1.4	12.2	3.2	2.5	0.6
25–34	42,530	11.0	1.7	7.4	3.8	2.2	18.2	24.2	9.1	1.4	11.5	4.0	2.5	1.4
35–44	41,652	12.3	1.5	8.3	4.7	3.0	20.5	22.3	12.3	1.1	13.0	5.7	2.8	2.0
45–54	29,737	15.9	2.4	9.3	7.5	4.6	17.0	21.4	15.0	1.7	14.6	7.0	2.5	2.9
55–64	21,537	18.2	2.4	12.6	7.5	4.8	15.3	20.9	10.4	1.2	10.7	5.0	2.1	1.5
65 and older	31,359	19.5	2.4	12.5	7.4	5.5	10.4	14.2	7.0	1.0	8.8	5.6	1.1	1.3
Sex														
Male	91,780	13.6	2.1	8.1	4.7	3.6	23.3	28.5	12.1	1.7	13.0	6.2	3.6	2.6
Female	99,882	14.0	1.6	9.7	6.1	3.4	11.2	13.5	9.6	1.0	10.9	4.2	1.1	0.9
Race/ethnicity														
White	162,526	13.6	1.6	9.2	5.8	3.4	16.6	21.8	11.2	1.4	12.0	5.4	2.5	1.8
Black	21,957	16.4	3.6	7.9	3.6	4.7	20.9	13.3	8.1	0.8	11.2	3.3	1.6	0.9
Spanish-speaking	14,144	11.0	1.7	6.9	4.8	2.0	17.0	17.9	9.7	0.7	10.9	3.7	1.3	1.0
Other	7,180	9.9	2.1	6.3	3.1	2.3	14.9	17.1	9.5	1.8	11.0	4.4	0.4	1.4
Education														
College graduate	39,600	13.2	2.1	7.9	6.0	3.7	21.5	25.2	19.7	4.1	19.6	10.5	4.6	6.2
Attended college	51,083	13.0	1.6	8.7	.2	2.9	18.2	22.1	13.1	1.1	14.5	6.0	3.1	1.1
High school graduate	64,414	13.8	1.8	9.8	5.7	3.7	15.8	20.5	7.3	0.4	8.3	2.8	1.5	0.3
Not high school graduate	36,567	15.5	1.7	8.7	4.6	3.7	12.8	13.9	4.2	0.3	6.3	2.1	0.2	0.0

(Table continues)

Table 4-4 *(Continued)*

	Total adult population (thousands)	Television watchers							Magazines / Newspapers					
		Network news		Documen- tary, prime	News specials	Sunday interviews	Sports		Newsweek	New York Times daily	Time	US News & World Report	USA Today	Wall Street Journal
		Early eve.[a]	Late night[b]				Pro Bas- ketball	Pro Football						
Employment														
Full-time	104,602	12.3	1.9	8.1	5.2	3.1	20.1	24.4	12.8	1.6	13.5	6.0	3.3	2.4
Part-time	18,438	14.4	1.4	8.0	4.4	2.5	15.7	16.7	10.3	1.6	11.6	3.7	1.5	1.1
Not Employed	68,622	15.9	1.8	10.4	6.1	4.3	12.7	16.0	7.9	0.8	9.5	4.2	1.0	0.7
Household Income														
Under $10,000	18,491	14.4	1.3	9.1	3.8	2.4	11.6	13.9	5.1	0.5	6.9	2.5	1.1	0.7
$10,000–19,999	28,635	15.8	1.8	8.5	5.2	4.6	11.3	14.0	6.0	0.4	7.5	3.0	0.8	—
$20,000–29,999	29,109	15.9	2.4	10.3	4.7	3.9	14.0	19.4	6.3	0.5	9.5	3.8	1.3	0.2
$30,000–39,999	26,273	13.7	1.4	8.3	5.5	3.3	17.8	21.3	9.7	1.0	10.7	4.9	2.3	0.8
$40,000–49,999	21,774	13.1	2.0	9.3	6.1	2.6	20.6	23.2	12.2	1.1	11.9	4.4	2.9	1.2
$50,000–59,999	17,867	12.7	1.8	10.2	5.1	3.7	20.4	24.5	12.0	1.2	13.6	6.8	2.8	1.8
$60,000–74,999	18,628	12.8	1.3	7.2	6.5	3.5	20.7	25.1	15.6	2.0	15.9	5.9	2.8	2.0
$75,000 or more	30,884	11.4	2.2	8.5	6.3	3.2	21.1	24.8	19.3	3.5	18.8	9.2	4.3	6.1
Total	191,663	13.8	1.8	8.9	5.4	3.5	17.0	20.6	10.8	1.3	11.9	5.1	2.3	1.7

Note: "—" indicates data not available. Data for earlier years can be found in previous editions of *Vital Statistics on American Politics*. Early news, late news: the average percentage viewing at least one of these news programs the weeknight before the survey. All percentages are based on 20,079 interviews for their Spring 1996 report. Percentages subject to sampling error; see sources. Total percentages for other categories: viewing CNN in the last seven days, 39.4 (Headline News, 19.9); viewing Court TV in the last seven days, 3.9; subscribes to cable TV, 64.3 (cable available in neighborhood, 91.9); has pay-TV, 29.7; has satellite dish, 3.8; listens to (any) radio weekday, 77.9; listens to (any) radio weekend, 60.4; reads any daily newspaper, 53.0; reads any Sunday newspaper, 62.9.

[a] Includes "ABC World News Tonight," "CBS Evening News," and "NBC Nightly News," Monday through Friday.
[b] Includes "ABC News Nightline," Monday through Friday.

Sources: Multimedia Audiences Report (New York: Mediamark Research, Inc., Spring 1996); *Television Audiences Report* (New York: Mediamark Research, Inc., Spring 1996).

Table 4-5 Use and Trustworthiness of Media, 1959–1994

	1959	1961	1963	1964	1967	1968	1971	1972	1974	1976	1978	1980	1982	1984	1986	1988	1990	1991	1992	1994
Source of most news[a]																				
Television	51	52	55	58	64	59	60	64	65	64	67	64	64	64	66	65	69	81	69	72
Newspapers	57	57	53	56	55	49	48	50	47	49	49	44	44	40	36	42	43	35	43	38
Radio	34	34	29	26	28	25	23	21	21	19	20	18	18	14	14	14	15	14	16	18
Magazines	8	9	6	8	7	7	5	6	4	7	5	5	5	4	4	4	3	4	4	8
People	4	5	4	5	4	5	4	4	4	5	5	4	4	4	4	5	7	6	6	—
Most believable[b]																				
Television	29	39	36	41	41	44	49	48	51	51	47	51	53	53	55	49	54	58	56	51
Newspapers	32	24	24	23	24	21	20	21	20	22	23	22	22	24	21	26	22	20	22	21
Radio	12	12	12	8	7	8	10	8	8	7	9	8	6	8	6	7	7	6	7	8
Magazines	10	10	10	10	8	11	9	10	8	9	9	9	8	7	7	5	5	5	4	5
Don't know/no answer	17	17	18	18	20	16	12	13	13	11	12	10	11	9	12	13	13	13	12	15

Note: "—" indicates not available.

[a] Question: "First, I'd like to ask you where you usually get most of your news about what's going on in the world today—from the newspapers or radio or television or magazines or talking to people or where?" (more than one answer permitted).
[b] Question: "If you got conflicting or different reports of the same news story from radio, television, the magazines, and the newspapers, which of the four versions would you be most inclined to believe—the one on the radio or television or magazines or newspapers?" (only one answer permitted).

Source: "America's Watching—Public Attitudes Toward Television 1993" (New York: Network Television Association and the National Association of Broadcasters, 1993), 29, 31; "1995," 17, 35.

Table 4-6 Public Use of Media to Follow Presidential Campaigns, 1952–1996 (percent)

Media	1952	1956	1960	1964	1968	1972	1976	1980	1984	1988	1992	1996
Read newspaper articles about the election												
regularly[a]	—	—	44	40	37	26	28	—	—	—	—	—
often[b]	39	69	12	14	12	14	17	27	24	—	—	—
from time to time[b]	40	—	16	18	19	16	24	29	34	—	—	—
once in a great while[c]	—	—	7	6	7	4	10	17	19	—	—	—
none	21	31	21	22	25	40	22	27	23	—	—	—
Attention paid to newspaper articles about the presidential campaign												
great deal	—	—	—	—	—	—	—	—	8	6	9	5
quite a bit	—	—	—	—	—	—	—	—	14	12	15	11
some	—	—	—	—	—	—	—	—	28	22	20	19
very little	—	—	—	—	—	—	—	—	20	9	6	7
none	—	—	—	—	—	—	—	—	31	52	50	58
Listen to speeches or discussions on radio												
good many[d]	34	—	15	12	12	8	12	14	10	5	7	7
several[e]	—	45	17	23	16	21	20	22	20	10	11	14
one or two[f]	35	—	10	12	12	13	16	15	16	17	18	18
none	30	55	58	52	59	59	52	50	55	69	64	61
Watched programs about the campaign on television												
good many[d]	32	—	47	41	42	33	37	28	25	—	31	15
several[e]	—	74	29	34	34	41	38	37	37	—	39	32
one or two[f]	19	—	11	13	13	16	15	22	24	—	19	28
none	49	26	13	11	11	9	10	13	14	—	11	25

Attention paid to television news about the presidential campaign									
great deal	—	—	—	—	—	—	17	15	20
quite a bit	—	—	—	—	—	—	24	26	29
some	—	—	—	—	—	—	28	29	28
very little	—	—	—	—	—	—	11	13	11
none	—	—	—	—	—	—	20	17	13
Read about the campaign in magazines									
good many[d]	15	—	12	10	9	12	7	7	7
several[e]	—	31	15	16	12	24	15	19	16
one or two[f]	26	—	13	13	15	15	14	12	11
none	60	69	59	61	64	49	64	62	66
Attention paid to magazine articles about the presidential campaign									
great deal	—	—	—	—	—	3	3	4	3
quite a bit	—	—	—	—	—	4	6	7	7
some	—	—	—	—	—	7	11	10	15
very little	—	—	—	—	—	2	3	3	7
none	—	—	—	—	—	84	76	77	68

Note: "—" indicates question not asked or response category not offered.

[a] "Quite a lot, pretty much" in 1952; "yes" in 1956; "good many" in 1980–1984.
[b] "Not very much" in 1952; "several" in 1980–1984.
[c] "One or two" in 1980–1984.
[d] "Quite a lot, pretty much" in 1952.
[e] "Yes" in 1956.
[f] "Not very much" in 1952.

Source: Calculated by the editors from the National Election Studies codebooks and data sets (Ann Arbor, Mich.: Center for Political Studies, University of Michigan).

Table 4-7 Media Coverage of Presidential Nomination and General Election Contests, by State, 1980–1996

State	1980 nomination Percent of news coverage		1984 nomination Percent of news coverage	1988 nomination Percent of TV news	1988 general election		1992 nomination Percent of TV news	1992 general election Percent of TV news	1996 nomination Percent of TV news	1996 general election	
	CBS	UPI			Percent of TV news	Percent of electoral vote				Percent of TV news	Percent of electoral vote
Alabama		0	3	0	0	2	0	1	0	2	2
Alaska		0	0	0	0	1	0	0	1	0	1
Arizona	0	1	1	0	1	1	0	1	6	4	1
Arkansas	0	0	0	0	1	1	0	1	0	1	1
California	5	4	7	3	20	9	5	11	5	14	10
Colorado	0	0	0	1	1	1	2	2	2	3	1
Connecticut	2	2	2	2	1	1	3	1	1	0	1
Delaware	0	0	0	0	0	1	0	0	2	0	1
District of Columbia	1	2	0	1	1	1	0	1	0	0	1
Florida	3	2	1	2	2	4	4	7	5	8	5
Georgia	0	0	4	1	0	2	7	3	3	2	2
Hawaii	0	0	0	0	0	1	0	0	0	0	1
Idaho	0	0	0	0	0	1	0	0	0	0	1
Illinois	0	7	4	5	7	4	5	4	1	2	4
Indiana	1	1	2	1	0	2	0	1	0	2	2
Iowa	14	13	13	23	0	1	2	1	18	1	1
Kansas	0	1	0	0	0	1	1	0	0	0	1
Kentucky	0	1	0	1	1	2	0	2	0	3	1
Louisiana	0	0	1	0	0	2	2	2	3	1	2

Maine	4	3	2	1	0	1	2	0	1	0	1
Maryland	0	2	1	0	0	2	4	1	1	0	1
Massachusetts	7	3	3	0	2	2	0	0	1	1	2
Michigan	1	7	1	5	6	4	6	7	1	5	3
Minnesota	0	0	0	3	1	2	1	0	0	0	2
Mississippi	0	0	0	0	0	1	1	1	0	0	1
Missouri	0	0	1	0	2	2	0	4	0	3	2
Montana	0	0	0	0	0	1	0	0	0	0	1
Nebraska	0	1	1	0	0	1	0	0	0	0	1
Nevada	0	1	0	0	0	1	0	1	0	2	1
New Hampshire	14	15	19	17	0	1	23	1	22	3	1
New Jersey	1	0	5	1	5	3	1	5	0	5	3
New Mexico	0	0	1	0	1	1	0	1	0	3	1
New York	7	6	11	7	4	7	8	2	4	1	6
North Carolina	0	1	1	1	1	2	0	4	0	0	3
North Dakota	0	0	0	0	0	1	0	0	2	0	1
Ohio	4	2	2	2	9	4	1	7	2	8	4
Oklahoma	0	1	0	0	0	1	1	1	0	0	1
Oregon	1	1	0	0	1	1	0	1	1	1	1
Pennsylvania	9	7	6	4	5	5	4	4	0	4	4
Puerto Rico	1	2	0	0	0	0	0	0	0	0	0
Rhode Island	0	0	0	0	0	1	0	0	0	0	1
South Carolina	2	3	0	3	0	1	3	1	5	0	1
South Dakota	0	0	0	3	0	1	3	1	2	1	1
Tennessee	0	2	1	0	1	2	1	1	1	3	2
Texas	2	2	4	2	20	5	2	10	3	6	6
Utah	0	0	0	0	0	1	0	1	0	2	1
Vermont	1	1	2	1	0	1	0	0	1	0	1

(Table continues)

Table 4-7 *(Continued)*

State	1980 nomination Percent of news coverage CBS	1980 nomination Percent of news coverage UPI	1984 nomination Percent of news coverage	1988 nomination Percent of TV news	1988 general election Percent of TV news	1988 general election Percent of electoral vote	1992 nomination Percent of TV news	1992 general election Percent of TV news	1996 nomination Percent of TV news	1996 general election Percent of TV news	1996 general election Percent of electoral vote
Virginia	0	0	1	0	0	2	1	0	0	2	2
Washington	0	0	1	0	2	2	1	1	1	1	2
West Virginia	0	0	1	0	0	1	0	0	0	0	1
Wisconsin	5	5	1	4	1	2	2	2	0	1	2
Wyoming	0	0	1	1	0	1	0	0	0	0	1

Note: Media coverage in a given state is the proportion of seconds of TV coverage or of column inches of print coverage of primary, caucus, or general election contests that mention the state. For 1984, media coverage of multistate stories is calculated by proportionately allocating coverage. For 1988, 1992, and 1996 media coverage of the nomination tabulates state contests mentioned—one story may mention several state contests. Media coverage of the general election includes only those stories discussing the presidential contest in a state.

Sources: 1980 news coverage: Michael J. Robinson and Margaret A. Sheehan, *Over the Wire and on TV: CBS and UPI in Campaign 1980* (New York: Russell Sage Foundation, 1983), 176, 177 (copyright © Russell Sage Foundation, used with permission), percentages calculated by the editors; 1984 news coverage: William C. Adams, personal communication, content analysis of *New York Times* and of ABC, CBS, and NBC evening news summarized in *Television News Index and Abstracts* (Nashville, Tenn.: Vanderbilt Television News Archives, Vanderbilt University); 1988 news coverage: Center for Media and Public Affairs content analysis of the ABC, CBS, and NBC evening news from February 8, 1987 through June 7, 1988 (nomination) and June 8 through November 7, 1988 (general election); 1992 news coverage: Center for Media and Public Affairs content analysis of the ABC, CBS, and NBC evening news from January 1 through June 2, 1992 (nomination) and June 3 through November 2, 1992 (general election); 1996 news coverage: Center for Media and Public Affairs content analysis of the ABC, CBS, and NBC evening news from January 1 through March 26, 1996 (nomination contest) and September 2 through November 4, 1996 (general election); 1990s electoral vote: this volume, Table 1-8. For a discussion of data on television news coverage of the 1988 nominations, see S. Robert Lichter, Daniel Amundson, and Richard Noyes, *The Video Campaign: Network Coverage of the 1988 Primaries* (Washington, D.C.: American Enterprise Institute for Public Policy Research and Center for Media and Public Affairs, 1988). For a discussion of data on news coverage of the 1984 nominations, see William C. Adams, "As New Hampshire Goes . . .," in *Media and Momentum: The New Hampshire Primary and Nomination Politics,* ed. Gary R. Orren and Nelson W. Polsby (Chatham, N.J.: Chatham House, 1987), 42–59.

Table 4-8   Focus of Television News Coverage, 1996 Presidential Election

Period	Dates	Policy issues (percent)	Campaign issues (percent)	Horse race (percent)	Number of stories
Nomination contest					
1995	1/1–12/31	44	14	42	485
Pre-Iowa	1/1–2/11	42	18	40	192
New Hampshire	2/12–2/19	25	33	42	98
Arizona	2/20–2/27	32	20	48	89
South Carolina	2/28–3/1	55	10	35	18
Junior Tuesday	3/2–3/4	29	0	71	32
Super Tuesday	3/5–3/11	18	13	70	48
Midwest	3/12–3/18	30	10	60	23
California	3/19–3/26	52	12	36	34
Total nomination contest		39	16	45	1,019
Rest of nomination period					
End of March	3/27–3/31	80	20	0	8
April	4/1–4/30	76	3	21	38
May	5/1–5/31	50	27	23	102
June	6/1–6/30	55	35	9	115
July	7/1–7/31	54	24	21	112
Pre-convention	8/1–8/9	94	0	6	55
Republican convention	8/10–8/18	34	33	33	188
Interim	8/19–8/23	59	24	17	40
Democratic convention	8/24–9/1	50	27	23	151
Total for period	3/27–9/1	53	27	21	809
General Election					
Pre-debates	9/2–10/5	50	33	17	197
Debates	10/6–10/16	24	45	31	98
Final days	10/17–11/4	32	36	32	188
Total general election		39	36	25	483
Nomination and general election total		43	24	33	2,311

Note: "Policy issues" involve concerns such as those detailed in Table 4-9; "campaign issues" concern candidate character; "horse race" coverage focuses on the contest—who's ahead, who's behind. Stories may be classified in more than one category. In addition, presidential campaign coverage can be other than policy, campaign, or horse race. Comparable data for earlier elections can be found in previous editions of *Vital Statistics on American Politics.*

Source: Center for Media and Public Affairs content analysis of the ABC, CBS, and NBC evening news from January 1, 1995 through November 4, 1996.

Table 4-9   Television Coverage of Issues During the 1996 Presidential Campaign

Issue	1995	Pre-Iowa	New Hamp-shire	Arizona	South Caro-lina	Junior Tuesday	Super Tuesday	Mid-west	Cali-fornia	End March
General foreign policy	2	2	0	3	0	0	0	0	0	0
Persian Gulf	2	0	1	0	0	0	0	0	0	0
Defense spending	0	1	0	1	0	0	0	0	4	0
Asia	1	0	4	6	2	0	2	2	0	0
Russia/former USSR	1	0	0	0	0	0	2	0	0	0
Dealing with allies	1	0	0	0	2	0	0	0	0	0
Middle East	1	0	1	0	0	3	3	0	0	0
Central America	1	1	0	3	0	0	3	2	0	0
Mexico	0	1	4	3	0	0	0	2	3	0
Yugoslavia	3	3	1	1	0	0	0	0	0	0
Arms control	1	1	1	1	0	0	0	0	0	0
Terrorism	0	1	0	0	0	3	2	0	0	0
SDI	0	0	0	0	0	0	0	0	0	0
Foreign policy total	12	8	11	18	4	5	11	7	7	0
General economy	3	4	6	11	8	13	18	9	9	9
Taxes	7	19	12	5	16	15	15	23	11	18
Jobs	3	2	7	10	12	15	15	12	12	0
Health care	1	2	0	0	0	0	0	0	3	0
Social Security	1	2	0	0	0	0	0	2	0	0
Budget deficit	5	11	2	3	6	3	0	7	3	9
Other budget	7	3	2	0	0	3	0	0	7	9
Trade	2	2	12	18	18	25	9	7	4	0
Energy	0	0	0	0	0	0	0	0	0	0
Agriculture	0	2	0	1	0	0	0	2	0	0
Government shutdown	0	3	0	1	0	0	0	0	0	0
Inflation	0	1	0	1	0	0	0	0	0	0
Medicare	4	3	0	1	0	0	2	5	0	0
Welfare reform	5	3	3	2	0	0	3	5	1	0
Minimum wage	0	0	0	0	0	0	0	0	0	9
Economic total	39	58	45	52	59	73	63	72	49	55
Family values	3	2	2	1	2	3	2	2	1	0
Homelessness	0	0	0	0	0	0	0	0	0	0
Race relations	3	0	2	0	8	3	0	0	0	0
Affirmative action	8	2	1	1	2	0	2	0	3	0
Education	3	4	5	2	2	0	3	2	7	18
Children's issues	2	1	1	1	0	0	3	0	3	0
Abortion	11	8	7	6	6	13	11	0	4	9
Crime	3	4	2	4	0	3	0	0	5	0
Drugs	1	1	2	1	0	0	0	0	1	0
Gun control	4	1	1	1	0	0	0	0	7	0
Immigration	2	1	6	8	4	3	3	7	5	0
Women's issues	1	0	3	1	10	0	0	0	0	0
AIDS	0	0	0	1	0	0	0	0	0	0

April	May	June	July	Pre-con-vention	Republican conven-tion	Interim	Democratic conven-tion	Pre-debates	Debates	Final days	Number of stories
1	2	3	1	0	2	0	1	4	2	1	62
1	1	2	0	0	0	0	1	8	0	1	61
1	1	1	0	0	0	5	1	0	0	0	22
4	4	1	0	0	0	0	3	1	2	2	64
4	0	2	1	0	0	0	0	0	1	0	18
2	0	1	2	0	0	0	1	2	0	0	26
2	2	1	1	0	0	0	0	6	0	0	45
0	0	0	1	0	0	1	0	1	1	0	26
1	0	1	0	0	1	0	0	0	0	0	22
1	1	2	0	0	0	0	1	2	1	0	54
2	3	1	0	0	0	0	0	1	0	0	26
4	0	2	3	0	0	1	0	0	0	0	21
0	1	1	0	0	0	0	0	0	0	0	5
24	17	15	10	0	2	7	9	25	7	6	452
5	2	8	5	16	10	5	8	6	7	7	264
5	13	9	6	19	16	11	7	7	17	7	430
0	0	2	3	4	1	0	6	4	3	4	155
2	1	1	0	2	1	5	1	2	2	3	56
0	0	4	3	3	2	1	1	1	1	3	58
6	7	6	3	12	7	4	5	4	4	3	222
5	2	1	4	3	1	1	1	1	1	2	113
1	1	2	1	0	0	0	2	3	1	0	134
4	7	0	0	0	1	0	0	1	0	0	26
2	1	0	3	0	0	0	0	0	0	0	19
1	1	1	0	0	0	0	0	0	1	2	24
2	0	1	2	1	0	0	0	2	1	2	27
1	1	4	4	3	3	2	2	2	3	6	115
0	7	3	6	3	2	10	8	1	2	0	144
4	8	1	1	3	1	5	0	1	1	0	43
39	53	41	40	69	45	44	43	34	43	39	1830
1	2	2	4	1	1	0	2	2	3	2	85
0	0	1	0	1	0	0	1	0	2	1	10
0	0	2	1	2	3	4	1	1	2	2	62
0	0	1	0	3	6	2	1	0	1	4	116
1	3	5	4	1	5	1	6	5	7	9	172
1	4	1	4	3	1	13	8	4	2	5	117
7	6	12	9	8	17	0	2	2	1	2	293
4	5	5	5	1	2	2	6	6	4	3	146
6	1	1	3	0	0	7	5	9	8	4	101
4	0	2	5	1	1	0	3	3	2	1	82
1	1	2	6	4	6	7	1	2	2	2	120
0	0	1	1	1	1	1	1	1	2	1	38
0	0	0	0	0	0	1	0	0	0	1	8

(Table continues)

Table 4-9   *(Continued)*

Issue	1995	Pre-Iowa	New Hamp-shire	Arizona	South Caro-lina	Junior Tuesday	Super Tuesday	Mid-west	Cali-fornia	End March
Gay rights	1	2	4	1	0	0	0	0	0	0
Tobacco	0	0	0	0	0	0	0	0	0	0
Social total	42	26	35	28	33	23	23	12	36	27
Environment	1	3	1	1	0	0	2	2	7	0
Supreme Court	0	0	0	1	0	0	0	0	1	0
Campaign finance	1	0	2	0	0	0	0	5	0	18
Transportation	0	0	0	0	0	0	0	0	0	0
Role of government	3	4	4	2	4	0	2	0	0	0
Goverment ethics	2	1	0	0	0	0	0	2	0	0
Government management	1	0	1	0	0	0	0	0	0	0
Other total	7	8	9	3	4	0	3	9	8	18
Number of stories	790	364	161	159	51	40	65	43	75	11

Note: Issues were coded if the story mentioned that particular issue. More than one issue could be coded for each story. Table entries give each issue's times mentioned as a percentage of all issues mentioned within each time period. More precise indications of the time periods can be found in Table 4-8, this volume. Totals calculated before rounding. Comparable data for earlier elections can be found in previous editions of *Vital Statistics on American Politics*.

Source: Center for Media and Public Affairs content analysis of the ABC, CBS, and NBC evening news from January 1, 1995, through November 5, 1996.

April	May	June	July	Pre-con-vention	Republican conven-tion	Interim	Democratic conven-tion	Pre-debates	Debates	Final days	Number of stories
0	0	2	1	1	1	0	0	1	0	0	35
0	1	3	6	1	2	6	3	1	0	0	45
26	26	37	48	27	44	44	40	35	35	37	1,430
4	0	1	1	1	2	2	2	3	2	1	65
5	0	1	0	1	1	0	0	1	0	1	20
1	0	1	0	0	1	1	1	1	2	7	49
0	0	0	1	0	0	0	0	0	0	0	4
1	2	1	1	2	4	0	2	2	3	2	89
0	1	3	0	0	0	0	0	0	9	7	58
0	0	1	0	0	0	1	1	0	0	1	14
11	4	7	2	3	8	4	8	6	15	19	299
82	218	191	156	147	299	99	281	399	123	257	4,011

Table 4-10 Television News Coverage of the Candidates and Parties, 1995–1996 (percent)

Party/candidate	1995	Pre-Iowa	New Hampshire	Arizona	South Carolina	Junior Tuesday	Super Tuesday	Midwest	California	Total nomination contest
Democrats										
Clinton	96	94	92	97	100	100	88	100	96	95
Gore	4	6	8	3	0	0	12	0	4	5
Republicans										
Dole	34	29	26	30	29	30	37	43	82	32
Kemp	0	0	0	0	0	0	0	0	0	0
Alexander	8	10	22	19	16	20	7	0	0	12
Buchanan	9	14	24	34	33	28	29	30	18	18
Dorman	3	1	1	0	0	0	0	0	0	2
Forbes	3	25	16	16	20	20	22	28	0	14
Gramm	21	15	8	0	0	0	0	0	0	12
Keyes	2	2	2	1	2	0	0	0	0	2
Lugar	6	3	1	1	0	1	4	0	0	3
Specter	5	0	0	0	0	0	0	0	0	2
Taylor	0	1	0	0	0	0	1	0	0	1
Wilson	9	0	0	0	0	0	0	0	0	3
Reform										
Perot	100	100	100	0	0	100	100	100	100	100
Choate	0	0	0	0	0	0	0	0	0	0
Lamm	0	0	0	0	0	0	0	0	0	0
Democrats	22	21	10	11	0	0	11	0	21	17
Republicans	74	79	90	89	100	100	89	100	68	81
Reform	5	0	0	0	0	0	0	0	11	2

Note: Table entries for the candidates give each candidate's times mentioned as a percentage of all candidate mentions within each party for each time period. One story may contain several candidate mentions. Table entries for the parties indicate the stories focusing on a particular party as a percentage of all stories focusing on political parties in each time period. More precise indications of the time periods can be found in Table 4-8, this volume. Comparable data for earlier elections can be found in previous editions of *Vital Statistics on American Politics.*

Source: Center for Media and Public Affairs content analysis of the ABC, CBS, and NBC evening news from January 1, 1995, through November 5, 1996.

End March	April	May	June	July	Pre-convention	Republican convention	Interim	Democratic convention	Total for rest of nomination period	Pre-debates	Debates	Final days	Total general election
100	89	97	90	93	97	82	94	81	88	92	82	90	89
0	11	3	10	7	3	18	6	19	12	8	18	10	11
100	93	94	90	92	74	57	72	85	77	86	82	89	86
0	0	0	0	0	21	34	28	15	16	14	18	11	14
0	0	0	0	0	0	0	0	0	0	0	0	0	0
0	7	6	10	8	5	9	0	0	7	0	0	0	0
0	0	0	0	0	0	0	0	0	0	0	0	0	0
0	0	0	0	0	0	0	0	0	0	0	0	0	0
0	0	0	0	0	0	0	0	0	0	0	0	0	0
0	0	0	0	0	0	0	0	0	0	0	0	0	0
0	0	0	0	0	0	0	0	0	0	0	0	0	0
0	0	0	0	0	0	0	0	0	0	0	0	0	0
0	0	0	0	0	0	0	0	0	0	0	0	0	0
0	0	0	0	0	0	0	0	0	0	0	0	0	0
100	100	100	75	50	50	69	100	100	69	77	100	94	86
0	0	0	0	0	0	0	0	0	0	23	0	6	14
0	0	0	25	50	50	31	0	0	31	0	0	0	0
40	59	35	39	31	11	9	64	90	40	42	41	50	45
40	38	65	56	53	87	86	30	8	55	43	55	45	46
20	3	0	4	16	2	5	6	2	5	15	3	6	9

Table 4-11 Horse Race Judgments of the Presidential Candidates in Television News Coverage, 1995–1996 (percent)

Party/candidate	1995		Pre-Iowa		New Hampshire		Arizona		South Carolina		Junior Tuesday		Super Tuesday		Midwest		California		End of March		April	
Republicans																							
Dole	77	(183)	71	(167)	62	(95)	54	(121)	54	(28)	77	(86)	87	(130)	95	(39)	70	(43)	100	(6)	38	(29)
Buchanan	67	(24)	85	(74)	75	(84)	71	(106)	27	(11)	60	(35)	44	(34)	10	(10)	78	(9)	—	—	100	(1)
Forbes	96	(23)	79	(166)	33	(36)	64	(44)	90	(21)	71	(24)	52	(21)	31	(13)	—	—	—	—	—	—
Alexander	81	(16)	64	(22)	73	(59)	47	(30)	43	(7)	24	(21)	21	(14)	—	—	—	—	—	—	—	—
Gramm	82	(67)	27	(63)	17	(23)	—	—	—	—	—	—	—	—	—	—	—	—	—	—	—	—
Democrats																							
Clinton	55	(110)	79	(58)	93	(14)	100	(7)	—	—	100	(1)	100	(11)	86	(7)	91	(23)	100	(2)	89	(18)
Independent																							
Perot	79	(14)	—	—	0	(1)	—	—	—	—	—	—	—	—	—	—	100	(3)	50	(2)	—	—

	May		June		July		Pre-convention		Republican convention		Interim		Democratic convention		Pre-debates		Debates		Final days		Total 1996 election	
Republicans																						
Dole	27	(106)	37	(54)	15	(71)	30	(37)	59	(155)	50	(16)	17	(29)	19	(161)	18	(106)	30	(172)	51	(1,834)
Buchanan	50	(2)	33	(3)	67	(3)	—		47	(15)	—		—		—		—		—		67	(411)
Forbes	—		—		—		—		—		—		—		—		—		—		70	(348)
Alexander	—		—		—		—		—		—		—		—		—		—		56	(169)
Gramm	—		—		—		—		—		—		—		—		—		—		48	(153)
Democrats																						
Clinton	76	(54)	38	(56)	64	(45)	100	(11)	67	(61)	55	(31)	75	(118)	88	(170)	81	(89)	80	(158)	75	(1,044)
Independent																						
Perot	—		50	(2)	75	(20)	—		70	(27)	0	(7)	13	(8)	19	(57)	0	(2)	26	(38)	40	(181)

Note: "—" indicates no stories, in most instances because a candidate was not an active presidential contender. Table entries are percent positive of all clearly positive and negative assessments by news sources about the probability the candidate will become president. This excludes positive and negative assessments of the candidate in other contexts (see Table 4-12). Total number of judgments about whether the candidate will become president are given in parentheses. More precise indications of the time periods can be found in Table 4-8, this volume. Comparable data for earlier elections can be found in previous editions of *Vital Statistics on American Politics*.

Source: Center for Media and Public Affairs content analysis of the ABC, CBS, and NBC evening news from January 1, 1995, through November 5, 1996.

Table 4-12 Assessments of the Presidential Candidates in Television News Coverage, 1995–1996 (percent)

Party/candidate	1995	Pre-Iowa	New Hampshire	Arizona	South Carolina	Junior Tuesday	Super Tuesday	Midwest	California	End of March	April
Republicans											
Dole	49 (237)	39 (148)	46 (107)	42 (92)	42 (24)	63 (30)	47 (62)	73 (22)	86 (22)	64 (11)	43 (35)
Kemp	—	—	—	—	—	—	—	—	—	—	—
Buchanan	70 (37)	75 (44)	42 (96)	45 (165)	46 (24)	25 (24)	32 (47)	60 (5)	85 (13)	—	—
Forbes	78 (9)	37 (228)	31 (36)	75 (16)	45 (20)	50 (6)	77 (22)	56 (9)	—	—	—
Alexander	56 (16)	75 (28)	62 (71)	69 (13)	60 (5)	20 (5)	—	—	—	—	—
Gramm	54 (82)	80 (41)	75 (4)	—	—	—	—	—	—	—	—
Democrats											
Clinton	41 (277)	51 (94)	55 (20)	41 (22)	40 (5)	0 (4)	43 (23)	50 (10)	53 (34)	45 (11)	61 (38)
Gore	100 (1)	—	—	—	—	—	100 (2)	—	—	—	—
Independent											
Perot	67 (12)	—	—	—	—	—	—	33 (3)	0 (2)	100 (1)	—

	May	June	July	Pre-convention	Republican convention	Interim	Democratic convention	Pre-debates	Debates	Final days	Total 1996 election
Republicans											
Dole	49 (150)	56 (187)	43 (133)	44 (81)	72 (249)	55 (38)	40 (47)	46 (166)	44 (161)	50 (158)	51 (2,160)
Kemp	—	—	—	76 (34)	76 (101)	71 (7)	50 (2)	75 (12)	42 (12)	0 (2)	72 (170)
Buchanan	33 (3)	33 (6)	—	—	44 (18)	—	—	—	—	—	48 (482)
Forbes	—	—	—	—	—	—	—	—	—	—	43 (346)
Alexander	—	—	—	—	—	—	—	—	—	—	63 (138)
Gramm	—	—	—	—	—	—	—	—	—	—	63 (127)
Democrats											
Clinton	33 (144)	37 (132)	60 (102)	64 (22)	27 (62)	51 (77)	57 (242)	40 (371)	40 (229)	39 (275)	44 (2,194)
Gore	—	—	0 (1)	—	25 (8)	—	92 (12)	71 (7)	100 (1)	—	69 (32)
Independent											
Perot	—	100 (2)	70 (10)	—	31 (13)	75 (4)	0 (2)	50 (18)	—	36 (14)	49 (81)

Note: "—" indicates candidate was not an active presidential contender. Table entries are percent positive of all clearly positive and negative assessments by news sources, excluding horse race judgments (see Table 4-11). Total number of assessments about the candidate are given in parentheses. More precise indications of the time periods can be found in Table 4-8, this volume. Comparable data for earlier elections can be found in previous editions of *Vital Statistics on American Politics*.

Source: Center for Media and Public Affairs content analysis of the ABC, CBS, and NBC evening news from January 1, 1995, through November 5, 1996.

Table 4-13   National Nominating Conventions: Television Coverage and Viewership, 1952–1992

Year/party	Audience rating[a] (percent)	Average hours viewed by household	Network hours telecast[b]
1952			
Republicans	—	10.5	57.5
Democrats	—	13.1	61.1
1956			
Republicans	—	6.4	22.8
Democrats	—	8.4	37.6
1960			
Republicans	—	6.2	25.5
Democrats	—	8.3	29.3
1964			
Republicans	—	7.0	36.5
Democrats	—	6.4	23.5
1968			
Republicans	26.4	6.5	34.0
Democrats	28.5	8.5	39.1
1972			
Republicans	23.4	3.5	19.8
Democrats	18.3	5.8	36.7
1976			
Republicans	31.5	6.3	29.5
Democrats	25.2	5.2	30.4
1980			
Republicans	21.6	3.8	22.7
Democrats	27.0	4.4	24.1
1984			
Republicans	19.2	1.9	11.9
Democrats	23.4	2.5	12.9
1988			
Republicans	18.3	2.2	12.6
Democrats	19.8	2.3	12.8
1992			
Republicans	22.0	—	7.3
Democrats	20.5	—	8.0

Note: "—" indicates not available. As of July 1997, Nielsen Media Research, New York, was preparing a new edition of *Nielsen Tunes in to Politics,* which will give information on the 1996 election.

[a] Percentage of television households viewing the convention during an average minute. Through 1988, based on viewing of ABC, CBS, and NBC; for 1992, based on viewing the three networks plus PBS and CNN. C-SPAN viewing not included.
[b] Number of hours during which one or more of ABC, CBS, or NBC was broadcasting the convention. In 1988, CNN broadcast 30.0 hours of the Democratic convention and 14.5 hours of the Republican convention. In 1992, CNN broadcast 8.0 hours of each convention.

Sources: 1952–1964: *Network Television Audiences to Primaries, Conventions, Elections* (Northbrook, Ill.: A. C. Nielsen, 1976), 8, 9, 21; audience rating: *Nielsen Tunes in to Politics: Tracking the Presidential Years (1960–1992),* 1; hours viewed, hours telecast, 1968–1992: data supplied by A. C. Nielsen Co; *Nielsen Tunes in to Politics,* 1–3.

Table 4-14   Television Viewership of Presidential and Vice-Presidential Debates, 1960–1996

Year	Candidates	Date	Audience rating[a] (percent)	Persons (in millions)
1960	Nixon-Kennedy	Sept. 26	59.5	—
		Oct. 7	59.1	—
		Oct. 13	61.0	—
		Oct. 21	57.8	—
1976	Ford-Carter	Sept. 23	53.5	69.7
		Oct. 6	52.4	63.9
		Oct. 22	47.8	62.7
	Dole-Mondale	Oct. 15	35.5	43.2
1980	Carter-Reagan	Oct. 28	58.9	80.6
1984	Reagan-Mondale	Oct. 7	45.3	65.1
		Oct. 21	46.0	67.3
	Bush-Ferraro	Oct. 11	43.6	56.7
1988	Bush-Dukakis	Sept. 25	36.8	65.1
		Oct. 13	35.9	67.3
	Quayle-Bentsen	Oct. 5	33.6	46.9
1992	Bush-Clinton-Perot	Oct. 11[b]	38.3	62.4
		Oct. 15	46.3	69.9
		Oct. 19	45.2	67.3
	Quayle-Gore-Stockdale	Oct. 13	36.0	51.2
1996	Clinton-Dole	Oct. 6	31.6	46.1
		Oct. 16	26.1	36.3
	Gore-Kemp	Oct. 9	19.7	26.6

Note: "—" indicates not available. 1976–1988 debates include ABC, CBS, and NBC only; 1992 includes CNN (Oct. 6 does not include CBS, which broadcast baseball's All-Star Game). 1992 includes CNN (all three) and Fox (Oct. 6). PBS data not included. Combined audience estimates are based on comparable durations.

[a] Percentage of television households viewing the debates during an average minute.
[b] Does not include CBS.

Source: Nielsen Media Research, 1997.

Table 4-15 Newspaper Endorsements of Presidential Candidates, 1932–1996

Year/endorsement	Papers		Circulation	
	Number	Percentage	Number	Percentage
1932				
Hoover (R)	656	52	—	—
Roosevelt (D)	511	41	—	—
Uncommitted	94	7	—	—
1936				
Landon (R)	727	57	—	—
Roosevelt (D)	459	36	—	—
Uncommitted	87	7	—	—
1940				
Willkie (R)	813	64	—	—
Roosevelt (D)	289	23	—	—
Uncommitted	171	13	—	—
1944				
Dewey (R)	796	60	26,654,996	69
Roosevelt (D)	291	22	6,902,243	18
Uncommitted	237	18	5,356,807	14
1948				
Dewey (R)	771	65	35,152,807	79
Truman (D)	182	15	4,489,851	10
Thurmond	45	4	537,730	1
Wallace	3	0	60,233	0
Uncommitted	182	15	4,454,557	10
1952				
Eisenhower (R)	933	67	40,129,237	80
Stevenson (D)	202	15	5,466,781	11
Uncommitted	250	18	4,417,102	9
1956				
Eisenhower (R)	740	62	34,538,755	72
Stevenson (D)	189	15	6,122,491	13
Uncommitted	270	23	7,079,846	15
1960				
Nixon (R)	731	58	38,006,203	71
Kennedy (D)	208	16	8,448,677	16
Uncommitted	328	26	7,135,954	13
1964				
Goldwater (R)	359	35	8,977,214	21
Johnson (D)	440	42	26,997,400	62
Uncommitted	237	23	7,638,727	18
1968				
Nixon (R)	634	61	34,559,385	70
Humphrey (D)	146	14	9,572,948	19

Table 4-15 *(Continued)*

	Papers		Circulation	
Year/endorsement	Number	Percentage	Number	Percentage
Wallace	12	1	159,524	0
Uncommitted	250	24	5,201,845	11
1972				
Nixon (R)	753	71	30,560,535	77
McGovern (D)	56	5	3,044,534	8
Uncommitted	245	23	5,864,548	15
1976				
Ford (R)	411	62	20,951,798	62
Carter (D)	80	12	7,607,739	23
Uncommitted	168	26	5,074,069	15
1980				
Reagan (R)	443	42	17,561,333	49
Carter (D)	126	12	7,782,078	22
Anderson	40	4	1,614,740	4
Uncommitted	439	42	9,131,940	25
1984				
Reagan (R)	381	58	18,357,512	52
Mondale (D)	62	9	7,568,639	21
Uncommitted	216	33	9,611,058	27
1988				
Bush (R)	241	31	18,186,225	40
Dukakis (D)	103	13	11,644,600	25
Uncommitted	428	55	16,224,807	35
1992[a]				
Bush (R)	121	15	7,134,599	18
Clinton (D)	149	18	10,961,415	27
Uncommitted	542	67	22,225,342	55
1996[b]				
Dole (R)	111	19	4,741,645	13
Clinton (D)	65	11	4,581,337	13
Uncommitted	415	70	26,173,692	74

Note: "—" indicates not available.

[a] One newspaper—circulation 9,075—endorsed Ross Perot.
[b] One newspaper—circulation 3,300—endorsed Harry Browne.

Sources: Editor & Publisher, October 26, 1940, 7; November 4, 1944, 9; October 30, 1948, 11; November 1, 1952, 9; November 3, 1956, 11; November 5, 1960, 10; October 31, 1964, 10; November 2, 1968, 9; November 7, 1972, 9; October 30, 1976, 5; November 1, 1980, 10; November 3, 1984, 9; November 5, 1988, 9; October 24, 1992, 9; October 26, 1996, 8.

Figure 4-2   Newspaper Endorsements of Presidential Candidates: Democratic,
Republican, and Neutral, 1932–1996

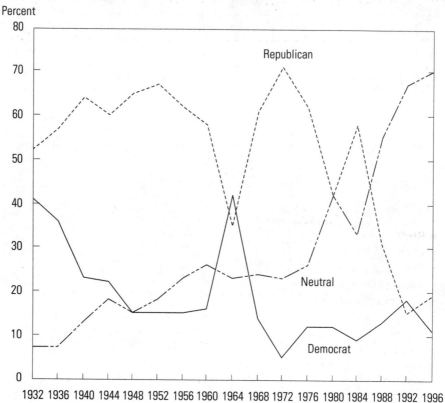

Source: This volume, Table 4-15.

5

Congress

- **Apportionment**
- **Membership Characteristics**
- **Staff**
- **Committees**
- **Bills and Laws**
- **Voting Patterns**
- **Current Members**

Statistics about Congress abound. Capsule descriptions of senators and representatives and their districts run to more than a thousand pages for each Congress (see, for example, *Politics in America* and the *Almanac of American Politics*). Elections are held every two years, generating mounds of electoral and financial data. Recorded votes annually number more than four hundred in the House and more than three hundred in the Senate. It is thus hardly surprising that votes for Congress, votes in Congress, congressional members themselves, and all those who surround them or contribute to their activities have been subject to extensive statistical scrutiny.

Election-related material constitutes one of the largest collections of data about Congress; various aspects of these data are provided in several chapters of this book. Election results, including material associated specifically with congressional elections such as losses by the president's party at midterm, are provided in Chapter 1; information pertaining to the funding of congressional campaigns is provided in Chapter 2. Chapter 3 covers individual voting behavior in congressional elections, as well as public judgments of the institution—so-called congressional approval (see Figure 3-6).

Congress also generates many other kinds of statistics. Simply apportioning members among the states (Table 5-1 and Figure 5-1) has led to a surprising amount of controversy and statistical calculation, which resulted in a fascinating, book-length treatment.[1] As the composition of Congress changes to include more women and minorities, these and other characteristics have also been tabulated and analyzed (Tables 5-2 and 5-3).

As Congress becomes a larger and more complex operation, more interest has been expressed in its structure and workload. These aspects of Congress are represented here with information about staff size (Figure 5-2), numbers of committees and their leadership (Table 5-4), numbers of measures considered and passed (Figure 5-3 and Table 5-5), and numbers of votes (Table 5-6). Although these, too, at first might be considered insignificant or analytically useless tabulations, analyses of the relationships among committee staffs, congressional voting, voter behavior, and legislative output suggest otherwise.

Voting by the members of Congress is of obvious interest. Indeed, cohesion within and contrasts between the political parties were the topics of some of the first statistical treatments of political subjects.[2] Increased numbers of roll calls and other recorded votes (Table 5-6) have done nothing to dampen this tradition. Party unity and presidential support by individual representatives and senators (Tables 5-10 and 5-11) and for groups (Tables 5-7, 5-8, 5-9, and Figure 5-4) have become a standard part of congressional analyses.

For the statistically minded, the study of Congress has long been an inviting prospect. The traditional topics are still interesting because the turnover of personnel, the constant change in congressional leadership and of the president, changes in regional strength, and so on make Congress anything but static. In addition, reforms of congressional procedures and of campaign finance since Watergate, technological changes that have resulted in electronic voting and the televising of proceedings in both chambers, and changes in the size and scope of the government bureaucracy Congress must deal with are adequate reasons to scrutinize anew the data underlying one's understanding of Congress.

Notes

1. Michel Balinski and H. P. Young, *Fair Representation* (New Haven, Conn.: Yale University Press, 1982).
2. Stuart Rice, *Quantitative Methods in Politics* (New York: Knopf, 1928).

Table 5-1 Apportionment of Membership in the House of Representatives, 1789–1990

State	1789[a]	1790	1800	1810	1820	1830	1840	1850	1860	1870	1880	1890	1900	1910	1930[b]	1940	1950	1960	1970	1980	1990
Alabama	—	—	—	1[c]	3	5	7	7	6	8	8	9	9	10	9	9	9	8	7	7	7
Alaska	—	—	—	—	—	—	—	—	—	—	—	—	—	—	—	—	1[c]	1	1	1	1
Arizona	—	—	—	—	—	—	—	—	—	—	—	—	—	1[c]	1	2	2	3	4	5	6
Arkansas	—	—	—	—	—	1[c]	1	2	3	4	5	6	7	7	7	7	6	4	4	4	4
California	—	—	—	—	—	—	—	2	3	4	6	7	8	11	20	23	30	38	43	45	52
Colorado	—	—	—	—	—	—	—	—	—	1[c]	1	2	3	4	4	4	4	4	5	6	6
Connecticut	5	7	7	7	6	6	4	4	4	4	4	4	5	5	6	6	6	6	6	6	6
Delaware	1	1	1	2	1	1	1[c]	1	1	1	1	1	1	1	1	1	1	1	1	1	1
Florida	—	—	—	—	—	—	1[c]	1	1	2	2	2	3	4	5	6	8	12	15	19	23
Georgia	3	2	4	6	7	9	8	8	7	9	10	11	11	12	10	10	10	10	10	10	11
Hawaii	—	—	—	—	—	—	—	—	—	—	—	—	—	—	—	—	1[c]	2	2	2	2
Idaho	—	—	—	—	—	—	—	—	—	—	1[c]	1	1	2	2	2	2	2	2	2	2
Illinois	—	—	—	1[c]	1	3	7	9	14	19	20	22	25	27	27	26	25	24	24	22	20
Indiana	—	—	—	1[c]	3	7	10	11	11	13	13	13	13	13	12	11	11	11	11	10	10
Iowa	—	—	—	—	—	—	2[c]	2	6	9	11	11	11	11	9	8	8	7	6	6	5
Kansas	—	—	—	—	—	—	—	—	1[c]	3	7	8	8	8	7	6	6	5	5	5	4
Kentucky	—	2[c]	6	10	12	13	10	10	9	10	11	11	11	11	9	9	8	7	7	7	6
Louisiana	—	—	—	1[c]	3	3	4	4	5	6	6	6	7	8	8	8	8	8	8	8	7
Maine	—	—	—	7[c]	7	8	7	6	5	5	4	4	4	4	3	3	3	2	2	2	2
Maryland	6	8	9	9	9	8	6	6	5	6	6	6	6	6	6	6	7	8	8	8	8
Massachusetts	8	14	17	13[d]	13	12	10	11	10	11	12	13	14	16	15	14	14	12	12	11	10
Michigan	—	—	—	—	—	1[c]	3	4	6	9	11	12	12	13	17	17	18	19	19	18	16
Minnesota	—	—	—	—	—	—	—	2[c]	2	3	5	7	9	10	9	9	9	8	8	8	8
Mississippi	—	—	—	1[c]	1	2	4	5	5	6	7	7	8	8	7	7	6	5	5	5	5
Missouri	—	—	—	—	1[c]	2	5	7	9	13	14	15	16	16	13	13	11	10	10	9	9
Montana	—	—	—	—	—	—	—	—	—	—	1[c]	1	1	2	2	2	2	2	2	2	1

(Table continues)

Table 5-1 (*Continued*)

State	1789[a]	1790	1800	1810	1820	1830	1840	1850	1860	1870	1880	1890	1900	1910	1930[b]	1940	1950	1960	1970	1980	1990
Nebraska	—	—	—	—	—	—	—	—	1[c]	1	3	6	6	6	5	4	4	3	3	3	3
Nevada	—	—	—	—	—	—	—	—	1[c]	1	1	1	1	1	1	1	1	1	1	2	2
New Hampshire	3	4	5	6	6	5	4	3	3	3	2	2	2	2	2	2	2	2	2	2	2
New Jersey	4	5	6	6	6	6	5	5	5	7	7	8	10	12	14	14	14	15	15	14	13
New Mexico	—	—	—	—	—	—	—	—	—	—	—	—	—	1[c]	1	2	2	2	2	3	3
New York	6	10	17	27	34	40	34	33	31	33	34	34	37	43	45	45	43	41	39	34	31
North Carolina	5	10	12	13	13	13	9	8	7	8	9	9	10	10	11	12	12	11	11	11	12
North Dakota	—	—	—	—	—	—	—	—	—	—	1[c]	1	2	3	2	2	2	2	1	1	1
Ohio	—	—	1[c]	6	14	19	21	21	19	20	21	21	21	22	24	23	23	24	23	21	19
Oklahoma	—	—	—	—	—	—	—	—	—	—	—	—	5[c]	8	9	8	6	6	6	6	6
Oregon	—	—	—	—	—	—	—	1[c]	1	1	1	2	2	3	3	4	4	4	4	5	5
Pennsylvania	8	13	18	23	26	28	24	25	24	27	28	30	32	36	34	33	30	27	25	23	21
Rhode Island	1	2	2	2	2	2	2	2	2	2	2	2	2	3	2	2	2	2	2	2	2
South Carolina	5	6	8	9	9	9	7	6	4	5	7	7	7	7	6	6	6	6	6	6	6
South Dakota	—	—	—	—	—	—	—	—	—	—	2[c]	2	2	3	2	2	2	2	2	1	1
Tennessee	—	1	3	6	9	13	11	10	8	10	10	10	10	10	9	10	9	9	8	9	9
Texas	—	—	—	—	—	—	2[c]	2	4	6	11	13	16	18	21	21	22	23	24	27	30
Utah	—	—	—	—	—	—	—	—	—	—	—	1[c]	1	2	2	2	2	2	2	3	3
Vermont	—	2	4	6	5	5	4	3	3	3	2	2	2	2	1	1	1	1	1	1	1
Virginia	10	19	22	23	22	21	15	13	11	9	10	10	10	10	9	9	10	10	10	10	11
Washington	—	—	—	—	—	—	—	—	—	—	1[c]	2	3	5	6	6	7	7	7	8	9
West Virginia	—	—	—	—	—	—	—	—	1[c]	3	4	4	5	6	6	6	6	5	4	4	3
Wisconsin	—	—	—	—	—	—	2[c]	3	6	8	9	10	11	11	10	10	10	10	9	9	9
Wyoming	—	—	—	—	—	—	—	—	—	—	1[c]	1	1	1	1	1	1	1	1	1	1
Total	65	106	142	186	213	242	232	237	243	293	332	357	391	435	435	435	437[e]	435	435	435	435
Apportionment ratio[f]	30	33	33	35	40	48	71	93	127	131	152	174	194	211	281	301	345	410	469	521	574

Note: "—" indicates state not yet admitted to Union. Apportionment effective with congressional election two years after census.

[a] Original apportionment made in Constitution, pending first census.

[b] No apportionment was made in 1920.

[c] Representation accorded newly admitted states by Congress, pending the next census.

[d] Twenty members were assigned to Massachusetts, but seven of these were credited to Maine when that area became a state.

[e] Normally 435, but temporarily increased two seats by Congress when Alaska and Hawaii became states.

[f] In thousands.

Sources: Congressional Quarterly Weekly Report (1990), 4240; *Congressional Quarterly's Guide to Congress,* 3d ed. (Washington, D.C.: Congressional Quarterly, 1982), 699; U.S. Bureau of the Census, *Historical Statistics of the United States* (Washington, D.C.: U.S. Government Printing Office, 1975), 1085.

Figure 5-1 Apportionment of Membership in the House of Representatives, by Region, 1910 and 1990

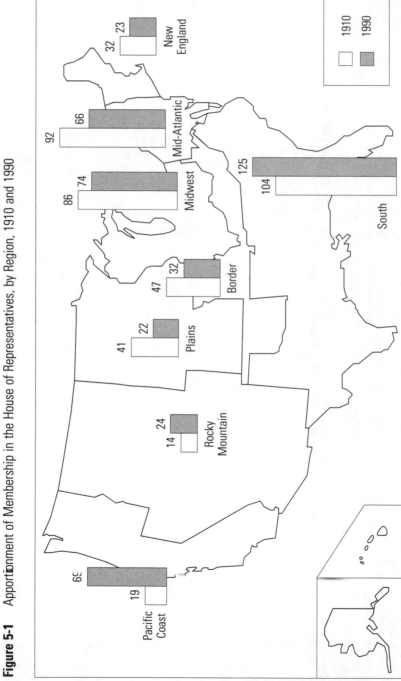

Source: This volume, Table 5-1.

Table 5-2   Members of Congress: Female, Black, Hispanic, Marital Status, and Age, 1971–1997

					Age					
Congress	Female	Black	His-panic	Not married[a]	Under 40	40–49	50–59	60–69	70–79	80 and over
Representatives										
92d (1971)	12	12	5	26	40	133	152	86	19	3
93d (1973)	14	15	5	34	45	132	154	80	20	2
94th (1975)	18	16	5	54	69	138	137	75	14	2
95th (1977)	18	16	5	56	81	121	147	71	15	0
96th (1979)	16	16	6	69	86	125	145	63	14	0
97th (1981)	19	16	6	86	94	142	132	54	12	1
98th (1983)	21	20	10	68	86	145	132	57	13	1
99th (1985)	22	19	11	69	71	154	131	59	17	2
100th (1987)	23	22	11	64	63	153	137	56	24	2
101st (1989)	25	23	11	—	41	163	133	74	20	2
102d (1991)	29	25	10	—	39	153	133	86	20	4
103d (1993)	48	38	17	—	47	152	129	91	13	3
104th (1995)	49	39	18	—	53	153	136	80	12	1
105th (1997)	51	37	18	—	47	145	147	82	10	2
Senators										
92d (1971)	1	1	1	3	4	24	32	23	16	1
93d (1973)	0	1	1	4	3	25	37	23	11	1
94th (1975)[b]	0	1	1	6	5	21	35	24	15	0
95th (1977)	0	1	0	9	6	26	35	21	10	2
96th (1979)	1	0	0	5	10	31	33	17	8	1
97th (1981)	2	0	0	7	9	35	36	14	6	0
98th (1983)	2	0	0	10	7	28	39	20	3	3
99th (1985)	2	0	0	8	4	27	38	25	4	2
100th (1987)	2	0	0	11	5	30	36	22	5	2
101st (1989)	2	0	0	—	0	30	40	22	6	2
102d (1991)	2	0	0	—	0	22	47	24	5	2
103d (1993)	6	1	0	—	1	16	49	22	11	1
104th (1995)	8	1	0	—	1	14	41	27	16	1
105th (1997)	9	1	0	—	1	21	39	26	12	1

Note: "—" indicates not available. As of beginning of first session of each Congress. Figures for representatives exclude vacancies. The counts above exclude nonvoting delegates and commissioners from American Samoa, Guam, Puerto Rico, the Virgin Islands, and Washington, D.C.

[a] Single, widowed, or divorced.
[b] Includes Sen. John Durkin (D-N.H.), seated September 1975.

Sources: Hispanic (1971–1985): Congressional Quarterly, *American Leaders, 1789–1987* (Washington, D.C.: Congressional Quarterly, 1987), 55; female and black (1971–1997) and Hispanic (1987–1997), *Congressional Quarterly Weekly Report* (1970), 2756; (1972), 2991; (1974), 3104; (1976), 3155; (1978), 3252; (1980), 3318; (1982), 2805;(1984), 2921; (1986), 2863; (1988), 3294; (1990), 3835–3836; (January 16, 1993, Supplement), 12; (November 12, 1994, Supplement), 10; (1997), 28; not married and age (1971–1989): U.S. Bureau of the Census, *Statistical Abstract of the United States, 1988* (Washington, D.C.: U.S. Government Printing Office, 1987), 244; *1990,* 257; age (1991–1997): calculated by the editors from *Congressional Quarterly Weekly Report* (1991), 118–127; (January 16, 1993, Supplement), 12, 160–168; (1995), 541–549; (1997), 497–505.

Table 5-3 Members of Congress: Seniority and Occupation, 1987–1997

Representatives

Seniority and occupation[a]	100th (1987)	101st (1989)	102d (1991)	103d (1993)	104th (1995)	105th (1997) Dem.	105th (1997) Rep.	105th (1997) Total
Seniority[a]								
Under 2 years	51	38	55	115	92	46	33	79
2–9 years	221	230	176	139	189	84	129	214[b]
10–19 years	114	117	149	134	109	48	52	100
20–29 years	37	35	42	34	36	22	12	34
30 years or more	12	13	13	13	9	5	1	6
Total	435	435[c]	435	435	435	205	227	435[c]
Occupation								
Agriculture	20	19	20	19	19	8	14	22
Business or banking	142	138	157	131	163	55	126	181
Education	38	42	57	66	76	40	33	74[b]
Journalism	20	17	25	24	15	4	7	12[b]
Law	184	184	183	181	170	87	85	172
Public service/politics	94	94	61	86	102	54	46	100

Senators

Seniority and occupation[a]	100th (1987)	101st (1989)	102d (1991)	103d (1993)	104th (1995)	105th (1997) Dem.	105th (1997) Rep.	105th (1997) Total
Seniority[a]								
Under 2 years	14	11	6	15	12	7	9	16
2–9 years	41	34	33	31	37	13	26	39
10–19 years	36	43	47	38	31	14	12	26
20–29 years	7	10	10	11	15	7	7	14
30 years or more	2	2	4	5	5	4	1	5
Total	100	100	100	100	100	45	55	100
Occupation								
Agriculture	5	4	8	9	9	2	6	8
Business or banking	28	28	31	27	24	8	25	33
Education	12	11	10	12	10	5	8	13
Journalism	8	8	10	8	8	2	7	9
Law	62	63	61	58	54	26	27	53
Public service/politics	20	20	4	12	12	9	17	26

Note: Members of Congress may state more than one occupation; therefore, sum may be greater than total. Not all occupations reported are listed. Data for earlier years can be found in previous editions of *Vital Statistics on American Politics.*

[a] Represents consecutive years of service.
[b] Includes Rep. Bernard Sanders (I-Vt.).
[c] Includes two vacancies.

Sources: U.S. Bureau of the Census, *Statistical Abstract of the United States, 1988* (Washington, D.C.: U.S. Government Printing Office, 1987), 244; *Congressional Quarterly Weekly Report* (1988), 3295; (1989), 41–44; (1990), 3837; (1991), 127–130; (January 16, 1993, Supplement), 13, 170–173; (November 12, 1994, Supplement), 11; (1995), 550–553; (1997), 29, 506–509.

Figure 5-2   Congressional Staff, 1930–1993

Number of employees

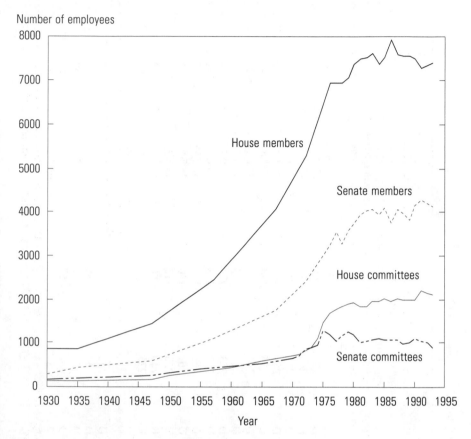

Year

Source: Norman Ornstein et al., eds., *Vital Statistics on Congress, 1995–1996* (Washington, D.C.: Congressional Quarterly, 1995), Tables 5-2 and 5-5.

Table 5-4 Number of Committees and Majority Party Chairmanships, 1955–1998

Congress		Number of committees[a]	Party in majority	Number of majority party members	Number of majority party members chairing standing committees and subcommittees	Percentage of majority party members chairing standing committees and subcommittees	Number of majority party members chairing all committees and subcommittees	Percentage of majority party members chairing all committees and subcommittees
House								
84th	(1955–1956)	130	D	232	63	27.2	75	32.3
90th	(1967–1968)	185	D	247	111	44.9	117	47.4
92d	(1971–1972)	175	D	254	120	47.2	131	51.6
94th	(1975–1976)	204	D	289	142	49.1	150	51.9
96th	(1979–1980)	193	D	276	144	52.2	149	54.0
97th	(1981–1982)	174	D	243	121	49.8	125	51.4
98th	(1983–1984)	172	D	267	124	46.4	127	47.6
99th	(1985–1986)	191	D	253	129	51.0	131	51.8
100th	(1987–1988)	192	D	258	128	49.6	132	51.2
101st	(1989–1990)	189	D	260	134	51.5	137	52.7
102d	(1991–1992)	185	D	267	130	48.7	135	50.6
103d	(1993–1994)	146	D	258	113	43.8	116	45.0
104th	(1995–1996)	110	R	230	86	37.4	86	37.4
105th	(1997–1998)	112	R	225	100	44.4	100	44.4
Senate								
84th	(1955–1956)	133	D	48	42	87.5	42	87.5
90th	(1967–1968)	155	D	64	55	85.9	58	90.6
92d	(1971–1972)	181	D	55[b]	51	92.7	52	94.5
94th	(1975–1976)	205	D	62[b]	57	91.9	57	91.9
96th	(1979–1980)	130	D	59[b]	58	98.3	58	98.3
97th	(1981–1982)	136	R	53	51	96.2	52	98.1

98th (1983–1984)	137	R	54	52	96.3	52	96.3
99th (1985–1986)	120	R	53	49	92.4	49	92.4
100th (1987–1988)	118	D	54	47	87.0	47	87.0
101st (1989–1990)	118	D	55	46	83.6	46	83.6
102d (1991–1992)	119	D	56	50	89.3	50	89.3
103d (1993–1994)	111	D	57	46	80.7	46	80.7
104th (1995–1996)	92	R	54	44	81.5	44	81.5
105th (1997–1998)	92	R	54	49	90.7	49	90.7

[a] Includes standing committees, subcommittees of standing committees, select and special committees, subcommittees of select and special committees, joint committees, and subcommittees of joint committees.

[b] Includes Harry Byrd Jr. (I-Va.), elected as an Independent.

Sources: 84th–103d: Norman J. Ornstein et al., eds., *Vital Statistics on Congress, 1993–1994* (Washington, D.C.: Congressional Quarterly, 1994), 113, 117–118; 104th–105th calculated by the editors from *Congressional Quarterly Weekly Report*, supplement to vol. 53, no. 12 (March 25, 1995), vol. 55, no. 12 (March 22, 1997).

Table 5-5   Bills, Acts, and Resolutions, 1947–1996

Congress		Measures introduced			Measures enacted		
		Bills	Joint resolutions	Total	Public	Private	Total
80th	(1947–1948)	10,108	689	10,797	906	457	1,363
81st	(1949–1951)	14,219	769	14,988	921	1,103	2,024
82d	(1951–1952)	12,062	668	12,730	594	1,023	1,617
83d	(1953–1954)	14,181	771	14,952	781	1,002	1,783
84th	(1955–1956)	16,782	905	17,687	1,028	893	1,921
85th	(1957–1958)	18,205	907	19,112	936	784	1,720
86th	(1959–1960)	17,230	1,031	18,261	800	492	1,292
87th	(1961–1962)	17,230	1,146	18,376	885	684	1,569
88th	(1963–1964)	16,079	1,401	17,480	666	360	1,026
89th	(1965–1966)	22,483	1,520	24,003	810	473	1,283
90th	(1967–1968)	24,786	1,674	26,460	640	362	1,002
91st	(1969–1970)	24,631	1,672	26,303	695	246	941
92d	(1971–1972)	21,363	1,606	22,969	607	161	768
93d	(1973–1974)	21,950	1,446	23,396	651	123	774
94th	(1975–1976)	19,762	1,334	21,096	588	141	729
95th	(1977–1978)	18,045	1,342	19,387	633	170	803
96th	(1979–1980)	11,722	861	12,583	613	123	736
97th	(1981–1982)	10,582	908	11,490	473	56	529
98th	(1983–1984)	10,134	1,022	11,156	623	54	677
99th	(1985–1986)	8,697	1,188	9,885	664	24	688
100th	(1987–1988)	8,515	1,073	9,588	713	48	761
101st	(1989–1990)	9,257	1,095	10,352	650	16	666
102d	(1991–1992)	9,601	909	10,510	589	14	603
103d	(1993–1994)	7,883	661	8,544	465	8	473
104th	(1995–1996)	6,545	263	6,808	333	4	337

Note: Measures exclude simple and concurrent resolutions.

Sources: 80th–99th: United States Congress, *Calendars of the U.S. House of Representatives and History of Legislation*, 99th Cong., Final ed., 19–57 through 19–68; 100th–102d: successive issues of *Congressional Quarterly Almanac.*

Figure 5-3   Proportion of Measures Introduced That Were Passed, 1789-1996

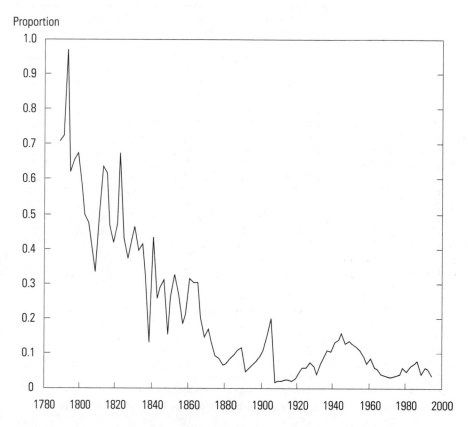

Note: Measures include acts, bills, and joint resolutions. Prior to 1824 only bills and acts are included. Figures are for each Congress.

Sources: 1789–1968: U.S. Bureau of the Census, *Historical Statistics of the United States,* Series Y189-198 (Washington, D.C.: U.S. Government Printing Office, 1975), 1081–1082; 1969–1994: Table 5-5, this volume.

Table 5-6 Recorded Votes in the House and the Senate, 1947–1996

Year	House	Senate	Year	House	Senate
1947	84	138	1972	329	532
1948	75	110	1973	541	594
1949	121	226	1974	537	544
1950	154	229	1975	612	602
1951	109	202	1976	661	688
1952	72	129	1977	706	635
1953	71	89	1978	834	516
1954	76	181	1979	672	497
1955	73	88	1980	681	546
1956	74	136	1981	371	497
1957	100	111	1982	488	469
1958	93	202	1983	533	381
1959	87	215	1984	463	292
1960	93	207	1985	482	381
1961	116	207	1986	488	359
1962	124	227	1987	511	420
1963	119	229	1988	465	379
1964	113	312	1989	379	312
1965	201	259	1990	536	326
1966	193	238	1991	444	280
1967	245	315	1992	488	270
1968[a]	233	280	1993	615	395
1969	177	245	1994	507	329
1970	266	422	1995	885	613
1971	320	423	1996	455	306

Note: The count of recorded votes prior to 1980 excludes quorum calls.

[a] The Senate recorded vote total does not include one "yea-and-nay" vote that was ruled invalid for lack of a quorum.

Sources: 1947–1979: Norman J. Ornstein et al., eds., *Vital Statistics on Congress, 1989–1990* (Washington, D.C.: Congressional Quarterly, 1990), 158; 1980–1996: *Congressional Quarterly Weekly Report* (1996), 2836.

Table 5-7 Conservative Coalition Votes and Victories, 1957–1996
(percent)

Year	House		Senate	
	Votes	Victories	Votes	Victories
1957	16	81	11	100
1958	15	64	19	86
1959	13	91	19	65
1960	20	35	22	67
1961	30	74	32	48
1962	13	44	15	71
1963	13	67	19	44
1964	11	67	17	47
1965	25	25	24	39
1966	19	32	30	51
1967	22	73	18	54
1968	22	63	25	80
1969	25	71	28	67
1970	17	70	26	64
1971	31	79	28	86
1972	25	79	29	63
1973	25	67	21	54
1974	22	67	30	54
1975	28	52	28	48
1976	17	59	26	58
1977	22	60	29	74
1978	20	57	23	46
1979	121	73	18	65
1980	16	67	20	75
1981	21	88	21	95
1982	16	78	20	90
1983	18	71	12	89
1984	14	75	17	94
1985	13	84	16	93
1986	11	78	20	93
1987	9	88	8	100
1988	8	82	10	97
1989	11	80	12	95
1990	10	74	11	95
1991	9	86	14	95
1992	10	88	14	87
1993	7	98	10	90
1994	7	92	10	72
1995	13	100	9	95
1996	11	100	12	97

Note: "Votes" is the percentage of all roll call votes on which a majority of voting southern Democrats and a majority of voting Republicans—the Conservative Coalition—opposed the stand taken by a majority of voting northern Democrats. "Victories" is the percentage of Conservative Coalition votes won.

Sources: 1957–1992: Norman J. Ornstein et al., eds., *Vital Statistics on Congress, 1993–1994* (Washington, D.C.: Congressional Quarterly, 1994), 203; 1993–1994: *Congressional Quarterly Weekly Report* (1993), 3435; (1994), 3627; (1996), 202, 3436.

Figure 5-4   Party Votes in the House, 1877–1996

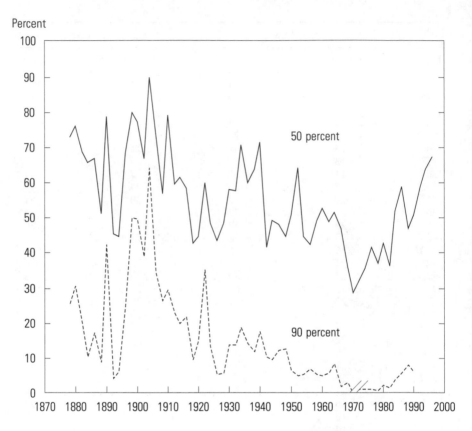

Percent

Note: Figures shown by Congress. A party vote occurs when the specified percentage (or more) of one party votes against the specified percentage (or more) of the other party.

Sources: 1877–1886 and 90 percent vote from 1972–1990: Brinck Kerr, "Structural Determinants of Party Voting in the U.S. Congress, 1877–1990," Ph.D. dissertation, Texas A&M University, 1993; 1887–1969: Joseph Cooper, David William Brady, and Patricia A. Hurley, "The Electoral Basis of Party Voting: Patterns and Trends in the U.S. House of Representatives, 1887–1969," in *The Impact of the Electoral Process,* ed. Louis Maisel and Joseph Cooper (Beverly Hills: Sage, 1977), 139; 1970–1990: Congressional Quarterly, *Congressional Quarterly Almanac* (Washington, D.C.: Congressional Quarterly, annual volumes); 1991–1996: *Congressional Quarterly Weekly Report* (1992), 3906, (1993), 3480, (1994), 3658, (1996), 199, 3432.

Table 5-8   Party Unity and Polarization in Congressional Voting, 1954–1996 (percent)

Year	House	Senate	Year	House	Senate
1954	38	47	1976	36	37
1955	41	30	1977	42	42
1956	44	53	1978	33	45
1957	59	36	1979	47	47
1958	40	44	1980	38	46
1959	55	48	1981	37	48
1960	53	37	1982	36	43
1961	50	62	1983	56	44
1962	46	41	1984	47	40
1963	49	47	1985	61	50
1964	55	36	1986	57	52
1965	52	42	1987	64	41
1966	41	50	1988	47	42
1967	36	35	1989	55	35
1968	35	32	1990	49	54
1969	31	36	1991	55	49
1970	27	35	1992	64	53
1971	38	42	1993	65	67
1972	27	36	1994	62	52
1973	42	40	1995	73	69
1974	29	44	1996	56	62
1975	48	48			

Note: Data indicate the percentage of all recorded votes on which a majority of voting Democrats opposed a majority of voting Republicans.

Sources: Congressional Quarterly Weekly Report (1996), 3462.

Table 5-9   Party Unity in Congressional Voting, 1954–1996 (percent)

	House			Senate		
Year	All Democrats	Southern Democrats	Repub-licans	All Democrats	Southern Democrats	Repub-licans
1954	80	—	84	77	—	89
1955	84	68	78	82	78	82
1956	80	79	78	80	75	80
1957	79	71	75	79	81	81
1958	77	67	73	82	76	74
1959	85	77	85	76	63	80
1960	75	62	77	73	60	74
1961	—	—	—	—	—	—
1962	81	—	80	80	—	81
1963	85	—	84	79	—	79
1964	82	—	81	73	—	75
1965	80	55	81	75	55	78
1966	78	55	82	73	52	78
1967	77	53	82	75	59	73
1968	73	48	76	71	57	74
1969	71	47	71	74	53	72
1970	71	52	72	71	49	71
1971	72	48	76	74	56	75
1972	70	44	76	72	43	73
1973	75	55	74	79	52	74
1974	72	51	71	72	41	68
1975	75	53	78	76	48	71
1976	75	52	75	74	46	72
1977	74	55	77	72	48	75
1978	71	53	77	75	54	66
1979	75	60	79	76	62	73
1980	78	64	79	76	64	74
1981	75	57	80	77	64	85
1982	77	62	76	76	62	80
1983	82	67	80	76	70	79
1984	81	68	77	75	61	83
1985	86	76	80	79	68	81
1986	86	76	76	74	59	80
1987	88	78	79	85	80	78
1988	88	81	80	85	78	74
1989	86	77	76	79	69	79
1990	86	78	78	82	75	77
1991	86	78	81	83	73	83
1992	86	79	84	82	70	83
1993	89	83	88	87	78	86
1994	88	83	88	86	77	81
1995	84	76	93	84	75	91
1996	84	75	90	86	76	91

Note: "—" indicates not available. Data show percentage of members voting with a majority of their party on party unity votes. Party unity votes are those roll calls on which a majority of Democrats vote against a majority of Republicans. Percentages are calculated to eliminate the impact of absences as follows: unity = (unity)/(unity + opposition).

Sources: 1954–1992: Norman J. Ornstein et al., eds., *Vital Statistics on Congress, 1993–1994* (Washington, D.C.: Congressional Quarterly, 1994), 201–202; 1993–1994: *Congressional Quarterly Weekly Report* (1993), 3479; (1994), 3659; (1996), 245, 3461.

Table 5-10 The 105th Congress: The House of Representatives

State/district/ representative	Party	Year born	Year first elected	% vote in 1996 Primary	% vote in 1996 General	Campaign expenditures (1995–1996)	Voting ratings[a] VP	PS	PU	CC	ADA	CCUS	ACU
Alabama													
1. Callahan	R	1932	1984	U	64	402,128	97	38	94	100	0	100	100
2. Everett	R	1937	1992	U	63	983,814	98	34	95	100	5	94	100
3. Riley	R	1944	1996	64	51	868,833	-	-	-	-	-	-	-
4. Aderholt	R	1965	1996	49	50	763,117	-	-	-	-	-	-	-
5. Cramer	D	1947	1990	U	56	1,006,341	99	65	59	98	40	63	55
6. Bachus	R	1947	1992	U	71	511,226	98	38	93	98	5	94	95
7. Hilliard	D	1942	1992	U	71	223,582	98	80	93	39	85	31	15
Alaska													
AL. Young	R	1933	1973	58	59	1,176,954	94	40	91	100	0	81	89
Arizona													
1. Salmon	R	1958	1994	U	60	456,089	99	33	92	92	10	88	100
2. Pastor	D	1943	1991	U	65	405,526	96	79	90	44	85	38	5
3. Stump	R	1927	1976	U	67	233,997	99	34	97	98	0	94	100
4. Shadegg	R	1949	1994	74	67	512,249	100	30	96	90	5	88	100
5. Kolbe	R	1942	1984	70	69	415,550	99	49	88	86	5	94	90
6. Hayworth	R	1958	1994	U	48	1,499,443	100	37	96	94	0	94	100
Arkansas													
1. Berry	D	1942	1996	52	53	871,389	-	-	-	-	-	-	-
2. Snyder	D	1947	1996	51	52	798,145	-	-	-	-	-	-	-
3. Hutchinson	R	1950	1996		56	366,628	-	-	-	-	-	-	-
4. Dickey	R	1939	1992	U	64	452,572	92	25	96	92	0	100	100

(Table continues)

Table 5-10 (Continued)

State/district/representative	Party	Year born	Year first elected	% vote in 1996 Primary	% vote in 1996 General	Campaign expenditures (1995–1996)	VP	PS	PU	CC	ADA	CCUS	ACU
California													
1. Riggs	R	1950	1990	U	50	1,390,399	94	40	86	80	10	81	85
2. Herger	R	1945	1986	84	61	536,724	98	33	96	94	0	100	100
3. Fazio	D	1942	1978	82	54	2,320,330	93	84	89	57	80	25	0
4. Doolittle	R	1950	1990	U	60	604,778	97	28	95	100	5	94	100
5. Matsui	D	1941	1978	U	70	814,857	95	87	93	42	85	19	0
6. Woolsey	D	1937	1992	U	62	542,131	99	84	98	4	95	19	0
7. Miller	D	1945	1974	U	72	434,745	94	81	96	4	90	13	0
8. Pelosi	D	1940	1987	U	84	465,863	94	83	98	2	95	13	0
9. Dellums	D	1935	1970	85	77	415,090	94	76	97	2	100	0	0
10. Tauscher	D	1951	1996	75	49	2,571,595	-	-	-	-	-	-	-
11. Pombo	R	1961	1992	U	59	470,749	99	29	95	98	5	94	100
12. Lantos	D	1928	1980	U	72	591,305	93	87	97	15	95	13	0
13. Stark	D	1931	1972	U	65	630,357	88	74	95	0	80	6	0
14. Eshoo	D	1942	1992	U	65	544,566	98	83	92	12	85	29	0
15. Campbell	R	1952	1988	U	59	2,177,865	99	54	73	43	40	88	60
16. Lofgren	D	1947	1994	U	66	191,393	99	77	91	16	85	31	5
17. Farr	D	1941	1993	88	59	563,235	98	84	94	27	90	31	0
18. Condit	D	1948	1989	U	66	678,001	99	53	52	82	35	63	70
19. Radanovich	R	1955	1994	U	67	618,220	91	34	96	98	0	94	100
20. Dooley	D	1954	1990	U	57	662,818	98	81	74	67	55	44	15
21. Thomas	R	1941	1978	79	66	768,689	98	42	90	100	5	94	90
[22. Capps[b]	D	1934	1996	U	48	904,831	-	-	-	-	-	-	-]
23. Gallegly	R	1944	1986	U	60	294,940	93	38	95	94	0	100	100
24. Sherman	D	1954	1996	54	50	1,364,516	-	-	-	-	-	-	-
25. McKeon	R	1939	1992	85	62	384,011	99	33	95	96	0	100	100

26. Berman	D	1941	1982	84	66	408,096	90	88	94	21	90	19	0
27. Rogan	R	1957	1996	88	50	763,574	-	-	-	-	-	-	-
28. Dreier	R	1952	1980	U	61	396,104	99	33	98	98	0	100	100
29. Waxman	D	1939	1974	U	68	365,082	92	83	97	6	90	13	0
30. Becerra	D	1958	1992	U	72	223,890	91	84	98	9	85	23	0
31. Martinez	D	1929	1982	U	67	83,015	94	79	78	57	80	31	10
32. Dixon	D	1934	1978	U	82	97,495	98	84	91	40	90	19	0
33. Roybal-Allard	D	1941	1992	U	82	144,278	97	83	97	12	90	25	0
34. Torres	D	1930	1982	U	68	207,398	94	84	95	27	100	14	0
35. Waters	D	1938	1990	U	86	235,851	88	74	95	13	85	19	0
36. Harman	D	1945	1992	24	52	1,579,938	90	67	75	66	60	60	26
37. Millender-McDonald	D	1938	1996	U	85	327,257	98	84	93	28	83	20	0
38. Horn	R	1931	1992	U	53	470,077	98	50	72	73	40	80	63
39. Royce	R	1951	1992	U	63	489,076	98	34	90	74	15	88	100
40. Lewis	R	1934	1978	77	65	239,448	94	46	88	100	5	94	83
41. Kim	R	1939	1992	58	59	579,673	100	34	98	98	0	100	100
42. Brown	D	1920	1962	78	50	722,544	96	90	96	26	90	25	0
43. Calvert	R	1953	1992	74	55	594,665	94	33	93	98	0	100	95
44. Bono	R	1935	1994	U	58	458,527	98	37	94	98	0	94	95
45. Rohrabacher	R	1947	1988	U	61	272,859	98	28	92	78	15	93	100
46. Sanchez	D	1960	1996	35	47	811,219	-	-	-	-	-	-	-
47. Cox	R	1952	1988	U	66	527,738	96	31	97	91	5	88	100
48. Packard	R	1931	1982	U	66	264,625	95	40	93	96	0	93	94
49. Bilbray	R	1951	1994	U	53	1,122,073	97	45	82	73	20	94	74
50. Filner	D	1942	1992	55	62	1,142,370	91	86	97	12	90	29	0
51. Cunningham	R	1941	1990	86	65	425,525	98	31	95	91	10	81	100
52. Hunter	R	1948	1980	U	65	632,305	93	30	96	98	10	94	100
Colorado													
1. DeGette	D	1957	1996	56	57	889,219	-	-	-	-	-	-	-
2. Skaggs	D	1943	1986	U	57	778,880	99	85	93	33	90	19	0

(Table continues)

Table 5-10 (Continued)

State/district/representative	Party	Year born	Year first elected	% vote in 1996		Campaign expenditures (1995–1996)	Voting ratings[a]						
				Primary	General		VP	PS	PU	CC	ADA	CCUS	ACU
3. McInnis	R	1953	1992	U	69	270,892	96	38	92	88	5	88	100
4. Schaffer	R	1962	1996	40	56	464,165	-	-	-	-	-	-	-
5. Hefley	R	1935	1986	77	72	329,794	99	30	95	94	10	94	100
6. Schaefer	R	1936	1983	U	62	760,648	98	33	97	98	0	100	100
Connecticut													
1. Kennelly	D	1936	1982	U	74	543,033	98	84	87	50	80	25	10
2. Gejdenson	D	1948	1980	U	52	1,177,255	98	83	92	33	90	20	0
3. DeLauro	D	1943	1990	U	71	424,582	99	84	93	29	85	19	0
4. Shays	R	1945	1987	U	60	552,597	100	53	69	33	30	69	60
5. Maloney	D	1948	1996	U	52	614,440	-	-	-	-	-	-	-
6. Johnson	R	1935	1982	U	50	931,406	98	58	74	78	20	81	55
Delaware													
AL. Castle	R	1939	1992	U	70	376,350	100	57	76	71	25	88	60
Florida													
1. Scarborough	R	1963	1994	U	73	428,856	94	31	89	79	10	94	95
2. Boyd	D	1945	1996	64	59	807,103	-	-	-	-	-	-	-
3. Brown	D	1946	1992	U	61	330,201	94	84	90	59	90	31	0
4. Fowler	R	1942	1992	89	U	280,593	92	36	92	96	10	92	95
5. Thurman	D	1951	1992	U	62	521,859	100	77	84	75	75	25	15
6. Stearns	R	1941	1988	U	67	301,045	99	33	94	90	5	88	100
7. Mica	R	1943	1992	U	62	539,973	99	33	96	94	0	100	100
8. McCollum	R	1944	1980	U	67	421,409	99	33	94	96	0	100	95
9. Bilirakis	R	1930	1982	80	69	846,392	99	33	91	90	5	94	90

10. Young	R	1930	1970	U	67	265,355	73	40	92	90	5	85	88
11. Davis	D	1957	1996	56	58	935,314	-	-	-	-	-	-	-
12. Canady	R	1954	1992	U	62	213,131	99	37	93	94	5	94	85
13. Miller	R	1942	1992	U	64	387,149	98	39	92	82	10	88	95
14. Goss	R	1938	1988	U	73	372,563	97	39	92	84	10	88	95
15. Weldon	R	1953	1994	U	51	774,408	99	38	93	94	5	100	100
16. Foley	R	1954	1994	U	64	613,392	99	43	84	78	10	94	90
17. Meek	D	1926	1992	U	89	257,039	97	81	91	46	85	33	5
18. Ros-Lehtinen	R	1952	1989	U	U*	163,902	95	48	77	76	30	73	60
19. Wexler	D	1961	1996	65	66	872,367	-	-	-	-	-	-	-
20. Deutsch	D	1957	1992	U	65	435,604	97	84	87	46	70	53	18
21. Diaz-Balart	R	1954	1992	U	U	130,085	97	51	77	90	30	60	60
22. Shaw	R	1939	1980	U	62	548,109	97	40	90	92	10	94	95
23. Hastings	D	1936	1992	U	73	276,708	94	86	93	47	95	20	0

Georgia

1. Kingston	R	1955	1992	U	68	452,178	96	31	92	90	5	86	100
2. Bishop	D	1947	1992	59	54	774,474	98	73	75	90	60	44	30
3. Collins	R	1944	1992	U	61	485,354	100	32	98	98	5	94	100
4. McKinney	D	1955	1992	67	58	1,015,197	96	80	98	4	100	20	0
5. Lewis	D	1940	1986	U	U	207,661	99	84	98	10	100	19	0
6. Gingrich	R	1943	1978	U	58	5,577,715	100	25	97	100	0	100	100
7. Barr	R	1948	1994	U	58	1,272,303	97	30	97	98	5	94	100
8. Chambliss	R	1943	1994	U	53	1,081,914	100	35	96	100	0	100	100
9. Deal	R	1942	1992	U	66	865,898	100	37	92	94	5	81	90
10. Norwood	R	1941	1994	U	52	1,622,486	94	31	98	100	0	100	100
11. Linder	R	1942	1992	U	64	780,653	98	35	96	98	0	100	100

Hawaii

1. Abercrombie	D	1938	1990	72	50	674,404	99	78	90	47	90	25	0
2. Mink	D	1927	1990	60	60	315,187	97	78	95	25	95	25	5

(Table continues)

Table 5-10 *(Continued)*

State/district/ representative	Party	Year born	Year first elected	% vote in 1996 Primary	General	Campaign expenditures (1995–1996)	Voting ratings[a] VP	PS	PU	CC	ADA	CCUS	ACU
Idaho													
1. Chenoweth	R	1938	1994	68	50	1,129,263	95	28	92	92	10	88	95
2. Crapo	R	1951	1992	86	69	755,679	98	30	95	96	0	100	95
Illinois													
1. Rush	D	1946	1992	89	86	156,219	93	84	96	10	95	25	0
2. Jackson	D	1965	1995	U	94	729,699	100	85	96	12	100	19	0
3. Lipinski	D	1937	1982	U	65	455,967	97	65	63	59	70	38	40
4. Gutierrez	D	1954	1992	71	94	261,252	93	83	95	6	100	14	0
5. Blagojevich	D	1956	1996	50	64	1,552,073	-	-	-	-	-	-	-
6. Hyde	R	1924	1974	84	64	434,160	98	39	93	94	10	100	90
7. Davis	D	1941	1996	33	82	410,662	-	-	-	-	-	-	-
8. Crane	R	1930	1969	75	62	534,151	97	35	98	96	0	100	100
9. Yates	D	1909	1948	84	63	184,005	90	79	96	9	85	7	0
10. Porter	R	1935	1980	68	69	726,615	97	42	81	58	25	75	80
11. Weller	R	1957	1994	U	52	1,116,062	99	41	84	84	5	87	84
12. Costello	D	1949	1988	U	72	506,257	98	67	75	60	70	25	30
13. Fawell	R	1929	1984	U	60	537,449	98	43	85	78	10	100	85
14. Hastert	R	1942	1986	U	64	968,055	99	37	96	100	0	100	100
15. Ewing	R	1935	1991	U	57	664,934	97	35	94	94	0	100	100
16. Manzullo	R	1944	1992	U	60	786,063	98	34	94	82	5	94	100
17. Evans	D	1951	1982	U	52	629,624	99	75	95	14	95	19	0
18. LaHood	R	1945	1994	U	59	699,963	99	39	84	76	10	88	80
19. Poshard	D	1945	1988	U	67	237,030	100	61	68	63	70	44	45
20. Shimkus	R	1958	1996	51	50	647,796	-	-	-	-	-	-	-

Indiana													
1. Visclosky	D	1949	1984	84	69	318,769	98	75	82	41	85	19	15
2. McIntosh	R	1958	1994	86	58	1,050,616	95	36	95	96	0	100	100
3. Roemer	D	1956	1990	U	58	525,727	99	68	64	63	60	56	40
4. Souder	R	1950	1994	82	58	438,384	97	37	92	92	10	75	95
5. Buyer	R	1958	1992	U	65	227,204	97	37	94	98	5	94	95
6. Burton	R	1938	1982	U	75	491,082	98	35	96	94	10	94	100
7. Pease	R	1951	1996	30	62	586,488	-	-	-	-	-	-	-
8. Hostettler	R	1961	1994	82	50	528,325	96	38	95	90	20	88	95
9. Hamilton	D	1931	1964	86	56	967,859	100	63	56	88	45	56	45
10. Carson	D	1938	1996	49	53	572,617	-	-	-	-	-	-	-
Iowa													
1. Leach	R	1942	1976	U	53	369,864	99	58	69	59	40	69	37
2. Nussle	R	1960	1990	U	53	679,904	100	33	96	90	5	94	95
3. Boswell	D	1934	1996	58	49	634,351	-	-	-	-	-	-	-
4. Ganske	R	1949	1994	U	52	2,334,251	94	45	84	61	20	94	83
5. Latham	R	1948	1994	U	65	477,173	99	32	96	94	0	100	95
Kansas													
1. Moran	R	1954	1996	76	73	430,261	-	-	-	-	-	-	-
2. Ryun	R	1947	1996	62	52	415,606	-	-	-	-	-	-	-
3. Snowbarger	R	1949	1996	44	50	465,869	-	-	-	-	-	-	-
4. Tiahrt	R	1951	1994	U	50	903,348	98	35	93	88	5	94	100
Kentucky													
1. Whitfield	R	1943	1994	U	54	897,338	98	38	89	98	5	94	85
2. Lewis	R	1946	1994	U	58	639,397	99	37	95	96	5	94	100
3. Northup	R	1948	1996	U	50	1,181,546	-	-	-	-	-	-	-
4. Bunning	R	1931	1986	U	68	886,717	99	33	96	98	5	81	100

(Table continues)

Table 5-10 (*Continued*)

State/district/ representative	Party	Year born	Year first elected	% vote in 1996 Primary	% vote in 1996 General	Campaign expenditures (1995–1996)	VP	PS	PU	CC	ADA	CCUS	ACU
5. Rogers	R	1937	1980	U	U	132,717	98	39	91	100	10	81	95
6. Baesler	D	1941	1992	U	56	574,074	98	73	70	76	60	40	25
Louisiana													
1. Livingston	R	1943	1977	U	+	1,042,853	96	39	92	98	0	88	95
2. Jefferson	D	1947	1990	U	+	301,082	91	79	90	54	85	31	5
3. Tauzin	R	1943	1980	U	+	612,332	92	35	93	98	0	93	90
4. McCrery	R	1949	1988	71	+	823,121	95	37	94	98	0	100	95
5. Cooksey	R	1941	1996	34	58	898,479	-	-	-	-	-	-	-
6. Baker	R	1948	1986	69	+	554,968	93	34	94	100	0	100	95
7. John	D	1960	1996	26	53	604,865	-	-	-	-	-	-	-
Maine													
1. Allen	D	1945	1996	52	55	933,425	-	-	-	-	-	-	-
2. Baldacci	D	1955	1994	U	72	581,219	100	86	89	47	80	31	10
Maryland													
1. Gilchrest	R	1946	1990	65	62	259,366	99	46	84	76	20	100	80
2. Ehrlich	R	1957	1994	83	62	844,918	98	33	94	96	10	94	100
3. Cardin	D	1943	1986	90	67	577,270	97	83	87	38	75	25	11
4. Wynn	D	1951	1992	85	85	343,875	99	84	91	37	90	31	0
5. Hoyer	D	1939	1981	84	57	1,155,840	99	86	87	69	85	13	5
6. Bartlett	R	1926	1992	85	57	253,966	99	30	95	96	0	100	100
7. Cummings	D	1951	1996	37	83	691,787	99	76	94	18	92	22	0
8. Morella	R	1931	1986	65	61	559,807	96	73	56	38	50	60	30

Voting ratings[a]

Massachusetts

District	Party					Votes							
1. Olver	D	1936	1991	U	53	1,005,595	98	85	98	6	95	19	0
2. Neal	D	1949	1988	U	72	227,105	95	81	93	18	75	20	11
3. McGovern	D	1959	1996	U	53	806,939	-	-	-	-	-	-	-
4. Frank	D	1940	1980	85	72	334,002	96	79	94	4	100	13	0
5. Meehan	D	1956	1992	86	U	308,067	93	87	93	8	85	19	0
6. Tierney	D	1951	1996	U	48	776,359	-	-	-	-	-	-	-
7. Markey	D	1946	1976	U	70	351,683	97	81	97	0	95	6	0
8. Kennedy	D	1952	1986	U	84	1,952,906	98	84	95	4	95	13	0
9. Moakley	D	1927	1972		72	769,122	90	78	93	12	65	25	6
10. Delahunt	D	1941	1996	38	54	1,072,986	-	-	-	-	-	-	-

Michigan

District	Party					Votes							
1. Stupak	D	1952	1992	U	71	458,509	99	73	84	37	75	25	20
2. Hoekstra	R	1953	1992	U	65	185,831	99	34	91	66	10	88	95
3. Ehlers	R	1934	1993	U	69	265,960	99	44	79	63	25	94	79
4. Camp	R	1953	1990	U	65	555,815	99	37	89	72	0	100	95
5. Barcia	D	1952	1992	U	70	200,556	99	71	69	75	45	60	47
6. Upton	R	1953	1986	U	68	399,520	100	39	82	55	10	94	85
7. Smith	R	1934	1992	75	42	263,739	96	35	89	77	10	93	95
8. Stabenow	D	1950	1996	U	54	1,497,300	-	-	-	-	-	-	-
9. Kildee	D	1929	1976	U	59	816,337	100	76	85	51	75	31	15
10. Bonior	D	1945	1976	U	54	1,513,432	99	79	95	16	95	19	5
11. Knollenberg	R	1933	1992	U	61	608,882	99	38	93	98	0	94	95
12. Levin	D	1931	1982	U	57	1,313,913	99	89	94	31	85	19	0
13. Rivers	D	1956	1994	U	57	1,099,549	99	77	91	18	95	19	5
14. Conyers	D	1929	1964	U	86	267,039	92	76	97	2	90	13	0
15. Kilpatrick	D	1945	1996	51	88	174,457	-	-	-	-	-	-	-
16. Dingell	D	1926	1955	U	62	1,854,280	98	78	85	52	70	31	25

(Table continues)

Table 5-10 *(Continued)*

State/district/ representative	Party	Year born	Year first elected	% vote in 1996 Primary	% vote in 1996 General	Campaign expenditures (1995–1996)	VP	PS	PU	CC	ADA	CCUS	ACU
Minnesota													
1. Gutknecht	R	1951	1994	U	53	927,715	98	37	89	81	5	94	100
2. Minge	D	1942	1992	U	55	616,673	99	73	78	30	70	38	15
3. Ramstad	R	1946	1990	U	70	494,908	95	46	79	48	35	88	70
4. Vento	D	1940	1976	U	57	559,370	99	89	97	6	95	13	0
5. Sabo	D	1938	1978	U	64	515,970	99	87	96	18	90	13	0
6. Luther	D	1945	1994	U	56	850,638	100	81	84	22	80	19	0
7. Peterson	D	1944	1990	U	68	532,229	98	61	61	63	55	63	53
8. Oberstar	D	1934	1974	U	67	538,159	98	76	88	22	80	20	20
Mississippi													
1. Wicker	R	1951	1994	U	68	524,101	98	35	96	100	0	100	100
2. Thompson	D	1948	1993	U	60	361,452	96	81	91	64	90	25	5
3. Pickering	R	1963	1996	56	61	1,167,906	-	-	-	-	-	-	-
4. Parker	R	1949	1988	U	61	288,719	99	37	95	100	0	100	100
5. Taylor	D	1953	1989	94	58	451,833	99	53	45	86	30	63	80
Missouri													
1. Clay	D	1931	1968	78	70	366,550	89	76	96	12	80	19	6
2. Talent	R	1956	1992	U	61	1,165,814	96	32	93	90	10	100	100
3. Gephardt	D	1941	1976	75	59	3,110,509	88	82	93	35	85	27	6
4. Skelton	D	1931	1976	U	64	770,607	98	66	58	100	40	60	50
5. McCarthy	D	1947	1994	U	67	220,339	97	84	87	22	80	25	5
6. Danner	D	1934	1992	77	69	112,970	98	63	67	63	55	56	45
7. Blunt	R	1950	1996	56	65	985,764	-	-	-	-	-	-	-

8. Emerson	R	1950	1996	51	50	806,205	—	—	—	—	—	—	—
9. Hulshof	R	1958	1996	50	49	686,450	—	—	—	—	—	—	—
Montana													
AL. Hill	R	1946	1996	44	52	943,062	—	—	—	—	—	—	—
Nebraska													
1. Bereuter	R	1939	1978	U	70	394,292	99	51	82	82	20	81	60
2. Christensen	R	1963	1994	U	57	1,722,490	96	35	94	90	5	88	100
3. Barrett	R	1929	1990	U	77	203,582	100	41	92	96	0	94	95
Nevada													
1. Ensign	R	1958	1994	U	50	1,904,413	97	40	80	68	5	88	85
2. Gibbons	R	1944	1996	42	59	724,036	—	—	—	—	—	—	—
New Hampshire													
1. Sununu	R	1964	1996	28	50	545,865	—	—	—	—	—	—	—
2. Bass	R	1952	1994	66	50	625,147	99	34	91	80	0	100	100
New Jersey													
1. Andrews	D	1957	1990	U	76	414,266	98	77	83	43	65	31	25
2. LoBiondo	R	1946	1994	U	60	890,526	100	44	76	53	25	81	70
3. Saxton	R	1943	1984	U	64	533,850	98	40	85	83	15	94	84
4. Smith	R	1953	1980	U	64	284,776	96	46	82	76	30	75	80
5. Roukema	R	1929	1980	75	71	496,610	95	53	68	44	50	56	53
6. Pallone	D	1951	1988	U	61	658,367	100	81	91	25	90	25	10
7. Franks	R	1951	1992	U	55	1,305,753	99	52	72	40	35	81	63
8. Pascrell	D	1937	1996	U	51	952,722	—	—	—	—	—	—	—
9. Rothman	D	1952	1996	79	56	797,632	—	—	—	—	—	—	—
10. Payne	D	1934	1988	82	84	404,017	97	78	98	6	95	19	0
11. Frelinghuysen	R	1946	1994	U	66	581,895	98	54	80	81	30	87	75

(Table continues)

Table 5-10 (Cor tinued)

State/district/ representative	Party	Year born	Year first elected	% vote in 1996 Primary	% vote in 1996 General	Campaign expenditures (1995–1996)	VP	PS	PU	CC	ADA	CCUS	ACU
12. Pappas	R	1960	1996	38	50	591,536	-	-	-	-	-	-	-
13. Menendez	D	1954	1992	93	79	379,469	95	80	94	27	85	19	5
New Mexico													
1. Schiff	R	1947	1988	U	57	603,316	92	56	76	87	25	80	63
2. Skeen	R	1927	1980	70	56	539,969	99	42	89	98	5	100	90
[3. Richardson[c]	D	1947	1982	U	67	526,898	94	81	82	78	75	40	15]
New York													
1. Forbes	R	1952	1994	U	55	918,162	96	43	76	91	15	73	84
2. Lazio	R	1958	1992	U	64	696,180	99	46	76	76	15	87	75
3. King	R	1944	1992	88	55	645,951	99	49	83	85	20	69	79
4. McCarthy	D	1944	1996	U	57	967,221	-	-	-	-	-	-	-
5. Ackerman	D	1942	1983	U	64	1,123,926	94	89	96	33	85	31	0
6. Flake	D	1945	1986	U	85	165,311	83	86	94	26	80	8	6
7. Manton	D	1932	1984	U	71	374,982	97	75	80	66	65	33	26
8. Nadler	D	1947	1992	82	82	780,423	95	77	96	4	100	7	0
9. Schumer	D	1950	1980	U	75	487,841	95	83	91	24	90	31	5
10. Towns	D	1934	1982	U	91	533,824	90	79	97	9	85	20	0
11. Owens	D	1936	1982	U	92	129,983	95	80	98	2	95	19	0
12. Velazquez	D	1953	1992	U	85	236,564	98	79	96	2	100	6	0
[13. Molinari[d]	R	1958	1990	U	62	557,586	82	41	84	81	20	92	88]
14. Maloney	D	1948	1992	U	72	599,406	97	86	96	13	85	20	5
15. Rangel	D	1930	1970	U	91	1,086,065	93	82	97	8	95	13	0
16. Serrano	D	1943	1990	U	96	149,752	97	82	96	12	95	19	0
17. Engel	D	1947	1988	77	85	374,074	94	84	95	22	95	25	0

Voting ratings[a]

18. Lowey	D	1988	1937	U	64	1,138,456	98	86	95	10	90	31	0
19. Kelly	R	1994	1936	53	46	906,904	100	47	83	84	10	88	70
20. Gilman	R	1972	1922	U	57	682,959	98	61	63	78	35	63	45
21. McNulty	D	1988	1947	57	66	628,000	93	72	83	39	60	33	22
22. Solomon	R	1978	1930	U	60	640,080	96	37	96	98	5	81	95
23. Boehlert	R	1982	1936	65	64	610,166	99	56	68	78	50	69	50
24. McHugh	R	1992	1948	U	71	172,883	98	42	85	88	10	81	79
25. Walsh	R	1988	1947	U	55	698,021	99	47	79	96	20	81	68
26. Hinchey	D	1992	1938	U	55	994,042	98	78	93	20	95	19	5
27. Paxon	R	1988	1954	U	60	1,553,754	92	35	98	100	0	100	100
28. Slaughter	D	1986	1929	U	57	868,969	96	84	94	18	90	25	5
29. LaFalce	D	1974	1939	U	62	443,052	96	83	91	24	80	25	5
30. Quinn	R	1992	1951	U	55	752,713	96	58	70	80	35	81	58
31. Houghton	R	1986	1926	U	72	699,270	91	61	77	83	20	63	60
North Carolina													
1. Clayton	D	1992	1934	U	66	300,049	98	86	94	38	100	13	5
2. Etheridge	D	1996	1941	U	53	730,969	-	-	-	-	-	-	-
3. Jones	R	1994	1943	U	63	593,793	99	30	93	94	5	94	100
4. Price	D	1996	1940	U	54	1,168,542	-	-	-	-	-	-	-
5. Burr	R	1994	1955	U	62	697,067	99	32	96	96	5	88	100
6. Coble	R	1984	1931	52	73	498,224	100	30	95	88	15	88	90
7. McIntyre	D	1996	1956	U	53	490,063	-	-	-	-	-	-	-
8. Hefner	D	1974	1930	U	55	555,614	99	71	76	94	55	38	30
9. Myrick	R	1994	1941	U	63	547,194	99	33	96	92	10	88	100
10. Ballenger	R	1986	1926	U	70	244,447	99	33	95	100	0	100	100
11. Taylor	R	1990	1941	U	58	481,658	93	33	95	100	5	87	100
12. Watt	D	1992	1945	U*	71	148,001	98	84	98	16	90	19	0
North Dakota													
AL. Pomeroy	D	1992	1952	U	55	971,332	98	81	80	67	80	31	11

(Table continues)

Table 5-10 *(Continued)*

State/district/representative	Party	Year born	Year first elected	% vote in 1996 Primary	% vote in 1996 General	Campaign expenditures (1995–1996)	Voting ratings[a] VP	PS	PU	CC	ADA	CCUS	ACU
Ohio													
1. Chabot	R	1953	1994	U	54	983,163	98	35	87	67	15	88	100
2. Portman	R	1955	1993	U	72	256,544	96	37	92	90	10	94	100
3. Hall	D	1942	1978	U	64	247,426	89	71	79	52	65	33	15
4. Oxley	R	1944	1981	U	65	639,496	95	37	93	98	5	100	100
5. Gillmor	R	1939	1988	U	61	327,472	95	40	91	93	15	73	84
6. Strickland	D	1941	1996	U	51	714,172	-	-	-	-	-	-	-
7. Hobson	R	1936	1990	86	68	620,093	98	38	90	94	0	88	90
8. Boehner	R	1949	1990	U	70	1,312,440	98	34	97	98	0	94	100
9. Kaptur	D	1946	1982	U	77	253,432	94	75	84	31	75	33	15
10. Kucinich	D	1946	1996	77	49	692,867	-	-	-	-	-	-	-
11. Stokes	D	1925	1968	U	81	361,175	82	80	95	14	65	17	0
12. Kasich	R	1952	1982	88	64	1,578,812	96	41	91	86	15	94	95
13. Brown	D	1952	1992	U	60	607,543	98	84	96	6	95	13	0
14. Sawyer	D	1945	1986	80	54	523,412	98	88	93	37	90	25	0
15. Pryce	R	1951	1992	86	71	384,780	95	40	89	88	5	94	85
16. Regula	R	1924	1972	84	69	154,379	99	48	86	94	15	81	75
17. Traficant	D	1941	1984	U	91	156,597	99	57	51	92	55	44	50
18. Ney	R	1954	1994	U	50	879,110	99	39	90	88	10	88	85
19. LaTourette	R	1954	1994	U	55	1,025,247	98	45	85	90	15	88	80
Oklahoma													
1. Largent	R	1955	1994	U	68	345,612	95	30	96	92	10	86	100
2. Coburn	R	1948	1994	U	55	1,354,299	98	29	91	86	10	80	89
3. Watkins	R	1938	1996	79	51	1,106,300	-	-	-	-	-	-	-
4. Watts	R	1957	1994	U	58	1,363,291	98	32	93	98	0	100	100

5. Istook	R	1950	1992	U	70	306,411	97	32	96	98	10	94	100
6. Lucas	R	1960	1994	U	64	439,969	99	34	96	100	0	100	100
Oregon													
1. Furse	D	1936	1992	99	52	1,370,710	94	81	93	12	80	33	5
2. Smith	R	1931	1996		62	412,394	-	-	-	-	-	-	-
3. Blumenauer	D	1948	1996	78	67	507,414	95	86	94	9	78	20	0
4. DeFazio	D	1947	1986	100	66	301,211	96	71	89	18	95	19	5
5. Hooley	D	1939	1996	51	51	1,019,312	-	-	-	-	-	-	-
Pennsylvania													
1. Foglietta	D	1928	1980	73	88	485,748	92	86	96	9	85	20	5
2. Fattah	D	1956	1994	U	88	412,478	93	83	98	6	95	25	0
3. Borski	D	1948	1982	91	69	317,799	97	82	86	37	80	20	10
4. Klink	D	1951	1992	U	64	506,560	98	63	75	62	65	20	30
5. Peterson	R	1938	1996	38	60	858,637	-	-	-	-	-	-	-
6. Holden	D	1957	1992	U	59	609,346	96	61	62	78	45	63	47
7. Weldon	R	1947	1986	83	67	362,252	88	45	85	88	15	85	84
8. Greenwood	R	1951	1992	60	59	614,221	97	49	78	80	25	88	60
9. Shuster	R	1932	1972	U	74	1,213,304	98	35	93	92	0	100	100
10. McDade	R	1931	1962	53	60	724,776	51	42	87	95	5	67	75
11. Kanjorski	D	1937	1984	U	68	342,141	99	68	78	55	65	25	30
12. Murtha	D	1932	1974	U	70	785,486	96	77	65	90	55	25	25
13. Fox	R	1947	1994	U	49	1,659,723	99	44	77	66	35	81	65
14. Coyne	D	1936	1980	66	61	1,027,674	98	81	94	10	100	19	0
15. McHale	D	1950	1992	U	55	366,847	100	72	77	53	70	38	20
16. Pitts	R	1939	1996	45	59	616,874	-	-	-	-	-	-	-
17. Gekas	R	1930	1982	U	72	110,578	99	35	96	98	0	100	100
18. Doyle	D	1953	1994	74	56	528,291	99	66	66	63	55	44	32
19. Goodling	R	1927	1974	55	63	305,541	97	37	88	88	10	94	95

(Table continues)

223

Table 5-10 *(Continued)*

State/district/ representative	Party	Year born	Year first elected	% vote in 1996 Primary	% vote in 1996 General	Campaign expenditures (1995–1996)	Voting ratings[a] VP	PS	PU	CC	ADA	CCUS	ACU
20. Mascara	D	1930	1994	U	54	577,217	99	70	70	76	60	38	35
21. English	R	1956	1994	U	51	1,262,645	98	46	81	83	10	88	74
Rhode Island													
1. Kennedy	D	1967	1994	U	69	1,051,719	98	75	86	35	85	13	10
2. Weygand	D	1948	1996	48	64	785,547	-	-	-	-	-	-	-
South Carolina													
1. Sanford	R	1960	1994	U	96	97,231	99	44	84	63	10	81	95
2. Spence	R	1928	1970	U	90	303,421	99	35	96	100	5	88	100
3. Graham	R	1955	1994	U	60	644,451	99	35	96	98	0	100	100
4. Inglis	R	1959	1992	U	71	143,966	97	34	95	94	10	87	100
5. Spratt	D	1942	1982	U	54	855,622	99	73	80	75	60	31	25
6. Clyburn	D	1940	1992	88	69	196,440	97	84	91	65	95	25	5
South Dakota													
AL. Thune	R	1961	1996	59	58	773,125	-	-	-	-	-	-	-
Tennessee													
1. Jenkins	R	1936	1996	18	64	457,975	-	-	-	-	-	-	-
2. Duncan	R	1947	1988	U	71	260,818	99	32	82	60	30	88	85
3. Wamp	R	1957	1994	U	56	942,237	99	31	89	75	15	88	100
4. Hilleary	R	1959	1994	U	58	1,183,570	99	32	93	86	0	94	95
5. Clement	D	1943	1988	U	72	299,403	98	73	69	86	60	50	30
6. Gordon	D	1949	1984	89	54	1,609,419	99	63	66	80	45	56	50
7. Bryant	R	1948	1994	U	64	649,783	99	35	96	98	0	100	100

225

	Party						94	67	63	100	45	56	47
8. Tanner	D	1944	1988	U	67	395,726	94	-	-	-	-	-	47
9. Ford	D	1970	1996	60	61	679,843	-	-	-	-	-	-	-
Texas													
1. Sandlin	D	1952	1996	56	52	1,691,255	-	-	-	-	-	-	-
2. Turner	D	1946	1996	59	52	919,505	-	-	-	-	-	-	-
3. Johnson	R	1930	1991		73	625,107	96	38	96	98	5	94	100
4. Hall	D	1923	1980	U	64	527,260	99	44	29	92	15	94	90
5. Sessions	R	1955	1996		53	1,091,122	-	-	-	-	-	-	-
6. Barton	R	1949	1984		77	890,468	96	37	94	94	15	88	89
7. Archer	R	1928	1970		81	278,951	98	35	97	96	5	94	100
8. Brady	R	1955	1996		59	1,094,498	-	-	-	-	-	-	-
9. Lampson	D	1945	1996		53	1,612,625	-	-	-	-	-	-	-
10. Doggett	D	1946	1994	U	56	410,302	98	90	90	29	80	19	0
11. Edwards	D	1951	1990	U	57	844,126	98	73	72	92	60	50	20
12. Granger	R	1943	1996	69	58	1,001,836	-	-	-	-	-	-	-
13. Thornberry	R	1958	1994	U	67	565,578	100	35	97	100	0	94	100
14. Paul	R	1935	1996	54	51	1,927,756	-	-	-	-	-	-	-
15. Hinojosa	D	1940	1996	52	62	715,391	-	-	-	-	-	-	-
16. Reyes	D	1944	1996	51	71	587,193	-	-	-	-	-	-	-
17. Stenholm	D	1938	1978	U	52	804,936	99	53	50	90	50	63	65
18. Jackson-Lee	D	1950	1994		77	477,866	92	88	93	43	90	27	5
19. Combest	R	1945	1984	U	80	440,379	100	35	96	100	0	100	95
20. Gonzalez	D	1916	1961	U	64	86,231	99	84	84	68	80	38	15
21. Smith	R	1947	1986	U	76	443,571	95	35	95	98	10	93	100
22. DeLay	R	1947	1984		68	1,621,708	95	35	96	98	0	93	100
23. Bonilla	R	1954	1992	U	62	779,893	97	36	90	96	0	94	85
24. Frost	D	1942	1978		56	1,963,529	96	83	79	90	65	38	10
25. Bentsen	D	1959	1994		57	1,654,345	99	81	78	82	75	31	10
26. Armey	R	1940	1984		74	1,673,388	98	38	96	96	0	94	100
27. Ortiz	D	1937	1982	70	65	407,316	94	67	70	94	60	43	37

(Table continues)

Table 5-10 (Continued)

State/district/representative	Party	Year born	Year first elected	% vote in 1996 Primary	% vote in 1996 General	Campaign expenditures (1995–1996)	VP	PS	PU	CC	ADA	CCUS	ACU
[28. Tejeda[e]	D	1945	1992	U	75	222,182	97	69	72	90	60	38	37]
29. Green	D	1947	1992		68	552,655	93	78	82	70	60	38	28
30. Johnson	D	1935	1992		55	416,694	98	87	91	55	80	25	0
Utah													
1. Hansen	R	1932	1980	C	68	274,156	96	41	94	98	0	100	100
2. Cook	R	1946	1996	52	55	1,061,793	-	-	-	-	-	-	-
3. Cannon	R	1950	1996	56	51	1,826,849	-	-	-	-	-	-	-
Vermont													
AL. Sanders	I	1941	1990	U	55	942,438	98	75	95	14	100	19	0
Virginia													
1. Bateman	R	1928	1982	80	U	534,156	98	41	91	96	15	94	85
2. Pickett	D	1930	1986	C	65	266,059	99	68	57	92	45	63	50
3. Scott	D	1947	1992	C	82	176,104	98	85	90	59	90	31	0
4. Sisisky	D	1927	1982	C	79	223,771	97	61	52	100	35	67	55
5. Goode	D	1946	1996	C	60	485,194	-	-	-	-	-	-	-
6. Goodlatte	R	1952	1992	C	67	566,763	100	30	93	88	5	100	95
7. Bliley	R	1932	1980	C	75	1,092,570	97	34	94	100	0	100	100
8. Moran	D	1945	1990	C	66	319,334	96	77	83	45	65	31	20
9. Boucher	D	1946	1982	C	65	576,709	95	73	78	72	65	44	15
10. Wolf	R	1939	1980	C	72	251,763	98	38	90	88	5	81	95
11. Davis	R	1949	1994	C	64	1,333,607	98	52	78	84	15	94	79

Voting ratings[a]

	Party					Vote							
Washington													
1. White	R	1953	1994	50	54	1,671,909	98	44	92	88	0	88	95
2. Metcalf	R	1927	1994	52	49	797,442	98	38	86	80	0	75	90
3. Smith	R	1950	1994	52	50	1,216,368	95	36	90	90	5	79	84
4. Hastings	R	1941	1994	55	53	734,640	98	33	97	98	0	100	100
5. Nethercutt	R	1944	1994	51	56	1,071,823	96	33	94	98	0	93	95
6. Dicks	D	1940	1976	67	66	477,269	95	88	84	59	65	19	0
7. McDermott	D	1936	1988	79	81	190,250	97	82	97	8	95	27	0
8. Dunn	R	1941	1992	65	65	1,146,933	94	38	94	92	0	100	100
9. Smith	D	1965	1996	49	50	711,722	-	-	-	-	-	-	-
West Virginia													
1. Mollohan	D	1943	1982	U	U	195,128	93	72	71	77	65	25	15
2. Wise	D	1948	1982	86	69	376,555	95	85	82	64	70	25	10
3. Rahall	D	1949	1976	U	U	145,980	100	70	81	51	75	19	20
Wisconsin													
1. Neumann	R	1954	1994	U	51	1,211,134	99	43	85	51	15	69	95
2. Klug	R	1953	1990	U	57	1,261,546	99	46	75	51	40	81	75
3. Kind	D	1963	1996	46	52	497,919	-	-	-	-	-	-	-
4. Kleczka	D	1943	1984	85	58	862,686	99	78	84	25	75	44	10
5. Barrett	D	1953	1992	U	73	153,139	99	86	89	2	85	25	5
6. Petri	R	1940	1979	U	73	364,660	99	46	83	65	20	88	100
7. Obey	D	1938	1969	U	57	862,370	98	77	85	31	75	19	25
8. Johnson	D	1943	1996	59	52	289,624	-	-	-	-	-	-	-
9. Sensenbrenner	R	1943	1978	U	74	261,644	100	37	85	61	20	81	100
Wyoming													
AL. Cubin	R	1946	1994	U	55	679,599	96	31	96	98	0	100	100

(Notes continue)

Table 5-10 *(Continued)*

Note: "–" indicates a newly elected representative (no basis for voting ratings). Brackets indicate former members of the 105th Congress. Information as of November 19, 1997. "AL" indicates at large; "R" indicates Republican; "D" indicates Democrat; "U" indicates lack of opposition other than write-in candidates; "U*" indicates unopposed, name did not appear on ballot; "+" indicates Louisiana where the primary is open to candidates of all parties (if a candidate wins 50 percent or more of the vote in the primary, that candidate is declared the winner and no general election is held); "C" indicates candidate nominated by party convention rather than primary.

[a] Voting ratings based on recorded votes in 1996. "VP" indicates voting participation score (percentage of recorded votes on which a representative voted "yea" or "nay"). "PS" indicates presidential support score (percentage of the votes on which the president took a position that the representative supported the president). "PU" indicates party unity score (percentage of the votes on which a representative supported his or her party when a majority of voting Democrats opposed a majority of voting Republicans). "CC" indicates conservative coalition score (percentage of the votes on which a representative voted in agreement with majorities of voting Republicans and southern Democrats against a majority of nonsouthern Democrats). Group ratings indicate the percentage of the time a representative supported the group-preferred position on votes the group selects. "ADA" (Americans for Democratic Action) is a liberal group, "AFL-CIO" (American Federation of Labor-Congress of Industrial Organizations) is a labor group, "CCUS" (Chamber of Commerce of the United States) is a business group, and "ACU" (American Conservative Union) is a conservative group. Voting participation and "ADA" scores are lowered by a member's failure to vote. Failure to vote does not lower the other scores.

[b] Seat is vacant as of November 1997 due to the death of Rep. Walter Capps.

[c] Bill Redmond (R) was sworn in May 20, 1997, to replace Rep. Bill Richardson, who had resigned to become the new ambassador to the United Nations.

[d] Vito Fossella (R) was sworn in November 5, 1997, to replace Rep. Susan Molinari, who had resigned earlier in the year.

[e] Ciro D. Rodriguez (D) was sworn in April 17, 1997, after the death of Rep. Frank Tejeda.

Source: Congressional Quarterly.

Table 5-11 The 105th Congress: The Senate

State/senator	Party	Year born	Year first elected	% vote in last election		Last campaign expenditures[a]	Voting ratings[b]						
				Primary	General		VP	PS	PU	CC	ADA	CCUS	ACU
Alabama													
Shelby	R	1934	1986	U	65	2,451,191	98	33	94	92	5	77	90
Sessions	R	1946	1996	59	52	3,862,359	-	-	-	-	-	-	-
Alaska													
Stevens	R	1923	1970	59	77	2,711,710	98	45	90	92	20	85	80
Murkowski	R	1933	1980	81	53	1,663,865	94	36	96	97	15	92	95
Arizona													
McCain	R	1936	1986	U	56	3,481,915	98	32	95	89	0	100	95
Kyl	R	1942	1994	99	54	4,138,203	98	23	98	97	5	100	100
Arkansas													
Bumpers	D	1925	1974	65	60	1,878,472	92	88	91	21	85	17	0
Hutchinson	R	1949	1996		53	1,604,014	-	-	-	-	-	-	-
California													
Feinstein	D	1933	1992	74	47	14,407,179	99	90	81	53	95	38	20
Boxer	D	1940	1992	44	48	10,368,600	99	90	94	18	100	23	5
Colorado													
Campbell	R	1933	1992	U	52	1,561,347	92	48	82	86	45	82	78
Allard	R	1943	1996	57	51	2,233,429	-	-	-	-	-	-	-
Connecticut													
Dodd	D	1944	1980	U	59	4,122,268	98	81	89	38	85	38	10
Lieberman	D	1942	1988	U	67	3,238,026	99	90	76	63	75	54	35
Delaware													
Roth	R	1921	1970	U	56	2,233,279	98	43	90	86	10	85	85
Biden	D	1942	1972	U	60	1,966,313	99	92	79	42	80	46	20

(Table continues)

Table 5-11 (Continued)

State/senator	Party	Year born	Year first elected	% vote in last election Primary	% vote in last election General	Last campaign expenditures[a]	Voting ratings[b] VP	PS	PU	CC	ADA	CCUS	ACU
Florida													
Graham	D	1936	1986	84	65	2,979,552	100	86	81	61	85	46	15
Mack	R	1940	1988	U	70	3,735,719	93	34	93	100	0	100	100
Georgia													
Coverdell	R	1939	1992	50	51	3,193,774	100	34	98	97	5	92	100
Cleland	D	1942	1996	U	49	2,926,391	-	-	-	-	-	-	-
Hawaii													
Inouye	D	1924	1962	76	57	2,971,128	95	86	87	51	85	33	11
Akaka	D	1924	1990	U	72	418,630	100	88	95	26	95	31	5
Idaho													
Craig	R	1945	1990	U	57	2,809,897	100	32	98	97	0	100	95
Kempthorne	R	1951	1992	57	57	1,305,338	100	32	98	97	0	100	95
Illinois													
Moseley-Braun	D	1947	1992	38	53	6,594,570	99	84	89	24	90	46	5
Durbin	D	1944	1996	65	56	4,966,804	-	-	-	-	-	-	-
Indiana													
Lugar	R	1932	1976	U	67	4,063,703	99	31	90	92	5	85	95
Coats	R	1943	1990	U	57	3,802,077	97	30	96	89	10	100	100
Iowa													
Grassley	R	1933	1980	U	70	2,322,262	100	32	92	82	15	92	90
Harkin	D	1939	1984	U	52	5,276,708	100	85	91	18	80	38	10
Kansas													
Brownback	R	1956	1996	55	54	2,269,550	-	-	-	-	-	-	-
Roberts	R	1936	1996	78	62	2,305,898	-	-	-	-	-	-	-

Kentucky														
Ford	D	1924	1974	U*	63	2,076,069	100	83	79	74	70	74	79	83
McConnell	R	1942	1984	89	55	4,669,642	99	39	95	95	10	95	95	39
Louisiana														
Breaux	D	1944	1986	73	+	1,446,199	99	78	70	84	60	84	70	78
Landrieu	D	1955	1996	20	50	2,715,287	-	-	-	-	-	-	-	-
Maine														
Snowe	R	1947	1994	100	60	2,041,834	100	53	72	79	35	79	72	53
Collins	R	1952	1996	55	49	1,621,475	-	-	-	-	-	-	-	-
Maryland														
Sarbanes	D	1933	1976	79	59	2,698,928	100	90	94	18	95	18	94	90
Mikulski	D	1936	1986	77	71	3,161,104	99	90	92	32	95	32	92	90
Massachusetts														
Kennedy	D	1932	1962	99	58	10,540,244	99	88	94	8	90	8	94	88
Kerry	D	1943	1984	U	52	10,962,607	99	92	92	18	95	18	92	92
Michigan														
Levin	D	1934	1978	U	58	5,965,017	100	86	94	29	85	29	94	86
Abraham	R	1952	1994	52	52	4,453,648	100	37	95	95	15	95	95	37
Minnesota														
Wellstone	D	1944	1990	86	50	5,979,224	100	85	92	11	95	11	92	85
Grams	R	1948	1994	58	49	2,439,798	98	36	98	92	5	92	98	36
Mississippi														
Cochran	R	1937	1978	95	71	828,693	96	40	93	94	5	94	93	40
Lott	R	1941	1988	95	69	2,138,544	99	34	97	97	5	97	97	34
Missouri														
Bond	R	1939	1986	83	52	4,577,895	99	37	95	100	10	100	95	37
Ashcroft	R	1942	1994	83	60	4,063,927	99	29	98	89	5	89	98	29
Montana														
Baucus	D	1941	1978	U	50	3,748,502	99	90	73	45	85	45	73	90
Burns	R	1935	1988	U	62	3,157,084	99	29	97	95	5	95	97	29

(Table continues)

Table 5-11 *(Continued)*

| State/senator | Party | Year born | Year first elected | % vote in last election | | Last campaign expenditures[a] | Voting ratings[b] | | | | | | |
				Primary	General		VP	PS	PU	CC	ADA	CCUS	ACU
Nebraska													
Kerrey	D	1943	1988	U	55	4,471,081	97	86	88	32	85	23	5
Hagel	R	1946	1996	62	56	3,564,316	-	-	-	-	-	-	-
Nevada													
Reid	D	1939	1986	53	51	2,725,713	99	78	79	53	85	31	15
Bryan	D	1937	1988	U	51	3,021,834	100	78	82	50	85	38	10
New Hampshire													
Smith	R	1941	1990	99	49	1,718,413	98	29	96	92	5	92	100
Gregg	R	1947	1992	50	48	875,675	98	34	91	89	5	92	75
New Jersey													
Lautenberg	D	1924	1982	81	50	7,278,332	98	90	93	11	95	15	0
Torricelli	D	1951	1996	U	53	9,134,854	-	-	-	-	-	-	-
New Mexico													
Domenici	R	1932	1972	U	65	3,110,548	95	42	90	94	20	83	85
Bingaman	D	1943	1982	U	54	3,227,352	99	84	88	37	95	15	0
New York													
Moynihan	D	1927	1976	75	55	5,784,736	97	81	90	19	90	31	10
D'Amato	R	1937	1980	U	49	9,175,533	97	48	87	89	25	69	75
North Carolina													
Helms	R	1921	1972	U	53	7,798,520	99	25	97	97	5	85	100
Faircloth	R	1928	1992	48	50	2,952,102	98	21	96	89	5	92	95
North Dakota													
Conrad	D	1948	1986	U	58	1,927,866	99	83	87	39	85	23	15
Dorgan	D	1942	1992	U	59	1,124,512	100	80	84	37	85	38	20
Ohio													
Glenn	D	1921	1974	U	51	3,999,271	99	88	90	18	95	23	10

DeWine	R	1947	1994	52	53	6,274,663	100	41	88	92	15	85	85
Oklahoma													
Nickles	R	1948	1980	U	59	3,316,336	100	34	99	97	0	100	100
Inhofe	R	1934	1994	75	57	2,510,946	98	28	100	97	0	100	100
Oregon													
Wyden	D	1949	1996	50	48	2,752,879	100	95	92	24	95	38	15
Smith	R	1952	1996	78	50	3,764,272	-	-	-	-	-	-	-
Pennsylvania													
Specter	R	1930	1980	65	49	8,854,815	99	59	64	66	50	77	50
Santorum	R	1958	1994	82	49	6,732,849	98	40	93	92	15	77	95
Rhode Island													
Chafee	R	1922	1976	69	65	1,896,589	99	60	64	68	40	92	60
Reed	D	1949	1996	86	63	2,732,011	-	-	-	-	-	-	-
South Carolina													
Thurmond	R	1902	1954	60	53	2,385,185	100	39	97	95	5	92	95
Hollings	D	1922	1966	U	50	3,642,045	98	82	82	59	70	46	20
South Dakota													
Daschle	D	1947	1986	U	65	2,878,375	100	93	94	24	90	38	0
Johnson	D	1946	1996	U	51	2,990,554	-	-	-	-	-	-	-
Tennessee													
Thompson	R	1942	1994	94	61	3,469,369	98	36	96	92	0	100	85
Frist	R	1952	1994	44	56	9,517,424	99	40	96	97	0	100	95
Texas													
Gramm	R	1942	1984	85	55	6,289,591	93	25	99	97	0	100	100
Hutchison	R	1943	1993	84	61	6,114,755	100	34	98	95	5	92	100
Utah													
Hatch	R	1934	1976	U	69	3,456,031	99	32	94	97	5	92	100
Bennett	R	1933	1992	51	55	4,439,376	97	36	92	97	5	92	95
Vermont													
Leahy	D	1940	1974	U	54	950,331	97	75	88	33	90	23	5
Jeffords	R	1934	1988	U	50	1,043,626	98	53	58	59	50	62	45

(Table continues)

Table 5-11 (*Continued*)

State/senator	Party	Year born	Year first elected	% vote in last election		Last campaign expenditures[a]	Voting ratings[b]						
				Primary	General		VP	PS	PU	CC	ADA	CCUS	ACU
Virginia													
Warner	R	1927	1978	65	52	5,196,091	100	42	93	89	5	85	95
Robb	D	1939	1988	58	46	5,501,697	99	85	76	79	80	46	20
Washington													
Gorton	R	1928	1980	53	56	4,792,764	99	45	90	95	15	100	85
Murray	D	1950	1992	28	54	1,342,038	98	89	95	18	90	17	0
West Virginia													
Byrd	D	1917	1958	85	69	1,550,354	100	81	82	32	70	23	15
Rockefeller	D	1937	1984	88	77	2,538,473	97	93	93	30	85	46	16
Wisconsin													
Kohl	D	1935	1988	90	58	7,374,312	100	88	84	32	75	69	20
Feingold	D	1953	1992	70	53	1,979,454	100	86	87	16	95	31	10
Wyoming													
Thomas	R	1933	1994	U	59	1,068,335	99	29	98	95	5	92	100
Enzi	R	1944	1996	32	54	953,572	-	-	-	-	-	-	-

Note: "–" indicates a newly elected senator (no basis for voting ratings). Information as of July 16, 1997. "R" indicates Republican; "D" indicates Democrat; "U" indicates lack of opposition other than write-in candidates; "U*" indicates unopposed, name did not appear on ballot; "+" indicates Louisiana where the primary is open to candidates of all parties (if a candidate wins 50 percent or more of the vote in the primary, that candidate is declared the winner and no general election is held).

[a] Figures for campaign expenditures cover from January 1 of the year preceding the last campaign (or whenever the campaign registered with the Federal Election Commission during the election cycle) through December 31 of the election year.
[b] For a description of the voting ratings, see footnote a, Table 5-10, this volume.

Source: Congressional Quarterly.

6

Presidency and Executive Branch

- **Presidents**
- **Ratings**
- **Backgrounds**
- **Cabinet and Staff**
- **Congressional Relations**
- **Civil Service Employment**
- **Regulations**

The presidency poses special problems to those interested in the collection of statistical data. The scope and variety of data available on the presidency are limited by the singularity of the president and the difference the individual president makes on the office's organization and operation. Moreover, the modern presidency has evolved since Franklin Roosevelt took office in the 1930s. Since then the emergence of the United States as a world power, the expansion of television, the growth of government, and the alteration of the presidential selection process have further changed the demands on and expectations of the presidency. Hence, for data on many points, the recent occupants of the Oval Office are just too few to sustain statistical analysis.

In spite of these seemingly insurmountable handicaps, the visibility of the president provides a considerable amount of relevant data. Of all elected officials, for example, only presidents have public judgments about how well they are doing prominently and repeatedly displayed: the twists and turns in the public approval ratings of a president's job performance are themselves news items. Consequently, elsewhere in this book a series of figures are devoted to this subject alone—showing overall presidential approval scores for ten presidents (Figure 3-4), and detailed ratings for Jimmy Carter, Ronald Reagan, George Bush, and Bill Clinton (Figure 3-5). But presidents are not judged only by the public or only while they are in office. At various times and in various ways, historians and political scientists have rated all the U.S. presidents (Table 6-2).

Apart from approval ratings (and of course presidential elections), the presidency has not been subjected to extensive statistical scrutiny. However, perhaps because the number of presidents has now reached forty-one individuals (Table 6-1), some additional areas are beginning to receive systematic study. The president's relationship with Congress is one such area. Information about presidential "victories" on votes in Congress (Table 6-7), the extent to which the president is supported by his own party and by the other party (Table 6-8), the number of vetoes presidents from Washington to Clinton have exercised (Table 6-9), and presidential success in having nominations approved (Tables 6-10 and 6-11) are all regularly tabulated and increasingly analyzed.

As discussed in Chapter 4, media coverage of the president is also beginning to receive systematic study. In part this study results from the extreme visibility of the president and of the federal government in general (Figure 4-1 and Table 4-14); it is also due to changing relationships between the president and the press, as indicated, for example, by the considerable decline in press conferences since the 1930s (Table 4-3).

Compilations of various presidential characteristics and activities also have become more numerous or more meaningful with the larger number who have served as president. How individuals get to be president, for example, has been a subject of considerable interest (Tables 6-3 and 6-4). As shown in Chapter 7, presidential appointments have been checked for their partisan characteristics (Table 7-6) and increasingly for their racial and sex distributions (Table 7-5).

The executive branch, apart from the president, has been subjected to little statistical analysis. Yet here, too, there is ample opportunity for meaningful tabulations, if not for t-tests and correlations. The tremendous size of the federal government (Tables 6-5 and 6-12) necessitates such an interest. The expanded involvement of the government in regulation (Tables 6-13 and 6-14), at least until the Reagan administration, also compels attention. But there are other more subtle and more significant messages in these data. For example, the changing emphases of the nation and of the priorities of particular presidents can be seen in such mundane listings as the size and composition of the White House staff over time (Table 6-6).

Thus, while the presidency provides data for conventional statistical analyses in only a few areas, a generous and increasing amount of numerical data provides considerable insight into what has traditionally been viewed as an office of impressive singularity.

Table 6-1 Presidents and Vice Presidents of the United States

President (political party)	Born	Died	Age at inauguration	Native of . . .	Elected from . . .	Term of service	Vice president
George Washington (F)	1732	1799	57	Va.	Va.	April 30, 1789–March 4, 1793	John Adams
George Washington (F)			61			March 4, 1793–March 4, 1797	John Adams
John Adams (F)	1735	1826	61	Mass.	Mass.	March 4, 1797–March 4, 1801	Thomas Jefferson
Thomas Jefferson (D-R)	1743	1826	57	Va.	Va.	March 4, 1801–March 4, 1805	Aaron Burr
Thomas Jefferson (D-R)			61			March 4, 1805–March 4, 1809	George Clinton
James Madison (D-R)	1751	1836	57	Va.	Va.	March 4, 1809–March 4, 1813	George Clinton
James Madison (D-R)			61			March 4, 1813–March 4, 1817	Elbridge Gerry
James Monroe (D-R)	1758	1831	58	Va.	Va.	March 4, 1817–March 4, 1821	Daniel D. Tompkins
James Monroe (D-R)			62			March 4, 1821–March 4, 1825	Daniel D. Tompkins
John Q. Adams (N-R)	1767	1848	57	Mass.	Mass.	March 4, 1825–March 4, 1829	John C. Calhoun
Andrew Jackson (D)	1767	1845	61	S.C.	Tenn.	March 4, 1829–March 4, 1833	John C. Calhoun
Andrew Jackson (D)			65			March 4, 1833–March 4, 1837	Martin Van Buren
Martin Van Buren (D)	1782	1862	54	N.Y.	N.Y.	March 4, 1837–March 4, 1841	Richard M. Johnson
W. H. Harrison (W)	1773	1841	68	Va.	Ohio	March 4, 1841–April 4, 1841	John Tyler
John Tyler (W)	1790	1862	51	Va.	Va.	April 6, 1841–March 4, 1845	
James K. Polk (D)	1795	1849	49	N.C.	Tenn.	March 4, 1845–March 4, 1849	George M. Dallas
Zachary Taylor (W)	1784	1850	64	Va.	La.	March 4, 1849–July 9, 1850	Millard Fillmore
Millard Fillmore (W)	1800	1874	50	N.Y.	N.Y.	July 10, 1850–March 4, 1853	
Franklin Pierce (D)	1804	1869	48	N.H.	N.H.	March 4, 1853–March 4, 1857	William R. King
James Buchanan (D)	1791	1868	65	Pa.	Pa.	March 4, 1857–March 4, 1861	John C. Breckinridge
Abraham Lincoln (R)	1809	1865	52	Ky.	Ill.	March 4, 1861–March 4, 1865	Hannibal Hamlin
Abraham Lincoln (R)			56			March 4, 1865–April 15, 1865	Andrew Johnson
Andrew Johnson (R)	1808	1875	56	N.C.	Tenn.	April 15, 1865–March 4, 1869	
Ulysses S. Grant (R)	1822	1885	46	Ohio	Ill.	March 4, 1869–March 4, 1873	Schuyler Colfax
Ulysses S. Grant (R)			50			March 4, 1873–March 4, 1877	Henry Wilson

(Table continues)

Table 6-1 (Continued)

President (political party)	Born	Died	Age at inauguration	Native of . . .	Elected from . . .	Term of service	Vice president
Rutherford B. Hayes (R)	1822	1893	54	Ohio	Ohio	March 4, 1877–March 4, 1881	William A. Wheeler
James A. Garfield (R)	1831	1881	49	Ohio	Ohio	March 4, 1881–Sept. 19, 1881	Chester A. Arthur
Chester A. Arthur (R)	1830	1886	50	Vt.	N.Y.	Sept. 20, 1881–March 4, 1885	
Grover Cleveland (D)	1837	1908	47	N.J.	N.Y.	March 4, 1885–March 4, 1889	Thomas A. Hendricks
Benjamin Harrison (R)	1833	1901	55	Ohio	Ind.	March 4, 1889–March 4, 1893	Levi P. Morton
Grover Cleveland (D)	1837	1908	55			March 4, 1893–March 4, 1897	Adlai E. Stevenson
William McKinley (R)	1843	1901	54	Ohio	Ohio	March 4, 1897–March 4, 1901	Garret A. Hobart
William McKinley (R)			58			March 4, 1901–Sept. 14, 1901	Theodore Roosevelt
Theodore Roosevelt (R)	1858	1919	42	N.Y.	N.Y.	Sept. 14, 1901–March 4, 1905	
Theodore Roosevelt (R)			46			March 4, 1905–March 4, 1909	Charles W. Fairbanks
William H. Taft (R)	1857	1930	51	Ohio	Ohio	March 4, 1909–March 4, 1913	James S. Sherman
Woodrow Wilson (D)	1856	1924	56	Va.	N.J.	March 4, 1913–March 4, 1917	Thomas R. Marshall
Woodrow Wilson (D)			60			March 4, 1917–March 4, 1921	Thomas R. Marshall
Warren G. Harding (R)	1865	1923	55	Ohio	Ohio	March 4, 1921–Aug. 2, 1923	Calvin Coolidge
Calvin Coolidge (R)	1872	1933	51	Vt.	Mass.	Aug. 3, 1923–March 4, 1925	
Calvin Coolidge (R)			52			March 4, 1925–March 4, 1929	Charles G. Dawes
Herbert Hoover (R)	1874	1964	54	Iowa	Calif.	March 4, 1929–March 4, 1933	Charles Curtis
Franklin D. Roosevelt (D)	1882	1945	51	N.Y.	N.Y.	March 4, 1933–Jan. 20, 1937	John N. Garner
Franklin D. Roosevelt (D)			55			Jan. 20, 1937–Jan. 20, 1941	John N. Garner
Franklin D. Roosevelt (D)			59			Jan. 20, 1941–Jan. 20, 1945	Henry A. Wallace
Franklin D. Roosevelt (D)			63			Jan. 20, 1945–April 12, 1945	Harry S. Truman
Harry S. Truman (D)	1884	1972	60	Mo.	Mo.	April 12, 1945–Jan. 20, 1949	
Harry S. Truman (D)			64			Jan. 20, 1949–Jan. 20, 1953	Alben W. Barkley
Dwight D. Eisenhower (R)	1890	1969	62	Texas	N.Y.	Jan. 20, 1953–Jan. 20, 1957	Richard M. Nixon
Dwight D. Eisenhower (R)			66		Pa.	Jan. 20, 1957–Jan. 20, 1961	Richard M. Nixon
John F. Kennedy (D)	1917	1963	43	Mass.	Mass.	Jan. 20, 1961–Nov. 22, 1963	Lyndon B. Johnson
Lyndon B. Johnson (D)	1906	1973	55	Texas	Texas	Nov. 22, 1963–Jan. 20, 1965	

Lyndon B. Johnson (D)			56			Jan. 20, 1965–Jan. 20, 1969	Hubert H. Humphrey
Richard M. Nixon (R)	1913	1994	56	Calif.	N.Y.	Jan. 20, 1969–Jan. 20, 1973	Spiro T. Agnew
Richard M. Nixon (R)			60			Jan. 20, 1973–Aug. 9, 1974	Spiro T. Agnew / Gerald R. Ford
Gerald R. Ford (R)	1913		61	Neb.	Mich.	Aug. 9, 1974–Jan. 20, 1977	Nelson A. Rockefeller
Jimmy Carter (D)	1924		52	Ga.	Ga.	Jan. 20, 1977–Jan. 20, 1981	Walter F. Mondale
Ronald Reagan (R)	1911		69	Ill.	Calif.	Jan. 20, 1981–Jan. 20, 1985	George Bush
Ronald Reagan (R)			73			Jan. 20, 1985–Jan. 20, 1989	George Bush
George Bush (R)	1924		64	Conn.	Texas	Jan. 20, 1989–Jan. 20, 1993	J. Danforth Quayle
William Clinton (D)	1924		46	Conn.	Ark.	Jan. 20, 1993–Jan. 20, 1997	Albert Gore, Jr.
William Clinton (D)	1946		50	Ark.		Jan. 20, 1997–	Albert Gore, Jr.

Note: "D" indicates Democrat, "D-R" indicates Democrat-Republican, "F" indicates Federalist, "N-R" indicates National Republican, "R" indicates Republican, and "W" indicates Whig.

Source: Congressional Quarterly, *Presidential Elections Since 1789*, 4th ed. (Washington, D.C.: Congressional Quarterly, 1987), 4; updated by the editors.

Table 6-2 Ratings of U.S Presidents

Schlesinger poll (1948)	Schlesinger poll (1962)	Maranell-Dodder poll (1970)	DiClerico poll (1977)	Tribune poll (1982)	Murray-Blessing poll[a] (1982)

Great
1. Lincoln
2. Washington
3. F. Roosevelt
4. Wilson
5. Jefferson
6. Jackson
 	
Near great
7. T. Roosevelt
8. Cleveland
9. J. Adams
10. Polk
 	
Average
11. J. Q. Adams
12. Monroe
13. Hayes
14. Madison
15. Van Buren
16. Taft
17. Arthur
18. McKinley
19. A. Johnson
20. Hoover
21. B. Harrison
	Great
	1. Lincoln
	2. Washington
	3. F. Roosevelt
	4. Wilson
	5. Jefferson
	
	Near great
	6. Jackson
	7. T. Roosevelt
	8. Polk
	   Truman (tie)
	9. J. Adams
	10. Cleveland
	
	Average
	11. Madison
	12. J. Q. Adams
	13. Hayes
	14. McKinley
	15. Taft
	16. Van Buren
	17. Monroe
	18. Hoover
	19. B. Harrison
	20. Eisenhower
	   Arthur (tie)
	21. A. Johnson
		Accomplishments of administration
		1. Lincoln
		2. F. Roosevelt
		3. Washington
		4. Jefferson
		5. T. Roosevelt
		6. Truman
		7. Wilson
		8. Jackson
		9. L. Johnson
		10. Polk
		11. J. Adams
		12. Kennedy
		13. Monroe
		14. Cleveland
		15. Madison
		16. Taft
		17. McKinley
		18. J. Q. Adams
		19. Hoover
		20. Eisenhower
		21. A. Johnson
		22. Van Buren
		23. Arthur
		24. Hayes
		25. Tyler
			Ten greatest presidents
			1. Lincoln
			2. Washington
			3. F. Roosevelt
			4. Jefferson
			5. T. Roosevelt
			6. Wilson
			7. Jackson
			8. Truman
			9. Polk
			10. J. Adams
				Ten best presidents
				1. Lincoln (best)
				2. Washington
				3. F. Roosevelt
				4. T. Roosevelt
				5. Jefferson
				6. Wilson
				7. Jackson
				8. Truman
				9. Eisenhower
				10. Polk (10th best)
				
				Ten worst presidents
				1. Harding (worst)
				2. Nixon
				3. Buchanan
				4. Pierce
				5. Grant
				6. Fillmore
				7. A. Johnson
				8. Coolidge
				9. Tyler
				10. Carter (10th worst)
					Great
					1. Lincoln
					2. F. Roosevelt
					3. Washington
					4. Jefferson
					
					Near great
					5. T. Roosevelt
					6. Wilson
					7. Jackson
					8. Truman
					
					Above average
					9. J. Adams
					10. L. Johnson
					11. Eisenhower
					12. Polk
					13. Kennedy
					14. Madison
					15. Monroe
					16. J. Q. Adams
					17. Cleveland
					
					Average
					18. McKinley

Below average
22. Tyler
23. Coolidge
24. Fillmore
25. Taylor
26. Buchanan
27. Pierce

Failure
28. Grant
29. Harding

Below average
22. Taylor
23. Tyler
24. Fillmore
25. Coolidge
26. Pierce
27. Buchanan

Failure
28. Grant
29. Harding

26. B. Harrison
27. Taylor
28. Buchanan
29. Fillmore
30. Coolidge
31. Pierce
32. Grant
33. Harding

19. Taft
20. Van Buren
21. Hoover
22. Hayes
23. Arthur
24. Ford
25. Carter
26. B. Harrison

Below average
27. Taylor
28. Reagan
29. Tyler
30. Fillmore
31. Coolidge
32. Pierce

Failure
33. A. Johnson
34. Buchanan
35. Nixon
36. Grant
37. Harding

Note: These ratings result from surveys of scholars and range in number from 49 to 846.
a The rating of President Reagan was obtained in a separate poll conducted in 1989.

Sources: Henry J. Abraham, *Justices and Presidents: Appointments to the Supreme Court*, 2d ed. (New York: Oxford University Press, 1985), 380–383 (copyright © Henry J. Abraham, 1974, 1985, reprinted by permission of Oxford University Press, Inc.); Tim H. Blessing, "Updating the Murray-Blessing Survey: The Presidential Performance Study Ranks Reagan," unpublished paper, Pennsylvania State University, 1991.

Table 6-3   Previous Public Positions Held by Presidents

Position	Number of presidents holding position prior to presidency	
	Pre-1900 (24)	Post-1900 (17)
Vice president	7	7
Cabinet member	7	3
U.S. representative	13	5
U.S. senator	9	5
U.S. Supreme Court justice	0	0
Federal judge	0	1
Governor	11	7
State legislator	16	5
State judge	1	2
Mayor	2	1
Diplomat, ambassador	7	2
Military general	11	1

Position	Last public position held prior to presidency	
	Pre-1900 (24)	Post-1900 (17)
Vice president		
Succeeded to presidency	4	5
Won presidency in own right	3	2
Congress		
House	1	0
Senate	3	2
Appointive federal office		
Military general	3	1
Cabinet secretary	3	2
Ambassador	2	0
Other civilian	1	0
Governor	4	5

Source: Compiled by the editors from Robert G. Ferris, *The Presidents*, rev. ed. (Washington, D.C.: National Park Service, 1977). In the list of generals, we have included Andrew Johnson (who had the rank of general when serving as military governor of Tennessee) and Chester A. Arthur (who held the rank of general when serving as quartermaster general); listed in various sources other than Ferris. Updated through President Bill Clinton.

Table 6-4   Latest Public Office Held by Candidates for Democratic and
Republican Presidential Nominations, 1936–1996

Public office[a]	Percentage of all persons polling at least 1 percent in Gallup Poll	Percentage of all presidential nominees
President[b]	1	8
Vice president	1	25
U.S. senator	37	17
Governor	22	42
Cabinet officer	15	0
U.S. representative	8	0
Mayor	3	0
U.S. Supreme Court justice	1	0
All others	2	0
No public office	11	8
Total	101	101
	(N = 158)	(N = 24)

[a] Last or current office at time person first polled at least 1 percent support for presidential nomination among fellow partisans or was first nominated.
[b] Presidents Truman and Ford received poll support for the presidential nomination only after they had actually served in the office.

Source: William R. Keech and Donald R. Matthews, *The Party's Choice: With an Epilogue on the 1976 Nominations* (Washington, D.C.: Brookings, 1976), 18; updated by the editors.

Table 6-5 The President's Cabinet, 1997

Cabinet office	Year established[a]	Current secretary[b]	Date confirmed	Number of paid civilian employees		Number of noncivil service positions[c]	Percentage of all positions
				1980[c]	1994[c]		
State	1789	Madeleine Albright	1/22/97	23,644	24,538	19,681	80
Treasury	1789	Robert Rubin	1/10/95	123,754	154,920	8,827	6
War	1789[d]						
Navy	1798[d]						
Interior	1849	Bruce Babbitt	1/21/93	79,505	67,913	8,678	13
Justice	1870	Janet Reno	3/11/93	56,426	104,244	40,541	39
Post Office	1872[e]						
Agriculture	1889[f]	Dan Glickman	3/30/95	122,839	98,733	7,891	8
Commerce and Labor	1903[f]						
Commerce	1913	William M. Daley	1/30/97	46,189	35,497	6,328	18
Labor	1913	Alexis Herman	4/30/97	23,717	15,722	733	5
Defense	1947	William R. Cohen	1/22/97	972,999	812,323	126,749	16
Health, Education and Welfare	1953[g]						
Health and Human Services	1979	Donna E. Shalala	1/21/93	158,644	58,173	12,734	22
Housing and Urban Development	1965	Andrew Cuomo	1/29/97	16,890	11,575	777	7
Transportation	1966	Rodney Slater	2/6/97	72,066	62,782	2,562	4
Energy	1977	Federico Peña	3/12/97	21,729	18,983	1,502	8
Education	1979	Richard W. Riley	1/21/93	7,370	4,795	637	13
Veterans Affairs	1989	Jesse Brown	1/21/93	235,501[h]	258,275	113,872	44

Note: The Cabinet also includes Vice President Albert Gore, Jr., Chief of Staff Erskine Bowles, Chair of the Council of Economic Advisors Janet Yellen, Environmental Protection Agency Administrator Carol Browner, Director of the Office of Management and Budget Franklin Raines, Ambassador to the United Nations

William Richardson, Director of the Central Intelligence Agency George Tenet, U.S. Trade Representative Charlene Barshefsky, Director of the Office of National Drug Control Policy Barry R. McCaffrey, Head of the Small Business Administration Aida Alvarez, Director of the Federal Emergency Management Agency James Lee Witt, and Counselor to the President Thomas "Mack" McLarty.

[a] Dates are when the department achieved cabinet status. Offices of Attorney General and Postmaster General were created in 1789, but executive departments were not created until later. A Department of Agriculture was established in 1862, but the commissioner did not achieve cabinet status until 1889.

[b] As of July 1, 1997.

[c] December 1980; January 1996. Noncivil service positions include excepted and senior executive service and are as of January 1996.

[d] Incorporated into Defense Department in 1947.

[e] Independent agency as of 1971.

[f] Split into separate departments in 1913.

[g] Split into Health and Human Services and Education in 1979.

[h] Figures are for the Veterans Administration, the agency that was upgraded on March 15, 1989, to the Department of Veterans Affairs.

Sources: Year established: Ronald C. Moe, "The Federal Executive Establishment: Evolution and Trends," prepared for the U.S. Senate Committee on Governmental Affairs by the Congressional Research Service (Washington, D.C.: U.S. Government Printing Office, 1980), 26–27; *Congressional Quarterly Weekly Report* (1988), 3059; secretary and date confirmed: *Congressional Quarterly Weekly Report*; employees and noncivil service positions: U.S. Office of Personnel Management, *Federal Civilian Workforce Statistics, Employment and Trends* (January 1981), 8–9, 11 (January 1996), Table 11; note: Office of Cabinet Secretary.

Table 6-6 White House Staff and the Executive Office of the President, 1943–1996

Year	White House	OMB/ Bureau of Budget[a]	Council of Economic Advisers	National Security Council	Office of Economic Opportunity	Office of Science and Technology	Office of Adminis- tration	Special Rep- resentative for Trade Negotiations	Office of Policy Development/ Domestic Council	Total executive office[b]
1943[c]	51	543									703
1944[c]	58	542									683
1945[c]	64	705									820
1946[c]	216	692	26								1,034
1947[c]	228	549	26								1,077
1948[c]	209	521	38	20							1,205
1949	243	517	36	17							1,240
1950	313	509	38	17							1,408
1951	246	518	37	21							1,326
1952	248	470	31	22							1,296
1953	247	417	28	28							1,183
1954	262	430	34	26							1,078
1955	366	422	33	27							1,221
1956	392	443	38	25							1,228
1957	399	441	35	65							1,255
1958	395	424	33	61							2,605
1959	406	432	33	64							2,735
1960	423	441	31	64							2,779
1961	439	456	45	43							1,586
1962	338	465	65	39		63					1,492
1963	376	485	57	43		48		30			1,572
1964	328	493	46	41		57		29			1,478
1965	292	506	45	39	1,768	75		24			3,307
1966	270	592	62	40	2,319	105		26			4,050
1967	271	570	56	38	2,951	58		24			4,747
1968	261	550	74	35	3,211	62		22			4,964

Year	1	2	3	4	5	6	7	8	9	10
1969	341	576	54	2,282	66	75		22		4,116
1970	491	636	57	2,633	82	77		26	26	4,808
1971	580	717	62	2,304	80	75		33	44	4,809
1972	583	703	58	2,066	80	76		38	53	5,721
1973	528	642	49	1,148	85			39	24	3,877
1974	560	646	46	1,090	87			45	32	2,868
1975	525	664	48		85	19		56	55	1,801
1976	534	694	39		79	44		55	43	1,796
1977	387	721	36		68	46		52	41	1,637
1978	381	617	35		76	44	197	58	55	1,679
1979	418	638	36		73	50	180	70	60	1,918
1980	426	631	38		74	13	182	131	68	2,013
1981	378	679	38		65	20	190	139	48	1,674
1982	374	617	35		59	23	196	138	46	1,608
1983	376	619	34		61	21	213	139	39	1,622
1984	371	605	28		63	17	196	147	40	1,593
1985	362	569	32		61	11	193	152	38	1,549
1986	365	537	36		69	11	200	144	40	1,526
1987	375	573	31		56	10	199	155	37	1,604
1988	357	573	35		63	20	232	162	32	1,594
1989	370	536	32		62	22	213	164	37	1,640
1990	391	568	35		60	39	215	172	37	1,729
1991	358	608	36		61	47	241	181	33	1,797
1992	392	553	34		62	35	247	185	42	1,869
1993	392	522	31		52	36	185	177	42	1,570
1994	381	544	29		49	34	182	166	38	1,577
1995	387	522	28		44	33	182	165	30	1,555
1996	387	527	30		43		185	161	28	1,582

Note: In almost all instances when no figures are shown, the office did not exist as a separate entity. Data as of December of the year indicated, except 1947 (January), 1960 (October).

[a] The Bureau of the Budget became the Office of Management and Budget in 1970.

[b] Includes offices not shown separately.

[c] Total executive office excludes personnel in war establishments or emergency war agencies.

Source: U.S. Office of Personnel Management, *Federal Manpower Statistics, Federal Civilian Workforce Statistics*, bimonthly release.

Table 6-7 Presidential Victories on Votes in Congress, 1953–1996

President (political party)/year	House and Senate victories	House		Senate	
		Victories	Number of votes	Victories	Number of votes
Eisenhower (R)					
1953	89.2%	91.2%	34	87.8%	49
1954	82.8	78.9	38	77.9	77
1955	75.3	63.4	41	84.6	52
1956	69.2	73.5	34	67.7	65
1957	68.4	58.3	60	78.9	57
1958	75.7	74.0	50	76.5	98
1959	52.9	55.6	54	50.4	121
1960	65.1	65.1	43	65.1	86
Average	69.9	68.4		70.7	
Total			354		605
Kennedy (D)					
1961	81.5	83.1	65	80.6	124
1962	85.4	85.0	60	85.6	125
1963	87.1	83.1	71	89.6	115
Average	84.6	83.7		85.2	
Total			196		364
Johnson (D)					
1964	87.9	88.5	52	87.6	97
1965	93.1	93.8	112	92.6	162
1966	78.9	91.3	103	68.8	125
1967	78.8	75.6	127	81.2	165
1968	74.5	83.5	103	68.9	164
Average	82.2	85.9		79.7	
Total			497		713
Nixon (R)					
1969	74.8	72.3	47	76.4	72
1970	76.9	84.6	65	71.4	91
1971	74.8	82.5	57	69.5	82
1972	66.3	81.1	37	54.3	46
1973	50.6	48.0	125	52.4	185
1974	59.6	67.9	53	54.2	83
Average	64.3	68.2		61.5	
Total			384		559
Ford (R)					
1974	58.2	59.3	54	57.4	68
1975	61.0	50.6	89	71.0	93
1976	53.8	43.1	51	64.2	53
Average	58.3	51.0		65.0	
Total			194		214

Table 6-7   *(Continued)*

President (political party)/year	House and Senate victories	House		Senate	
		Victories	Number of votes	Victories	Number of votes
Carter (D)					
1977	75.4%	74.7%	79	76.1%	88
1978	78.3	69.6	112	84.8	151
1979	76.8	71.7	145	81.4	161
1980	75.1	76.9	117	73.3	116
Average	76.6	73.1		79.7	
Total			453		516
Reagan (R)					
1981	82.4	72.4	76	88.3	128
1982	72.4	55.8	77	83.2	119
1983	67.1	47.6	82	85.9	85
1984	65.8	52.2	113	85.7	77
1985	59.9	45.0	80	71.6	102
1986	56.5	33.3	90	80.7	83
1987	43.5	33.3	99	56.4	78
1988	47.4	32.7	104	64.8	88
Average	62.2	45.6		77.9	
Total			721		760
Bush (R)					
1989	62.6	50.0	86	73.3	101
1990	46.8	32.4	108	63.4	93
1991	54.2	43.2	111	67.5	83
1992	43.0	37.1	105	53.3	60
Average	51.8	40.2		65.6	
Total			410		337
Clinton (D)					
1993	86.4	87.3	102	85.4	89
1994	86.4	87.2	78	85.5	62
1995	36.2	26.3	133	49.0	102
1996	55.1	53.2	79	57.6	59
Average	66.0	63.5		69.4	
Total			392		312

Note: "R" indicates Republican; "D" indicates Democrat. Percentages based on the number of congressional votes supporting the president divided by the total number of votes on which the president had taken a position. The percentages differ slightly from those found in *Congressional Quarterly Almanac*, *Congressional Quarterly Weekly Report*, and Ornstein et al.'s *Vital Statistics on Congress* due to corrections and consistent rounding of percentages to one decimal place.

Sources: Congressional Quarterly Almanac (Washington, D.C.: Congressional Quarterly, various years); *Congressional Quarterly Weekly Report* (1992), 3894, (1993), 3473, (1994), 3620, (1996), 3428.

Table 6-8   Congressional Voting in Support of the President's Position, 1953–1996 (percent)

	House			Senate		
President/year	All Demo-crats	Southern Demo-crats	Repub-licans	All Demo-crats	Southern Demo-crats	Repub-licans
Eisenhower						
1953	55	—	80	55	—	78
1954	54	—	80	45	—	82
1955	58	—	67	65	—	85
1956	58	—	79	44	—	80
1957	54	—	60	60	—	80
1958	63	—	65	51	—	77
1959	44	—	76	44	—	80
1960	49	—	63	52	—	76
Kennedy						
1961	81	—	41	73	—	42
1962	83	71	47	76	63	48
1963	84	71	36	77	65	52
Johnson						
1964	84	70	42	73	63	52
1965	83	65	46	75	60	55
1966	81	64	45	71	59	53
1967	80	65	51	73	69	63
1968	77	63	59	64	50	57
Nixon						
1969	56	55	65	55	56	74
1970	64	64	79	56	62	74
1971	53	69	79	48	59	76
1972	56	59	74	52	71	77
1973	39	49	67	42	55	70
1974	52	64	71	44	60	65
Ford						
1974	48	52	59	45	55	67
1975	40	48	67	53	67	76
1976	36	52	70	47	61	73
Carter						
1977	69	58	46	77	71	58
1978	67	54	40	74	61	47
1979	70	58	37	75	66	51
1980	71	63	44	71	69	50

Table 6-8   *(Continued))*

President/year	House			Senate		
	All Demo-crats	Southern Demo-crats	Repub-licans	All Demo-crats	Southern Demo-crats	Repub-licans
Reagan						
1981	46	60	72	52	63	84
1982	43	55	70	46	57	77
1983	30	45	74	45	46	77
1984	37	47	64	45	58	81
1985	31	43	69	36	46	80
1986	26	37	69	39	56	90
1987	26	37	65	38	43	67
1988	28	34	61	51	58	73
Bush						
1989	38	49	72	56	66	84
1990	26	35	65	39	49	72
1991	35	43	74	42	53	84
1992	27	38	75	33	40	75
Clinton						
1993	79	80	40	89	85	30
1994	79	79	48	89	88	44
1995	79	73	22	84	80	29
1996	78	74	39	85	79	38

Note: "—" indicates not available. Percentages indicate number of congressional votes support-ing the president divided by the total number of votes on which the president took a position. The percentages are calculated to eliminate the effects of absences as follows: support = (sup-port)/(support + opposition).

Sources: 1953–1954: *Congressional Quarterly Almanac 1953* (Washington, D.C.: Congressional Quarterly, 1954), 78; *1954,* 48; 1955–1988: Norman J. Ornstein et al., eds., *Vital Statistics on Congress, 1989–1990* (Washington, D.C.: Congressional Quarterly, 1990), 196–197; 1989–1994: *Congressional Quarterly Weekly Report* (1990), 4208; (1992), 3896; (1994), 3654; (1996), 239, 3455.

Table 6-9   Presidential Vetoes, 1789–1996

Years	President	Regular vetoes	Vetoes overridden	Pocket vetoes	Total vetoes
1789–1797	Washington	2	0	0	2
1797–1801	Adams	0	0	0	0
1801–1809	Jefferson	0	0	0	0
1809–1817	Madison	5	0	2	7
1817–1825	Monroe	1	0	0	1
1825–1829	J. Q. Adams	0	0	0	0
1829–1837	Jackson	5	0	7	12
1837–1841	Van Buren	0	0	1	1
1841–1841	Harrison	0	0	0	0
1841–1845	Tyler	6	1	4	10
1845–1849	Polk	2	0	1	3
1849–1850	Taylor	0	0	0	0
1850–1853	Fillmore	0	0	0	0
1853–1857	Pierce	9	5	0	9
1857–1861	Buchanan	4	0	3	7
1861–1865	Lincoln	2	0	5	7
1865–1869	A. Johnson	21	15	8	29
1869–1877	Grant	45	4	48	93
1877–1881	Hayes	12	1	1	13
1881–1881	Garfield	0	0	0	0
1881–1885	Arthur	4	1	8	12
1885–1889	Cleveland	304	2	110	414
1889–1893	Harrison	19	1	25	44
1893–1897	Cleveland	42	5	128	170
1897–1901	McKinley	6	0	36	42
1901–1909	T. Roosevelt	42	1	40	82
1909–1913	Taft	30	1	9	39
1913–1921	Wilson	33	6	11	44
1921–1923	Harding	5	0	1	6
1923–1929	Coolidge	20	4	30	50
1929–1933	Hoover	21	3	16	37
1933–1945	F. Roosevelt	372	9	263	635
1945–1953	Truman	180	12	70	250
1953–1961	Eisenhower	73	2	108	181
1961–1963	Kennedy	12	0	9	21
1963–1969	L. Johnson	16	0	14	30
1969–1974	Nixon	26[a]	7	17	43
1974–1977	Ford	48	12	18	66
1977–1981	Carter	13	2	18	31
1981–1989	Reagan	39	9	39	78
1989–1992	Bush	29	1	17	46
1993–1996	Clinton	17	1	0	17
Total		1,465	105	1,067	2,532

[a] Two pocket vetoes, overruled in the courts, are counted here as regular vetoes.

Sources: Congressional Quarterly Weekly Report (1989), 7; (1992), 3925–3926; (1994), 3623; (1996), 10, 3386.

Table 6-10   Senate Action on Nominations, 1935–1996

		Senate action			
Congress		Number received	Con- firmed	Withdrawn	Rejected[a]	Unconfirmed
74th	(1935–1936)	22,487	22,286	51	15	135
75th	(1937–1938)	15,330	15,193	20	27	90
76th	(1939–1941)	29,072	28,939	16	21	96
77th	(1941–1942)	24,344	24,137	33	5	169
78th	(1943–1944)	21,775	21,371	31	6	367
79th	(1945–1946)	37,022	36,550	17	3	452
80th	(1947–1948)	66,641	54,796	153	0	11,692
81st	(1949–1951)	87,266	86,562	45	6	653
82d	(1951–1952)	46,920	46,504	45	2	369
83d	(1953–1954)	69,458	68,563	43	0	852
84th	(1955–1956)	84,173	82,694	38	3	1,438
85th	(1957–1958)	104,193	103,311	54	0	828
86th	(1959–1960)	91,476	89,900	30	1	1,545
87th	(1961–1962)	102,849	100,741	1,279	0	829
88th	(1963–1964)	122,190	120,201	36	0	1,953
89th	(1965–1966)	123,019	120,865	173	0	1,981
90th	(1967–1968)	120,231	118,231	34	0	1,966
91st	(1969–1971)	134,464	133,797	487	2	178
92d	(1971–1972)	117,053	114,909	11	0	2,133
93d	(1973–1974)[b]	134,384	131,254	15	0	3,069
94th	(1975–1976)	132,151	131,378	6	0	3,801
95th	(1977–1978)	137,504	124,730	66	0	12,713
96th	(1979–1980)	154,797	154,665	18	0	1,458
97th	(1981–1982)	186,264	184,844	55	7	1,346
98th	(1983–1984)	97,893	97,262	4	0	610
99th	(1985–1986)	99,614	95,811	16	0	3,787
100th	(1987–1988)	89,193	88,721	23	1	5,922
101st	(1989–1990)	93,368	88,078	48	1	7,951
102d	(1991–1992)	76,446	75,349	24	0	756
103d	(1993–1994)	77,384	76,122	1,080	0	2,741
104th	(1995–1996)	74,490	73,711	22	0	8,472

Note: Data for earlier years can be found in previous editions of *Vital Statistics on American Politics*.

[a] Includes only those nominations rejected outright by a vote of the Senate. Most nominations that fail to win approval of the Senate are unfavorably reported by committees and never reach the Senate floor, having been withdrawn. In some cases, the full Senate may vote to recommit a nomination to committee, in effect killing it.

[b] Forty-six nominations were returned to the president during the October–November 1974 recess in accordance with Senate Rule 38, which states: "[I]f the Senate shall adjourn or take a recess for more than thirty days, all nominations pending and not finally acted upon at the time of taking such adjournment or recess shall be returned by the Secretary to the President, and shall not again be considered unless they shall again be made to the Senate by the President."

Sources: 1929–1980: *Congressional Quarterly's Guide to Congress*, 3d ed. (Washington, D.C.: Congressional Quarterly, 1982), 195; 1981–1992: *Congressional Record* (daily ed.), Daily Digest, "Resume of Congressional Activity," 97th Cong. (1st sess., D1613; 2d sess., D1499); 98th Cong. (2d sess., D1348); 99th Cong. (1st sess., D1565; 2d sess., D1343); 100th Cong. (2d sess., D1400); 101st Cong. (1st sess., D1431; 2d sess., D1449); 102d Cong. (2d sess., D1336); 103d Cong. (2d sess., D1276); 104th Cong. (2d sess., D2).

Table 6-11   Senate Rejections of Cabinet Nominations

Nominee	Position	President	Date	Vote
Roger B. Taney	secretary of treasury	Jackson	6/23/1834	18–28
Caleb Cushing	secretary of treasury	Tyler	3/3/1843	19–27
Caleb Cushing	secretary of treasury	Tyler	3/3/1843	10–27
Caleb Cushing	secretary of treasury	Tyler	3/3/1843	2–29
David Henshaw	secretary of navy	Tyler	1/15/1844	6–34
James M. Porter	secretary of war	Tyler	1/30/1844	3–38
James S. Green	secretary of treasury	Tyler	6/15/1844	[a]
Henry Stanbery	attorney general	A. Johnson	6/2/1868	11–29
Charles B. Warren	attorney general	Coolidge	3/10/1925	39–41
Charles B. Warren	attorney general	Coolidge	3/16/1925	39–46
Lewis L. Strauss	secretary of commerce	Eisenhower	6/19/1959	46–49
John Tower	secretary of defense	Bush	3/9/1989	47–53

[a] Not recorded.

Source: Congressional Quarterly, *Congressional Quarterly's Guide to Congress*, 4th ed. (Washington, D.C.: Congressional Quarterly, 1991), 252.

Table 6-12   Number of Civilian Federal Government Employees and Percentage under Merit Civil Service, 1816–1996

Year	Total number of employees[a]	Percentage under merit	Year	Total number of employees[a]	Percentage under merit
1816	4,837	—	1949	2,102,109	84.3
1821	6,914	—	1950	1,960,708	84.5
1831	11,491	—	1951	2,482,666	86.4
1841	18,038	—	1952	2,600,612	86.4
1851	26,274	—	1953	2,558,416	83.6
1861	36,672	—	1954	2,407,676	82.7
1871	51,020	—	1955	2,397,309	83.6
1881	100,020	—	1956	2,398,736	85.1
1891	157,442	21.5	1957	2,417,565	85.5
1901	239,476	44.3	1958	2,382,491	85.3
1910	388,708	57.2	1959	2,382,807	85.7
1911	395,905	57.5	1960	2,398,704	85.5
1912	400,150	54.3	1961	2,435,804	86.1
1913	396,494	71.3	1962	2,514,197	85.9
1914	401,887	72.8	1963	2,527,960	85.6
1915	395,429	73.9	1964	2,500,503	86.1
1916	399,381	74.3	1965	2,527,915	85.2
1917	438,500	74.5	1966	2,759,019	85.8
1918	854,500	75.2	1967	3,002,461	82.8
1919[b]	794,271	86.6	1968	3,055,212	84.1
1920[c]	655,265	75.9	1969	3,076,414	82.9
1921[c]	561,142	79.9	1970	2,981,574	82.3
1922	543,507	77.4	1971	2,862,894	84.1
1923	536,900	76.6	1972[d]	2,779,261	61.6
1924	543,484	76.5	1973	2,732,377	62.0
1925	553,045	76.6	1974[e]	2,893,118	57.0
1926	548,713	77.0	1975[e]	2,896,944	57.4
1927	547,127	77.3	1976[e]	2,883,134	57.6
1928	560,772	77.0	1977[e]	2,893,334	57.1
1929	579,559	88.2	1978[e]	2,929,100	57.3
1930	601,319	87.9	1979[e]	2,949,630	56.6
1931	609,746	76.8	1980	3,121,769	56.1
1932	605,496	77.2	1981	2,947,428	58.7
1933	603,587	75.6	1982	2,917,095	59.2
1934	698,649	64.5	1983	2,920,514	59.2
1935	780,582	58.3	1984	2,959,317	58.7
1936	867,432	57.5	1985	3,059,987	57.2
1937	895,993	59.4	1986	3,061,210	56.6
1938	882,226	63.8	1987	3,125,635	56.2
1939	953,891	69.5	1988	3,126,171	56.0
1940	1,042,420	69.7	1989[f]	3,151,334	56.2
1941	1,437,682	68.9	1990	3,503,550	50.5
1942	2,296,384	—	1991	3,138,180	56.4
1943	3,299,414	—	1992	3,134,915	56.7
1944	3,332,356	—	1993	3,050,711	56.7
1945	3,816,310	—	1994	2,992,840	55.4
1946	2,696,529	—	1995	2,958,447	54.8
1947	2,111,001	80.2	1996	2,888,623	53.7
1948	2,071,009	82.4			

(Notes continue)

Table 6-12   *(Continued)*

Note: "—" indicates not available. As of June, except where indicated.

[a] Excludes employees of the Central Intelligence Agency and the National Security Agency.
[b] As of November.
[c] As of July.
[d] Under Postal Reorganization Act of 1970, U.S. Postal Service employees were changed from competitive (merit) service to excepted service.
[e] Excludes those employees in temporary and indefinite competitive status. In June 1973, 3.6 percent of federal civilian employees were in such service; in June 1980, 2.9 percent were.
[f] As of May.

Sources: 1816–1970: U.S. Bureau of the Census, *Historical Statistics of the United States* (Washington, D.C.: U.S. Government Printing Office, 1975), 1102–1103; 1971–1996: U.S. Office of Personnel Management, *Federal Civilian Workforce Statistics, Employment and Trends*, bimonthly release.

Table 6-13   Major Regulatory Agencies

Agency	Year established	Agency head		Number of employees[a]
		Number	Title	
Consumer Product Safety Commission	1972	3	commissioner	462
Environmental Protection Agency	1970	1	administrator	17,157
Equal Employment Opportunity Commission	1965	5	commissioner	2,622
Federal Communications Commission	1934	5	commissioner	2,064
Federal Deposit Insurance Corporation	1933	5	board of director	9,207
Federal Energy Regulatory Commission	1977	5	commissioner	1,339
Federal Reserve System	1913	7	governor	1,734
Federal Trade Commission	1914	5	commissioner	950
Food and Drug Administration	1906	1	commissioner	9,381
National Labor Relations Board	1935	5	board of director	1,956
Occupational Safety and Health Administration	1970	1	assistant secretary	2,073
Securities and Exchange Commission	1934	5	commissioner	2,797

Note: The Interstate Commerce Commission, established in 1887, was terminated on December 30, 1995 (*Congressional Quarterly Weekly Report*, January 6, 1996, 58).

[a] As of January 1997.

Sources: Year established, agency head: Congressional Quarterly, *Federal Regulatory Directory* (Washington, D.C.: Congressional Quarterly, 1994), passim; number of employees: U.S. Office of Personnel Management, *Federal Civilian Workforce Statistics, Employment and Trends* (January 1995), and unpublished data from the agencies.

Table 6-14   Number of Pages in the *Federal Register*, 1940–1996

Year	Pages	Year	Pages
1940	5,307	1979	77,497
1945	15,508	1980	87,012
1950	9,562	1981	63,554
1955	10,196	1982	58,493
1960	14,479	1983	57,703
1965	17,206	1984	50,997
1966	16,850	1985	53,479
1967	21,087	1986	47,418
1968	20,068	1987	49,653
1969	20,464	1988	53,375
1970	20,032	1989	53,821
1971	25,442	1990	53,618
1972	28,920	1991	67,716
1973	35,586	1992	62,919
1974	45,422	1993	69,684
1975	60,221	1994	68,107
1976	57,072	1995	67,518
1977	63,629	1996	69,366
1978	61,261		

Source: Compiled from successive volumes of the *Federal Register* (Washington, D.C.: U.S. Government Printing Office).

7

The Judiciary

- **Federal and State Court Structures**
- **Supreme Court Justices**
- **Ratings**
- **Supreme Court Caseloads**
- **Federal Court Judges**
- **Federal Court Caseloads**
- **Laws Overturned**

The judiciary, although one of the three "separate but equal" branches of government, is often considered remote from the political push and pull that characterizes the other two. Preoccupation with process, precedent, and the meaning of the law gives the courts a strikingly different appearance. But grappling with the constitutionality of abortion or the death penalty and pouring practical meaning into ambiguous, generally worded statutes enacted by legislatures put the courts squarely in the midst of the political process.

Even if courts can be considered political, are statistics essential to understanding the courts? They are for two reasons. First, the courts themselves have to deal with statistics. A 1987 Supreme Court decision, for example, considered the question of racially disparate patterns in the imposition of the death penalty—Georgia defendants who killed whites were eleven times as likely to be sentenced to die as those who killed blacks.[1] The Court held that the statistics were not relevant to this particular case. Although the numbers may have been accurate and meaningful, they did not show that there was racial discrimination against the defendant being tried.

This example should not give the impression that courts disdain statistics. In fact, as one federal judge wrote, "In the problem of racial discrimination, statistics often tell much, and Courts listen."[2] Cases often turn on conclusions drawn from numerical data—voting rights (Table 1-30), reapportionment and redistricting (Tables 1-18, 1-29, and 5-1), and school desegregation (Table 10-14) are but three areas in which this is true.

259

Statistics also can promote understanding of the courts. A single case does not lend itself to statistical analysis, but the large number, the hierarchy (Figure 7-1), the geographical spread (Figure 7-2) of the federal courts, and the even greater variety of state courts and appointment methods (Table 7-1) suggest that numerical summarization aids comprehension. In addition, precisely because of the judicial emphasis on precedents, there are perhaps better records of previous activities than in most other areas of government.

The characteristics of those on the federal bench are one area of interest. Although the nature of the courts might suggest that appointments are merely a matter of judicial qualifications, the record indicates otherwise. Federal judicial appointments have always been subject to partisan considerations (Tables 7-2 and 7-6), and other characteristics of federal judges have been shown to vary with the appointing president (Table 7-5). Partisan and ideological differences also explain part of the frustration presidents have encountered with nominations to the Supreme Court (Table 7-4). Nor are more subjective judgments ignored in characterizing court appointees. Just as historians have judged presidents, legal scholars have evaluated Supreme Court justices (Table 7-3).

The growing caseload of the courts has become a major concern in recent years, and, while individual "horror" stories may be more dramatic (when Chief Justice Warren E. Burger retired in 1986 he noted that in a recent week he had worked more than one hundred hours), statistical evidence tells an even more convincing story. The caseload of the courts has indeed climbed dramatically in recent years (Tables 7-7 through 7-10 and Figure 7-3). Cases filed in the district courts rose by 59 percent between 1980 and 1985, while the number of judges rose by only 2 percent (Table 7-9).

There is also considerable information on the nature of judicial work. For example, civil rather than criminal cases account for the increased workload (Table 7-10). One can also see from the distribution of types of cases in the federal courts that a district court judge must be prepared to hear and decide cases on a wide range of topics (Table 7-11). Dramatic changes also have occurred in the kinds of cases courts must deal with and in the ways they have responded. The Supreme Court has struck down more federal, state, and local laws on constitutional grounds in this century than in the nineteenth (Table 7-12). Within this century, however, doctrinal trends have changed. For example, since the 1930s the Court has rejected far fewer economic regulatory laws and has increasingly struck down laws restricting civil liberties (Figure 7-4).

As they are with the executive and the legislature, statistics are a necessary component for understanding the courts and their decisions.

Notes

1. *McCleskey v. Kemp,* 481 U.S. 279.
2. *Alabama v. United States,* 304 F.2d 201 (1961).

Figure 7-1 The United States Federal Court System

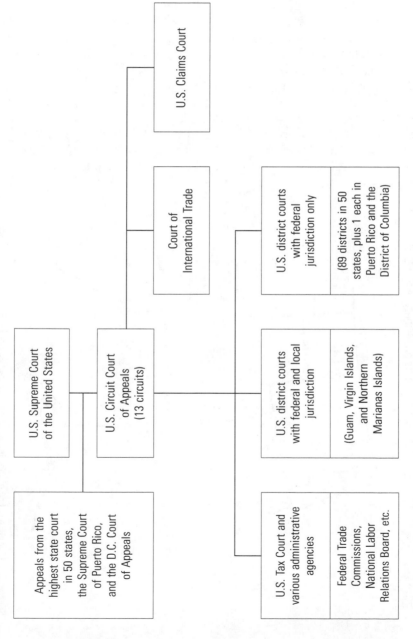

Source: Administrative Office of the United States Courts.

262

Figure 7-2 The Thirteen Federal Judicial Circuits and Ninety-four U.S. District Courts

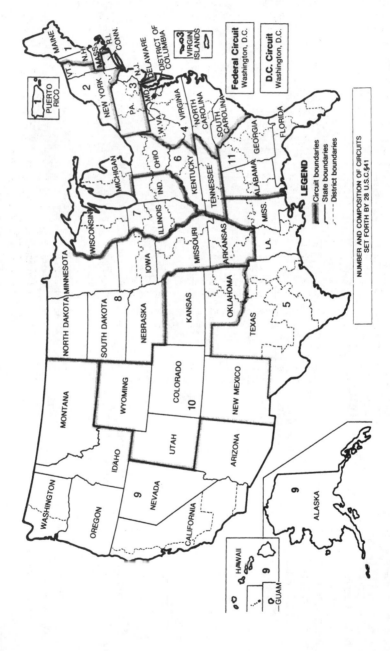

Source: Administrative Office of the United States Courts (January 1983).

Table 7-1   Principal Methods of Judicial Selection for State Courts

Partisan election	Nonpartisan election	Legislative election	Gubernatorial appointment	Merit plan
Alabama[a]	Georgia[a]	Connecticut[a]	California	Alaska[a]
Arkansas	Idaho[a]	Rhode Island[c]	Delaware	Arizona[a]
Illinois[a]	Kentucky	South Carolina[a]	Maine[a]	Colorado[a]
Mississippi[a]	Louisiana	Virginia	Massachusetts	Florida[a,b]
North Carolina[b]	Michigan[a]		New Hampshire	Hawaii
Pennsylvania[a]	Minnesota		New Jersey[a]	Indiana[a]
Tennessee[a,b]	Montana		New York[a,d]	Iowa[a]
Texas[a]	Nevada			Kansas[a]
West Virginia	North Dakota			Maryland
	Ohio[a]			Missouri[a]
	Oregon[a]			Nebraska
	Washington[a]			New Mexico
	Wisconsin[a]			Oklahoma[a,b]
				South Dakota[a]
				Utah
				Vermont
				Wyoming[a]

Note: "Merit plan" typically involves appointment by governor from a list of candidates submitted by an independent or quasi-independent judiciary council or commission.

[a] Minor court judges chosen by other methods.
[b] Most but not all major judicial positions selected this way.
[c] Supreme Court justices only.
[d] Appellate judges only.

Source: Council of State Governments, *Book of the States, 1996–1997* (Lexington, Ky.: Council of State Governments, 1996), 133–135.

Table 7-2 Supreme Court Justices of the United States

Seat number and justice	Party	Home state	Years on Court	Age at nomination	Years of previous judicial experience
Washington appointees					
1 John Jay	Federalist	New York	1789–1795	44	2
2 John Rutledge	Federalist	South Carolina	1789–1791	50	6
3 William Cushing	Federalist	Massachusetts	1789–1810[a]	57	29
4 James Wilson	Federalist	Pennsylvania	1789–1798[a]	47	0
5 John Blair, Jr.	Federalist	Virginia	1789–1796	57	11
6 James Iredell	Federalist	North Carolina	1790–1799[a]	38	0.5
2 Thomas Johnson	Federalist	Maryland	1791–1793	59	1.5
2 William Paterson	Federalist	New Jersey	1793–1806[a]	47	0
1 John Rutledge	Federalist	South Carolina	1795	55	6[b]
5 Samuel Chase	Federalist	Maryland	1796–1811[a]	55	8
1 Oliver Ellsworth	Federalist	Connecticut	1796–1800	51	5
J. Adams appointees					
4 Bushrod Washington	Federalist	Virginia	1798–1829[a]	36	0
6 Alfred Moore	Federalist	North Carolina	1799–1804	44	1
1 John Marshall	Federalist	Virginia	1801–1835[a]	45	3
Jefferson appointees					
6 William Johnson	Jeffersonian	South Carolina	1804–1834[a]	32	6
2 H. Brockholst Livingston	Jeffersonian	New York	1806–1823[a]	49	0
7 Thomas Todd	Jeffersonian	Kentucky	1807–1826[a]	42	6
Madison appointees					
5 Gabriel Duvall	Jeffersonian	Maryland	1811–1835	58	6
3 Joseph Story	Jeffersonian	Massachusetts	1811–1845[a]	32	0
Monroe appointee					
2 Smith Thompson	Jeffersonian	New York	1823–1843[a]	55	16

J. Q. Adams appointee				
7 Robert Trimble	Jeffersonian	Kentucky	1826–1828[a]	11
Jackson appointees				
7 John McLean	Democrat	Ohio	1829–1861[a]	6
4 Henry Baldwin	Democrat	Pennsylvania	1830–1844[a]	0
6 James Wayne	Democrat	Georgia	1835–1867[a]	5
1 Roger B. Taney	Democrat	Maryland	1836–1864[a]	0
5 Philip P. Barbour	Democrat	Virginia	1836–1841[a]	8
Van Buren appointees				
8 John Catron	Democrat	Tennessee	1837–1865[a]	10
9 John McKinley	Democrat	Alabama	1837–1852[a]	0
5 Peter V. Daniel	Democrat	Virginia	1841–1860[a]	0
Tyler appointee				
2 Samuel Nelson	Democrat	New York	1845–1872	22
Polk appointees				
3 Levi Woodbury	Democrat	New Hampshire	1845–1851[a]	6
4 Robert C. Grier	Democrat	Pennsylvania	1846–1870	13
Fillmore appointee				
3 Benjamin R. Curtis	Whig	Massachusetts	1851–1857	0
Pierce appointee				
9 John A. Campbell	Democrat	Alabama	1853–1861	0
Buchanan appointee				
3 Nathan Clifford	Democrat	Maine	1858–1881[a]	0
Lincoln appointees				
7 Noah H. Swayne	Republican	Ohio	1862–1881	0
5 Samuel F. Miller	Republican	Iowa	1862–1890[a]	0
9 David Davis	Republican	Illinois	1862–1877	14

(Table continues)

Table 7-2 (Continued)

Seat number and justice	Party	Home state	Years on Court	Age at nomination	Years of previous judicial experience
10 Stephen J. Field	Democrat	California	1863–1897	46	6
1 Salmon P. Chase	Republican	Ohio	1864–1873[a]	56	0
Grant appointees					
4 William Strong	Republican	Pennsylvania	1870–1880	61	11
6 Joseph P. Bradley	Republican	New Jersey	1870–1892[a]	56	0
2 Ward Hunt	Republican	New York	1873–1882	62	8
1 Morrison R. Waite	Republican	Ohio	1874–1888[a]	57	0
Hayes appointees					
9 John M. Harlan	Republican	Kentucky	1877–1911[a]	44	1
4 William B. Woods	Republican	Georgia	1880–1887[a]	56	12
Garfield appointee					
7 Stanley Matthews	Republican	Ohio	1881–1889[a]	56	4
Arthur appointees					
3 Horace Gray	Republican	Massachusetts	1881–1902	53	18
2 Samuel Blatchford	Republican	New York	1882–1893[a]	62	15
Cleveland appointees (first term)					
4 Lucius Q. C. Lamar	Democrat	Mississippi	1883–1893[a]	62	0
1 Melville W. Fuller	Democrat	Illinois	1888–1910[a]	55	0
Harrison appointees					
7 David J. Brewer	Republican	Kansas	1889–1910[a]	52	19
5 Henry B. Brown	Republican	Michigan	1891–1906	54	16
6 George Shiras, Jr.	Republican	Pennsylvania	1892–1903	60	0
4 Howell E. Jackson	Democrat	Tennessee	1893–1895[a]	60	7

	Party	State	Years		
Cleveland appointees (second term)					
2 Edward D. White	Democrat	Louisiana	1894–1910[a]	48	1.5
4 Rufus W. Peckham	Democrat	New York	1895–1909[a]	57	9
McKinley appointee					
8 Joseph McKenna	Republican	California	1898–1925	54	5
T. Roosevelt appointees					
3 Oliver W. Holmes	Republican	Massachusetts	1902–1932	61	20
6 William R. Day	Republican	Ohio	1903–1922	53	7
5 William H. Moody	Republican	Massachusetts	1906–1910	52	0
Taft appointees					
4 Horace H. Lurton	Democrat	Tennessee	1909–1914[a]	65	26
7 Charles E. Hughes	Republican	New York	1910–1916	48	0
1 Edward D. White	Democrat	Louisiana	1910–1921[a]	65	1.5[b]
2 Willis Van Devanter	Republican	Wyoming	1910–1937	51	8
5 Joseph R. Lamar	Democrat	Georgia	1910–1916[a]	53	2
9 Mahlon Pitney	Republican	New Jersey	1912–1922	54	11
Wilson appointees					
4 James C. McReynolds	Democrat	Tennessee	1914–1941	52	0
5 Louis D. Brandeis	Republican	Massachusetts	1916–1939	59	0
7 John H. Clarke	Democrat	Ohio	1916–1922	59	2
Harding appointees					
1 William H. Taft	Republican	Ohio	1921–1930	63	13
7 George Sutherland	Republican	Utah	1922–1938	60	0
6 Pierce Butler	Democrat	Minnesota	1923–1939[a]	56	0
9 Edward T. Sanford	Republican	Tennessee	1923–1930[a]	57	14
Coolidge appointee					
8 Harlan Fiske Stone	Republican	New York	1925–1941	52	0

(Table continues)

Table 7-2 *(Continued)*

Seat number and justice	Party	Home state	Years on Court	Age at nomination	Years of previous judicial experience
Hoover appointees					
1 Charles E. Hughes	Republican	New York	1930–1941	67	0
9 Owens J. Roberts	Republican	Pennsylvania	1930–1945	55	0
3 Benjamin N. Cardozo	Democrat	New York	1932–1938[a]	61	18
F. Roosevelt appointees					
2 Hugo L. Black	Democrat	Alabama	1937–1971[a]	51	1.5
7 Stanley F. Reed	Democrat	Kentucky	1938–1957	53	0
3 Felix Frankfurter	Independent	Massachusetts	1939–1962	56	0
5 William O. Douglas	Democrat	Connecticut	1939–1975	40	0
6 Frank Murphy	Democrat	Michigan	1940–1949[a]	49	7
4 James F. Byrnes	Democrat	South Carolina	1941–1942	62	0[b]
1 Harlan Fiske Stone	Republican	New York	1941–1946[a]	68	0[b]
8 Robert H. Jackson	Democrat	New York	1941–1954[a]	49	0
4 Wiley B. Rutledge	Democrat	Iowa	1943–1949[a]	48	4
Truman appointees					
9 Harold H. Burton	Republican	Ohio	1945–1958	57	0
1 Fred M. Vinson	Democrat	Kentucky	1946–1953[a]	56	5
6 Tom C. Clark	Democrat	Texas	1949–1967	49	0
4 Sherman Minton	Democrat	Indiana	1949–1956	58	8
Eisenhower appointees					
1 Earl Warren	Republican	California	1953–1969	62	0
8 John M. Harlan	Republican	New York	1955–1971	55	1
4 William J. Brennan	Democrat	New Jersey	1956–1990	50	7
7 Charles E. Whittaker	Republican	Missouri	1957–1962	56	3
9 Potter Stewart	Republican	Ohio	1958–1981	43	4

	Party	State		Age	Previous judicial experience (years)
Kennedy appointees					
7 Byron R. White	Democrat	Colorado	1962–1993	44	0
3 Arthur J. Goldberg	Democrat	Illinois	1962–1965	54	0
L. Johnson appointees					
3 Abe Fortas	Democrat	Tennessee	1965–1969	55	0
6 Thurgood Marshall	Democrat	New York	1967–1991	59	4
Nixon appointees					
1 Warren E. Burger	Republican	Minnesota	1969–1986	61	13
3 Harry A. Blackmun	Republican	Minnesota	1970–1994	61	11
2 Lewis F. Powell, Jr.	Democrat	Virginia	1971–1987	64	0
8 William H. Rehnquist	Republican	Arizona	1971–1986	47	0
Ford appointee					
5 John Paul Stevens	Republican	Illinois	1976–	55	5
Reagan appointees					
9 Sandra Day O'Connor	Republican	Arizona	1981–	51	6.5
1 William H. Rehnquist	Republican	Arizona	1986–	61	0[b]
8 Antonin Scalia	Republican	Illinois	1986–	50	4
2 Anthony Kennedy	Republican	California	1988–	51	12
Bush appointees					
4 David H. Souter	Republican	New Hampshire	1990–	50	13
6 Clarence Thomas	Republican	Georgia	1991–	43	1
Clinton appointees					
7 Ruth Bader Ginsburg	Democrat	New York	1993–	60	13
3 Stephen B. Breyer	Democrat	Massachusetts	1994–	55	15

Note: Seat number 1 is always held by the chief justice of the United States.

[a] Died in office.
[b] Prior to appointment to associate justice.

Sources: Sheldon Goldman, *Constitutional Law: Cases and Essays* (New York: Harper and Row, 1987); previous judicial experience: Abraham, *Justices and Presidents*, 56–58 (copyright © Henry J. Abraham, 1974, 1985, reprinted by permission of Oxford University Press, Inc.); *Congressional Quarterly's Guide to Congress*, 786–788; updated by the editors.

Table 7-3 Ratings of Supreme Court Justices

Great	Near great	Average			Below average	Failure
J. Marshall	W. Johnson	Jay	McKinley	Shiras	T. Johnson	Van Devanter
Story	Curtis	J. Rutledge	Daniel	Peckham	Moore	McReynolds
Taney	Miller	Cushing	Nelson	McKenna	Trimble	Butler
Harlan I	Field	Wilson	Woodbury	Day	Barbour	Byrnes
Holmes	Bradley	Blair	Grier	Moody	Woods	Burton
Hughes	Waite	Iredell	Campbell	Lurton	H. E. Jackson	Vinson
Brandeis	E. D. White	Paterson	Clifford	J. R. Lamar		Minton
Stone	Taft	S. Chase	Swayne	Pitney		Whittaker
Cardozo	Sutherland	Ellsworth	Davis	J. H. Clarke		
Black	Douglas	Washington	S. P. Chase	Sanford		
Frankfurter	R. H. Jackson	Livingston	Strong	Roberts		
Warren	W. B. Rutledge	Todd	Hunt	Reed		
		Harlan II	Duvall	Matthews		
		Brennan	Thompson	Gray		
		Fortas	McLean	Blatchford		
		Murphy	Brewer	Baldwin		
		T. C. Clark	B. R. White	Wayne		
		Stewart	Goldberg	Catron		
		L. Q. C. Lamar	T. Marshall	Brown		
		Fuller				

Note: Ratings reflect evaluations made in June 1970 by sixty-five law school deans and professors of law, history, and political science with expertise in the judicial process.

Source: Albert P. Blaustein and Roy M. Mersky, *The First One Hundred Justices: Statistical Studies on the Supreme Court of the United States* (Hamden, Conn.: Shoe String Press, Archon Books, 1978), 37–40.

Table 7-4   Supreme Court Nominations That Failed

Nominee	Date of nomination	President	Action
William Paterson	1793	Washington	withdrawn
John Rutledge	1795	Washington	rejected, 10–14
Alexander Wolcott	1811	Madison	rejected, 9–24
John Crittenden	1828	J. Q. Adams	postponed
Roger B. Taney	1835	Jackson	postponed
John Spencer	1844	Tyler	rejected, 21–26
R. Walworth	1844	Tyler	withdrawn
Edward King	1844	Tyler	postponed
Edward King	1844	Tyler	withdrawn
John Read	1845	Tyler	not acted on
G. Woodward	1845	Polk	rejected, 20–29
Edward Bradford	1852	Fillmore	not acted on
George Badger	1853	Fillmore	postponed
William Micou	1853	Fillmore	not acted on
Jeremiah Black	1861	Buchanan	rejected, 25–26
Henry Stanbery	1866	A. Johnson	not acted on
Ebenezer Hoar	1869	Grant	rejected, 24–33
George Williams	1873	Grant	withdrawn
Caleb Cushing	1874	Grant	withdrawn
Stanley Matthews	1881	Hayes	not acted on
W. B. Hornblower	1893	Cleveland	rejected, 24–30
Wheeler H. Peckham	1894	Cleveland	rejected, 32–41
John J. Parker	1930	Hoover	rejected, 39–41
Abe Fortas[a]	1968	L. Johnson	withdrawn
Homer Thornberry	1968	L. Johnson	not acted on
C. Haynsworth	1969	Nixon	rejected, 45–55
G. H. Carswell	1970	Nixon	rejected, 45–51
Robert Bork	1987	Reagan	rejected, 42–58
Douglas Ginsburg	1987	Reagan	not submitted[b]

Note: Twenty-nine of the 145 presidential nominations have failed to obtain Senate confirmation. However, five nominees declined appointment after having been nominated (Harrison, 1789; W. Cushing, 1796; Jay, 1800; Lincoln, 1811; Adams, 1811) and two withdrew after being confirmed (W. Smith, 1837; Conkling, 1882).

[a] In 1968, Fortas, an associate justice, was nominated for chief justice.
[b] Publicly announced but withdrawn before the president formally submitted his nomination to the Senate.

Source: Congressional Quarterly's Guide to the U.S. Supreme Court, 2d ed. (Washington, D.C.: Congressional Quarterly, 1990), 652; updated by the editors.

Table 7-5 Characteristics of Federal District and Appellate Court Appointees, Presidents Johnson to Clinton (percent)

	Johnson appointees	Nixon appointees	Ford appointees	Carter appointees	Reagan appointees	Bush appointees	Clinton appointees
District courts							
Occupation							
Politics/government	21.3	10.6	21.2	5.0	13.4	10.8	10.7
Judiciary	31.1	28.5	34.6	44.6	36.9	41.9	44.4
Large law firm	2.5	11.2	9.6	13.9	17.9	25.7	17.2
Moderate firm	18.9	27.9	25.0	19.8	19.0	14.9	16.6
Small/solo firm	23.0	19.0	9.6	13.4	10.0	4.7	7.7
Other	3.3	2.8	0.0	3.5	2.8	2.0	3.6
Experience							
Judicial	34.4	35.2	42.3	54.0	46.2	46.6	49.7
Prosecutorial	45.9	41.9	50.0	38.1	44.1	39.2	37.9
Neither	33.6	36.3	30.8	30.7	28.6	31.8	31.4
Political affiliation							
Democrat	94.3	7.3	21.2	90.6	4.8	5.4	90.5
Republican	5.7	92.7	78.8	4.5	91.7	88.5	2.4
Independent or other	0.0	0.0	0.0	5.0	3.4	6.1	7.1
Past party activism	49.2	48.6	50.0	60.9	59.0	60.8	53.9
Religion							
Protestant	58.2	73.2	73.1	60.4	60.3	64.2	—
Catholic	31.1	18.4	17.3	27.7	30.0	28.4	—
Jewish	10.7	8.4	9.6	11.9	9.3	7.4	—
Race/ethnicity							
White	93.4	95.5	88.5	78.7	92.4	89.2	72.2
Black	4.1	3.4	5.8	13.9	2.1	6.8	19.5
Asian-American	0.0	0.0	3.9	0.5	0.7	0.0	1.2
Hispanic	2.5	1.1	1.9	6.9	4.8	4.0	6.5
Sex							
Female	1.6	0.6	1.9	14.4	8.3	19.6	30.2
Number of appointees	122.0	179.0	52.0	202.0	290.0	148.0	169.0

Courts of Appeals

Occupation						
Politics/government	10.0	8.3	5.4	6.4	10.8	3.4
Judiciary	57.5	75.0	46.4	55.1	59.5	58.6
Large law firm[a]	5.0	8.3	10.7	14.1	16.2	17.2
Moderate firm[a]	17.5	8.3	16.1	9.0	10.8	10.3
Small/solo firm[a]	7.5	0.0	5.4	1.3	0.0	0.0
Other	2.5	0.0	16.1	14.1	2.7	10.3
Experience						
Judicial	65.0	75.0	53.6	60.3	62.2	69.0
Prosecutorial	47.5	25.0	32.1	28.2	29.7	37.9
Neither	20.0	25.0	39.3	34.6	32.4	20.7
Political affiliation						
Democrat	95.0	8.3	82.1	0.0	5.4	86.2
Republican	5.0	91.7	7.1	96.2	89.2	3.4
Independent or other	0.0	0.0	10.7	1.3	5.4	10.3
Past party activism	57.5	58.3	73.2	65.4	70.3	48.3
Religion						
Protestant	60.0	58.3	60.7	55.1	59.4	—
Catholic	25.0	33.3	23.2	30.8	24.3	—
Jewish	15.0	8.3	16.1	14.1	16.3	—
Race/ethnicity						
White	95.0	100.0	78.6	97.4	89.2	72.4
Black	5.0	0.0	16.1	1.3	5.4	13.8
Asian-American	0.0	0.0	1.8	0.0	0.0	3.4
Hispanic	0.0	0.0	3.6	1.3	5.4	10.3
Sex						
Female	2.5	0.0	19.6	5.1	18.9	31.0
Number of appointees	40.0	12.0	56.0	78.0	37.0	29.0

Note: "—" indicates not available.

[a] Large law firm: twenty-five or more partners and associates; moderate: five to twenty-four; small: two to four.

Source: Sheldon Goldman, "Bush's Judicial Legacy: The Final Imprint," *Judicature* 76 (April–May 1993), 287, 293; Sheldon Goldman and Elliot Slotnick, "Clinton's First Term Judiciary: Many Bridges to Cross," *Judicature* 80 (May–June 1997), 261, 269.

Table 7-6   Federal Judicial Appointments of Same Party as President, Presidents Cleveland to Clinton

President	Party	Percentage
Cleveland	Democrat	97.3
Harrison	Republican	87.9
McKinley	Republican	95.7
T. Roosevelt	Republican	95.8
Taft	Republican	82.2
Wilson	Democrat	98.6
Harding	Republican	97.7
Coolidge	Republican	94.1
Hoover	Republican	85.7
F. Roosevelt	Democrat	96.4
Truman	Democrat	93.1
Eisenhower	Republican	95.1
Kennedy	Democrat	90.9
Johnson	Democrat	94.5
Nixon	Republican	92.8
Ford	Republican	81.2
Carter	Democrat	88.8
Reagan	Republican	92.7
Bush	Republican	88.6
Clinton	Democrat	89.9

Source: Cleveland–Kennedy: Henry J. Abraham, *Justices and Presidents: Appointments to the Supreme Court,* 3d ed. (New York: Oxford University Press, 1991), 68 (copyright © Henry J. Abraham, 1974, 1985, 1991, reprinted by permission of Oxford University Press, Inc.); Johnson–Clinton: calculated from Table 7-5, this volume.

Figure 7-3   Cases Filed in the U.S. Supreme Court, 1938–1995

Number of cases

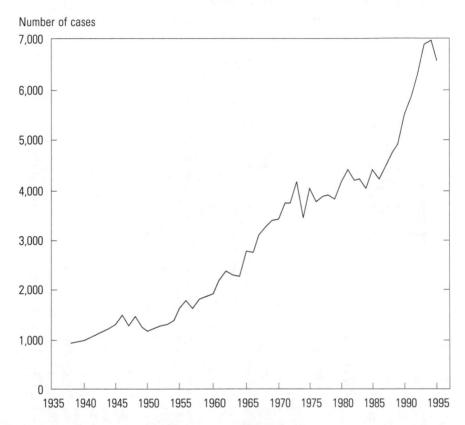

Sources: 1938–1969: successive volumes of *Statistical Abstract of the United States;* 1970–1983: Office of the Clerk of the Supreme Court; 1984–1995; reprinted with permission from *The United States Law Week,* vol. 56, 3102, vol. 59, 3064, vol. 61, 3098, vol. 63, 3134, vol. 65, 3100 (copyright © by the Bureau of National Affairs).

Table 7-7 Caseload of the U.S. Supreme Court, 1970–1995

Action	1970	1975	1980	1983	1984	1985	1986	1987	1988	1989	1990	1991	1992	1993	1994	1995
Appellate cases on docket	1,903	2,352	2,749	2,688	2,575	2,571	2,547	2,577	2,587	2,416	2,351	2,451	2,441	2,442	2,515	2,456
From prior term	325	431	527	520	539	400	476	440	466	384	365	365	379	342	377	361
Docketed during present term	1,578	1,921	2,222	2,168	2,036	2,171	2,071	2,137	2,141	2,032	1,986	2,086	2,062	2,100	2,138	2,095
Cases acted upon[a]	1,613	1,900	2,324	2,220	2,253	2,185	2,189	2,224	2,271	2,096	2,042	2,125	2,140	2,099	2,185	2,130
Granted review	214	244	167	140	167	166	152	157	130	103	114	103	83	78	83	92
Denied, dismissed, or withdrawn	1,285	1,538	1,999	1,902	1,953	1,863	1,876	1,919	1,973	1,881	1,802	1,914	1,920	1,947	2,016	1,945
Summarily decided	114	118	90	71	59	78	71	66	75	44	81	52	84	34	52	62
Cases not acted upon	290	452	425	468	322	386	358	353	316	320	309	326	301	343	330	326
Pauper cases on docket	2,289	2,395	2,371	2,394	2,416	2,577	2,564	2,675	3,056	3,316	3,951	4,307	4,792	5,332	5,574	5,098
Cases acted upon[a]	1,802	1,997	2,027	1,992	2,067	2,189	2,250	2,263	2,638	2,891	3,436	3,768	4,261	4,621	4,983	4,514
Granted review	41	28	17	9	18	20	15	23	17	19	27	17	14	21	10	13
Denied, dismissed, or withdrawn	1,683	1,903	1,968	1,968	2,050	2,136	2,186	2,210	2,577	2,824	3,369	3,716	4,209	4,566	4,955	4,439
Summarily decided	78	66	32	10	14	24	38	21	32	35	28	22	25	30	14	55
Cases not acted upon	487	398	344	402	329	388	314	412	418	425	515	539	531	711	591	584
Original cases on docket	20	14	24	18	15	10	12	16	14	14	14	12	12	12	11	11
Cases disposed of during term	7	7	7	7	8	2	1	5	2	2	3	1	1	1	2	5
Total cases available for argument	267	280	264	269	271	276	270	280	254	204	201	196	166	145	136	145
Cases disposed of	160	181	162	189	184	175	179	175	173	147	131	130	120	105	97	93
Cases argued	151	179	154	184	175	171	175	167	170	146	125	127	116	99	94	90
Cases dismissed or remanded without argument	9	2	8	5	9	4	4	8	3	1	6	3	4	6	3	3
Cases remaining	107	99	102	80	87	101	91	105	81	57	70	66	46	40	39	52
Cases decided by signed opinion	126	160	144	174	159	161	164	151	156	143	121	120	111	93	91	87

277

Cases decided per curiam opinion	22	16	8	6	11	10	10	9	12	3	4	3	4	6	3	3
Number of signed opinions	109	138	123	151	139	146	145	139	133	129	112	107	107	84	82	75
Total cases on docket	4,212	4,761	5,144	5,100	5,006	5,158	5,123	5,268	5,657	5,746	6,316	6,770	7,245	7,786	8,100	7,565

Note: The Supreme Court begins its regular annual session on the first Monday in October. This session, known as the October term, lasts about nine months. The year shown indicates when the term began.

[a] For 1980–1995, includes cases granted review and carried over to next term, not shown separately.

Sources: 1970–1983: U.S. Bureau of the Census, *Statistical Abstract of the United States, 1977* (Washington, D.C.: U.S. Government Printing Office, 1976), 184; *1987*, 168; 1984–1995: reprinted with permission from *The United States Law Week* (Washington, D.C.: The Bureau of National Affairs), vol. 56, 3102; vol. 59, 3064; vol. 61, 3098; vol. 63, 3134; vol. 65, 3100 (copyright © by The Bureau of National Affairs, Inc.).

Table 7-8 Caseloads of U.S. Courts of Appeals, 1980–1996

	1980	1985	1989	1990	1991	1992	1993	1994	1995	1996
Number of judgeships	132	156	156	156	167	167	167	167	167	167
Number of sitting senior judges	42	45	54	60	65	66	70	73	80	78
Number of vacant judgeship months	217.1	275.0	92.7	153.3	216.2	237.8	213.4	238.9	185.5	154.8
Appeals filed										
Prisoner	3,704	6,532	9,620	10,019	10,932	11,847	12,795	13,061	14,985	16,996
All other civil	12,141	18,660	19,089	18,631	18,987	20,716	21,639	21,218	21,630	21,279
Criminal	4,405	4,989	8,403	9,655	10,249	11,215	11,862	10,674	10,162	10,889
Administrative	2,950	3,179	2,788	2,553	2,859	3,235	3,928	3,369	3,295	2,827
Total	23,200	33,360	39,900	40,858	43,027	47,013	50,224	48,322	50,072	51,991
Appeals terminated										
Consolidations and cross appeals	2,704	2,669	2,910	3,839	3,757	4,007	3,607	3,816	3,177	2,998
Procedural	6,170	12,349	14,483	14,008	14,862	16,769	18,422	18,149	18,856	20,089
On the merits										
Prisoner	2,267	2,835	4,585	4,988	5,584	5,509	6,157	6,634	7,242	7,521
Other civil	5,861	9,208	10,065	9,563	9,756	9,942	10,087	10,987	11,293	11,292
Criminal	2,718	3,070	4,154	5,223	6,393	6,777	7,791	7,932	7,652	6,949
Administrative	1,167	1,256	1,312	1,169	1,288	1,369	1,726	1,666	1,585	1,564
Total on the merits	12,013	16,369	20,116	20,943	23,021	23,597	25,761	27,219	27,772	27,326
Total	20,887	31,387	37,509	38,790	41,640	44,373	47,790	49,184	49,805	50,413
Pending appeals	20,252	24,758	30,614	32,299	33,455	36,068	38,233	37,294	37,536	38,888
Per active judge[a]										
Termination on the merits	227	308	356	367	391	399	428	459	449	435
Procedural terminations	—	103	106	99	93	103	109	113	105	109

Note: "__" indicates not available. Data for other years can be found in previous editions of *Vital Statistics on American Politics.*

[a] Includes only judges active during the entire twelve-month period.

Sources: Director of the Administrative Office of the United States Courts, *Federal Court Management Statistics 1985* (Washington, D.C.: U.S. Government Printing Office, 1985), 29–30; *1991,* 27–31; *1992,* 29–30; *1990; 1993; 1995; 1996.*

Table 7-9 Caseloads of U.S. District Courts, 1980–1996

	1980	1985	1989	1990	1991	1992	1993	1994	1995	1996
Overall										
Filings	188,487	299,164	257,259	251,166	241,420	265,612	264,038	267,799	281,681	304,535
Terminations	180,245	293,545	255,473	245,014	240,952	263,034	259,238	258,712	259,336	283,383
Pending	199,019	272,636	267,440	273,301	274,010	262,805	252,697	257,183	268,197	279,781
Number (and percentage) of civil										
cases over three years old	20,592	16,726	23,137	25,672	28,421	17,249	18,451	14,086	13,538	16,152
	(11.7)	(6.6)	(9.7)	(10.6)	(11.8)	(7.7)	(8.3)	(6.2)	(5.6)	(6.4)
Number of judgeships	516	575	575	575	649	649	649	649	649	647
Vacant judgeship months	956.2	895.8	374.1	540.1	988.7	1,313.4	1,199.6	1,104.3	642.0	571.7
Per judgeship										
Civil filings	327	476	393	381	320	355	354	364	383	416
Criminal felony filings	38	44	54	56	52	54	53	49	51	55
Total filings	365	520	447	437	372	409	407	413	434	471
Pending cases	386	474	465	475	422	405	389	396	413	432
Terminations	349	511	444	426	371	405	399	399	400	438
Trials completed	38	36	35	35	31	32	30	27	27	27
Median time from filing to disposition (months)										
Criminal felony	3.7	3.7	5.2	5.4	5.7	5.9	6.3	6.5	6.6	6.8
Civil	8	7	9	9	9	9	8	8	8	7
Median time from issue to trial (months)										
Civil only[a]	15	14	13	14	15	15	16	18	18	18

Note: Data for other years can be found in previous editions of *Vital Statistics on American Politics.*

[a] Time is computed from the date that the answer or response is filed to the date trial begins.

Sources: Director of the Administrative Office of the United States Courts, *Federal Court Management Statistics 1985* (Washington, D.C.: U.S. Government Printing Office, 1985), *1993, 1995, 1996.*

Table 7-10   Number of Civil and Criminal Cases Filed in U.S. District
Courts, 1950–1996

	Civil cases		Criminal cases	
Year	Commenced	Terminated	Commenced	Terminated
1950	44,454	42,482	36,383	37,675
1955	48,308	47,959	35,310	38,990
1960	49,852	48,847	28,137	30,512
1965	67,678	63,137	31,569	33,718
1970	87,321	79,466	38,102	36,356
1975	117,320	103,787	41,108	49,212
1980	168,789	160,481	28,932	29,297
1981	180,576	177,975	31,328	30,221
1982	206,193	189,473	32,682	31,889
1983	241,842	215,356	35,913	33,985
1984	261,485	243,113	36,845	35,494
1985	273,670	269,848	39,500	37,139
1986	254,828	266,765	41,490	39,328
1987	239,185	238,001	43,292	42,287
1988	239,634	238,753	44,585	42,115
1989	233,529	235,219	45,995	42,810
1990	217,879	213,922	48,904	44,295
1991	207,742	211,713	47,035	41,569
1992	230,509	231,304	48,356	44,147
1993	230,597	227,316	46,098	45,280
1994	238,590	227,015	45,269	44,924
1995	248,335	229,820	45,788	41,527
1996	269,132	250,387	47,889	45,499

Note: Data are for the twelve-month period ending on June 30 of the year shown.

Sources: 1950–1975: *Statistical Abstract of the United* States, *1971* (Washington, D.C.: U.S. Government Printing Office, 1971), 152, *1976,* 168; 1980–1996: Director of the Administrative Office of the United States Courts, *Annual Report of the Director of the Administrative Office of the United States Courts* (Washington, D.C.: U.S. Government Printing Office, 1987), 7, 13; (1989), 7, 12; (1991), 7, 10; (1992) 4, 6; (1994), (1996).

Table 7-11 Types of Civil and Criminal Cases in U.S. District Courts, 1996

Civil cases	Percentage	Criminal cases	Percentage
Contract actions	13.3	Embezzlement	2.7
Recovery of overpayments		Fraud	16.2
and enforcement of		Drunk driving and traffic	10.7
judgments	(1.9)	Narcotics	25.6
Other contract actions	(11.4)	Larceny and theft	7.8
Tort actions	22.2	Homicide, robbery, assault,	
Product liability		and burglary	4.9
personal injury	(10.2)	Forgery and counterfeiting	2.1
Other personal injury	(10.4)	Weapons and firearms	6.7
Personal property damage	(1.5)	Immigration	11.7
Statutory actions	62.2	Escape	1.5
Prisoner petitions	(25.4)	Auto theft	0.5
Civil rights	(15.6)	All other	9.6
Social security	(3.5)		
Labor laws	(5.6)	Total number of	
Tax suits	(0.8)	criminal cases	47,146
Bankruptcy	(1.7)		
Other statutory	(9.6)		
Real property actions	2.3		
Total number of			
civil cases	269,132		

Note: Data are for the twelve-month period ending on September 30, 1996. Data for earlier years can be found in previous editions of *Vital Statistics on American Politics.*

Source: Director of the Administrative Office of the United States Courts, *Annual Report of the Director of the Administrative Office of the United States Courts* (Washington, D.C.: Government Printing Office, 1996).

Table 7-12 Federal, State, and Local Laws Declared Unconstitutional by the Supreme Court, by Decade, 1789–1996

Years	Federal	State and local
1789–1799	0	0
1800–1809	1	1
1810–1819	0	7
1820–1829	0	8
1830–1839	0	3
1840–1849	0	9
1850–1859	1	7
1860–1869	4	23
1870–1879	7	36
1880–1889	4	46
1890–1899	5	36
1900–1909	9	40
1910–1919	6	118
1920–1929	15	139
1930–1939	13	93
1940–1949	2	58
1950–1959	5	60
1960–1969	16	149
1970–1979	20	193
1980–1989	16	162
1990–1996	10	45
Total	134	1,233

Sources: Lawrence Baum, *The Supreme Court,* 4th ed. (Washington, D.C.: CQ Press, 1992), 188, 190; Lawrence Baum, personal communication.

Figure 7-4   Economic and Civil Liberties Laws Overturned by the Supreme Court by Decade, 1900–1996

Number of laws

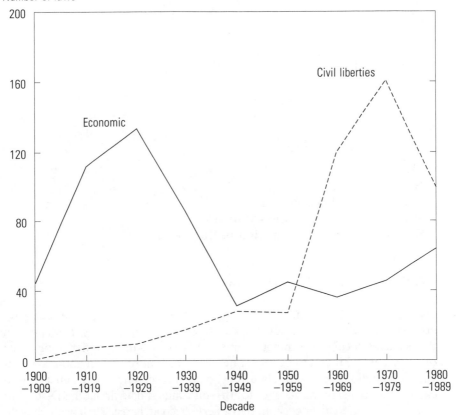

Note: Civil liberties category does not include laws supportive of civil liberties. Laws include federal, state, and local. From 1990–1996, twenty-one economic and thirty civil liberties laws were overturned.

Sources: Lawrence Baum, *The Supreme Court,* 4th ed. (Washington, D.C.: CQ Press, 1992), 197; Lawrence Baum, personal communication.

8

Federalism

- **Historical Data**
- **State Constitutional Provisions**
- **States and the Federal Constitution**
- **State and Local Governments and Employees**
- **Taxes**
- **Spending**
- **Intergovernmental Revenue Flows**

From a statistical point of view, a major problem in studying American government below the federal level is that there are fifty state governments and thousands of local governmental units (Table 8-9). Among other things, this often makes it difficult to get accurate, up-to-date information about all relevant jurisdictions. Even for state-level data, a researcher often must turn to each of the fifty state capitals, or to fifty-one units if data about the District of Columbia are needed, or even more if Puerto Rico and areas such as the Northern Marianas Islands are included, as might be necessary for studying delegates to the national party conventions. If the researcher's interest is in counties, cities, school districts, and the like, the data collection task can be enormous—well beyond the capacity of one person.

Fortunately, organizations and publications devoted to data collection have stepped to the fore. Some, such as the Council of State Governments and the International City Management Association, are well established. The former has published the *Book of the States* since 1935, and the latter the *Municipal Year Book* since 1934. Other sources are newer, such as Congressional Quarterly's magazine *Governing,* which began publication in 1987. The U.S. Census Bureau also offers systematic collections of data covering increasingly longer spans. Two examples are the *State and Metropolitan Area Data Book* (published biennially since 1980) and the *County and City Data Book* (published with varying frequency since 1952). Such groups and publications make data collection far easier, and more systematic, and ensure higher quality than in the past.

Even when data are available, a researcher still can be frustrated by the inevitable variety that occurs across units. Simple tables or one-sentence summaries are often inadequate. As was shown in Tables 2-2 and 2-3, which concern financing state election campaigns, there is enormous variation among states. Similarly, the listing of state fiscal discipline measures (Table 8-5) notes that provisions for passing tax bills and borrowing vary, without giving the exact requirement in each state. So much variation exists on this single point—a two-thirds majority of the legislators present and voting, two-thirds of the total number of legislators, 60 percent of the legislators present, and so on—that this book leaves it to the original sources to present the particulars.

Therefore, in studying state and local governments, their interrelationships, and their relations with the federal government, a researcher must pay attention to details. Even more than usual it is essential to read footnotes and check several sources. Differences in data collection procedures, the timing of data collection, and variations in detail of reports all become important. The user must also keep in mind the purpose for examining the data. It takes a careful researcher to know when variations can be ignored and when they become so frequent or so large that they must be an explicit part of the analysis.

Despite improvements in data collection, it is still necessary to go directly to states and localities for some information. Fortunately, this too has become easier. Publications such as the *National Directory of State Agencies* and the *State Information Book* give names and titles of specific individuals and offices, typically with addresses and phone numbers. While this will still not make a project involving twenty-five or fifty states easy, at least one can gather missing information or exact details about specific states and localities.

The recent surge in availability of information has now made possible a serious look at cities, counties, states, regions, and the relationships among all these governments. The tables in this book emphasize three topics. First, information is given about specific states, often with an eye toward how states rank relative to one another. This includes information about their constitutions, elected officials, provisions for direct democracy, and economic provisions (Tables 8-1 through 8-8, 8-10, 8-12, and 10-8). Second, data are provided about states and localities as a whole and how they differ from the federal government and from each other (Tables 8-9 through 8-11, 8-13, and Figures 8-1 through 8-3). Third, considerable emphasis is given to intergovernmental relationships because of the growing fiscal interdependence between federal and state governments, state and local units, and even directly between federal and local governments (Figure 8-4, and Tables 8-14 through 8-18).

As these tables amply demonstrate, students as well as professionals now have access to systematic information about all fifty states and increasingly about localities. Although users may have to make extra effort to absorb all the details provided by these tables, they are rewarded by the new possibilities for research and understanding.

Table 8-1   The States: Historical Data and Current Populations

State	Population[a]	Date organized as territory	Date admitted to Union	Chrono- logical order of admission to Union
Alabama	4,040,587	March 3, 1817	December 14, 1819	22
Alaska	550,043	August 24, 1912	January 3, 1959	49
Arizona	3,665,228	February 24, 1863	February 14, 1912	48
Arkansas	2,350,725	March 2, 1819[b]	June 15, 1836	25
California	29,760,021		September 9, 1850	31
Colorado	3,294,394	February 28, 1861	August 1, 1876	38
Connecticut	3,287,116	—	January 9, 1788[c]	5
Delaware	666,168	—	December 7, 1787[c]	1
Florida	12,937,926	March 30, 1822	March 3, 1845	27
Georgia	6,478,216	—	January 2, 1788[c]	4
Hawaii	1,108,229	June 14, 1900	August 21, 1959	50
Idaho	1,006,749	March 4, 1863	July 3, 1890	43
Illinois	11,430,602	February 3, 1809	December 3, 1818	21
Indiana	5,544,159	May 7, 1800	December 11, 1816	19
Iowa	2,776,755	June 12, 1838	December 28, 1846	29
Kansas	2,477,574	May 30, 1854[b]	January 29, 1861	34
Kentucky	3,685,296		June 1, 1792	15
Louisiana	4,219,973	March 26, 1804[b]	April 30, 1812	18
Maine	1,227,928		March 15, 1820	23
Maryland	4,781,468	—	April 28, 1788[c]	7
Massachusetts	6,016,425	—	February 6, 1788[c]	6
Michigan	9,295,297	January 11, 1805	January 26, 1837	26
Minnesota	4,375,099	March 3, 1849	May 11, 1858	32
Mississippi	2,573,216	April 7, 1798	December 10, 1817	20
Missouri	5,117,073	June 4, 1812	August 10, 1821	24
Montana	799,065	May 26, 1864	November 8, 1889	41
Nebraska	1,578,385	May 30, 1854	March 1, 1867	37
Nevada	1,201,833	March 2, 1861	October 31, 1864	36
New Hampshire	1,109,252	—	June 21, 1788[c]	9
New Jersey	7,730,188	—	December 18, 1787[c]	3
New Mexico	1,515,069	September 9, 1850	January 6, 1912	47
New York	17,990,455	—	July 26, 1788[c]	11
North Carolina	6,628,637	—	November 21, 1789[c]	12
North Dakota	638,800	March 2, 1861	November 2, 1889	39
Ohio	10,847,115	May 7, 1800	March 1, 1803	17
Oklahoma	3,145,585	May 2, 1890	November 16, 1907	46
Oregon	2,842,321	August 14, 1848	February 14, 1859	33
Pennsylvania	11,881,643	—	December 12, 1787[c]	2
Rhode Island	1,003,464	—	May 29, 1790[c]	13
South Carolina	3,486,703	—	May 23, 1788[c]	8

Table 8-1 *(Continued)*

State	Population[a]	Date organized as territory	Date admitted to Union	Chrono-logical order of admission to Union
South Dakota	696,004	March 2, 1861	November 2, 1889	40
Tennessee	4,877,185	June 8, 1790[d]	June 1, 1796	16
Texas	16,986,510	[b]	December 29, 1845	28
Utah	1,722,850	September 9, 1850	January 4, 1896	45
Vermont	562,758	[b]	March 4, 1791	14
Virginia	6,187,358	—	June 25, 1788[c]	10
Washington	4,866,692	March 2, 1853	November 11, 1889	42
West Virginia	1,793,477	[b]	June 20, 1863	35
Wisconsin	4,891,769	April 20, 1836	May 29, 1848	30
Wyoming	453,588	July 25, 1868	July 10, 1890	44
Total	248,709,873			

Note: "—" indicates one of the original thirteen states.

[a] As of 1990.
[b] No territorial status before admission to Union.
[c] Date of ratification of U.S. Constitution.
[d] Date Southwest Territory (identical boundaries as Tennessee's) was created.

Sources: Council of State Governments, *Book of the States, 1992–1993* (Lexington, Ky.: Council of State Governments, 1992), 659–660; population: U.S. Bureau of the Census, *1990 Census of Population and Housing: Summary Population and Housing Characteristics* (Washington, D.C.: U.S. Government Printing Office, 1992), Series 1990 CPH-1-1, 360.

Table 8-2 State Constitutions

State	Number of constitutions[a]	Dates of adoption	Present constitution Effective date	Present constitution Estimated length (number of words)	Number of amendments Submitted to voters	Number of amendments Adopted
Alabama	6	1819, 1861, 1865, 1868, 1875, 1901	November 28, 1901	220,000	818	582
Alaska	1	1956	January 3, 1959	15,988	34	25
Arizona	1	1911	February 14, 1912	28,876	218	119
Arkansas	5	1836, 1861, 1864, 1868, 1874	October 30, 1874	40,720	171	81
California	2	1847, 1879	July 4, 1879	54,645	823	491
Colorado	1	1876	August 1, 1876	45,679	265	128
Connecticut	4	1818, 1965	December 30, 1965	9,564	29[b]	28
Delaware	4	1776, 1792, 1831, 1897	June 10, 1897	19,000		127
Florida	6	1839, 1861, 1865, 1868, 1886, 1968	January 7, 1969	25,100	97	69
Georgia	10	1777, 1789, 1798, 1861, 1865, 1868, 1877, 1945, 1976, 1982	July 1, 1983	25,000	58	44
Hawaii	1	1950	August 21, 1959	20,774	110	86
Idaho	1	1889	July 3, 1890	23,239	194	114
Illinois	4	1818, 1848, 1870, 1970	July 1, 1971	13,700	16	10
Indiana	2	1816, 1851	November 1, 1851	10,230	70	38
Iowa	2	1846, 1857	September 3, 1857	13,430	52	49
Kansas	1	1859	January 29, 1861	11,900	119	91
Kentucky	4	1792, 1799, 1850, 1891	September 28, 1891	27,234	66	33
Louisiana	11	1812, 1845, 1852, 1861, 1864, 1868, 1879, 1898, 1913, 1921, 1974	January 1, 1975	54,112	112	72

Maine	1	1819	March 15, 1820	13,500	194	164
Maryland	4	1776, 1851, 1864, 1867	October 5, 1867	41,349	241	207
Massachusetts	1	1780	October 25, 1780	36,700	145	117
Michigan	4	1835, 1850, 1908, 1963	January 1, 1964	25,246	54	20
Minnesota	1	1857	May 11, 1858	23,700	208	113
Mississippi	4	1817, 1832, 1869, 1890	November 1, 1890	23,508	152	119
Missouri	4	1820, 1865, 1875, 1945	March 30, 1945	42,000	139	86
Montana	2	1889, 1972	July 1, 1973	11,866	38	21
Nebraska	2	1866, 1875	October 12, 1875	20,048	294	198
Nevada	1	1864	October 31, 1864	20,770	189	115
New Hampshire	2	1776, 1784	June 2, 1784	9,200	280	143
New Jersey	3	1776, 1844, 1947	January 1, 1948	17,800	60	47
New Mexico	1	1911	January 6, 1912	27,200	252	127
New York	4	1777, 1822, 1846, 1894	January 1, 1895	51,700	284	215
North Carolina	3	1776, 1868, 1970	July 1, 1971	11,000	35	27
North Dakota	1	1889	November 2, 1889	20,564	238	132
Ohio	2	1802, 1851	September 1, 1851	36,900	259	157
Oklahoma	1	1907	November 16, 1907	68,800	300	151
Oregon	1	1857	February 14, 1859	26,090	397	201
Pennsylvania	5	1776, 1790, 1838, 1873, 1968	1968[c]	21,675	27	21
Rhode Island	2	1842	May 2, 1843	19,026	105	59
South Carolina	7	1776, 1778, 1790, 1861, 1865, 1868, 1895	January 1, 1896	22,500	650	465
South Dakota	1	1889	November 2, 1889	25,000	196	101
Tennessee	3	1796, 1835, 1870	February 23, 1870	15,300	55	32
Texas	5	1845, 1861, 1866, 1869, 1876	February 15, 1876	80,806	532	364
Utah	1	1895	January 4, 1896	11,000	134	84
Vermont	3	1777, 1786, 1793	July 9, 1793	6,880	210	52
Virginia	6	1776, 1830, 1851, 1869, 1902, 1970	July 1, 1971	18,500	31	26
Washington	1	1889	November 11, 1889	29,400	159	89

(Table continues)

Table 8-2 *(Continued)*

| | | | Present constitution | | Number of amendments | |
| | *Number of constitutions*[a] | *Dates of adoption* | *Effective date* | *Estimated length (number of words)* | *Submitted to voters* | *Adopted* |
State						
West Virginia	2	1863, 1872	April 9, 1872	26,000	113	66
Wisconsin	1	1848	May 29, 1848	15,531	177	129
Wyoming	1	1889	July 10, 1890	31,800	104	62

Note: Constitutions as of January 1, 1996. For more details on the constitutions, see source.

[a] The constitutions include those Civil War documents customarily listed by the individual states. In Connecticut and Rhode Island, colonial charters served as the first constitutions.

[b] Proposed amendments are not submitted to the voters in Delaware.

[c] Certain sections of the constitution were revised in 1967–1968. Amendments proposed and adopted are since 1968.

Source: Council of State Governments, *Book of the States, 1996–1997* (Lexington, Ky.: Council of State Governments, 1996), 3.

Table 8-3 Governors' Terms, Limits, Powers, and Other Statewide Elected Officials

State	Length of term in 1900	Length of term in 1995	Year of change	Maximum number of consecutive terms	Item veto[a]	Other statewide elected officials[b] Number of officials	Other statewide elected officials[b] Number of agencies
Alabama	2[c]	4	1902	2	yes	9	7
Alaska	[c]	4		2[d]	yes	1	0
Arizona	2	4	1970	2[c]	yes	8	6
Arkansas	2	4	1984	2[f]	yes	6	6
California	4	4		2[f]	yes	7	7
Colorado	2	4	1958	2[e]	yes	4	4
Connecticut	2	4	1950	No limit	yes	5	5
Delaware	4	4		2[f]	yes	1	1
Florida	4	4		2	no	7	7
Georgia	2[c]	4	1942	2[d]	yes	12	8
Hawaii		4		2	yes	1	1
Idaho	2	4	1946	No limit	yes	6	6
Illinois	4	4		No limit	yes	5	5
Indiana	4	4		[g]	no	6	6
Iowa	2	4	1974	No limit	yes	7	6
Kansas	2	4	1974	2	yes	5	5
Kentucky	4	4		2	yes	6	6
Louisiana	4	4		2	yes	7	7
Maine	2	4	1958	2[d]	no	0	0
Maryland	4	4		2[d]	yes	3	3
Massachusetts	1	4	1920, 1966[h]	2[d]	yes	5	7
Michigan	2	4	1966	2	yes	35	6
Minnesota	2	4	1962	No limit	yes	5	5
Mississippi	4	4		2	yes	7	7

(Table continues)

Table 8-3 (Continued)

State	Length of term in 1900	Length of term in 1995	Year of change	Maximum number of consecutive terms	Item veto[a]	Other statewide elected officials[b] Number of officials	Number of agencies
Missouri	4	4		2[f]	yes	5	5
Montana	4	4		2[i]	yes	5	5
Nebraska	2	4	1966	2[d]	yes	5	5
Nevada	4	4		2	no	5	5
New Hampshire	2	2		No limit	no	0	0
New Jersey	3[c]	4	1949	2[d]	yes	0	0
New Mexico	4	4	1916, 1970	2[d]	yes	9	7
New York	2	4	1938	No limit	yes	3	3
North Carolina	4	4		2	yes	9	9
North Dakota	2	4	1964	No limit	yes	13	16
Ohio	2[c]	4	1958	2[f]	yes	5	5
Oklahoma	4	4		2	yes	10	8
Oregon	4	4		2[g]	yes	5	5
Pennsylvania	4	4		2	yes	4	4
Rhode Island	1	4	1912, 1995[h]	2	no	4	4
South Carolina	2	4	1926	2	yes	8	10
South Dakota	2	4	1974	2	yes	9	7
Tennessee	1	4	1954	2	yes	0	0
Texas	2	4	1974	No limit	yes	9	7
Utah	4	4		3[j]	yes	4	14
Vermont	2	2		No limit	no	5	5
Virginia	4	4		1[f]	yes	2	2
Washington	4	4		1[k]	yes	8	8
West Virginia	4	4		2	yes	5	6
Wisconsin	2	4	1970	No limit	yes	5	5
Wyoming	4	4		No limit[i]	yes	4	4

[a] Provisions to override vary, requiring as many as two-thirds of the legislators elected. For details, see source.

[b] Popularly elected executive branch officials and the number of agencies involving these officials.

[c] Oklahoma was admitted to the Union in 1907, Arizona and New Mexico in 1912, and Alaska and Hawaii in 1959. Oklahoma, Alaska, and Hawaii have always had four-year gubernatorial terms. Arizona started with two years. New Mexico started with four years, went to two years in 1916 and back to four years in 1970.

[d] After two consecutive terms, must wait four years before being eligible again. In Massachusetts, provision begins with governor elected in 1998. Governor Weld may serve one more term if elected.

[e] Because the term limit was passed during their administrations, Governor Symington (Arizona) and Governor Romer (Colorado) have been grandfathered. After their third term, they will not be eligible to run again.

[f] Two terms only, whether or not consecutive, except Virginia: one term only, successive terms forbidden.

[g] Cannot serve more than eight years in any twelve-year period.

[h] Massachusetts went from one year to two years in 1920 and from two years to four years in 1966. Rhode Island went from two years to four years in 1995.

[i] Cannot serve more than eight years in any sixteen-year period.

[j] Governor Leavitt may serve three additional terms after his present term.

[k] Cannot serve more than eight years in any fourteen-year period.

Sources: Council of State Governments, *Book of the States, 1996–1997* (Lexington, Ky.: Council of State Governments, 1996), 17–18, 22–23; length of term in 1900 and year of change: *Congressional Quarterly's Guide to U.S. Elections,* 2d ed. (Washington, D.C.: Congressional Quarterly, 1985), 454.

Table 8-4   State Provisions for Initiative, Referendum, and Recall

State	Initiative[a]	Referendum[b]	Recall[c]
Alabama			
Alaska	indirect	legislature and petition	all but judges
Arizona	indirect	legislature and petition	all elected officials
Arkansas	direct	legislature and petition	
California	direct	legislature and petition	all elected officials
Colorado	direct	legislature	all elected officials
Connecticut		legislature	
Delaware		legislature	
Florida	direct	legislature	
Georgia		legislature	all elected officials
Hawaii		legislature	
Idaho	direct	legislature and petition	all but judges
Illinois	direct	legislature	
Indiana		legislature	
Iowa		legislature	
Kansas		legislature	all but judges
Kentucky		legislature and petition	
Louisiana		legislature	all but certain judges
Maine	indirect	legislature and petition	
Maryland		legislature and petition	
Massachusetts	indirect	legislature and petition	
Michigan	both	legislature and petition	all but certain judges
Minnesota		legislature	
Mississippi	indirect	legislature	
Missouri	direct	legislature and petition	
Montana	direct	legislature and petition	all elected or appointed officials
Nebraska	direct	legislature and petition	
Nevada	both	legislature and petition	all public officers
New Hampshire		legislature	
New Jersey		legislature	all elected officials
New Mexico		legislature and petition	
New York		legislature	
North Carolina		legislature	
North Dakota	direct	legislature and petition	all elected officials exc. Congress
Ohio	both	legislature and petition	
Oklahoma	direct	legislature and petition	
Oregon	direct	legislature and petition	all elected officials exc. Congress
Pennsylvania		legislature	
Rhode Island		legislature	certain elected officials
South Carolina		legislature	
South Dakota	direct	legislature and petition	certain municipal officials
Tennessee		legislature	
Texas		legislature	

Table 8-4   *(Continued)*

State	Initiative[a]	Referendum[b]	Recall[c]
Utah	both	legislature and petition	
Vermont		legislature	
Virginia		legislature	
Washington	both	legislature and petition	all but certain judges
West Virginia		legislature	
Wisconsin		legislature	all elected officials
Wyoming	indirect	legislature and petition	

Note: Initiative and referendum provisions may apply to Constitution, statutes, or both. See source for details.

[a] Initiative: Allows proposed state laws to be placed on a ballot by citizen petition and enacted or rejected by the electorate. "Direct" means measures may be placed on the ballot with a specific number of signatures and no legislative action; requirements for number of signatures vary. "Indirect" means a measure must be submitted to the legislature for consideration before it can be placed on the ballot.

[b] Referendum: State law passed by the legislature is referred to voters before it goes into effect. Referendum may be held by citizen petition or voluntary submission by the legislature. For certain types of decisions, such as tax increases, referendum may be a constitutional requirement.

[c] Recall: Voters are allowed to remove state elective officials in a recall election. Number of signatures needed ranges from 10 to 40 percent; percentage is based on last vote for the office in question or general election. Sometimes percentage is modified by geographical or jurisdictional restrictions.

Source: Council of State Governments, *Book of the States, 1996–1997* (Lexington, Ky.: Council of State Governments, 1996), 209, 221–222.

Table 8-5 State Fiscal Discipline Measures

State	Legislature must pass or governor must sign a balanced budget	Legislative votes required to pass budget	Extraordinary vote required to pass . . .	Governor may item-veto appropriations bills	Governor may reduce budget without legislative approval	Taxes automatically adjusted for inflation[a]	May carry over a deficit	Scope of sunset legislation
Alabama	x	Majority		x	x			C
Alaska	x	Majority		x				C
Arizona	x	Majority		x	x		x	S
Arkansas	x	3/4 elected	T	x				
California		2/3 elected	T,B	x		x	x	R
Colorado	x	Majority		x	x			C
Connecticut	x	Majority		x	x			R
Delaware	x	Majority	T	x	x			R
Florida	x	Majority		x	x			R
Georgia	x	Majority		x	x			R
Hawaii	x	Maj. elected		x	x			
Idaho	x	Majority		x	x			R
Illinois	x	3/5 elected	B	x			x	C
Indiana		Majority			x			
Iowa		Majority		x	x	x		
Kansas	x	Majority		x	x			R
Kentucky	x	Majority	T	x				C
Louisiana	x	Majority	T	x	x	x	x	C
Maine	x	Majority						R
Maryland	x	Majority		x	x		x	R
Massachusetts	x	Majority		x	x			
Michigan	x	Majority		x		x	x	
Minnesota	x	Majority	x	x	x	x	x	S
Mississippi	x	Majority	T	x	x			
Missouri	x	Majority		x	x			

State		Vote requirement						
Montana	x	Majority		x	x		x	
Nebraska	x	3/5 elected	B	x	x		x	
Nevada	x	Majority				x		
New Hampshire		Majority		x				
New Jersey	x	Majority		x	x			
New Mexico	x	Majority		x	x			R
New York		Majority		x	x			
North Carolina	x	Majority		x				
North Dakota	x	Majority		x	x			
Ohio	x	Majority		x	x			
Oklahoma	x	Majority	T	x	x		x	R,C
Oregon	x	Majority		x	x	x	x	S
Pennsylvania	x	Maj. elected		x				
Rhode Island	x	2/3 both houses	B	x				
South Carolina	x	Majority		x	x			R
South Dakota	x	Majority	T	x	x	x	x	
Tennessee	x	Majority		x	x			C
Texas	x	Majority		x	x			S
Utah	x	Majority		x	x			R
Vermont		Majority		x			x	S
Virginia		Majority		x				
Washington		Majority		x	x			C
West Virginia	x	Majority		x	x			S
Wisconsin	x	Majority		x	x		x	
Wyoming		Majority			x	x		
Total	41		12	37	43	9	11	25

Note: "T" indicates tax bills, "B" indicates state borrowing, "C" indicates comprehensive, "R" indicates regulatory, "S" indicates selective. There is considerable variation with respect to each type of measure. For example, an extraordinary vote may not be generally required but may be necessary for emergency budget requests; some states may carry over a deficit but for only a year; some states include sunset clauses in specific legislation, and so on. Considerable detail about each mechanism can be found in the source.

[a] Automatic adjustment of tax brackets, personal exemption, or standard deductions.

Source: Council of State Governments, Book of the States, 1996–1997 (Lexington, Ky.: Council of State Governments, 1996), 98–100, 122–124, 230–231, 263–264.

Table 8-6   Incorporation of the Bill of Rights to Apply to State
Governments

Year	Issue and amendment	Supreme Court case	Vote
[1868 Fourteenth Amendment to Constitution passed][a]			
1897	Eminent domain (V)	*Chicago, Burlington & Quincy RR v. Chicago* 166 U.S. 266	9:0
1927	Freedom of speech (I)	*Fiske v. Kansas* 274 U.S. 380	9:0
1931	Freedom of press (I)	*Near v. Minnesota* 283 U.S. 697	5:4
1932	Counsel in capital criminal cases (VI)	*Powell v. Alabama* 287 U.S. 45	7:2
1934	Free exercise of religion (I)	*Hamilton v. Regents of the U. of California* 293 U.S. 245	9:0
1937	Freedom of assembly and petition (I)	*De Jonge v. Oregon* 299 U.S. 253	8:0
1947	Separation of church and state (I)	*Everson v. Board of Education of Ewing Township* 330 U.S. 1	5:4
1948	Public trial (VI)	*In re Oliver* 33 U.S. 257	7:2
1961	Unreasonable searches and seizures (IV)	*Mapp v. Ohio* 367 U.S. 643	6:3
1962	Cruel and unusual punishment (VIII)	*Robinson v. California* 370 U.S. 660	6:2
1963	Counsel in all criminal cases (VI)	*Gideon v. Wainwright* 372 U.S. 335	9:0
1964	Self-incrimination (V)	*Malloy v. Hogan* 378 U.S. 1	5:4
		Murphy v. Waterfront Commission 378 U.S. 52	9:0
1965	Right to confront adverse witnesses (VI)	*Pointer v. Texas* 380 U.S. 400	7:2
1967	Impartial jury (VI)	*Parker v. Gladden* 385 U.S. 363	8:1
1967	Obtaining and confronting favorable witnesses (VI)	*Washington v. Texas* 388 U.S. 14	9:0
1967	Speedy trial (VI)	*Klopfer v. North Carolina* 386 U.S. 213	9:0
1968	Jury trial in non-petty criminal cases (VI)	*Duncan v. Louisiana* 391 U.S. 145	7:2
1969	Double jeopardy (V)	*Benton v. Maryland* 395 U.S. 784	7:2

Note: Enumerated rights not incorporated: grand jury indictment, trial by jury in civil cases, excessive fines and bail, right to bear arms, and safeguards on quartering troops in private homes.

[a] The Fourteenth Amendment's due process clause is the basis for applying the Bill of Rights to the states.

Sources. Henry J. Abraham, *The Judiciary: The Supreme Court in the Governmental Process,* 9th ed. (Dubuque, Iowa: William C. Brown, 1994); votes: *United States Reports* (Washington, D.C.: U.S. Government Printing Office, various years).

Table 8-7   Length of Time Between Congressional Approval and
Actual Ratification of the Twenty-seven Amendments
to the U.S. Constitution

Amendment		Time required for ratification	Year ratified
I–X	Bill of Rights	2 years, 2$^{1}/_{2}$ months	1791
XI	Lawsuits against states	11 months	1795
XII	Presidential elections	6$^{1}/_{2}$ months	1804
XIII	Abolition of slavery	10 months	1865
XIV	Civil rights	2 years, 1 month	1868
XV	Suffrage for all races	11 months	1870
XVI	Income tax	3 years, 6$^{1}/_{2}$ months	1913
XVII	Senatorial elections	11 months	1913
XVIII	Prohibition	1 year, 1 month	1919
XIX	Women's suffrage	1 year, 2 months	1920
XX	Terms of office	11 months	1933
XXI	Repeal of prohibition	9$^{1}/_{2}$ months	1933
XXII	Limit on presidential terms	3 years, 11 months	1951
XXIII	Washington, D.C., vote	9 months	1961
XXIV	Abolition of poll taxes	1 year, 4 months	1964
XXV	Presidential succession	1 year, 10 months	1967
XXVI	Eighteen-year-old suffrage	3 months	1971
XXVII	Congressional salaries	203 years	1992

Sources: Congressional Research Service, *The Constitution of the United States: Analysis and Interpretation* (Washington, D.C.: U.S. Government Printing Office, 1973), 23–44 (92d Cong., 2d sess., S. Doc. 92-82); *Congressional Quarterly Weekly Report* (1992), 1423.

Table 8-8   State Action on Proposed Constitutional Amendments

	Proposed amendment				
State	Reappor-tionment[a]	Equal rights[b]	Balanced budget[c]	Ban abortion[d]	Line-item veto[e]
Alabama	yes	n.a.	r	yes	n.a.
Alaska	n.a.	yes	yes	n.a.	n.a.
Arizona	yes	n.a.	yes	n.a.	yes
Arkansas	yes	n.a.	yes[f]	yes	n.a.
California	n.a.	yes	n.a.[f]	n.a.	n.a.
Colorado	yes	yes	yes	n.a.	n.a.
Connecticut	n.a.	yes	n.a.	n.a.	n.a.
Delaware	n.a.	yes	yes	yes	n.a.
Florida	yes	n.a.	r	n.a.	n.a.
Georgia	yes	n.a.	yes	n.a.	n.a.
Hawaii	n.a.	yes	n.a.	n.a.	n.a.
Idaho	yes	r	yes[f]	yes	yes
Illinois	r[g]	n.a.	n.a.[f]	n.a.	yes
Indiana	yes	yes	yes	yes	n.a.
Iowa	yes	yes	yes	n.a.	n.a.
Kansas	r[g]	yes	yes[f]	n.a.	yes
Kentucky	yes	r	n.a.[f]	yes	n.a.
Louisiana	yes	n.a.	r	yes	yes
Maine	n.a.	yes	n.a.	n.a.	n.a.
Maryland	r[g]	yes	yes	n.a.	n.a.
Massachusetts	n.a.	yes	n.a.	yes	n.a.
Michigan	n.a.	yes	n.a.	n.a.	yes
Minnesota	yes	yes	n.a.	n.a.	n.a.
Mississippi	yes	n.a.	yes	yes	n.a.
Missouri	yes	n.a.	yes[f]	yes	n.a.
Montana	yes	yes	n.a.[f]	n.a.	n.a.
Nebraska	yes	r	yes	yes	n.a.
Nevada	yes	n.a.	r[g]	yes	yes
New Hampshire	yes	yes	yes	n.a.	n.a.
New Jersey	n.a.	yes	n.a.	yes	n.a.
New Mexico	yes	yes	yes	n.a.	n.a.
New York	n.a.	yes	n.a.	n.a.	n.a.
North Carolina	r[g]	n.a.	yes	n.a.	n.a.
North Dakota	yes	yes	yes	n.a.	n.a.
Ohio	n.a.	yes	n.a.	n.a.	n.a.
Oklahoma	yes	n.a.	yes	yes	n.a.
Oregon	n.a.	yes	yes	n.a.	n.a.
Pennsylvania	n.a.	yes	yes	yes	n.a.
Rhode Island	n.a.	yes	n.a.	yes	n.a.
South Carolina	yes	n.a.	yes	n.a.	n.a.
South Dakota	yes	r	yes	yes	yes
Tennessee	yes	r	yes	yes	yes
Texas	r[g]	yes	yes	n.a.	n.a.

Table 8-8   *(Continued)*

State	Proposed amendment				
	Reapportionment[a]	Equal rights[b]	Balanced budget[c]	Ban abortion[d]	Line-item veto[e]
Utah	yes	n.a.	yes	yes	n.a.
Vermont	n.a.	yes	n.a.	n.a.	n.a.
Virginia	yes	n.a.	yes	n.a.	yes
Washington	r[g]	yes	n.a.	n.a.	n.a.
West Virginia	n.a.	yes	n.a.	n.a.	n.a.
Wisconsin	n.a.	yes	n.a.	n.a.	n.a.
Wyoming	yes	yes	yes	n.a.	n.a.

Note: "Yes" indicates state legislature approved the amendment or sent a petition to Congress for a constitutional convention; "n.a." indicates no action was taken or the state legislature rejected the amendment or a proposal to petition for a convention; and "r" indicates previous appeal was rescinded. The equal rights amendment was initiated by Congress and submitted to the states for ratification. The other proposed amendments were initiated by petition from state legislatures.

[a] Reapportionment: States acted to petition Congress for a constitutional convention on this issue following two Supreme Court "one-person, one-vote" decisions concerning how states were apportioned for their state legislatures. As a result, some states called for a convention to consider an amendment that would allow one house of a state legislature to be apportioned on a basis other than population.

[b] Equal rights: This amendment had a time limit for approval, which expired. As proposed by Congress and voted on by the states, it read: "Section 1. Equality of rights under the law shall not be denied or abridged by the United States or by any State on account of sex. Section 2. The Congress shall have the power to enforce, by appropriate legislation, the provisions of this article. Section 3. This amendment shall take effect two years after the date of ratification."

[c] Balanced budget: This proposed amendment has various forms. In its simplest form, Congress would be required to approve a balanced federal budget each year. In other forms there is a provision that a three-fifths majority of Congress could vote not to balance the budget in any given year.

[d] Abortion: Some states have called for a constitutional convention to consider an amendment that would ban abortions. The most common approach among the various proposed amendments is to apply the constitutional protection of due process against the denial of life and property to unborn children.

[e] Some states have called for a constitutional convention to consider an amendment that would give the president a line-item veto.

[f] The state did not endorse the call for a constitutional convention but petitioned Congress to propose a balanced budget amendment to the states.

[g] Passed by only one house of each of the state legislature.

Sources: Reapportionment: *Congressional Quarterly Weekly Report* (1969), 1372–1373; equal rights: Congressional Research Service, *The Constitution of the United States: Analysis and Interpretation* (Washington, D.C.: U.S. Government Printing Office, 1973), 43 (92d Cong., 2d sess., S. Doc. 92-82); balanced budget: Congressional Research Service, "Constitutional Convention: Political and Legal Questions," September 18, 1990; abortion and line-item veto: *Congressional Record* citations to state communications relating to constitutional conventions.

Figure 8-1   Number of Government Employees: Federal, State, and Local, 1929–1992

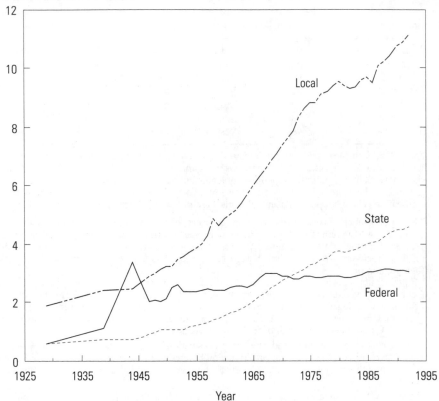

Number of employees (millions)

Sources: 1929–1944, 1949, 1952, 1954, 1959, 1964, 1969–1988: U.S. Advisory Commission on Intergovernmental Relations, *Significant Features of Fiscal Federalism, 1990,* vol. 2 (Washington, D.C.: U.S. Advisory Commission on Intergovernmental Relations, 1990), 177; 1989–1992: *1994,* 151; other years: U.S. Bureau of the Census, *Historical Statistics of the United States,* Series Y189-198 (Washington, D.C.: U.S. Government Printing Office, 1975), 1100.

Table 8-9 Federal, State, and Local Governments: Number of Units and Employees

				Local government					
Year	Federal	State	County	Municipal	School district	Township and town	Special district[a]	Total	Total
1942									
Number	1	48	3,050	16,220	108,579	18,919	8,299 [d]	155,067	155,116
Employees (thousands)[b]	2,664	503[c]	333[c]	872[c]	—	223[c,d]		1,428[c]	5,915
1952[d]									
Number	1	50	3,052	16,807	67,355	17,202	12,340 [c]	116,756	116,807
Employees (thousands)	2,583	1,060	573	1,341	1,234	312[c]		3,461	7,105
1957[d]									
Number	1	50	3,050	17,215	50,454	17,198	14,424 [c]	102,341	102,392
Employees (thousands)[e]	2,439	1,300	726	1,539	1,651	394[c]		4,307	8,047
1962									
Number	1	50	3,043	18,000	34,678	17,142	18,323 [c]	91,186	91,237
Employees (thousands)	2,539	1,680	862	1,696	2,161	449[c]		5,169	9,388
1967									
Number	1	50	3,049	18,048	21,782	17,105	21,264 [c]	81,248	81,299
Employees (thousands)	2,993	2,335	1,077	1,993	2,919	549[c]		6,539	11,867
1972									
Number	1	50	3,044	18,517	15,781	16,991	23,885	78,218	78,269
Employees (thousands)	2,832	2,957	1,369	2,376	3,587	348	327	8,007	13,759
1977									
Number	1	50	3,042	18,862	15,174	16,822	25,962	79,862	79,913
Employees (thousands)	2,839	3,491	1,761	2,469	4,127	361	402	9,120	15,459

(Table continues)

Table 8-9 *(Continued)*

			Local government							
Year	Federal	State	County	Municipal	School district	Township and town	Special district[a]	Total	Total
1982									
Number	1	50	3,041	19,076	14,851	16,734	28,078	81,780	81,831
Employees (thousands)	2,862	3,744	1,824	2,397	4,194	356	478	9,249	15,841
1987									
Number	1	50	3,042	19,200	14,721	16,691	29,532	83,166	83,217
Employees (thousands)	3,121	4,115	1,963	2,541	4,620	414	537	10,076	17,311
1992									
Number	1	50	3,043	19,279	14,422	16,656	31,555	84,955	85,006
Employees (thousands)	3,047	4,595	2,253	2,665	5,134	424	627	11,103	18,745

Note: "—" indicates not available. A census of governmental units is conducted every five years.

[a] Special districts include independent public housing authorities, local irrigation units, power authorities, and other such bodies.
[b] Month for employee counts varies across years. For details, see sources. Numbers include full- and part-time employees.
[c] Employees in other than education.
[d] Townships and special districts are combined.
[e] Adjusted to include units in Alaska and Hawaii.

Sources: 1942–1967: U.S. Bureau of the Census, *Historical Statistics of the United States* (Washington, D.C.: United States Government Printing Office, 1975), 1086, 1100; 1972–1989 governmental units: U.S. Bureau of the Census, *Census of Governments, 1987* (Washington, D.C.: U.S. Government Printing Office, 1988), vi; (1993), 3; 1972–1992 employees: U.S. Office of Personnel Management, *Federal Manpower Statistics, Federal Civilian Workforce Statistics* (Washington, D.C.: U.S. Government Printing Office), various years; U.S. Bureau of the Census, *Public Employment in 1985* (Washington, D.C.: U.S. Government Printing Office, 1986), 2; *1987*, vii; *1989*, vii; *1992*, vi, ix.

Table 8-10 Tax Capacity and Tax Efforts of the States

	1967		1975		1980		1982		1984		1986		1988		1991	
State	TC	TE	TC	TE	TC	TE	TC	TE	TC	TE	TC	TE	TC	TE	TC	TE
Alabama	70	89	77	79	76	85	74	87	73	90	74	86	76	84	81	81
Alaska	99	104	155	76	260	166	313	180	250	141	177	168	159	127	178	119
Arizona	95	109	92	108	89	117	96	92	99	95	99	99	99	96	99	103
Arkansas	77	83	78	78	79	86	79	81	75	87	78	91	74	84	78	82
California	124	108	110	119	117	102	116	99	119	93	118	95	116	94	115	95
Colorado	104	106	106	90	113	90	121	81	121	82	117	83	107	89	109	86
Connecticut	117	93	110	99	112	100	117	99	124	99	135	94	143	90	130	99
Delaware	123	90	124	84	111	89	115	84	123	77	121	81	124	84	125	80
District of Columbia	121	90	118	94	111	131	115	145	120	138	122	143	123	154	123	157
Florida	104	84	102	74	100	74	104	72	105	74	105	77	104	82	103	86
Georgia	80	92	86	89	82	96	84	96	89	89	94	89	94	89	91	95
Hawaii	99	135	107	124	117	105	114	108	118	99	113	105	114	112	146	95
Idaho	91	105	89	90	87	88	86	85	78	91	77	90	76	93	82	94
Illinois	114	84	112	99	108	102	99	107	97	110	96	106	99	102	102	100
Indiana	99	95	98	92	92	84	89	88	87	95	87	94	87	93	90	93
Iowa	104	104	106	93	105	96	96	105	87	112	84	113	83	113	93	100
Kansas	105	96	109	85	109	88	106	88	100	95	96	96	91	104	93	100
Kentucky	80	85	85	84	83	89	82	88	77	89	76	89	81	88	83	100
Louisiana	94	90	97	87	109	78	113	82	102	81	90	91	83	90	89	89
Maine	81	105	84	104	80	111	84	107	88	105	95	99	98	105	95	102
Maryland	101	103	101	106	99	109	100	106	105	100	108	99	109	108	106	103
Massachusetts	98	121	98	129	96	135	101	119	111	105	124	103	129	94	117	101
Michigan	104	100	101	106	97	116	93	120	93	129	96	118	95	112	94	107
Minnesota	95	119	97	117	102	111	99	111	101	124	102	108	104	112	101	112
Mississippi	64	98	70	96	69	96	71	92	70	95	65	97	65	94	68	92
Missouri	97	86	96	84	94	84	91	82	89	85	93	82	90	86	91	85
Montana	105	93	103	92	112	92	110	97	95	101	88	103	85	102	91	78
Nebraska	110	78	106	85	97	102	97	93	93	99	91	96	90	98	95	99

(Table continues)

Table 8-10 (*Continued*)

State	1967 TC	1967 TE	1975 TC	1975 TE	1980 TC	1980 TE	1982 TC	1982 TE	1984 TC	1984 TE	1986 TC	1986 TE	1988 TC	1988 TE	1991 TC	1991 TE
Nevada	171	71	145	70	154	60	151	63	146	65	147	65	135	69	128	73
New Hampshire	110	81	102	75	97	75	100	75	110	69	119	62	126	66	110	84
New Jersey	107	97	109	103	105	112	106	113	114	109	121	103	124	101	119	112
New Mexico	94	92	97	85	107	83	115	82	103	85	91	88	83	99	87	96
New York	108	138	98	160	90	167	92	170	98	158	107	152	109	152	103	156
North Carolina	78	94	85	86	80	97	82	94	87	89	88	92	91	93	93	87
North Dakota	92	97	101	92	108	79	115	83	106	93	94	89	86	91	91	92
Ohio	100	82	104	80	97	87	92	94	90	105	91	103	91	97	93	96
Oklahoma	102	80	98	73	117	72	126	78	113	76	98	85	89	89	87	93
Oregon	106	101	100	96	103	93	99	95	94	103	93	98	91	99	100	97
Pennsylvania	91	99	98	93	93	104	89	106	88	105	90	101	94	97	96	95
Rhode Island	91	105	88	112	84	123	81	133	86	123	92	111	99	104	89	115
South Carolina	64	97	77	85	75	95	74	96	77	95	79	94	79	96	83	90
South Dakota	91	107	94	87	90	88	87	91	83	87	78	95	78	95	86	83
Tennessee	78	87	84	79	79	84	77	86	81	81	84	84	84	83	82	82
Texas	98	75	111	68	124	65	130	66	117	69	104	79	96	88	97	87
Utah	87	111	86	89	86	101	86	97	81	106	80	107	78	106	82	94
Vermont	88	119	94	108	84	104	89	102	95	94	99	91	105	100	105	97
Virginia	86	90	93	87	95	88	94	90	96	88	101	85	104	91	103	91
Washington	112	106	98	101	103	94	102	93	99	103	98	103	98	102	108	99
West Virginia	75	96	89	85	94	82	92	86	79	100	76	98	78	88	77	102
Wisconsin	94	124	98	115	95	116	87	128	89	133	86	134	90	119	90	118
Wyoming	141	79	154	70	196	74	201	105	181	105	151	117	123	94	134	81

Note: Tax capacity (TC) measures a state's underlying economic resources and speaks to the ability to raise revenue. The tax capacity is the amount of revenue each state would raise if it applied a national average set of tax rates for twenty-six commonly used tax bases. The index above is the per capita tax capacity divided by the per capita average for all states, with the index for the average set at 100. Tax effort (TE) is the ratio of a state's actual tax collections to its tax capacity. The relative index of tax effort is created by dividing each state's tax effort by the average for all states. One hundred is the index for the U.S. average. For a more complete explanation, see the source. Data for additional years can be found in previous editions of *Vital Statistics on American Politics*.

Source: U.S. Advisory Commission on Intergovernmental Relations, *Significant Features of Fiscal Federalism, 1992*, vol. 2 (Washington, D.C.: U.S. Advisory Commission on Intergovernmental Relations, 1992), 268–269; 1994, 182–183.

Table 8-11   Federal, State, and Local Taxes, by Source, 1957–1992 (percent)

Jurisdiction/ year	Property taxes	Sales, gross receipts, and customs	Individual and corporate income taxes	All other taxes
Federal				
1957		15.9	81.3	2.7
1967		13.7	83.0	3.3
1977		9.5	86.8	3.7
1982		11.3	85.7	3.0
1983		11.7	85.5	2.8
1984		11.9	85.1	3.0
1985		10.8	86.4	2.8
1986		10.0	87.3	2.7
1987		9.0	88.3	2.7
1988		9.4	88.1	2.6
1989		8.5	89.1	2.3
1990		8.5	88.6	2.8
1991		9.1	88.2	2.7
1992		9.8	87.5	2.7
State				
1957	3.3	58.1	17.5	21.1
1967	2.7	58.2	22.4	16.8
1977	2.2	51.8	34.3	11.7
1982	1.9	48.4	36.7	12.9
1983	1.9	48.9	36.7	12.4
1984	2.0	48.7	37.8	11.5
1985	1.9	48.9	37.7	11.5
1986	1.9	49.3	37.6	11.2
1987	1.9	48.5	39.2	10.4
1988	1.9	49.3	38.6	10.3
1989	1.9	48.7	39.7	9.8
1990	1.9	48.9	39.2	9.9
1991	2.0	49.4	38.5	10.0
1992	2.0	49.6	38.5	10.0
Local				
1957	86.7	7.2	1.3	4.8
1967	86.6	6.7	3.2	3.5
1977	80.5	11.1	5.0	3.4
1982	76.0	14.3	5.9	3.9
1983	76.0	14.5	5.7	3.9
1984	75.0	14.8	5.8	4.3
1985	74.2	15.6	5.9	4.3
1986	74.0	15.6	5.9	4.5
1987	73.7	15.5	6.1	4.7
1988	74.1	15.2	6.0	4.7
1989	74.3	15.1	6.0	4.6
1990	74.5	15.3	5.7	4.6
1991	75.3	14.9	5.6	4.2
1992	75.6	14.7	5.5	4.1

Source: U.S. Advisory Commission on Intergovernmental Relations, *Significant Features of Fiscal Federalism, 1992,* vol. 2 (Washington, D.C.: U.S. Advisory Commission on Intergovernmental Relations, 1992), 126–127, *1994,* 70–71.

Table 8-12 State Lottery Revenues

State/year[a]	Date established	Gross revenue (millions)	Net proceeds (millions)	Net proceeds as a percentage of state's own source revenue	Where the revenues go
Arizona					
1982	July 1981	$114.1	$45.9	1.9	
1992		234.2	91.1	1.6	Transportation
California					
1986	October 1985	1,675.7	685.6	1.8	
1992		1,278.1	469.2	0.8	Education
Colorado					
1983	January 1983	128.7	47.0	1.9	Parks and recreation,
1992		224.9	76.2	1.5	capital construction
Connecticut					
1982	February 1972	159.7	62.5	2.1	
1992		515.8	204.4	2.6	General fund
Delaware					
1982	October 1975	23.5	8.5	1.0	
1992		74.5	27.7	1.4	General fund
District of Columbia					
1984	August 1982	50.7	12.6	1.6	
1992		139.2	47.3	0.2	General fund
Florida					
1988	January 1988	621.3	200.7	1.5	Education
1992		2,071.9	865.2	4.8	Education
Georgia	—	—	—	—	
Idaho	July 1989				
1990		66.3	24.2	1.6	
1992		52.0	13.9	0.8	Permanent building fund

State / Year	Date				Purpose
Illinois					
1982	July 1974	310.1	141.5	1.0	
1992		1,475.8	609.2	3.5	Education
Indiana					
1990	October 1989	378.6	132.4	1.6	"Build Indiana" fund
1992		359.5	116.2	1.3	
Iowa					
1986	August 1985	77.2	26.3	0.8	
1992		151.0	39.7	0.8	Economic development
Kansas					
1988	November 1987	62.2	19.6	0.6	
1992		73.1	19.7	0.5	Economic development
Kentucky					
1989	April 1989	118.2	45.7	0.9	
1990		401.9	104.2	1.6	Education
Louisiana					
1992	—	356.0	139.7	2.1	General fund
Maine					
1982	June 1974	9.7	2.4	0.3	
1992		114.1	41.3	1.7	General fund
Maryland					
1982	May 1973	434.1	208.3	4.9	
1992		770.8	347.5	4.0	General fund
Massachusetts					
1982	March 1972	210.0	69.4	1.2	
1992		1,610.9	482.7	3.5	Local government
Michigan					
1982	November 1972	483.1	198.3	2.4	
1992		1,120.9	473.3	3.0	Education

(Table continues)

Table 8-12 (Continued)

State/year[a]	Date established	Gross revenue (millions)	Net proceeds (millions)	Net proceeds as a percentage of state's own source revenue	Where the revenues go
Minnesota					
1990	April 1990	64.0	8.0	0.1	Environmental trust fund
1992		279.9	54.8	0.6	
Missouri					
1986	January 1986	196.5	80.0	1.7	General fund
1992		207.5	67.0	1.0	
Montana					
1988	June 1987	20.6	7.6	0.7	Local schools
1992		26.3	5.7	0.4	Education, environment
Nebraska	—	—	—	—	
New Hampshire	March 1964				
1982		13.3	5.3	1.0	Education
1992		99.4	36.3	2.4	
New Jersey	January 1970				
1982		$480.8	$214.9	3.0	Education
1992		1,287.0	573.8	3.2	
New York					
1982	June 1967	386.9	179.0	1.0	Education
1992		1,881.0	858.0	2.2	
Ohio					
1982	August 1974	345.3	149.6	2.0	Education
1992		1,700.6	729.6	4.4	
Oregon					
1986	April 1985	83.1	21.3	0.7	Economic development
1992		244.4	49.4	0.9	

	Date[a]				Use
Pennsylvania	March 1972				Senior citizens
1982		523.8	226.7	2.4	programs
1992		1,315.1	650.0	3.0	
Rhode Island	May 1974				
1982		33.8	16.6	1.2	General fund
1992		57.5	22.6	1.2	
South Dakota	September 1987				
1988		24.8	12.8	1.1	General fund
1992		60.5	43.5	4.5	General fund
Texas	—	—	—	—	
Vermont	February 1978				
1982		3.5	8.7	0.2	
1992		48.6	16.7	1.4	General fund
Virginia	June 1988				General fund,
1989		388.5	141.0	1.6	capital improvements
1992		826.0	289.6	2.8	
Washington	November 1982				
1983		166.8	69.7	1.4	General fund
1992		302.2	109.2	1.0	
West Virginia	January 1986				
1986		53.0	22.1	1.0	General fund
1992		85.9	28.6	0.9	
Wisconsin	June 1988				
1989		230.4	97.5	1.2	Property tax relief
1992		425.9	140.8	1.5	

Note: "—" indicates not available.

[a] First year listed is either 1982 or first year of operation.

Source: Significant Features of Fiscal Federalism, 1992, vol. 2 (Washington, D.C.: U.S. Advisory Commission on Intergovernmental Relations, 1992), 170, 172–173, 1994, 106–109.

Figure 8-2   Federal, State, and Local Government Expenditures as a Percentage of GDP, 1930–1996

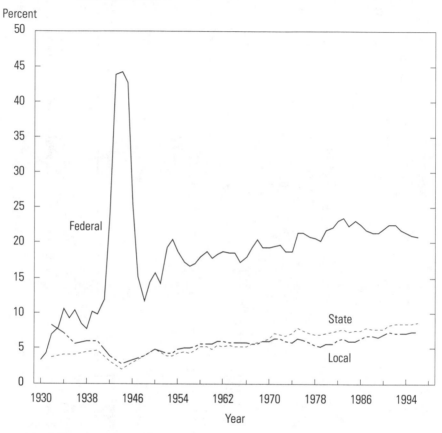

Note: The comprehensive revision of the national income and product accounts by the Bureau of Economic Analysis (released in January 1996) makes these numbers differ from previously reported figures. See Florence H. Campi, "State and Local Government Fiscal Position, 1995," *Survey of Current Business,* (September 1996), 42–47, and "Preview of the Comprehensive Revision of the National Income and Product Accounts: Recognition of Government Investment and Incorporation of a New Methodology for Calculating Depreciation," *Survey of Current Business* (September 1995), 33–41.

Sources: State and local expenditures: *Facts and Figures on Government Finance* (Washington, D.C.: Tax Foundation, 1997), 6; federal outlays and gross domestic product: Office of Management and Budget, *Budget of the U.S. Government, Fiscal Year 1998, Historical Tables* (Washington, D.C.: U.S. Government Printing Office, 1997), 21–22.

Table 8-13 State and Local Government Expenditures, by Function, 1902–1993 (percent)

Function	1902	1940	1952	1962	1972	1977	1982	1987	1990	1991	1992	1993
Education	23.3	23.5	27.0	31.5	34.6	31.7	29.4	29.3	29.6	29.2	28.5	28.4
Highways	16.0	14.0	15.1	14.7	10.0	7.1	6.6	6.8	6.3	6.1	5.8	5.6
Public welfare	3.4	10.3	9.0	7.2	11.1	11.1	11.1	10.5	11.0	12.0	13.5	13.8
Health	1.6	1.4	1.4	0.9	1.4	1.7	2.0	2.2	2.5	2.5	2.6	2.7
Hospitals	3.9	4.0	5.7	5.2	5.5	5.4	5.8	5.2	5.2	5.1	5.1	5.2
Police protection	4.6	3.2	3.0	3.0	3.2	3.2	3.2	3.2	3.1	3.1	3.0	3.0
Fire protection	3.7	2.1	1.9	1.6	1.4	1.4	1.3	1.4	1.4	1.3	1.3	1.3
Natural resources	0.8	1.9	2.5	1.9	1.6	1.3	1.3	1.3	1.3	1.2	1.1	1.1
Corrections	—	—	1.1	1.1	1.1	1.3	1.6	2.2	2.5	2.6	2.5	2.5
Sanitation and sewerage	4.7	1.8	3.2	2.8	2.5	2.9	2.9	2.8	2.9	2.9	2.8	2.4
Housing and community development	—	—	2.0	1.6	1.4	1.0	1.6	1.5	1.6	1.6	1.5	1.5
Parks and recreation	2.6	1.4	1.0	1.3	1.2	1.5	1.4	1.4	1.5	1.5	1.4	1.3
Financial administration	122.9	5.0	3.9	1.5	1.3	1.4	1.5	1.7	1.7	1.6	1.6	1.6
Other government administration	—	—	—	1.8	1.8	1.9	2.7	2.9	2.9	3.0	2.8	2.7
Social insurance administration	—	0.6	0.6	0.6	0.6	0.5	0.4	0.4	0.3	0.3	0.3	0.3

(Table continues)

Table 8-13 *(Continued)*

Function	1902	1940	1952	1962	1972	1977	1982	1987	1990	1991	1992	1993
Interest on general debt	6.2	5.8	1.8	2.9	3.2	3.5	3.8	5.4	5.1	4.9	4.8	4.6
Utilities	7.5	11.8	9.9	7.7	6.0	7.5	9.2	8.5	7.7	7.4	7.1	6.7
Liquor store expenditure	—	—	—	—	—	—	—	0.4	0.3	0.3	0.3	0.3
Insurance trust expenditure	—	6.1	5.5	6.9	5.5	8.1	7.5	6.6	6.5	7.0	7.9	8.1
Other	8.9	5.0	4.2	4.8	6.7	7.7	6.7	6.8	6.6	6.4	6.1	6.4
Total direct expenditure (millions)	$1,095	$11,240	$30,863	$70,547	$190,496	$324,554	$524,817	$772,864	$972,662	$1,060,167	$1,147,075	$1,207,125

Note: "—" indicates not available. For 1902–1952, financial administration includes other government administration. For 1902–1982, utilities includes liquor store expenditures.

Sources: 1902–1982: U.S. Bureau of the Census, *Census of Governments, 1982* (Washington, D.C.: U.S. Government Printing Office, 1985), 32–33; 1987–1989: U.S. Bureau of the Census, *Governmental Finances in 1986–87* (Washington, D.C.: U.S. Government Printing Office, 1988), 13; *1989–90*, 45; *1990–91*, 45; *1991–92*, 4; 1993: United States Total State & Local Government Finances by Level of Government, *http://www.census.gov/ftp/pub/govs/estimate/93stlus.txt* (as of May 27, 1997).

Figure 8-3   Surpluses and Deficits in Federal, State, and Local Government Finances, 1960–1996

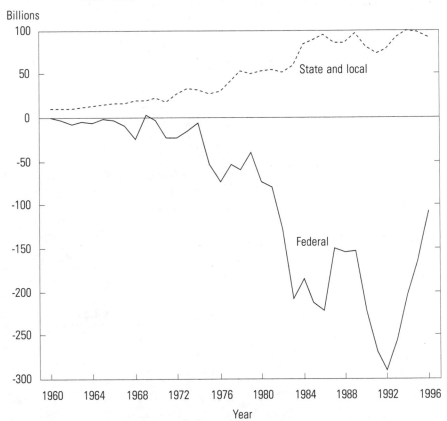

Note: The comprehensive revision of the national income and product accounts by the Bureau of Economic Analysis (released in January 1996) makes these numbers differ from previously reported figures. See Florence H. Campi, "State and Local Government Fiscal Position, 1995," *Survey of Current Business*, (September 1996), 42–47, and "Preview of the Comprehensive Revision of the National Income and Product Accounts: Recognition of Government Investment and Incorporation of a New Methodology for Calculating Depreciation," *Survey of Current Business* (September 1995), 33–41.

Source: Office of Management and Budget, *Budget of the U.S. Government, Fiscal Year 1998, Historical Tables* (Washington, D.C.: U.S. Government Printing Office, 1997), 267.

Figure 8-4   State and Local Government Surpluses Compared to Federal Grants-in-Aid, 1960–1996

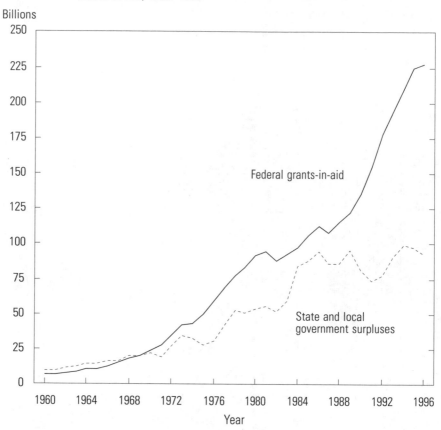

Billions

Note: The comprehensive revision of the national income and product accounts by the Bureau of Economic Analysis (released in January 1996) makes these numbers differ from previously reported figures. See Florence H. Campi, "State and Local Government Fiscal Position, 1995," *Survey of Current Business,* (September 1996), 42–47, and "Preview of the Comprehensive Revision of the National Income and Product Accounts: Recognition of Government Investment and Incorporation of a New Methodology for Calculating Depreciation," *Survey of Current Business* (September 1995), 33–41.

Source: Office of Management and Budget, *Budget of the U.S. Government, Fiscal Year 1998, Historical Tables* (Washington, D.C.: U.S. Government Printing Office, 1997), 194–195, 265.

Table 8-14   Federal Grants-in-Aid Outlays, 1950–2002

		Federal grants as a percentage of			
		Federal outlays[a]		State and	Gross
	Total grants-in-aid		Domestic	local	domestic
Year	(billions)	Total	programs[b]	expenditures[c]	product
1950	$2.3	5.3	—	—	0.8
1955	3.2	4.7	—	—	0.8
1960	7.0	7.6	18.0	19.0	1.4
1965	10.9	9.2	18.0	20.0	1.6
1970	24.1	12.3	23.0	24.0	2.4
1975	49.8	15.0	22.0	27.0	3.2
1980	91.4	15.5	22.0	31.0	3.4
1981	94.7	14.0	—	—	3.1
1982	88.1	11.8	—	—	2.7
1983	92.4	11.4	—	—	2.7
1984	97.6	11.5	—	—	2.6
1985	105.9	11.2	18.0	25.0	2.6
1986	112.3	11.3	—	—	2.6
1987	108.4	10.8	—	—	2.4
1988	115.3	10.8	—	—	2.3
1989	121.9	10.7	—	—	2.3
1990	135.3	10.8	17.0	21.0	2.4
1991	154.5	11.7	—	—	2.6
1992	178.1	12.9	—	—	2.9
1993	193.6	13.7	—	—	3.0
1994	210.6	14.4	—	—	3.1
1995	225.0	14.8	22.0	25.0	3.1
1996	227.8	14.6	21.0	24.0	3.0
1997 est.	244.8	15.0	21.0	—	3.1
1998 est.	258.8	15.3	21.0	—	3.1
1999 est.	270.0	15.3	21.0	—	3.1
2000 est.	276.4	15.2	21.0	—	3.1
2001 est.	282.6	15.3	21.0	—	3.0
2002 est.	290.5	15.5	20.0	—	2.9

Note: "—" indicates not available. Amounts in current dollars. Fiscal years.

[a] Includes off-budget outlays; all grants are on-budget.
[b] Excludes outlays for national defense, international affairs, and net interest.
[c] As defined in the national income and product accounts.

Sources: Total grants, total federal outlays, and GDP: Office of Management and Budget, *Budget of the United States Government, Fiscal Year 1998, Historical Tables* (Washington, D.C.: U.S. Government Printing Office, 1997), 194–195; domestic programs and state and local expenditures: Office of Management and Budget, *Budget of the United States Government, Fiscal Year 1998, Analytical Perspectives* (Washington, D.C.: U.S. Government Printing Office, 1997), 196.

Table 8-15 Federal Grants-in-Aid to State and Local Governments, by Function, 1940–1998 (percent)

Function	1940	1945	1950	1955	1960	1965	1970	1975	1980	1985	1990	1995	1998 est.
Health	3	11	5	4	3	6	16	18	17	23	32	42	43
Income security	39	52	59	54	38	32	24	19	20	26	27	24	24
Education, training, employment and social services	3	14	7	10	8	10	27	24	24	17	17	15	15
Transportation	19	4	21	19	43	38	19	12	14	16	14	11	10
Natural resources and environment	—	1	1	1	2	2	2	5	6	4	3	2	2
Community and regional development	32	14	—	2	2	6	7	6	7	5	4	3	3
General purpose fiscal assistance	1	1	2	3	2	2	2	14	9	7	2	1	1
Agriculture	3	3	5	7	4	5	3	1	1	2	1	1	1
Other	—	—	—	—	—	—	—	1	2	1	1	—	2
Total	100	100	100	100	102	101	100	100	100	101	100	99	100

Note: "—" indicates 0.5 percent or less.

Sources: 1940–1990: Office of Management and Budget, *Budget Baselines, Historical Data, and Alternatives for the Future* (Washington, D.C.: U.S. Government Printing Office, 1993), 429–432; 1995: Office of Management and Budget, *Budget of the U.S. Government, Fiscal Year 1997, Analytical Perspectives* (Washington, D.C.: U.S. Government Printing Office, 1996), 172–177; 1998: *1998,* 198–203.

Table 8-16 Flow of Federal Funds to and from the States, 1965–1994

State	1965–1967	1969–1971	1974–1976	1982–1984	1986–1988	1989–1991	1992–1994
Alabama	1.52	1.49	1.31	1.29	1.37	1.41	1.38
Alaska	1.01	2.76	1.82	1.01	1.16	1.19	1.26
Arizona	1.33	1.19	1.18	1.14	1.20	1.21	1.19
Arkansas	1.29	1.20	1.19	1.27	1.33	1.27	1.26
California	1.32	1.24	1.15	1.09	0.98	0.89	0.94
Colorado	1.33	1.24	1.05	0.91	1.10	1.18	1.05
Connecticut	0.92	0.88	0.92	1.02	0.84	0.77	0.69
Delaware	0.54	0.60	0.71	0.83	0.76	0.68	0.70
District of Columbia	2.16	2.99	3.23	—	5.07	5.38	5.42
Florida	1.15	1.09	0.96	1.09	1.02	1.00	1.05
Georgia	1.52	1.29	1.08	1.09	1.02	0.96	1.04
Hawaii	1.38	1.53	1.56	1.38	1.40	1.24	1.17
Idaho	1.15	0.96	1.03	1.13	1.31	1.36	1.19
Illinois	0.59	0.63	0.70	0.70	0.72	0.72	0.75
Indiana	0.75	0.81	0.74	0.83	0.89	0.89	0.89
Iowa	1.00	0.83	0.81	0.80	1.09	1.05	1.05
Kansas	1.44	1.14	0.96	1.02	1.10	1.03	1.03
Kentucky	1.32	1.14	1.17	1.10	1.23	1.27	1.21
Louisiana	1.33	1.19	1.07	0.90	1.08	1.26	1.30
Maine	1.14	1.04	1.19	1.30	1.21	1.22	1.38
Maryland	1.34	1.39	1.31	1.27	1.25	1.19	1.25
Massachusetts	0.90	0.95	1.04	1.10	1.02	0.99	0.99
Michigan	0.58	0.61	0.76	0.78	0.74	0.77	0.82
Minnesota	0.93	0.89	0.87	0.85	0.92	0.87	0.81
Mississippi	1.68	1.73	1.65	1.61	1.72	1.70	1.72
Missouri	1.09	1.10	1.12	1.43	1.31	1.32	1.28
Montana	1.53	1.18	1.17	1.07	1.37	1.43	1.38
Nebraska	1.26	0.91	0.91	0.95	1.16	1.10	1.05
Nevada	0.86	0.75	0.85	0.92	0.99	0.86	0.81
New Hampshire	0.83	0.97	0.90	0.98	0.76	0.70	0.74
New Jersey	0.71	0.75	0.79	0.70	0.64	0.63	0.68
New Mexico	1.68	1.67	1.47	1.80	2.07	2.02	1.95
New York	0.62	0.78	0.93	0.92	0.84	0.80	0.83
North Carolina	1.21	0.99	1.00	0.95	0.94	0.94	0.98
North Dakota	2.04	1.51	1.32	1.06	1.56	1.55	1.50
Ohio	0.70	0.75	0.76	0.85	0.93	0.94	0.92
Oklahoma	1.36	1.35	1.23	0.88	1.10	1.21	1.24
Oregon	0.80	0.84	0.91	0.89	0.97	0.95	0.94
Pennsylvania	0.71	0.85	0.95	0.96	0.97	0.95	1.00
Rhode Island	1.17	1.14	1.07	1.05	0.99	1.00	1.07
South Carolina	1.58	1.25	1.22	1.25	1.25	1.31	1.26
South Dakota	1.67	1.26	1.33	1.24	1.51	1.42	1.30
Tennessee	1.12	1.01	0.98	1.20	1.18	1.15	1.15
Texas	1.35	1.31	0.96	0.78	0.89	0.98	0.96

(Table continues)

Table 8-16   *(Continued)*

State	1965– 1967	1969– 1971	1974– 1976	1982– 1984	1986– 1988	1989– 1991	1992– 1994
Utah	1.32	1.53	1.28	1.27	1.45	1.40	1.17
Vermont	1.11	1.02	1.16	1.10	0.94	0.88	0.94
Virginia	1.73	1.68	1.46	1.52	1.56	1.40	1.39
Washington	1.24	1.10	1.20	1.09	1.16	1.03	0.93
West Virginia	1.02	1.09	1.21	1.07	1.27	1.40	1.47
Wisconsin	0.67	0.71	0.76	0.82	0.84	0.85	0.83
Wyoming	1.50	1.10	1.00	0.75	1.04	1.13	1.04

Note: Numbers are the estimated amount of federal expenditures in each state for each $100 of federal taxes paid by residents of each state. Includes all federal expenditures that can be allocated by state. All figures adjusted proportionally so that overall there is $1.00 of revenue for each $1.00 of expenditure. Three-year averages (two-year for 1992–1993) for expenditures and revenue were used to ensure that unusually high or low figures in a particular state in any single year would not unduly influence the flow-of-fund ratios. The 1965–1976 figures are based on detailed analyses that take into account the precise location of taxes and expenditures (e.g., where procurement spending actually occurred as indicated by subcontracts, not just the major contract). Calculations for the 1982–1993 figures do not incorporate such adjustments (personal communication from Michael Lawson).

Sources: 1965–1984: U.S. Advisory Commission on Intergovernmental Relations, *Significant Features of Fiscal Federalism, 1985–86* (Washington, D.C.: U.S. Advisory Commission on Intergovernmental Relations, 1986), 178; 1986–1994: calculated by the editors from Bureau of the Census, Department of Commerce, *Federal Expenditures by State for Fiscal Year 1987* (Washington, D.C.: U.S. Government Printing Office, 1988), 1; *1988,* 1; *1989,* 1; *1990,* 1; *1991,* 1; *1992,* 1; *1993,* 1; *1994,* 1; and Paul G. Merski, "The 1992 Federal Tax Burden by State," *Tax Foundation Special Report,* May 1992, 6; and *Facts and Figures on Government Finance* (Washington, D.C.: Tax Foundation, 1994), 83–84; Tax Foundation, "Total Fiscal Tax Burden by State," 1995.

Table 8-17   Fiscal Dependency of Lower Levels on Higher Levels of Government, 1927–1994

Year	Intergovernmental revenue as a percentage of total revenue		
	State from federal	Local from federal	Local from state[a]
1927	5.0	[b]	9.4
1934	27.3	1.3	20.7
1940	11.6	3.6	21.4
1946	9.4	0.1	21.9
1952	13.9	1.2	26.0
1957	14.2	1.2	25.2
1962	18.9	1.8	25.2
1965	20.2	2.2	32.5
1967	22.3	2.7	28.5
1970	21.6	2.9	30.2
1972	23.8	4.0	30.6
1973	24.2	6.1	31.0
1974	22.5	7.1	31.1
1975	23.0	6.8	32.0
1976	22.9	7.6	31.5
1977	22.4	8.4	30.7
1978	22.3	9.0	30.1
1979	22.1	8.8	31.6
1980	22.3	8.2	31.5
1981	21.8	7.8	30.9
1982	20.0	6.7	30.2
1983	19.3	6.2	29.1
1984	19.2	5.7	28.9
1985	19.2	5.4	28.9
1986	19.3	4.7	29.2
1987	18.5	4.2	29.1
1988	18.5	3.5	29.4
1989	18.4	3.3	29.6
1990	18.7	3.2	29.7
1991	20.4	3.1	29.8
1992	21.4	3.1	30.3
1993	22.0	3.1	30.3
1994	22.7	3.3	30.2

[a] Includes indirect federal aid passed through the states.
[b] Less than 0.1 percent.

Sources: 1927–1992: Calculated by the editors from U.S. Advisory Commission on Intergovernmental Relations, *Significant Features of Fiscal Federalism, 1994,* vol. 2 (Washington, D.C.: U.S. Advisory Commission on Intergovernmental Relations, 1994), 44; 1993–1994: *http://www. census.gov/govs/estimate* (as of August 6, 1997).

Table 8-18   Variations in Local Dependency on State Aid, 1993–1994 (percent)

Rank	State	Percentage	Rank	State	Percentage
1	New Mexico	51.4	27	Ohio	33.5
2	California	45.4	28	Louisiana	33.4
3	Delaware	45.0	29	Pennsylvania	33.2
4	West Virginia	43.6	30	New Jersey	33.2
5	Arkansas	43.1	31	Oregon	31.7
6	North Carolina	42.2	32	Maine	31.4
7	Kentucky	41.9	33	Virginia	31.4
8	Minnesota	41.2	34	South Carolina	31.3
9	Mississippi	41.1	35	Texas	31.1
10	Wisconsin	40.4	36	Michigan	30.9
11	Arizona	40.3	37	Tennessee	30.8
12	Montana	40.1	38	Missouri	30.7
13	Washington	39.7	39	Georgia	29.3
14	Wyoming	39.1	40	Illinois	28.9
15	Idaho	38.6	41	Connecticut	28.3
16	Nevada	38.3	42	Rhode Island	27.8
17	Oklahoma	38.1	43	Maryland	27.3
18	Alaska	37.3	44	Colorado	27.3
19	Utah	35.9	45	Florida	27.0
20	North Dakota	35.5	46	Nebraska	26.2
21	New York	34.9	47	Vermont	25.8
22	Massachusetts	34.6	48	South Dakota	22.5
23	Indiana	34.0	49	New Hampshire	13.3
24	Alabama	33.7	50	Hawaii	12.6
25	Iowa	33.7		Total	34.8
26	Kansas	33.6			

Note: Percentages reflect state transfers (including "pull-through" monies from the federal government) as a percentage of total local general revenues. Where ties occur, the rank order was determined by the second decimal.

Source: U.S. Bureau of the Census, "State and Local Government Finance Estimates, by State: 1993–1994" as reported at *http://www.census.gov/govs/www/esti94.html* (as of July 25, 1997).

9

Foreign and Military Policy

- **Diplomacy**
- **Treaties and Agreements**
- **Military Engagements**
- **Military Personnel**
- **Expenditures**
- **Military Sales and Assistance**
- **Foreign Aid**
- **Investment and Trade**
- **Immigration**

Even if one sought to understand only U.S. domestic politics, data on international relations would be essential. In the 1960 presidential campaign, for example, John Kennedy made the "missile gap" a major issue: the United States was falling behind the Soviet Union in its missile arsenal, and this imperiled the defense of the free world. The actual existence of that missile gap has been disputed, but the charge fit in with Kennedy's pledge to get the country moving again and played well to the public in the aftermath of Sputnik and the U-2 incident. Similarly, Ronald Reagan made increased military spending a cornerstone of his campaign platform in 1980.

One might think that statistics relating to foreign policy, especially the military aspects, are difficult or impossible to find, that secrecy prevents publication of important information about our defense capabilities. There are instances in which this is the case. Performance capabilities of spy satellites and the "stealth" bomber are understandably kept secret. There are also secret diplomatic and military initiatives undertaken by the Central Intelligence Agency and other organizations that the public learns about later, if at all. In the 1980s the sale of weapons to Iran while the United States was publicly declaring that it would have nothing to do with that country, and the use of profits from these sales to support the Nicaraguan contras, is a case in point.

Despite these examples and the obvious need for secrecy in defense-related areas, a surprisingly wide array of data is available, in part because details about military hardware are not the only kinds of relevant information. As was especially evident during the 1960s, for example, public opinion about foreign policy is extraordinarily relevant and powerful information. As presented in Chapter 3, public opinion on U.S. involvement in Vietnam reveals a great deal about why President Lyndon Johnson declined to seek reelection in 1968 and why U.S. forces began to withdraw from Vietnam soon thereafter (Figure 3-15). In opposite fashion, opinions about our involvement in the 1991 Gulf War (Figure 3-15) indicate why President George Bush's presidential approval ratings were, temporarily as it turned out, extraordinarily high (Figure 3-5). Public opinion on defense spending has been politically relevant, although the pattern of changes in the late 1970s and 1980s suggests that Ronald Reagan was leading as well as responding to changes in public sentiments (Table 3-22).

Diplomatic structures and efforts, both current and historical (Tables 9-1 and 9-3), as well as international arms control and other agreements (Tables 9-2 and 9-4) are also relevant inasmuch as they are affected by and, in turn, affect domestic politics. The historical record of U.S. involvement abroad in both the distant and recent past (Tables 9-5 through 9-7) serves as a reminder that the end of the "new world order" has not signaled a complete withdrawal from foreign engagements. Likewise, the number and placement of U.S. troops abroad remain important issues (Table 9-8). More obviously, data on military personnel are sometimes directly related to domestic concerns, as for example a table on military personnel categorized by sex, race, and Hispanic origin (Table 9-9).

A variety of other information closely relates to both defense and domestic policy, and this kind of data is emphasized here. Defense spending, for example, involves more than whether the United States has spent enough to defend itself. Elementary economics courses use the phrase "guns or butter" to express the tradeoff between defense and nondefense spending. Every dollar spent for weaponry means a dollar less that can be spent for social programs, tax reductions, and other politically worthy causes. Therefore, information on defense spending (Table 9-10) is doubly relevant.

In presenting information about defense spending, two elements arise. The first is the concept of "constant" versus "current" dollars. Current dollars are what people deal with every day. The price asked for goods is the price paid; whether the price has gone up more or less than other prices is not especially relevant. People may be aware that prices of some goods have gone up (for example, oil and gasoline in the 1970s) or down (for example, many electronic products) more than others, but the price quoted is what is most significant. Constant dollars, in contrast, take into account what has happened to prices more generally (see Table 11-2 for the Consumer Price Index). Thus, for example, most food clearly costs more in current dollars than it did years ago; in the 1960s one never heard of a loaf of bread that cost $1.00. Yet relative to other prices, the cost of bread has been reduced. Its price may have only doubled in a given period of time while other prices have tripled. In a meaningful sense, therefore, bread and other foods are cheaper than they used to be; the "real" cost of bread has been reduced.

Another, perhaps simpler, way to express this is to say that constant dollar calculations take inflation into account. For defense spending, therefore, the question is: After taking inflation into account, has spending increased? If spending has risen only as fast as inflation, the new budget will buy only as much as the previous budget, even though nominally, that is, in current dollars, it is larger. Because this issue of real versus current dollars is so significant, Table 9-10 and many of the tables in Chapter 11 express expenditures both ways.

The second new element in presenting information about defense spending is that it is especially relevant to see what other countries are doing as well. Whether the United States is spending a lot or a little is a relative question. If foreign adversaries raise their spending, then perhaps the United States must do the same. As a consequence, information is presented on worldwide military expenditures (Table 9-11), even though the focus in this volume is on the United States.

Economic and social dimensions are also relevant to U.S. foreign and military policy, and data about these are widely available. The slippage of the U.S. trade balance (Table 9-15) and the increasing foreign investment in the United States and U.S. investment abroad (Table 9-14) are two aspects of the economic context of recent foreign policy discussions. Foreign aid, whether in the form of military (Table 9-12) or nonmilitary (Table 9-13) assistance, is another part of economic foreign policy. Immigration policy has social and economic implications, and changes in the flow of immigrants, along with future prospects, make it a most significant aspect of U.S. foreign relations (Table 9-16).

Despite the ending of the Cold War, public opinion about wars, international agreements, previous conflicts, levels of defense spending, foreign aid, the balance of trade, and so on—and the data about them—remain as relevant as ever. The emergence of the United States as a world power in the twentieth century has elevated the political significance of international relations so that no overview of American politics would be complete without a look at foreign and military policy. Foreign policy has often proved critical in domestic politics, and that accounts for the numbers presented here.

Table 9-1   U.S. Diplomatic and Consular Posts, 1781–1996

Year	Diplomatic	Consular
1781	4	3
1790	2	10
1800	6	52
1810	4	60
1820	7	83
1830	15	141
1840	20	152
1850	27	197
1860	33	282
1870	36	318
1880	35	303
1890	41	323
1900	41	318
1910	48	324
1920	45	368
1930	57	299
1940	58	264
1950	74	179
1960	99	166
1970	117	122
1980	133	100
1990	170	97
1992	185	99
1994	191	90
1996	192	80

Note: 1990–1996 figures are as of May, April, August, and February, respectively. For those years, diplomatic posts include embassies, countries with ambassadors without physical missions, branch offices, missions, and interest sections. Consular posts include consulates general and consulates.

Sources: U.S. Department of State, Office of Public Communication, *A Short History of the U.S. Department of State 1781–1981* (Washington, D.C.: U.S. Government Printing Office, 1981), 35. Updated from U.S. Department of State, *Key Officers of Foreign Service Posts* (Washington, D.C.: U.S. Government Printing Office, May 1990), vi; (1992), xi; (1994), xv; (1996), xv.

Table 9-2   Treaties and Executive Agreements Concluded by the United States, 1789–1996

Years	Number of treaties	Number of executive agreements
1789–1839	60	27
1839–1889	215	238
1889–1929	382	763
1930–1932	49	41
1933–1944 (F. Roosevelt)	131	369
1945–1952 (Truman)	132	1,324
1953–1960 (Eisenhower)	89	1,834
1961–1963 (Kennedy)	36	813
1964–1968 (L. Johnson)	67	1,083
1969–1974 (Nixon)	93	1,317
1975–1976 (Ford)	26	666
1977–1980 (Carter)	79	1,476
1981–1988 (Reagan)	125	2,840
1989–1992 (Bush)	67	1,350
1993–1996 (Clinton)	97	1,137

Note: Number of treaties includes those concluded during the indicated span of years. Some of these treaties did not receive the consent of the U.S. Senate. Varying definitions of what comprises an executive agreement and their entry-into-force date make the above numbers approximate.

Sources: 1789–1980: *Congressional Quarterly's Guide to Congress,* 291; 1981–1994: Office of the Assistant Legal Adviser for Treaty Affairs, U.S. Department of State.

Table 9-3   U.S.-Soviet Summit Meetings, 1945–1991

Date	Location	Leaders	Topic
July–August 1945	Potsdam	President Harry S. Truman, Soviet leader Josef Stalin, British prime ministers Winston Churchill and Clement R. Attlee	Partition and control of Germany
July 1955	Geneva	President Dwight D. Eisenhower, Soviet leader Nikolai A. Bulganin, British prime minister Anthony Eden, French premier Edgar Faure	Reunification of Germany, disarmament, European security
September 1959	Camp David, Md.	President Dwight D. Eisenhower, Soviet leader Nikita S. Khrushchev	Berlin problem
May 1960	Paris	President Dwight D. Eisenhower, Soviet leader Nikita S. Khrushchev, French president Charles de Gaulle, British prime minister Harold Macmillan	U-2 incident
June 1961	Vienna	President John F. Kennedy, Soviet leader Nikita S. Khrushchev	Berlin problem
June 1967	Glassboro, N.J.	President Lyndon B. Johnson, Soviet leader Aleksei N. Kosygin	Middle East
May 1972	Moscow	President Richard M. Nixon, Soviet leader Leonid I. Brezhnev	SALT I, antiballistic missile limitations
June 1973	Washington, D.C.	President Richard M. Nixon, Soviet leader Leonid I. Brezhnev	Détente
June–July 1974	Moscow and Yalta	President Richard M. Nixon, Soviet leader Leonid I. Brezhnev	Arms control
November 1974	Vladivostok	President Gerald R. Ford, Soviet leader Leonid I. Brezhnev	Arms control
June 1979	Vienna	President Jimmy Carter, Soviet leader Leonid I. Brezhnev	SALT II
November 1985	Geneva	President Ronald Reagan, Soviet leader Mikhail Gorbachev	Arms control, U.S.-Soviet relations

Table 9-3   *(Continued)*

Date	Location	Leaders	Topic
October 1986	Reykjavik	President Ronald Reagan, Soviet leader Mikhail Gorbachev	Arms control
December 1987	Washington, D.C.	President Ronald Reagan, Soviet leader Mikhail Gorbachev	Intermediate Nuclear Force (INF) Treaty, Afghanistan
May 1988	Moscow	President Ronald Reagan, Soviet leader Mikhail Gorbachev	Arms control, human rights
December 1988	New York	President Ronald Reagan, Soviet leader Mikhail Gorbachev	U.S.-Soviet relations
December 1989	Malta	President George Bush, Soviet leader Mikhail Gorbachev	Arms control, Eastern Europe
May–June 1990	Washington, D.C.	President George Bush, Soviet leader Mikhail Gorbachev	Arms control
September 1990	Helsinki	President George Bush, Soviet leader Mikhail Gorbachev	Middle East crisis
July 1991	Moscow	President George Bush, Soviet leader Mikhail Gorbachev	Arms control and Soviet economic and political future

Note: Prior to the dissolution of the Soviet Union, President George Bush and Soviet leader Mikhail Gorbachev met in Madrid at the opening of the Mideast Peace talks in October 1991. There was no specific agenda.

Source: *Congressional Quarterly's Guide to the U.S. Presidency* (Washington, D.C.: Congressional Quarterly, 1989), 520–521; updated by the editors.

Table 9-4   Arms Control and Disarmament Agreements

Issue	Participants
Nuclear weapons	
To prevent the spread of nuclear weapons	
Antarctic Treaty, 1959	39 states[a]
Outer Space Treaty, 1967	100 states[a]
Latin American Nuclear-Free Zone	
Treaty, 1967	30 states[a]
Nonproliferation Treaty, 1968	185 states[b]
Seabed Treaty, 1971	94 states[a]
To reduce the risk of nuclear war	
Hot Line and Modernization	
Agreements, 1963	United States and Soviet Union
Accidents Measures Agreement, 1971	United States and Soviet Union
Prevention of Nuclear War Agreement,	
1973	United States and Soviet Union
To limit nuclear testing	
Limited Test Ban Treaty, 1963	128 states[a]
Threshold Test Ban Treaty, 1974	United States and Soviet Union
Peaceful Nuclear Explosions Treaty,	
1976[b]	United States and Soviet Union
To limit nuclear weapons	
ABM Treaty (SALT I) and Protocol, 1972	United States and Soviet Union
SALT I Interim Agreement, 1972[c]	United States and Soviet Union
SALT II, 1979[d]	United States and Soviet Union
Intermediate Range Nuclear Force (INF)	
Missiles Treaty, 1988	United States and Soviet Union
Strategic Arms Reduction Treaty	
(START), 1991	United States, Russia, Bellarius, Kazakstan, Ukraine[f]
Strategic Arms Reduction Treaty, II	
(START II), 1993	United States and Russia[g]
Other weapons	
To prohibit use of gas	
Geneva Protocol, 1925	129 states[a]
To prohibit biological weapons	
Biological Weapons Convention, 1972	157 states[h]
To prohibit techniques changing the	
environment	
Environmental Modification	
Convention, 1977	62 states[a]
To control use of inhumane weapons	
Convention on Conventional Weapons,	
1981	73 states[i]
To limit conventional weapons	
Conventional Forces in Europe Treaty,	
1990	30 states[j]

Table 9-4   *(Continued)*

Issue	*Participants*
To ban use, development, production, stockpiling of chemical weapons Chemical Weapons Convention, 1993	164 states[k]

[a] Number of parties and signatories as of January 1996.

[b] Number of parties and signatories as of January 1997.

[c] Ratified by the United States and entered into force in December 1990.

[d] Expired by its terms on October 3, 1977.

[e] Never ratified. If the treaty had entered into force, it would have expired by its terms on December 31, 1985.

[f] Ratified by the United States in October 1992; entered into force December 1994.

[g] Ratified by the United States in January 1996.

[h] Number of parties and signatories as of November 1996.

[i] Convention entered into force December 1983. Number of parties and signatories as of December 1996. Full title of treaty is Convention on Prohibitions or Restrictions on the Use of Certain Conventional Weapons which may be Deemed to be Excessively Injurious or to have Indiscriminate Effects (and Protocols).

[j] Ratified by the United States in December 1991; entered into force November 1992.

[k] Ratified by the U.S. April 24, 1997; took effect April 29, 1997 with 164 countries having signed and 75 having ratified.

Sources: U.S. Arms Control and Disarmament Agency, *Arms Control and Disarmament Agreements,* 1990 ed. (Washington: U.S. Arms Control and Disarmament Agency, 1990), and unpublished data from Office of Treaty Affairs, U.S. State Department., and the U.S. Arms Control and Disarmament Agency; note k updated by the editors.

Table 9-5   Use of United States Armed Forces Abroad, 1798–1996

Decade	Number of instances	Example of use of armed forces
1798–1800	1	Undeclared naval war with France
1801–1810	4	Tripoli—First Barbary War
1811–1820	13	Caribbean—engagements with pirates, onshore and offshore
1821–1830	8	Cuba—fight, capture pirates
1831–1840	7	Fiji Islands—punish natives who attacked American explorers
1841–1850	8	China—after a clash at a trading post in Canton
1851–1860	22	Nicaragua—oppose William Walker's attempt to control country
1861–1870	13	Japan—several times, to protect American interests
1871–1880	5	Colombia—protect American interests in fighting over Panama
1881–1890	7	Hawaii—protect American interests
1891–1900	18	Philippine Islands—protect American interests; conquer islands
1901–1910	16	Colombia, Panama, Dominican Republic, Honduras, Nicaragua—protect American interests during civil turmoil
1911–1920	29	Honduras, China, Turkey, Mexico—protect American interests
1921–1930	15	Panama, Costa Rica—to prevent war over boundary dispute
1931–1940	7	Haiti—part of long-term stay to prevent chronic insurrection
1941–1950	13	Trieste—reinforce air forces after Yugoslav downing of plane
1951–1960	6	Korean War; Lebanon—protect against threatened insurrection
1961–1970	8	Vietnam War; Congo—airlift Congolese troops during rebellion
1971–1980	11	Lebanon—evacuate citizens fighting; Iran—rescue attempt
1981–1990	23	Libya—shoot down jets; Granada—restore law and order
1991–1994	5	Persian Gulf War; Somalia—food aid; Haiti—oust military; Bosnia—keep peace

Note: The count of instances is necessarily approximate; for example, numerous engagements with pirates in the Caribbean between 1814 and 1825 are counted as only one instance. Five of the instances were declared wars: the War of 1812 (1812–1815), the Mexican War (1846–1848), the Spanish-American War (1898), World War I (1917–1918), and World War II (1941–1945). Others might be considered undeclared wars: Undeclared Naval War with France (1798–1800), First Barbary War (1801–1805), Second Barbary War (1815), Korean War (1950–1953), Vietnam War (1964–1973), and Persian Gulf War (1991). (Actions that covered more than one decade are counted as occurring in each decade.)

Source: Ellen C. Collier, "Instances of Use of United States Armed Forces Abroad, 1798–1993" (Washington, D.C.: Congressional Research Service, 1993); updated by the editors based on reports in the *New York Times*.

Table 9-6 U.S. Personnel in Major Military Conflicts

Item	Civil War[a]	Spanish-American War	World War I	World War II	Korean conflict	Vietnam conflict	Gulf War
Personnel serving (thousands)	2,213	307[b]	4,735	16,113[c]	5,720[d]	8,744[e]	541[f]
Average duration of service (months)	20	8	12	33	19	23	7
Casualties (thousands)							
Battle deaths	140	[g]	53	292	34	47[h]	[g]
Wounds not mortal	282	2	204	671	103	153[h]	[g]
Draftees: classified (thousands)	777	0	24,234	36,677	9,123	75,717[e]	0
Examined	522	0	3,764	17,955	3,685	8,611	0
Rejected	160	0	803	6,420	1,189	3,880	0
Inducted	46	0	2,820	10,022	1,560	1,759	0
Cost (millions)[i]							
Current	$2,300	$270	$32,700	$360,000	$50,000	$140,600	$7,300[j]
Constant (1967)	8,500	1,100	100,000	816,300	69,300	148,800	1,790

Note: For Revolutionary War, the number of personnel serving is not known, but estimates range from 184,000 to 250,000; for War of 1812, 286,730 served; for Mexican War, 78,718 served.

a Union forces only. Estimates of the number serving in Confederate forces range from 600,000 to 1.5 million; cost for the Confederacy estimated at $1 million (current dollars) and $3.7 million (constant dollars).
b Covers April 21, 1898 to August 13, 1898.
c Covers December 1, 1941 to December 31, 1946.
d Covers June 25, 1950 to July 27, 1953.
e Covers August 4, 1964 to January 27, 1973.
f Covers August 1, 1990 to April 30, 1992.
g Fewer than 500.
h Covers January 1, 1961 to January 27, 1973.
i Original direct costs only. Excludes service-connected veterans' benefits and interest payments on war loans.
j Total costs estimated at $61.6 billion (in current dollars). Shown is the portion of that amount estimated to have been paid by the United States.

Sources: U.S. Bureau of the Census, *Statistical Abstract of the United States, 1994* (Washington, D.C.: U.S. Government Printing Office, 1994), 357, 362; U.S. Department of Defense, unpublished data.

Table 9-7 U.S. Military Forces and Casualties in Vietnam, 1957–1993

| | | Battle deaths | | | | Wounded nonfatal[a] | |
| | | | | | | Hospital care (thousands) | No hospital care (thousands) |
Year	Military forces (thousands)	Total[a]	Killed	Died of wounds	Died while missing[b]		
1957–1964	23.3[c]	279	197	10	72	0.8	0.8
1965	184.3	1,432	1,124	111	197	3.3	2.8
1966	385.3	5,047	4,142	579	326	16.5	13.6
1967	485.6	9,463	7,525	1,598	401	32.4	29.7
1968	536.1	14,623	12,624	979	959	46.8	46.0
1969	475.2	9,426	8,117	1,168	141	32.9	37.3
1970	234.6	4,230	3,486	555	189	15.2	15.4
1971	156.8	1,376	1,082	160	134	4.8	4.2
1972	24.2	361	205	28	128	0.6[d]	0.6[d]
1973–1993	0.0	1,118	0	22	1,068		
Total	[e]	47,355	38,502	5,210	3,615	153.3	150.4

Note: Military forces as of December 31. All U.S. forces withdrawn by January 27, 1973.

[a] Casualties from enemy action. Deaths exclude 10,803 servicemen who died in accidents or from disease.
[b] Includes 114 servicemen who died while captured.
[c] For 1964 only.
[d] Fewer than 50.
[e] Not applicable.

Sources: Military forces, battle deaths: U.S. Bureau of the Census, *Statistical Abstract of the United States, 1995* (Washington, D.C.: U.S. Government Printing Office, 1995), 365; wounded, nonfatal: *Statistical Abstract of the United States, 1987*, 328.

Table 9-8 U.S. Military Personnel Abroad or Afloat, by Country, 1972–1996 (thousands)

Country	1972	1975	1980	1985	1987	1988	1989	1990	1991	1992	1993	1994	1995	1996
Outside United States[a]	628	517	502	515	524	541	510	609	448	344	308	287	238	240
Europe[a,b]	298	314	332	358	354	356	341	310	285	205	166	138	118	115
Germany	210	220	244	247	251	249	249	228	203	134	105	88	73	49
Greece	3	4	4	4	3	3	3	2	1	1	1	c	c	1
Iceland	3	3	3	4	3	3	3	3	3	3	3	2	2	2
Italy	10	12	12	15	14	15	16	14	13	13	10	12	12	12
Spain	9	9	9	9	9	9	9	7	6	4	4	3	3	3
Turkey	7	7	5	5	5	5	5	4	6	5	4	4	3	3
United Kingdom	22	21	24	30	28	28	28	25	23	20	16	14	12	12
Afloat	28	30	22	36	31	33	21	18	20	17	17	9	8	4
East Asia and Pacific[a]	275	156	115	125	129	141	135	119	105	98	99	98	89	95
Japan (includes Okinawa)	65	48	46	47	50	50	50	47	45	46	46	45	39	43
Philippines	17	15	13	15	16	17	15	14	8	2	c	c	c	c
South Korea	41	42	39	42	45	46	44	41	40	36	35	37	36	37
Thailand	47	20	c	c	c	c	c	c	c	c	c	c	c	c
Vietnam	47	0	0	0	0	0	0	0	0	c	c	c	c	c
Afloat	51	28	16	20	17	28	25	16	11	13	17	15	13	15
U.S. outlying areas[d]	29	25	2	14	12	12	12	11	11	12	12	9	9	8
Troop dependents	342	365	369	385	386	373	389	400	365	303	273	229	223	214

Note: Data for additional years can be found in previous editions of *Vital Statistics on American Politics*.

[a] Includes troops in countries not shown.
[b] Western Europe and related areas.
[c] Fewer than 500.
[d] Primarily Guam and Puerto Rico.

Sources: 1972–1985: *Statistical Abstract of the United States, 1977* (Washington, D.C.: U.S. Government Printing Office, 1977), 370; *1982–1983*, 361; *1986*, 343; *1987*, 328; *1986–1994*: U.S. Department of Defense, *Selected Manpower Statistics, Fiscal Year 1986* (Washington, D.C.: U.S. Government Printing Office, 1987), 44–46, 51, 163; *1987, 1988*, 44–46, 51, 178; *1989*, 44–46, 51, 179; *1990, 1991, 1992, 1993*, 44–47, 51, 176; *1994*, 35–43, 177; *1995*: http://web1.whs.osd.mil/mmid/military/309a995.htm, 1–6; http://web1.whs.osd.mil/mmid/m01/sms4/ar.htm; *1996*: Department of Defense, *Worldwide Manpower Distribution by Geographical Area* (Washington, D.C.: U.S. Government Printing Office, 1996), 19–28, 75.

Table 9-9 U.S. Active Duty Forces, by Sex, Race, and Hispanic Origin, 1965–1996

Year	Female			Black			Hispanic[a]			Total[b]	
	Officers	Enlisted	Total	Officers	Enlisted	Total	Officers	Enlisted	Total	Officers (thousands)	Enlisted (thousands)
1965	3.1%	0.9%	1.2%	1.9%	10.5%	9.5%	—	—	—	339	2,317
1966	3.2	0.8	1.1	—	—	—	—	—	—	349	2,745
1967	3.3	0.8	1.0	2.1	9.9	8.9	—	—	—	385	2,992
1968	3.2	0.8	1.1	2.1	10.2	9.2	—	—	—	416	2,132
1969	3.1	0.9	1.1	2.1	9.6	8.7	—	—	—	419	3,041
1970	3.3	1.1	1.4	2.2	11.0	9.8	—	—	—	402	2,664
1971	3.5	1.3	1.6	2.3	12.1	10.7	1.3%	3.4%	3.1%	371	2,329
1972	3.8	1.6	1.9	2.4	13.5	11.9	1.2	4.0	3.6	336	1,987
1973	4.0	2.2	2.5	2.7	14.9	13.2	1.2	4.5	4.0	321	1,932
1974	4.3	3.3	3.5	3.0	16.2	14.4	1.3	4.5	3.9	303	1,860
1975	4.6	4.5	4.6	3.2	16.2	14.4	1.4	4.6	4.2	292	1,836
1976	5.0	5.3	5.2	3.6	17.1	15.2	1.3	4.6	4.2	281	1,801
1977	5.4	5.8	5.7	3.9	17.4	15.6	1.5	4.5	4.1	276	1,798
1978	6.2	6.5	6.5	4.3	19.3	17.3	1.6	4.5	4.1	274	1,788
1979	6.9	7.5	7.4	4.7	21.2	19.0	1.6	4.4	3.8	274	1,753
1980	7.7	8.5	8.4	5.0	21.9	19.6	1.2	4.0	3.6	278	1,759
1981	8.1	9.0	8.9	5.3	22.1	19.8	1.2	4.1	3.7	285	1,783
1982	8.6	9.0	9.0	5.3	22.0	19.7	1.2	4.1	3.7	292	1,804
1983	9.0	9.3	9.3	5.8	21.6	19.4	1.4	4.1	3.7	301	1,811
1984	9.4	9.5	9.5	6.2	21.1	19.0	1.4	3.9	3.6	304	1,820
1985	9.8	9.8	9.8	6.4	21.1	18.9	1.5	3.9	3.6	309	1,828
1986	10.1	10.0	10.1	6.5	21.2	19.1	1.7	4.1	3.7	311	1,845
1987	10.4	10.2	10.2	6.5	21.5	19.4	1.7	4.3	3.9	308	1,856
1988	10.7	10.4	10.4	6.7	22.0	19.8	1.8	4.5	4.1	305	1,819
1989	11.1	11.0	11.0	6.9	22.8	20.3	2.0	4.8	4.4	303	1,814

1990	11.4	10.9	10.9	6.9	22.9	20.5	2.1	5.0	4.6	304	1,762
1991	11.7	10.8	10.9	7.1	22.6	20.3	2.2	5.2	4.8	298	1,711
1992	12.0	11.3	11.4	7.2	22.0	19.8	2.3	5.5	5.0	281	1,551
1993	12.4	11.5	11.7	7.1	21.6	19.4	2.4	5.8	5.3	264	1,466
1994	12.8	12.0	12.1	7.3	21.4	19.2	2.6	6.0	5.4	253	1,380
1995	13.0	12.5	12.6	7.5	21.5	19.3	2.8	6.4	5.8	245	1,295
1996	13.4	13.2	13.2	7.8	21.8	19.6	3.0	6.9	6.3	233	1,225

Note: "—" indicates not available.

[a] Hispanics may be of any race. Data on percent Hispanic origin from 1971 to 1979 is based on male armed forces members only.
[b] Includes other races not shown separately.

Sources: 1965–1985: *Statistical Abstract of the United States, 1976* (Washington, D.C.: U.S. Government Printing Office, 1976), 336; *1980,* 375–376; *1984,* 353; *1986,* 341; *1987,* 327; 1986–1988: Department of Defense, unpublished data; 1989 (female, total enlisted): U.S. Department of Defense, *Selected Manpower Statistics, 1989* (Washington, D.C.: U.S. Government Printing Office, 1989), 78, 87, 101; 1989 (other): U.S. Department of Defense, *Defense 90 Almanac* (Washington, D.C.: U.S. Government Printing Office, 1990), 30; 1990–1996: Defense Equal Opportunity Management Institute, *Semi-Annual Race/Ethnic/Gender Profile of the Department of Defense Active Forces, Reserve Forces, and the United States Coast Guard* (Patrick Air Force Base, Fla.: Defense Equal Opportunity Management Institute, 1990), 24; (1991), 9; (1992)–(1996), 12.

Table 9-10   U.S. Defense Spending, 1940–2002

Year	Annual percentage change[a] Current dollars	Annual percentage change[a] Constant dollars	Defense outlays as a percentage of Federal outlays	Defense outlays as a percentage of Gross domestic product
1940	—	—	17.5	1.7
1941	276.5	234.1	47.1	5.7
1942	301.6	221.9	73.0	18.1
1943	159.5	134.8	84.9	38.0
1944	18.6	29.6	86.7	39.2
1945	4.9	12.5	89.5	39.1
1946	−48.6	−43.5	77.3	20.1
1947	−70.0	−71.8	37.1	5.7
1948	−28.9	−27.6	30.6	3.7
1949	45.1	39.8	33.9	5.0
1950	3.8	4.6	32.2	5.2
1951	72.3	67.2	51.8	7.5
1952	95.3	77.5	68.1	13.5
1953	14.5	3.5	69.4	14.5
1954	−6.6	−8.3	69.5	13.4
1955	−13.4	−14.3	62.4	11.1
1956	−0.5	−6.6	60.2	10.2
1957	6.8	−0.1	59.3	10.4
1958	3.1	−1.6	56.8	10.4
1959	4.7	−4.8	53.2	10.2
1960	−1.8	−5.6	52.2	9.5
1961	3.1	0.5	50.8	9.6
1962	5.4	3.3	49.0	9.4
1963	2.1	−2.0	48.0	9.1
1964	2.6	1.5	46.2	8.8
1965	−7.7	−7.6	42.8	7.5
1966	14.8	10.3	43.2	7.9
1967	22.9	18.2	45.4	9.0
1968	14.7	9.1	46.0	9.7
1969	0.7	−4.5	44.9	8.9
1970	−1.0	−6.8	41.8	8.3
1971	−3.4	−8.9	37.5	7.5
1972	0.4	−7.3	34.3	6.9
1973	−3.2	−8.7	31.2	6.0
1974	3.4	−4.7	29.5	5.7
1975	9.1	−1.8	26.0	5.7
1976	3.6	−3.3	24.1	5.3
TQ[b]	c	c	23.2	5.0
1977	8.5	−0.2	23.8	5.1
1978	7.5	0.5	22.8	4.8
1979	11.3	2.0	23.1	4.8
1980	15.2	3.4	22.7	5.1
1981	17.5	5.5	23.2	5.3
1982	17.7	9.1	24.8	5.9
1983	13.3	7.7	26.0	6.3

Table 9-10   *(Continued)*

| Year | Annual percentage change[a] | | Defense outlays as a percentage of | |
	Current dollars	Constant dollars	Federal outlays	Gross domestic product
1984	8.3	1.2	26.7	6.2
1985	11.1	6.5	26.7	6.4
1986	8.2	6.1	27.6	6.5
1987	3.1	1.6	28.1	6.3
1988	3.0	1.2	27.3	6.0
1989	4.5	1.3	26.6	5.9
1990	−1.4	−4.0	23.9	5.5
1991	−8.7	−12.7	20.7	4.8
1992	9.2	5.3	21.6	5.0
1993	−2.4	−4.1	20.7	4.7
1994	−3.3	−5.3	19.3	4.1
1995	−3.4	−5.7	17.9	3.8
1996	−2.4	−5.2	17.0	3.6
1997 est.	0.6	−1.9	16.4	3.4
1998 est.	−2.9	−5.3	15.4	3.2
1999 est.	0.8	−1.8	14.8	3.0
2000 est.	2.2	−0.4	14.7	3.0
2001 est.	0.3	−2.2	14.5	2.8
2002 est.	1.9	−0.7	14.5	2.7

Note: "—" indicates data not available.

[a] Change from prior year.
[b] Transition quarter, July–September.
[c] Not applicable.

Sources: Annual percentage change calculated from actual dollar amounts of defense spending in Table 11-3, this volume; percent of federal outlays and GDP; Office of Management and Budget, *Budget of the U.S. Government, Fiscal Year 1998 Historical Tables* (Washington, D.C.: U.S. Government Printing Office, 1997), 95–101.

Table 9-11 Worldwide Military Expenditures, 1984–1994

Country group	1984	1985	1986	1987	1988	1989	1990	1991	1992	1993	1994	Per capita	
												1984	1994
Current dollars (billions)[a]													
Worldwide, total[a]	$904.5	$952.2	$997.4	$1,029.6	$1,058.6	$1,068.9	$1,081.2	$1,027.3	$931.5	$867.1	$840.3	—	—
NATO[b]	377.5	405.7	432.6	447.8	455.8	475.2	485.5	468.5	489.9	480.0	469.3	—	—
United States	237.1	258.2	280.9	288.2	293.1	304.1	306.2	280.3	305.1	297.6	288.1	—	—
Warsaw Pact[c]	310.9	327.1	339.9	357.4	373.5	357.7	324.0	276.6	—	—	—	—	—
Soviet Union[d]	263.7	277.2	287.6	303.0	319.0	303.0	292.0	260.0	139.2	111.5	96.8	—	—
Constant (1991) dollars (billions)													
Worldwide, total	1,251.8	1,271.6	1,297.0	1,297.7	1,284.8	1,241.3	1,203.3	1,101.1	971.4	884.9	840.3	263	149
NATO[b]	522.5	541.7	562.6	564.4	553.1	551.8	540.3	502.2	510.9	489.9	469.3	825	668
United States	328.1	344.8	365.3	363.2	355.7	353.1	340.7	300.4	318.2	303.8	288.1	1,388	1,105
Warsaw Pact[c]	430.3	436.8	442.0	450.5	453.3	415.4	360.8	296.5	—	—	—	1,110	—
Soviet Union[d]	365.0	370.2	374.0	381.9	387.2	351.9	325.0	278.7	145.2	113.8	96.8	1,321	647
Percentage GNP[e]													
Worldwide, total[a]	5.5	5.4	5.4	5.2	4.9	4.6	4.4	4.0	3.6	3.2	3.0	—	—
NATO[b]	4.8	4.8	4.9	4.7	4.5	4.3	4.2	3.7	3.8	3.6	3.3	—	—
United States	6.2	6.4	6.6	6.3	6.0	5.8	5.5	4.9	5.1	4.7	4.3	—	—
Warsaw Pact[c]	12.1	12.2	12.0	12.1	11.8	10.7	9.8	9.3	—	—	—	—	—
Soviet Union[d]	13.0	13.1	12.8	12.9	12.7	11.5	11.0	10.3	—	—	—	—	—

Note: "—" indicates not available. Data for other years can be found in earlier editions of *Vital Statistics on American Politics.*

[a] Includes countries not in NATO (North Atlantic Treaty Organization) or the Warsaw Pact.

[b] NATO includes Belgium, Canada, Denmark, France, Iceland, Great Britain, Greece, Italy, Luxembourg, the Netherlands, Norway, Portugal, Spain, Turkey, the United States, and West Germany (Germany since 1991).

[c] The Warsaw Pact countries include Bulgaria, Czechoslovakia, East Germany, Hungary, Poland, Romania, and the Soviet Union. The Warsaw Pact was formally dissolved on July 1, 1991.

[d] Estimate based on partial or uncertain data. Expenditures for 1992 and later are for Russia.

[e] The meaning of military expenditures as a percentage of GNP differs between most Eastern and Western bloc countries because of differing estimating procedures.

Source: U.S. Arms Control and Disarmament Agency, *World Military Expenditures and Arms Transfers 1995* (Washington, D.C.: U.S. Government Printing Office, 1996), 53–99.

Table 9-12 U.S. Military Sales and Military Assistance to Foreign Governments, Principal Recipients, 1950–1995 (millions)

Country	Military sales								Military assistance[a]
	1950–1988	1989	1990	1991	1992	1993	1994	1995	1950–1995
Australia	$5,139.9	$582.6	$381.0	$205.2	$156.0	$232.9	$349.6	$303.5	$0.0
Belgium	2,101.1	135.6	156.0	163.2	37.0	51.1	95.1	20.1	1,203.8
Canada	2,361.4	143.6	102.8	163.9	106.9	122.1	153.6	116.7	0.0
China (Taiwan)	4,089.3	352.8	460.1	556.1	707.8	693.6	735.7	1,160.7	2,554.6
France	786.1	36.2	108.5	31.8	35.0	40.7	77.9	58.7	4,045.1
Germany	8,916.2	631.8	357.9	476.5	500.2	345.4	154.8	236.6	884.8
Greece	2,218.1	137.4	113.5	123.9	162.9	212.9	193.4	226.6	1,673.2
Indochina	8.5	0.0	0.0	0.0	0.0	0.0	0.0	0.0	709.0
Iran	10,660.9	0.0	0.0	0.0	0.0	0.0	0.0	0.0	766.7
Israel	11,129.4	230.3	146.3	242.4	720.8	787.2	451.6	331.6	160.0
Italy	1,135.5	63.6	61.3	61.2	52.1	47.9	105.9	55.7	2,243.7
Korea	3,754.6	315.7	327.5	230.4	309.0	305.6	373.6	430.7	5,471.7
Netherlands	3,703.9	386.6	375.3	370.7	318.9	115.2	215.7	188.6	1,178.1
Saudi Arabia	22,028.3	618.9	875.7	2,744.3	2,416.0	3,493.1	2,061.3	3,654.3	23.9
Thailand	1,797.5	211.1	175.4	179.2	101.6	106.3	137.6	346.4	1,169.0
Turkey	3,080.3	618.7	720.0	600.5	703.4	748.6	884.6	362.2	3,170.2
United Kingdom	5,158.7	130.5	205.3	243.0	153.6	183.5	176.6	108.4	1,012.9
Vietnam	1.2	0.0	0.0	0.0	0.0	0.0	0.0	0.0	14,773.9
Total[b]	118,732.7	7,120.4	7,621.7	8,563.9	10,110.7	10,909.6	9,269.6	11,616.4	55,193.4

Note: Figures exclude training. Amounts in current dollars.

[a] Military assistance, especially to Europe, has been very low for a decade or more.
[b] Includes countries not shown.

Source: U.S. Defense Security Assistance Agency, *Foreign Military Sales, Foreign Military Construction Sales, and Military Assistance Facts, September 30, 1995* (Washington, D.C.: U.S. Government Printing Office, 1995), 16–19, 78–81.

Table 9-13   U.S. Foreign Aid, Principal Recipients, 1962–1994 (millions)

Region/country	1962–1990	1991	1992	1993	1994
Asia[a]	$23,115	$749	$511	$375	$241
India	3,964	30	48	25	37
Indonesia	1,698	60	42	48	14
Korea	1,080	0	0	0	0
Pakistan	4,280	96	[b]	6	0
Philippines	2,388	328	201	83	46
Vietnam	4,490	1	1	[b]	1
Europe[a]	4,726	606	509	464	542
Turkey	2,786	250	1	200	0
Latin America[a]	17,600	1,075	855	780	438
Brazil	1,480	0	0	4	6
Costa Rica	1,312	42	24	9	4
Dominican Republic	897	14	16	20	11
El Salvador	2,536	180	234	172	56
Honduras	1,326	99	65	33	19
Jamaica	815	27	38	43	9
ROCAP[c]	705	21	12	17	7
Near East[a]	33,111	2,754	2,205	2,124	1,910
Egypt	12,896	783	893	748	592
Israel	16,414	1,850	1,200	1,200	1,200
Jordan	1,400	31	0	65	28
Morocco	461	50	41	33	18
Sub-Saharan Africa[a]	10,154	865	890	783	764
Cameroon	273	20	22	10	[b]
Chad	136	16	13	12	5
Kenya	619	25	20	16	18
Niger	288	28	29	17	19
Senegal	385	24	34	22	32
Somalia	389	1	11	28	8
Sudan	888	2	3	[b]	0
Zaire	579	22	0	0	[b]
Zambia	299	35	40	26	20
Zimbabwe	355	43	40	49	38
Oceania and other	89	20	20	23	16
Total[d]	110,306	7,668	6,819	7,059	7,330

Note: Amounts in current dollars. Shown are loans and grants made by the U.S. Agency for International Development and its predecessor agencies. Excluded are Food for Peace and "other" economic assistance. Data for individual years before 1991 can be found in earlier editions of *Vital Statistics on American Politics.*

[a] Includes countries not shown separately.
[b] Less than one million.
[c] Programs covering Costa Rica, El Salvador, Guatemala, Honduras, Nicaragua, and Panama.
[d] Includes interregional aid.

Source: U.S. Agency for International Development, *U.S. Overseas Loans and Grants and Assistance from International Organizations, Obligations and Loan Authorizations*, July 1, 1945–September 30, 1994 (Washington, D.C.: U.S. Government Printing Office, 1994), 4–203.

Table 9-14 Foreign Investment in the United States and U.S. Investment
Abroad, 1950–1995 (millions)

Year	All areas	Canada	Europe	Japan
Foreign direct investment in the United States				
1950	$3,391	$1,029	$2,228	—
1960	6,910	1,934	4,707	$88
1970	13,270	3,117	9,554	229
1980	83,046	12,162	54,688	4,723
1985	184,615	17,131	121,413	19,313
1986	220,414	20,318	144,181	26,824
1987	271,788	24,013	186,076	35,151
1988	314,754	26,566	208,942	51,126
1989	368,924	30,370	239,190	67,268
1990	396,702	30,037	250,973	81,775
1991	418,780	36,341	252,692	93,787
1992	425,636	37,845	251,206	97,537
1993	445,268	39,408	270,767	96,213
1994	502,410	42,133	309,415	104,529
1995	560,088	46,005	360,762	108,582
U.S. investment abroad				
1950	11,788	3,579	1,733	19
1960	32,778	11,198	6,681	254
1970	78,178	22,790	24,516	1,483
1980	215,578	44,978	96,539	6,243
1985	230,250	46,909	105,171	9,235
1986	259,562	49,994	122,165	11,332
1987	314,307	57,783	150,439	15,684
1988	333,501	62,610	156,932	17,927
1989	370,091	65,548	175,213	18,488
1990	430,521	69,508	214,739	22,599
1991	467,844	70,711	235,163	25,403
1992	498,991	68,832	246,228	26,590
1993	548,644	70,395	269,158	31,393
1994	621,044	74,987	310,031	36,677
1995	711,621	81,387	363,527	39,198

Note: "—" indicates not available. Amounts in current dollars. Data for additional years can be found in previous editions of *Vital Statistics on American Politics*.

Sources: 1950–1960: U.S. Department of Commerce, *Foreign Business Investments in the United States: A Supplement to Survey of Current Business* (Washington, D.C.: U.S. Government Printing Office, 1962), 34; *Survey of Current Business*, August 1962, 22; others from *Survey of Current Business*: August 1973, 50; September 1973, 24; August 1982, 21–22; August 1983, 24; August 1985, 63; August 1988, 65, 80; August 1990, 41, 62–64; August 1991, 47, 87; August 1992, 89, 123–125; August 1994, 99, 134–137; July 1996, 47, 50.

Table 9-15 U.S. Balance of Trade, 1946–1996 (millions)

Year	Merchandise trade balance[a]	Balance on current account[b]	Year	Merchandise trade balance[a]	Balance on current account[b]
1946	$6,697	$4,885	1972	−6,416	−5,795
1947	10,124	8,992	1973	911	7,140
1948	5,708	2,417	1974	−5,505	1,962
1949	5,339	873	1975	8,903	18,116
1950	1,122	−1,840	1976	−9,483	4,295
1951	3,067	884	1977	−31,091	−14,335
1952	2,611	614	1978	−33,927	−15,143
1953	1,437	−1,286	1979	−27,568	−285
1954	2,576	219	1980	−25,500	2,317
1955	2,897	430	1981	−28,023	5,030
1956	4,753	2,730	1982	−36,485	−11,443
1957	6,271	4,762	1983	−67,102	−43,985
1958	3,462	784	1984	−112,492	−98,951
1959	1,148	−1,282	1985	−122,173	−124,243
1960	4,892	2,824	1986	−145,081	−152,088
1961	5,571	3,822	1987	−159,557	−167,392
1962	4,521	3,387	1988	−126,959	−128,436
1963	5,224	4,414	1989	−115,245	−105,575
1964	6,801	6,823	1990	−109,030	−94,657
1965	4,951	5,431	1991	−74,068	−9,518
1966	3,817	3,031	1992	−96,106	−62,583
1967	3,800	2,583	1993	−132,609	−99,936
1968	635	611	1994	−166,121	−148,405
1969	607	399	1995	−173,424	−148,154
1970	2,603	2,331	1996	−187,674	−165,095
1971	−$2,260	−$1,433			

Note: Amounts in current dollars.

[a] "Merchandise trade balance" measures the difference between the value of goods the United States imports and the goods the United States exports.
[b] "Balance on current account" is the broadest trade gauge, measuring the difference in imports and exports of merchandise trade and trade in services; also includes certain one-way flows of money into the United States, such as pension payments.

Sources: U.S. President, *The Economic Report of the President* (Washington, D.C.: U.S. Government Printing Office, 1997), Table B-101; 1997: U.S. Department of Commerce, *News*, press release, "U.S. International Transactions: Fourth Quarter and Year 1996," March 13, 1997, 10.

Table 9-16 Immigrants, by Country, 1820–1995

| | Europe | | | | | | Other | | Total |
Year	North-western[a]	Central[b]	Southern[c]	Eastern[d]	Asia[e]	Canada	western hemisphere[f]	All other[g]	number (thousands)
1820–1830	62.8%	5.1%	2.1%	0.1%	—	1.6%	6.2%	22.0%	151.8
1831–1840	56.3	25.5	1.0	—	—	2.3	3.3	11.7	599.1
1841–1850	67.6	25.4	0.3	—	—	2.4	1.2	3.1	1,713.3
1851–1860	56.9	36.7	0.8	—	1.6%	2.3	0.6	1.1	2,598.2
1861–1870	53.7	34.4	0.9	0.1	2.8	6.6	0.5	0.8	2,314.8
1871–1880	48.1	28.6	2.7	1.4	4.4	13.6	0.7	0.4	2,812.2
1881–1890	44.3	35.4	6.3	4.2	1.3	7.5	0.6	0.3	5,246.6
1891–1900	30.9	32.4	19.1	14.2	1.9	0.1	1.0	0.5	3,687.6
1901–1910	17.8	28.2	26.4	20.1	2.8	2.0	2.1	0.2	8,795.4
1911–1920	14.9	18.3	25.5	17.7	3.4	12.9	7.0	0.4	5,735.8
1921–1930	21.2	20.8	14.0	4.3	2.4	22.5	14.4	0.4	4,107.2
1931–1940	15.9	30.8	15.9	3.3	3.0	20.5	9.8	0.9	528.4
1941–1950	25.4	26.3	7.7	0.6	3.5	16.6	17.7	2.1	1,035.0
1951–1960	17.7	26.0	10.6	2.9	6.1	10.9	22.5	3.1	2,515.5
1961–1970	12.2	11.2	12.2	1.3	13.2	8.6	38.9	2.3	3,321.7
1971–1980	4.3	4.0	8.0	1.8	35.9	2.6	40.4	3.1	4,493.3
1981–1990	3.9	3.1	2.3	1.6	37.0	2.1	47.1	3.0	7,338.1
1991–1995	3.7	3.8	1.7	5.8	29.7	2.0	49.8	3.4	5,203.3

(Notes continue)

Table 9-16 *(Continued)*

Note: "——" indicates less than 0.1 percent. Data for most years are for country of last permanent residence. See source for details.

[a] United Kingdom, Ireland, Norway, Sweden, Denmark, the Netherlands, Belgium, Switzerland, and France.
[b] Germany, Poland, Czechoslovakia, Yugoslavia, Hungary, and Austria.
[c] Italy, Spain, Portugal, and Greece.
[d] USSR, Romania, Turkey, and "other Europe."
[e] Cambodia, China, Taiwan, Hong Kong, India, Iran, Israel, Japan, Korea, Philippines, Thailand, Vietnam, and "other Asia."
[f] Mexico, Caribbean, and Central and South America.
[g] Africa, Australia, and New Zealand.

Source: U.S. Department of Justice, Immigration and Naturalization Service, *Statistical Yearbook of the Immigration and Naturalization Service, 1995* (Washington, D.C.: U.S. Government Printing Office, 1997), 28–30.

10

Social Policy

- **Population**
- **Medicare and Social Security**
- **Income Levels**
- **Public Aid**
- **Social Welfare Expenditures**
- **Integration in Schooling and Employment**
- **Abortion**
- **Crime and Punishment**

The study of social policies might fairly be described as controversies informed by, but not settled by, statistics. No matter what the area, those on all sides of an issue try to support their arguments with relevant data.

The data thought to be relevant to questions and controversies about social policy are of many kinds and can be characterized in a variety of ways. First, there is factual information showing, for example, how many whites, blacks, and Hispanics are below the poverty line (Table 10-6), how much money is spent on social welfare (Tables 10-10 and 10-11), and how many crimes were committed in a given year (Table 10-18). Second, there are data about public opinion (see Chapter 3) and social policy. Social policy concerns not only the actual crime rate but what people think about crime—for example, whether the courts are too easy on criminals (Table 3-20) and whether the death penalty is acceptable and desirable (Table 3-15). It matters not only what abortion rates are (Table 10-17), but also what people think and say about abortion (Table 3-16). One might also distinguish between data about the past or present and projections about the future. Much of the concern about Social Security payments and about health care costs is not about present payments but about what to expect in the future (Tables 10-2 and 10-3, Figure 10-2).

Social policies are inherently controversial, and so too are data relevant to such policies. Discussion over how to conduct the U.S. Census in the year 2000—should sampling techniques supplement the traditional complete enumeration method—illustrates the contentiousness that determining the basic facts of population counts (such as in Table 10-1 or Figure 10-1) can produce. Analysts often agree on a set of facts but disagree on the relevance of the material and its interpretation. Information about numbers of people on welfare (Table 10-9), about the proportion of women and minorities elected to political office (Table 1-21), about the extent of crime and the cost of prisons (Tables 10-18 and 10-20), and so on, does not automatically answer causal questions (why the situation is as it is) any more than it answers normative questions (whether the existing situation is good and what should be done). Moreover, the importance of future projections often leads to special problems of inference. Any projection must be based on assumptions about what the future will be like. A footnote in Table 10-3, for example, should underscore the fact that no one can be certain in 1997 what health or Social Security costs will be in 2070.

There are numerical and other data relevant to every social concern, though they are highly varied in type and always difficult to interpret. Consequently, information is provided here for a wide range of policies, including Medicare (Table 10-2), social security (Table 10-3 and Figure 10-2), income and poverty in general (Tables 10-4 through 10-6) and social welfare in particular (10-7 through 10-12), affirmative action in both the schools and in employment (Table 10-4 and Tables 10-13 through 10-16), abortion (Table 10-17), and crime and punishment (Tables 10-18 through 10-20). Often, of course, a given set of data is relevant to more than one question. Information about poverty rates, for example, is relevant both to questions about social welfare and affirmative action. Since most debates about social policy involve expenditures, spending for other kinds of programs such as defense (Table 9-10), as well as overall taxation policies (Table 11-7), are also relevant.

In the face of enormous problems of inference, of controversy about almost every fact, and of the need to deal with future unknowns, one might well ask whether all these numbers are useful or necessary when discussing social policies. There are at least two answers to this question. The first is highly pragmatic. Some analysts will surely have factual information at their disposal; those who do not or cannot understand data and are unable or unwilling to provide any of their own will be hostage to others' information and interpretations.

From a more theoretical perspective, one can note that although data are always subject to some error and interpretation, people often do agree on the facts and on roughly how they should be interpreted. There is no disagreement, for example, that—barring major unforeseen catastrophes or extremely large and unlikely changes in immigration—there will be a considerably smaller ratio of young people to old people in the first half of the next century. Knowing this does not solve the problems implicit in this fact, but it tells analysts that there will be problems and that the country needs to be thinking of solutions. It also suggests possible solutions—raising the retirement age, lowering

Social Security payments, raising Social Security taxes, encouraging private pension plans so that the elderly need less government support, and so on.

In the area of social policy, as in other areas, data do not speak for themselves. They must be analyzed and interpreted. The facts alone will settle few arguments about causality or about normative questions. Still, data and an ability to interpret them are essential ingredients in the arsenal of any well-educated social analyst, commentator, or student.

Figure 10-1   U.S. Population: Total, Urban, and Rural, 1790–2050

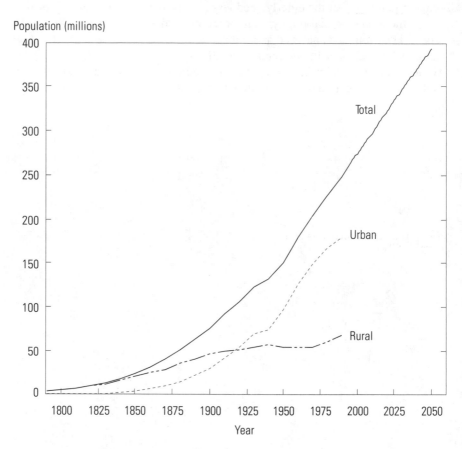

Population (millions)

Note: The Census Bureau makes three projections—a low, middle, and high series—based on alternate assumptionsm regarding births, deaths, and immigration. The projection shown is the middle series. For comparison, in 2050, the low series shows a population of 282,524,000 and the high series shows a population of 518,903,000.

Sources: Total, urban, and rural population, 1790–1990: *http://www.census.gov/population/censusdata/table-4.pdf* (as of July 1997); 1996–2050: U.S. Bureau of the Census, Current Population Reports, Series P25-1130, "Population Projections of the United States by Age, Sex, Race, and Hispanic Origin: 1995 to 2050," as reported at *http://www.census.gov/population/projections/nation/npaltsrs.txt* (as of July 9, 1997).

Table 10-1   U.S. Population, 1790–1990

Year	Resident population	Year	Resident population
1790	3,929,214	1900	75,994,575
1800	5,308,483	1910	91,972,266
1810	7,239,881	1920	105,710,620
1820	9,638,453	1930	122,775,046
1830	12,866,020	1940	131,669,275
1840	17,069,453	1950	150,697,361
1850	23,191,876	1960	179,323,175
1860	31,443,321	1970	203,235,298
1870	39,818,449	1980	226,545,805
1880	50,155,783	1990	248,709,873
1890	62,947,714		

Sources: 1790–1970: U.S. Bureau of the Census, *Historical Statistics of the United States* (Washington, D.C.: U.S. Government Printing Office, 1975), 11; 1980: U.S. Bureau of the Census, *1980 Census of Population*: *General Population Characteristics* (Washington, D.C.: U.S. Government Printing Office, 1980), Series PC80-1-B1, 1–19; 1990: U.S. Bureau of the Census, *1990 Census of Population and Housing*: *Summary Population and Housing Characteristics* (Washington, D.C.: U.S. Government Printing Office, 1990), Series 1990 CPH-1-1, 360.

Table 10-2   Hospital Insurance Trust Fund: Income, Expenditures, and Balance, 1991–2006 (billions)

Year	Income	Disbursements	Net increase in fund	Fund at end of year
1991	$88.8	$72.6	$16.3	$115.2
1993	98.2	94.4	3.8	127.8
1996	124.6	129.9	−5.3	124.9
1997	127.4	140.2	−12.8	112.2
1998	131.4	151.5	−20.1	92.1
1999	135.4	164.1	−28.6	63.4
2000	139.7	177.7	−37.9	25.5
2001	143.8	192.8	−48.9	−23.4
2002	147.9	208.8	−60.8	−84.3
2003	151.8	225.9	−74.1	−158.3
2004	155.4	244.0	−88.6	−246.9
2005	159.2	262.9	−103.7	−350.7
2006	162.3	283.2	−121.0	−471.6

Note: The Hospital Insurance Program (Medicare Part A) pays for inpatient hospital care and other related care for those aged sixty-five or older and for the long-term disabled. It represents more than half of all Medicare expenses. Income for the fund is derived from a 1.45 percent payroll tax on employees and employers. Figures for 1993 represent actual experience. Figures for 1994 and beyond are "intermediate" projections; see source for details. Amounts in current dollars.

Source: U.S. Congress, House, "1992 Annual Report of the Board of Trustees of the Federal Hospital Insurance Trust Fund," 102d Cong., 2d sess., House Document 102-280, April 13, 1992, 14; (1994), 103d Cong., 2d sess., House Document 103-230, April 12, 1994, 14; (1996) Hospital Insurance Trustees Report, *http://www.hefa.gov/pubforms//hi/tabiid3.htm* (as of May 14, 1997).

Table 10-3 Social Security (OASDI) Covered Workers and Beneficiaries, 1945–2070

Year	Covered workers[a] (thousands)	Beneficiaries[b]			Covered workers per OASDI beneficiary	Beneficiaries per 100 covered workers
		OASI	DI	Total		
1945	46,390	1,106	—	1,106	41.9	2
1950	48,280	2,930	—	2,930	16.5	6
1955	65,200	7,563	—	7,563	8.6	12
1960	72,530	13,740	522	14,262	5.1	20
1965	80,680	18,509	1,648	20,158	4.0	25
1970	93,090	22,618	2,568	25,186	3.7	27
1975	100,200	26,998	4,125	31,123	3.2	31
1980	112,212	30,385	4,734	35,119	3.2	31
1985	120,429	32,776	3,874	36,650	3.3	30
1986	123,260	33,349	3,972	37,321	3.3	30
1987	126,283	33,918	4,035	37,953	3.3	30
1988	130,137	34,343	4,077	38,420	3.4	30
1989	132,471	34,754	4,105	38,859	3.4	29
1990	133,637	35,266	4,204	39,470	3.4	30
1991	132,905	35,785	4,388	40,173	3.3	30
1992	133,936	36,314	4,716	41,030	3.3	31
1993	136,119	36,758	5,083	41,841	3.3	31
1994	138,849	37,082	5,435	42,517	3.3	31
1995	140,905	37,376	5,731	43,107	3.3	31
1996	141,925	37,708	5,982	43,690	3.2	31
1997	142,820	38,048	6,272	44,320	3.2	31
1998	144,160	38,357	6,550	44,907	3.2	31
1999	145,244	38,668	6,827	45,495	3.2	31
2000	146,344	38,999	7,103	46,102	3.2	32
2005	152,415	41,015	8,554	49,569	3.1	33
2010	157,859	44,496	9,891	54,387	2.9	34
2015	161,050	50,352	10,563	60,915	2.6	38
2020	162,360	57,628	10,848	68,476	2.4	42
2025	163,259	64,343	11,248	75,591	2.2	46
2030	164,451	69,680	11,277	80,957	2.0	49
2035	166,417	72,889	11,253	84,142	2.0	51
2040	168,323	73,845	11,437	85,282	2.0	51
2045	169,650	74,442	11,978	86,420	2.0	51
2050	170,563	75,694	12,302	87,996	1.9	52
2055	171,223	77,855	12,533	90,388	1.9	53
2060	171,959	80,211	12,496	92,707	1.9	54
2065	172,720	82,070	12,548	94,618	1.8	55
2070	173,480	83,605	12,712	96,317	1.8	56

Note: "—" indicates not available; "OASI" indicates Old-Age and Survivors' Insurance; "DI" indicates Disability Insurance. Projections (1996–2070) are the so-called Intermediate projections. See source for further details.

[a] Workers who pay OASDI taxes at some time during the year.
[b] Beneficiaries with monthly benefits in current-payment status as of June 30.

Source: 1996 OASDI Trustees Report, Table II. F19, *http://www.ssa.gov/OACT/TR/tbiif19.html* (as of May 20, 1997).

Figure 10-2   Social Security Receipts, Spending, and Reserve Estimates, 1996–2025

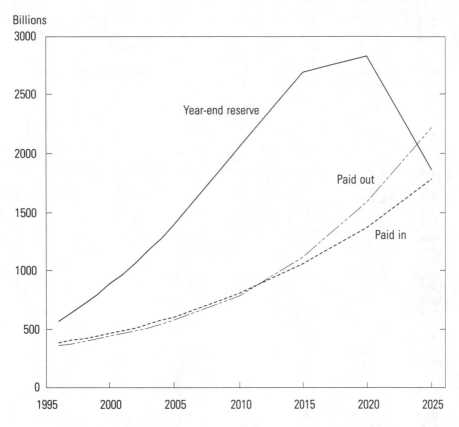

Note: In billions of current dollars. The combined OASI and DI Trust Funds (Social Security) are estimated to become exhausted during 2029 under intermediate cost projections. For details see source.

Source: OASDI Trustees Report, Table III.B3, *http://www.ssa.gov/OACT/TR/tbiiib3.html* (as of May 20, 1997).

Table 10-4 Median Family Income, by Race and Hispanic Origin, 1950–1995

Year	Median income in current dollars				Median income in constant (1995) dollars				Annual percentage change in median income of all families	
	All families[a]	White	Black	Hispanic origin[b]	All families[a]	White	Black	Hispanic origin[b]	Current dollars	Constant dollars
1950	$3,319	$3,445	$1,869[c]	—	$19,306	$20,039	$10,872	—	—	—
1955	4,418	4,613	2,544[c]	—	23,138	24,159	13,323	—	6.6[d]	3.9[d]
1960	5,620	5,835	3,230[c]	—	26,599	27,617	15,287	—	5.4[d]	3.0[d]
1965	6,957	7,251	3,993[c]	—	31,001	32,311	17,793	—	4.8[d]	3.2[d]
1970	9,867	10,236	6,279	—	36,410	37,772	23,170	—	8.4[d]	3.1[d]
1971	10,285	10,672	6,440	—	36,367	37,736	22,772	—	4.2	-0.2
1972	11,116	11,549	6,864	$8,183	38,155	39,641	23,560	$28,088	8.1	4.8
1973	12,051	12,595	7,269	8,715	38,910	40,667	23,470	28,139	8.4	2.0
1974	12,902	13,408	8,006	9,540	37,886	39,371	23,509	28,013	7.1	-3.5
1975	13,719	14,268	8,779	9,551	37,202	38,691	23,806	25,900	6.3	-2.6
1976	14,958	15,537	9,242	10,259	38,377	39,863	23,712	26,321	9.0	3.1
1977	16,009	16,740	9,563	11,421	38,604	40,367	23,060	27,541	7.0	0.5
1978	17,640	18,368	10,879	12,566	39,827	41,471	24,562	28,371	10.2	2.3
1979	19,587	20,439	11,574	14,169	40,339	42,093	23,836	29,180	11.0	-0.2
1980	21,023	21,904	12,674	14,716	38,930	40,561	23,469	27,251	7.3	-5.5
1981	22,388	23,517	13,266	16,401	37,868	39,778	22,439	27,742	6.5	-3.5
1982	23,433	24,603	13,598	16,227	37,356	39,221	21,677	25,868	4.7	-1.4
1983	24,674	25,837	14,561	16,930	37,754	39,534	22,280	25,905	5.3	2.0
1984	26,433	27,686	15,431	18,832	38,772	40,610	22,634	27,623	7.1	2.7
1985	27,735	29,152	16,786	19,027	39,283	41,290	23,775	26,949	4.9	1.3
1986	29,458	30,809	17,604	19,995	40,962	42,840	24,479	27,803	6.2	4.3

(Table continues)

Table 10-4 (*Continued*)

	Median income in current dollars				Median income in constant (1995) dollars				Annual percentage change in median income of all families	
Year	All families[a]	White	Black	Hispanic origin[b]	All families[a]	White	Black	Hispanic origin[b]	Current dollars	Constant dollars
1987	30,970	32,385	18,406	20,300	41,548	43,446	24,693	27,233	5.1	1.4
1988	32,191	33,915	19,329	21,769	41,470	43,691	24,901	28,044	3.9	-0.2
1989	34,213	35,975	20,209	23,446	42,049	44,214	24,838	28,816	6.3	1.4
1990	35,353	36,915	21,423	23,431	41,223	43,044	24,980	27,321	3.3	-2.0
1991	35,939	37,783	21,548	23,895	40,214	42,277	24,111	26,737	1.7	-2.4
1992	36,812	38,909	21,161	23,901	39,727	42,005	22,923	25,586	2.4	-1.9
1993	36,959	39,300	21,542	23,654	38,980	41,449	22,720	24,947	0.4	-1.9
1994	38,782	40,884	24,696	24,318	39,881	42,043	25,398	25,007	4.9	2.3
1995	40,611	42,646	25,970	24,750	40,611	42,646	25,970	24,570	4.7	1.8

Note: "—" indicates not available.

a Includes other races not shown separately.
b Persons of Hispanic origin may be of any race.
c For 1950–1965, black and other races.
d Calculated by annualizing the five-year change.

Sources: *1950–1965: Statistical Abstract of the United States, 1987* (Washington, D.C.: U.S. Government Printing Office), 436; 1970–1995: U.S. Bureau of the Census, Current Population Reports, "Money Income in the United States: 1995" (Washington, D.C.: U.S. Government Printing Office, 1996), Series P-60, no. 193, 13–16, B2, B9–B10.

Table 10-5   Persons Below the Poverty Line, 1995

Group	Percentage of group that is poor	Group as a percentage of all poor people
Race/ethnicity		
White	11.2	67.1
White (not of Hispanic origin)	8.5	44.7
Black	29.3	27.1
Hispanic origin[a]	30.3	23.5
Family status		
Female householder, no husband present		
White	29.7	19.3
Black	48.2	18.0
Hispanic[a]	52.8	8.4
All other families		
White	6.6	29.0
Black	10.8	4.5
Hispanic[a]	22.1	11.8
Age		
Under 18	20.8	40.3
65 or over	10.5	9.1
Dwelling		
Metropolitan residents	13.4	77.8
Nonmetropolitan residents	15.6	22.2
Region		
Northeast	12.5	17.7
Midwest	11.0	18.6
South	15.7	39.7
West	14.9	24.0
All persons	13.8	100.0

[a] Persons of Hispanic origin may be of any race.

Source: U.S. Bureau of the Census, Poverty 1995, *http://www.census.gov/hhes/poverty/pov95/povest1.html* (as of May 13, 1997), and Historical Poverty Tables—Persons, *http://www.census.gov/hhes/poverty/histpov/hstpov2.html* (as of May 23, 1997).

Table 10-6 Persons Below the Poverty Level, by Race and Hispanic Origin, 1959–1995 (percent)

Year	White	Black	Hispanic origin[a]	Total[b]
1959	18.1	55.1	—	22.4
1960	17.8	—	—	22.2
1961	17.4	—	—	21.9
1962	16.4	—	—	21.0
1963	15.3	—	—	19.5
1964	14.9	—	—	19.0
1965	13.3	—	—	17.3
1966	11.3	41.8	—	14.7
1967	11.0	39.3	—	14.2
1968	10.0	34.7	—	12.8
1969	9.5	32.2	—	12.1
1970	9.9	33.5	—	12.6
1971	9.9	32.5	—	12.5
1972	9.0	33.3	—	11.9
1973	8.4	31.4	21.9	11.1
1974	8.6	30.3	23.0	11.2
1975	9.7	31.3	26.9	12.3
1976	9.1	31.1	24.7	11.8
1977	8.9	31.3	22.4	11.6
1978	8.7	30.6	21.6	11.4
1979	9.0	31.0	21.8	11.7
1980	10.2	32.5	25.7	13.0
1981	11.1	34.2	26.5	14.0
1982	12.0	35.6	29.9	15.0
1983	12.1	35.7	28.0	15.2
1984	11.5	33.8	28.4	14.4
1985	11.4	31.3	29.0	14.0
1986	11.0	31.1	27.3	13.6
1987	10.4	32.4	28.0	13.4
1988	10.1	31.3	26.7	13.0
1989	10.0	30.7	26.2	12.8
1990	10.7	31.9	28.1	13.5
1991	11.3	32.7	28.7	14.2
1992	11.9	33.4	29.6	14.8
1993	12.2	33.1	30.6	15.1
1994	11.7	30.6	30.7	14.5
1995	11.2	29.3	30.3	13.8

Note: "—" indicates not available.

[a] Persons of Hispanic origin may be of any race.
[b] Includes other races not shown separately.

Source: 1959–1993: U.S. Bureau of the Census, Current Population Reports, "Income, Poverty, and Valuation of Noncash Benefits: 1993" (Washington, D.C.: U.S. Government Printing Office, 1995), Series P-60, no. 188, D13–D16; 1994-1995, *http://www.census.gov/hhes/poverty/pov95/povest1.html* (as of May 13, 1997).

Table 10-7   Aid to Families with Dependent Children Versus the
Poverty Line, 1936–1995

Year	Average monthly benefit per family	Yearly benefit	Average poverty threshold
1936	$28.15	$337.80	—
1940	31.98	383.76	—
1945	48.18	578.16	—
1950	71.33	855.96	—
1955	84.17	1,010.04	—
1960	105.75	1,269.00	$3,022
1961	110.97	1,331.64	3,054
1962	116.30	1,395.60	3,089
1963	120.19	1,442.28	3,128
1964	126.88	1,522.56	3,169
1965	133.20	1,598.40	3,223
1966	142.83	1,713.96	3,335
1967	155.19	1,862.28	3,410
1968	168.41	2,020.92	3,553
1969	174.89	2,098.68	3,743
1970	183.13	2,197.56	3,968
1971	187.16	2,245.92	4,137
1972	188.87	2,266.44	4,275
1973	190.91	2,290.92	4,540
1974	204.27	2,451.24	5,038
1975	219.44	2,633.28	5,500
1976	236.10	2,833.20	5,815
1977	246.27	2,955.24	6,191
1978	253.89	3,046.68	6,662
1979	262.86	3,154.32	7,412
1980	280.03	3,360.36	8,414
1981	282.04	3,384.48	9,287
1982	303.02	3,636.24	9,862
1983	312.82	3,753.84	10,178
1984	325.44	3,905.28	10,609
1985	342.15	4,105.80	10,989
1986	355.04	4,260.48	11,203
1987	361.37	4,336.44	11,611
1988	374.07	4,488.84	12,092
1989	383.14	4,597.68	12,674
1990	391.67	4,700.04	13,359
1991	390.44	4,685.28	13,924
1992	373.71	4,484.52	14,335
1993	377.24	4,526.88	14,763
1994	377.78	4,533.36	15,141
1995 (prelim.)	—	—	15,570

Note: "—" indicates not available. Poverty threshold is the annual income for a family of four. Amounts in current dollars.

Source: U.S. Department of Health and Human Services, Social Security Administration, *Social Security Bulletin, Annual Statistical Supplement, 1996* (Washington, D.C.: U.S. Government Printing Office, 1996), 169, 357.

Table 10-8   Benefits and Recipients of Public Aid and Food Stamps, by State, 1996

State	Maximum AFDC grant (per month)[a]	Food stamp benefit (per month)[b]	Combined benefits as a percentage of 1993 poverty threshold[c]	Public aid recipients (percentage of population)[d]	Food stamp recipients (percentage of population)[e]
Alabama	$164	$313	44	6.6	11.7
Alaska	923	321	92	7.2	8.1
Arizona	347	313	61	5.9	9.6
Arkansas	204	313	48	6.3	10.9
California	607	245	79	11.6	9.6
Colorado	421	301	67	4.3	6.3
Connecticut	636	236	81	6.6	6.7
Delaware	338	313	60	5.0	8.2
District of Columbia	420	301	67	17.2	17.1
Florida	303	313	57	6.6	9.4
Georgia	280	313	55	7.9	10.6
Hawaii	712	471	95	7.2	11.1
Idaho	317	313	58	3.4	6.5
Illinois	377[f]	313	64	8.1	9.2
Indiana	288	313	56	4.8	6.5
Iowa	426	299	67	5.0	6.1
Kansas	429[f]	313	69	4.6	6.4
Kentucky	262	313	53	9.1	12.3
Louisiana	190	313	47	10.0	14.8
Maine	418	301	66	7.3	10.5
Maryland	373[f]	313	63	6.0	7.3
Massachusetts	565	257	76	7.1	6.0
Michigan[g]	459[f]	289	69	8.4	9.3
Minnesota	532	267	74	4.9	6.2
Mississippi	120	313	40	10.5	16.2
Missouri	292	313	56	6.9	10.1
Montana	425	299	67	5.4	8.0
Nebraska	364	313	63	3.8	6.1
Nevada	348	313	61	3.9	5.9
New Hampshire	550	262	75	3.3	4.4
New Jersey	424[f]	307	68	5.8	6.7
New Mexico	389	310	65	8.7	13.6
New York[h]	577[f]	270	78	10.1	11.5
North Carolina	272	313	54	6.9	8.1
North Dakota	431	298	67	3.6	6.2
Ohio	341[f]	313	60	7.7	9.1
Oklahoma	307	313	57	6.0	10.8
Oregon	460[f]	313	71	4.7	8.9
Pennsylvania	421	301	67	7.1	8.9
Rhode Island	554[f]	299	79	8.6	9.1
South Carolina	200	313	47	6.5	9.7
South Dakota	430	298	67	4.2	6.6
Tennessee	185	313	46	8.2	12.0

Table 10-8   *(Continued)*

State	Maximum AFDC grant (per month)[a]	Food stamp benefit (per month)[b]	Combined benefits as a percentage of 1993 poverty threshold[c]	Public aid recipients (percentage of population)[d]	Food stamp recipients (percentage of population)[e]
Texas	188	313	46	6.0	11.9
Utah	426	299	67	3.3	5.5
Vermont	650	232	82	6.8	9.4
Virginia	354	313	62	4.7	7.9
Washington	546[f]	289	77	6.8	8.9
West Virginia	253	313	52	9.4	16.1
Wisconsin	517	272	73	6.3	5.1
Wyoming	360	313	62	4.3	6.8

Note: The first two columns are maximum potential AFDC and food stamp benefits for a one-parent family of three persons. In most states the AFDC and food stamps amounts apply also to two-parent families of three (where the second parent is incapacitated or, as permitted in almost half the states, unemployed). Some, however, increase benefits for such families.

[a] In states with area differentials, figure shown is for areas with highest benefit. As of January 1996.
[b] Food stamp benefits are based on maximum AFDC benefits shown. For assumptions about deductions, see the source. As of January 1996.
[c] Based on the Census Bureau's 1996 poverty threshold for a family of three persons, $12,980, converted to a monthly rate of $1,082. For Alaska, this threshold is $16,220; for Hawaii, $14,930.
[d] Persons receiving AFDC (average monthly number, 1995) or Supplemental Security Income (December 1995).
[e] As of July 1996.
[f] Part of the AFDC cash benefit has been designated as energy aid and is disregarded by the state in calculating food stamp benefits. The amounts disregarded vary by state. See the source for further details.
[g] Wayne County only, columns 1–3.
[h] New York City only, columns 1–3.

Sources: Benefits, AFDC recipients: U.S. Congress, House, Background Material and Data on Programs Within the Jurisdiction of the Committee on Ways and Means, 104th Cong., 2d sess., November 4, 1996 (Washington, D.C.: U.S. Government Printing Office, 1996), 437–438, 460–462, SSI; recipients: U.S. Department of Health and Human Services, Social Security Administration, Social Security Bulletin, *Annual Statistical Supplement 1996* (Washington, D.C.: U.S. Government Printing Office, 1996), 129; food stamp recipients: U.S. Department of Agriculture, Food and Nutrition Service, Food Stamp Program, *http://www.usda.gov/fes/library/961007-1.txt* (as of May 8, 1997); state populations: U.S. Bureau of the Census, *http://www.census.gov:80/population/estimates/state/96agesex.txt* (as of May 8, 1997).

Table 10-9   Recipients of Social Insurance Programs, 1995

Program	Number of recipients (thousands)	Percentage of population[a]
Nonmeans-tested		
Social Security (OASDI)	43,387	15.8
Medicare (hospital insurance)[b]	36,544	13.4
Veterans programs	3,324	1.2
Railroad programs	803	0.3
State unemployment insurance	2,099	0.8
Means-tested		
Medicaid	36,282	13.2
Supplemental Security Income	6,517	2.4
Aid to Families with Dependent Children[b]	14,164	5.2
Food stamps	26,619	9.7
General assistance[b]	1,105	0.4

Note: "Means-tested" refers to the requirement of demonstration of financial need based on income and assets. People may receive benefits from more than one program. For example, in 1985, 16 percent of U.S. households received one or more means-tested benefits; in addition to the programs listed above, these include free or reduced-price school lunches and publicly owned or subsidized housing. OASDI beneficiaries as of December 31. Medicare enrollees as of July 1. Veterans program beneficiaries as of December 31. Railroad programs beneficiaries as of December 31 (except for unemployment). State unemployment insurance is the average weekly number in December. Medicaid is the number of recipients during the year. SSI is the number of recipients in December. AFDC is the average number of monthly recipients. Food stamp number is the average during the year. General assistance is the average monthly number.

[a] Population in the "Social Security area," which includes Puerto Rico and other outlying areas, adjusted for Census undercount; for details, see source.
[b] 1994.

Sources: U.S. Department of Health and Human Services, Social Security Administration, *Social Security Bulletin, Annual Statistical Supplement,* 1996 (Washington, D.C.: U.S. Government Printing Office, 1996), 198, 303, 327–328, 342, 357, 359, 365; *Social Security Bulletin, Summer 1996,* 121; note: U.S. Bureau of the Census, Current Population Reports, "Receipt of Selected Noncash Benefits: 1985" (Washington, D.C.: U.S. Government Printing Office, 1987), Series P-60, no. 155, 2.

Table 10-10   Social Welfare Expenditures, 1950–1992

Year	Federal		State and local		Total expenditures	
	Total (billions)	Percentage of total federal outlays	Total (billions)	Percentage of total state and local outlays	Total (billions)	Percentage of total GDP
1950	$10.5	26.2	$13.0	59.2	$23.5	8.8
1955	14.6	22.3	18.0	55.3	32.6	8.5
1960	25.0	28.1	27.3	60.1	52.3	10.3
1965	37.6	32.6	39.5	61.7	77.1	11.5
1966	45.2	34.9	42.6	60.0	87.8	11.9
1967	53.2	35.0	46.3	57.8	99.5	12.6
1968	60.2	35.1	53.4	60.0	113.6	13.4
1969	68.1	37.5	58.8	58.8	127.0	13.7
1970	77.1	40.0	68.4	57.9	145.6	14.8
1971	92.3	44.8	78.9	59.3	171.3	16.3
1972	105.9	47.2	84.4	60.4	190.3	16.6
1973	122.2	50.3	91.1	59.3	213.3	16.7
1974	136.7	52.1	101.9	58.1	238.7	17.0
1975	166.9	53.7	122.3	61.6	289.2	19.1
1976	196.7	56.8	134.8	63.2	331.5	19.7
1977	217.9	56.1	142.4	63.2	360.3	19.3
1978	239.4	55.2	154.4	63.2	393.8	18.2
1979	263.2	54.8	166.6	62.1	429.9	17.7
1980	303.2	54.4	189.5	62.9	492.7	18.6
1981	346.5	54.3	207.4	62.3	553.8	18.7
1982	370.2	52.9	230.9	61.1	601.1	19.2
1983	402.3	53.1	247.1	61.0	649.4	19.6
1984	421.2	50.8	256.9	59.9	678.1	18.3
1985	450.6	48.7	282.0	59.9	732.2	18.4
1986	472.8	48.6	309.0	64.2	781.8	18.5
1987	497.9	50.2	336.2	66.6	834.1	18.7
1988	527.0	49.5	360.5	67.0	887.5	18.5
1989	565.1	49.5	392.3	68.0	957.4	18.5
1990	616.6	49.2	434.1	—	1,050.2	19.2
1991	676.4	51.1	485.6	—	1,162.2	20.5
1992	749.3	54.2	515.8	—	1,265.1	21.3

Note: Amounts in current dollars.

Sources: 1950–1960: U.S. Department of Health and Human Services, Social Security Administration, *Social Security Bulletin,* November 1988 (Washington, D.C.: U.S. Government Printing Office, 1988), 27–28; 1965–1991: *Social Security Bulletin,* Winter 1992, 55–56; Spring 1994, 98–99, 101; Summer 1995, 67–70.

Table 10-11 Social Welfare Expenditures, by Category, 1950–1992

Year	Social insurance	Public aid	Health and medical programs[a]	Veterans programs	Education	Housing	Other social welfare[b]	All health and medical care[c]	Total social welfare outlays
Federal (millions)									
1950	$2,103	$1,103	$604	$6,386	$157	$15	$174	$1,362	$10,541
1955	6,385	1,504	1,150	4,772	485	75	252	1,948	14,623
1960	14,307	2,117	1,737	5,367	868	144	417	2,918	24,957
1965	21,807	3,594	2,660	6,011	2,470	238	812	4,482	37,592
1970	45,246	9,649	4,568	8,952	5,876	582	2,259	16,363	77,130
1975	99,715	27,276	7,888	16,570	8,629	2,541	4,264	33,469	166,882
1980	191,162	49,394	12,827	21,254	13,452	6,278	8,786	68,939	303,153
1985	310,175	63,480	17,842	26,704	13,796	11,059	7,548	122,139	450,604
1990	422,257	92,858	27,204	30,428	18,374	16,612	8,905	187,864	616,639
1991	453,534	113,235	29,668	32,331	19,084	18,696	9,831	—	676,380
1992	495,710	138,704	31,872	34,212	20,188	17,950	10,677	—	749,312
State and local (millions)									
1950	2,844	1,393	1,460	480	6,517	—	274	1,704	12,967
1955	3,450	1,499	1,953	62	10,672	15	367	2,473	18,017
1960	4,999	1,984	2,727	112	16,758	33	723	3,478	27,337
1965	6,316	2,670	3,495	20	25,638	80	1,254	4,942	39,473
1970	9,446	6,839	5,038	126	44,970	120	1,886	8,698	68,425
1975	23,298	14,171	8,837	449	72,205	631	2,683	17,932	122,274
1980	38,592	23,309	14,382	212	107,597	601	4,813	31,320	189,507
1985	59,420	34,882	21,531	338	158,251	1,540	6,004	49,146	281,966
1990	91,565	53,953	36,263	488	240,011	2,856	9,012	83,666	434,148
1991	107,641	68,104	38,504	526	258,063	2,826	9,949	—	485,613
1992	121,266	69,241	39,163	555	272,011	2,668	10,855	—	515,758

Total (millions)

Year									Total
1950	4,947	2,496	2,064	6,866	6,674	15	448	3,065	23,508
1955	9,835	3,003	3,103	4,834	11,157	89	619	4,421	32,640
1960	19,307	4,101	4,464	5,479	17,626	177	1,139	6,395	52,293
1965	28,123	6,264	6,155	6,031	28,108	318	2,066	9,424	77,065
1970	54,692	16,488	9,606	9,078	50,846	702	4,145	25,061	145,557
1975	123,013	41,447	16,742	17,019	80,834	3,172	6,947	51,401	289,174
1980	229,754	72,703	27,263	21,466	121,049	6,879	13,599	100,259	492,713
1985	369,595	98,361	39,373	27,042	172,048	12,599	13,522	171,285	732,246
1990	513,823	146,811	63,467	30,916	258,385	19,469	17,918	—	1,050,156
1991	561,175	181,339	68,172	32,857	277,147	21,523	19,780	—	1,162,239
1992	616,975	207,945	71,035	34,767	292,199	20,617	21,532	—	1,265,070

Percentage of total expenditures

Year									Total
1950	21.0	10.6	8.8	29.2	28.4	0.1	1.9	13.0	100.0
1955	30.1	9.2	9.5	14.8	34.2	0.3	1.9	13.5	100.0
1960	36.9	7.8	8.5	10.5	33.7	0.3	2.2	12.2	100.0
1965	36.5	8.1	8.0	7.8	36.5	0.4	2.7	12.2	100.0
1970	37.6	11.3	6.6	6.2	34.9	0.5	2.8	17.2	100.0
1975	42.5	14.3	5.8	5.9	28.0	1.1	2.4	17.8	100.0
1980	46.6	14.8	5.5	4.4	24.6	1.4	2.8	20.3	100.0
1985	50.5	13.4	5.4	3.7	23.5	1.7	1.8	23.4	100.0
1990	48.9	14.0	6.0	2.9	24.6	1.9	1.7	—	100.0
1991	48.3	15.6	5.9	2.8	23.8	1.9	1.7	—	100.0
1992	48.8	16.4	5.6	2.7	23.1	1.6	1.7	—	100.0

Percentage federal of total

Year									Total
1950	42.5	44.2	29.2	93.0	2.3	100.0	38.9	44.4	44.8
1955	64.9	50.1	37.1	98.7	4.3	84.3	40.7	44.1	44.8
1960	74.1	51.6	38.9	98.0	4.9	81.4	36.6	45.6	47.7
1965	77.5	57.4	43.2	99.7	8.8	74.8	39.3	47.6	48.8
1970	82.7	58.5	47.6	98.6	11.6	82.9	54.4	65.3	53.0

(Table continues)

Table 10-11 *(Continued)*

Year	Social insurance	Public aid	Health and medical programs[a]	Veterans programs	Education	Housing	Other social welfare[b]	All health and medical care[c]	Total social welfare outlays
1975	81.1	65.8	47.1	97.4	10.7	80.1	61.4	65.1	57.7
1980	83.2	67.9	47.1	99.0	11.1	91.2	64.6	68.7	61.5
1985	83.9	64.5	45.1	98.8	8.0	87.8	55.7	71.3	61.5
1990	82.2	63.3	42.9	98.4	7.1	85.3	49.7	—	58.7
1991	80.8	62.4	43.5	98.4	6.9	86.9	49.7	—	58.2
1992	80.3	66.7	44.9	98.4	6.9	87.1	49.6	—	59.2

Note: "—" indicates not available. Amounts in current dollars. Figures for fiscal years ending in year shown. Data for additional years can be found in earlier editions of *Vital Statistics on American Politics*.

[a] Excludes medical services parts of social insurance, public aid, veterans, and other social welfare.

[b] Includes outlays for vocational rehabilitation, institutional care, child nutrition and welfare, and social welfare expenditures not elsewhere classified.

[c] Combines health and medical programs with medical services included in social insurance, public aid, veterans, vocational rehabilitation, and antipoverty programs.

Sources: 1950–1965: U.S. Department of Health and Human Services, Social Security Administration, *Social Security Bulletin*, November 1988 (Washington, D.C.: U.S. Government Printing Office, 1988), 27–28; 1970–1992: *Social Security Bulletin*, Summer 1995, 67–69.

Table 10-12 Private Social Welfare Expenditures, by Category and as a Percentage of GDP, 1972–1993 (millions)

Year	Private[a] Health	Income maintenance[b]	Education	Welfare services[c]	Total	Public total[d]	Percentage of gross domestic product Private[e]	Public[f]	Total[g]
1972	$57,200	$15,955	$14,935	$7,545	$95,635	$190,315	7.9	16.6	23.7
1973	63,200	18,063	16,146	8,297	105,706	212,314	7.8	16.7	23.7
1974	69,400	19,660	17,718	8,970	115,748	237,132	7.9	17.0	24.1
1975	102,000	21,910	19,993	10,067	153,970	289,173	9.7	19.1	27.7
1976	113,900	25,004	22,095	11,748	172,747	331,425	9.8	19.7	28.4
1977	113,900	30,662	23,581	13,535	181,678	360,314	9.2	19.3	27.5
1978	113,900	36,743	26,361	16,590	193,594	393,830	8.7	18.2	25.9
1979	126,900	42,628	28,774	19,540	217,842	431,007	8.8	17.7	25.5
1980	145,000	51,169	32,667	22,776	251,612	492,714	9.3	18.6	26.9
1981	168,500	58,741	36,521	25,728	289,490	554,189	9.6	18.7	27.2
1982	191,300	70,096	40,570	28,067	330,033	601,345	10.5	19.2	28.5
1983	210,900	82,414	44,639	31,369	369,322	649,229	10.8	19.6	29.3
1984	230,000	93,235	48,435	34,699	406,369	678,112	10.8	18.3	27.9
1985	248,000	116,207	53,167	38,914	456,288	732,250	11.3	18.4	28.5
1986	270,954	143,495	58,541	43,211	516,201	781,725	11.7	18.5	28.9
1987	292,965	143,359	65,498	47,601	549,423	834,142	11.7	18.7	29.1
1988	333,128	148,533	72,137	52,579	606,377	887,542	12.0	18.5	29.2
1989	369,844	166,885	80,383	59,312	676,424	957,394	12.4	18.5	29.6
1990	413,145	164,397	87,864	64,583	729,989	1,050,155	12.7	19.2	30.5
1991	440,978	170,307	93,813	68,998	774,096	1,165,136	13.1	20.5	32.1
1992	477,024	186,655	100,491	76,022	840,192	—	13.5	21.3	33.3
1993	505,086	194,119	107,451	80,899	887,555	—	13.6	21.1	33.2

(Notes continue)

Table 10-12 *(Continued)*

Note: Amounts in current dollars.

[a] Calendar year basis.

[b] These expenditures represent outlays for private employee benefit plans including private pension plans, group life insurance, sickness and disability insurance, paid sick leave, and supplemental unemployment benefits.

[g] Expenditures include individual and family social services, adoption services, emergency and disaster services, child day care centers, senior citizen centers, residential care, recreation and group work, civic, social, and fraternal organizations, job training, and vocational rehabilitation.

[d] Fiscal year basis.

[e] Calendar year expenditures as a percentage of calendar year gross domestic product.

[f] Fiscal year expenditures as a percentage of federal fiscal year gross domestic product.

[g] The sum of public and private expenditures as a percentage of gross domestic product, after adjustment to eliminate overlap that occurs when public or private income maintenance payments are used to purchase medical care, educational services, or residential care.

Source: 1972–1985: U.S. Department of Health and Human Services. Social Security Administration, *Social Security Bulletin,* Spring 1994 (Washington, D.C.: U.S. Government Printing Office, 1994), 88; 1986–1993: *Social Security Bulletin, Annual Statistical Supplement, http://www.ssa.gov/statistics/hdabs96.html* (as of June 11, 1997).

Table 10-13 Persons Who Have Completed High School or College, by Race, Hispanic Origin, and Sex, 1940–1995 (percent)

| | 25 years and over | | | | | | 25–29 years | | | | | |
| | White | | Black[a] | | Hispanic[b] | | White | | Black[a] | | Hispanic[b] | |
Level/Year	Male	Female	Male	Female	Male	Female	Male	Female	Male	Female	Male	Female
Completed four years of high school or more												
1940	24.2	28.1	6.9	8.4	—	—	38.9	43.4	10.6	13.6	—	—
1947	33.2	36.7	12.7	14.5	—	—	52.9	56.8	19.6	24.7	—	—
1959	44.5	47.7	19.6	21.6	—	—	66.9	67.4	40.6	38.6	—	—
1970	57.2	57.6	32.4	34.8	—	—	79.2	76.4	54.5	57.9	—	—
1980	71.0	70.1	51.1	51.3	46.4	44.1	86.8	87.0	74.8	78.1	58.3	58.8
1990	79.1	79.0	65.8	66.5	50.3	51.3	84.6	88.1	81.5	81.8	56.6	59.9
1993	81.8	81.3	69.6	71.1	52.9	53.2	86.1	88.5	85.0	80.9	58.3	64.0
1994	82.1	81.9	71.7	73.8	53.4	53.2	84.7	88.3	82.9	85.1	58.0	63.0
1995	83.0	83.0	73.7	74.1	52.9	53.8	86.6	88.2	88.1	85.1	55.7	58.7
Completed four years of college or more[d]												
1940	5.9	4.0	1.4	1.2	—	—	7.5	5.3	1.5	1.7	—	—
1947	6.6	4.9	2.4	2.6	—	—	6.2	5.7	2.6	2.9	—	—
1959	11.0	6.2	3.8	2.9	—	—	15.9	8.1	5.6	3.7	—	—
1970	15.0	8.6	4.6	4.4	—	—	21.3	13.3	6.7	8.0	—	—
1980	22.1	14.0	7.7	8.1	9.7	6.2	25.5	22.0	10.5	12.5	8.4	6.9
1990	25.3	19.0	11.9	10.8	9.8	8.7	24.2	24.3	15.1	11.9	7.3	9.1
1993	25.7	19.7	11.9	12.4	9.5	8.5	24.4	25.1	12.6	13.8	7.1	9.8
1994	26.1	20.0	12.8	13.0	9.6	8.6	23.6	24.8	12.8	13.0	9.6	8.6
1995	27.2	21.0	13.6	12.9	10.1	8.4	25.4	26.6	13.6	12.9	10.1	8.4

Note: "—" indicates data not available.

[a] Data are for black and other races for 1940 to 1960; for 1970–1993, data are for black persons only.

[b] Persons of Hispanic origin may be of any race.

[c] Beginning 1992, high school graduate or more.

[d] Beginning 1992, bachelor's degree or more.

Source: U.S. Bureau of the Census, Current Population Reports, *http://www.census.gov:80/population/socdemo/education/table18.txt* (as of May 9, 1997).

Table 10-14   School Desegregation, by Region, 1968–1994

Region/year	Percentage of black students in schools more than 50 percent minority	Percentage of Hispanic students in schools more than 50 percent minority	Percentage of black students in schools 90–100 percent minority	Percentage of Hispanic students in schools 90–100 percent minority
South 1968	80.9	69.6	77.8	33.7
1972	55.3	69.9	24.7	31.4
1976	54.9	70.9	22.4	32.2
1980	57.1	76.0	23.0	37.3
1984	56.9	75.4	24.2	37.3
1986	58.0	75.2	25.1	38.6
1988	56.5	80.2	24.0	37.9
1991	60.8	76.8	26.6	38.6
1994	—	75.6	—	38.0
Change 1968 to 1991/94	−20.1	+6.0	−51.2	+4.3
Border 1968	71.6	—	60.2	—
1972	67.2	—	54.7	—
1976	60.1	—	42.5	—
1980	59.2	—	37.0	—
1984	62.5	—	37.4	—
1986	59.3	29.9	35.6	—
1988	59.6	—	34.5	—
1991	59.3	37.4	33.2	10.8
1994	—	40.8	—	12.3
Change 1968 to 1991/94	−12.3	—	−27.0	—
Northeast 1968	66.8	74.8	42.7	44.0
1972	69.9	74.4	46.9	44.1
1976	72.5	74.9	51.4	45.8
1980	79.9	76.3	48.7	45.8
1984	73.1	77.5	47.4	47.1
1986	72.8	78.2	49.8	46.4
1988	77.3	79.7	48.0	44.2
1991	76.2	78.1	50.1	46.2
1994	—	77.6	—	45.1
Change 1968 to 1991/94	+9.4	+2.8	+7.4	+1.1
Midwest 1968	77.3	31.8	58.0	6.8
1972	75.3	34.4	57.4	9.5
1976	70.3	39.3	51.1	14.1
1980	69.5	46.6	43.6	19.6
1984	70.7	53.9	43.6	24.2
1986	69.8	54.3	38.5	23.5
1988	70.1	52.3	41.8	24.9

Table 10-14   *(Continued)*

Region/year	Percentage of black students in schools more than 50 percent minority	Percentage of Hispanic students in schools more than 50 percent minority	Percentage of black students in schools 90–100 percent minority	Percentage of Hispanic students in schools 90–100 percent minority
1991	69.9	53.5	39.4	21.1
1994	—	53.1	—	21.8
Change 1968 to 1991/94	−7.4	+21.3	−18.6	+15.0
West 1968	72.2	42.4	50.8	11.7
1972	68.1	44.7	42.7	11.5
1976	67.4	52.7	36.3	13.3
1980	66.8	63.5	33.7	18.5
1984	66.9	68.4	29.4	22.9
1986	68.2	69.9	28.3	24.7
1988	67.1	71.3	28.6	27.5
1991	69.7	73.5	26.4	29.7
1994	—	75.9	—	32.1
Change 1968 to 1991/94	−2.5	+33.5	−24.4	+20.4
Total 1968	76.6	54.8	64.3	23.1
1972	63.6	56.6	38.7	23.3
1976	62.4	60.8	35.9	24.8
1980	62.9	68.1	33.2	28.8
1984	63.5	70.6	33.2	31.0
1986	63.3	71.5	32.5	32.2
1988	63.2	—	32.1	—
1991	66.0	73.4	33.9	34.0
1994	67.1	74.0	33.6	34.8
Change 1968 to 1991/94	−9.5	+19.2	−30.7	+11.7

Note: "—" indicates not available. Data are for 1968–1969 to 1994–1995 school years. For composition of regions, see Appendix Table A-4.

Sources: 1968–1980: Gary Orfield, testimony before the House Subcommittee on Civil and Constitutional Rights, *Civil Rights Implications of the Education Block Grant Program,* September 9, 1982, 67–72; 1984–1986: Reprinted with permission from Gary Orfield, Franklin Monfort, Melissa Aaron, "Status of School Desegregation 1968–1986" (Alexandria, Va.: National School Boards Association, 1989), 5, 7; 1988: Reprinted with permission from Gary Orfield and Franklin Monfort, "Status of School Desegregation: The Next Generation" (Alexandria, Va.: National School Boards Association, 1992), 3, 7–8; 1991: Gary Orfield, "The Growth of Segregation in American Schools: Changing Patterns of Separation and Poverty Since 1968" (Alexandria, Va: National School Boards Association, 1993), 9, copyright 1989, 1992, and 1993 National School Boards Association, all rights reserved; 1994: Gary Orfield, et al., "Deepening Segregation in American Public Schools." Harvard Project on School Desegregation," April 5, 1997, 11, 15.

Table 10-15   Federal Employment, by Government Service (GS) Salary
Level, Race, Hispanic Origin, and Sex, 1995

Government service (GS) salary level		Total number	Percentage black	Percentage Hispanic	Percentage female
GS-01	$12,669-15,844	3,235	31.9	19.4	69.4
GS-02	$14,243-17,928	6,412	30.5	9.7	65.6
GS-03	$15,542-20,204	34,144	27.2	7.9	67.4
GS-04	$17,447-22,685	99,720	29.2	7.1	71.6
GS-05	$19,520-25,379	163,707	25.4	7.3	72.3
GS-06	$21,758-28,283	107,402	25.6	6.1	75.3
GS-07	$24,178-31,432	144,416	22.8	6.5	66.6
GS-08	$26,777-34,814	43,924	24.8	7.1	65.1
GS-09	$29,577-38,451	142,687	16.1	6.8	50.7
GS-10	$32,571-42,345	16,729	15.0	4.6	44.9
GS-11	$35,786-46,523	205,840	12.9	5.9	44.4
GS-12	$42,890-55,760	248,313	11.1	4.5	34.0
GS-13	$51,003-66,303	173,007	9.0	3.7	27.5
GS-14	$60,270-78,351	91,116	6.7	2.9	22.4
GS-15	$70,894-92,161	52,572	5.1	2.8	19.1
Total, all pay plans		1,960,577	16.7	5.9	44.0
Total, GS and related		1,533,224	16.9	5.7	49.5

Note: Amounts in current dollars. Pay schedules effective January 1997.

Source: Office of Personnel Management, unpublished data.

Table 10-16 State and Local Government Employment and Salary, by Sex, Race, and Hispanic Origin, 1973–1995 (thousands)

| | Employment | | | | | | | Median annual salary | | | | | | |
| | | | | | Minority | | | | | | | Minority | | |
Year	Male	Female	White[a]	Total	Black[a]	Hispanic	Total[b]	Male	Female	White[a]	Total	Black[a]	Hispanic	Total[b]
1973	2,486	1,322	3,115	3,809	523	125	693	$9.6	$7.0	$8.8	$8.6	$7.4	$7.4	$7.5
1975	2,436	1,464	3,102	3,899	602	147	797	11.3	8.2	10.2	9.8	8.6	8.9	8.8
1977	2,737	1,678	3,480	4,415	705	175	935	12.4	9.1	11.3	10.9	9.5	9.9	9.7
1978	2,711	1,736	3,481	4,447	723	181	966	13.3	9.7	12.0	11.7	10.1	10.7	10.4
1979	2,761	1,816	3,568	4,576	751	192	1,008	14.1	10.4	12.8	12.3	10.6	11.4	10.9
1980	2,350	1,637	3,146	3,987	619	163	842	15.2	11.4	13.8	13.3	11.5	12.3	11.8
1981	2,740	1,925	3,591	4,665	780	205	1,074	17.7	13.1	16.1	15.6	13.3	14.7	13.5
1983	2,674	1,818	3,423	4,492	768	219	1,069	20.1	15.3	18.5	18.0	15.6	17.3	15.9
1984	2,700	1,880	3,458	4,580	799	233	1,121	21.4	16.2	19.6	19.1	16.5	18.4	17.4
1985	2,789	1,952	3,563	4,742	835	248	1,179	22.3	17.3	20.6	19.9	17.5	19.2	18.4
1986	2,797	1,982	3,549	4,779	865	259	1,230	23.4	18.1	21.5	—	18.7	20.2	19.6
1987	2,818	2,031	3,600	4,849	872	268	1,249	24.1	18.9	22.4	—	19.3	21.1	20.9
1989	3,030	2,227	3,863	5,257	961	308	1,394	26.1	20.6	24.1	—	20.7	22.7	22.1
1990	3,071	2,302	3,918	5,374	994	327	1,456	27.3	21.8	25.2	—	22.0	23.8	23.3
1991	3,110	2,349	3,965	5,459	1,011	340	1,494	28.4	22.7	26.4	25.5	22.7	24.5	—
1993[c]	2,820	2,204	3,588	5,024	948	341	1,436	30.6	24.3	28.5	27.7	24.2	26.8	—
1995	2,960	2,355	3,781	5,315	993	379	1,534	33.5	27.0	31.4	30.5	26.8	28.6	—

Note: "—" indicates not available. Full-time employment as of June 30, excludes school systems and educational institutions. Amounts in current dollars.

[a] Non-Hispanic.

[b] Includes other minority groups, not shown separately.

[c] Reporting changes occurred in 1993 that affect comparability of 1993 and later numbers to earlier entries.

Sources: 1973–1991: U.S. Equal Employment Opportunity Commission, *State and Local Government Information Report* (Washington, D.C.: U.S. Government Printing Office), annual volumes; 1993–1995: U.S. Equal Employment Opportunity Commission, *Job Patterns for Minorities and Women in State and Local Government,* 1994 and 1996.

Table 10-17   Frequency of Legal Abortions, 1973–1992

	Total		White		Nonwhite	
Year	Number of abortions (thousands)	Percentage of pregnancies terminated by abortion	Number of abortions (thousands)	Percentage of pregnancies terminated by abortion	Number of abortions (thousands)	Percentage of pregnancies terminated by abortion
1973	744.6	19.3	548.8	17.4	195.8	25.9
1974	898.6	22.0	629.3	19.6	269.3	31.6
1975	1,034.2	24.9	701.2	21.5	333.0	35.9
1976	1,179.3	26.5	784.9	23.0	394.4	38.9
1977	1,316.7	28.6	888.8	25.0	427.9	40.4
1978	1,409.6	29.2	969.4	26.1	440.2	39.6
1979	1,497.7	29.6	1,062.4	27.1	435.3	38.2
1980	1,553.9	30.0	1,093.6	27.4	460.3	39.2
1981	1,577.3	30.1	1,107.8	27.4	469.6	39.2
1982	1,573.9	30.0	1,095.3	27.1	478.7	39.2
1983	1,575.0	30.4	1,084.4	27.4	490.6	40.1
1984	1,577.2	29.7	1,086.6	26.8	490.6	39.2
1985	1,588.6	29.7	1,075.6	26.5	512.9	39.7
1986	1,574.0	29.4	—	25.9	—	39.8
1987	1,559.1	28.8	1,017.3	25.2	541.8	39.3
1988	1,590.8	28.6	1,025.7	25.0	565.1	38.9
1989	1,567.0	27.5	1,006.0	23.6	561.0	39.4
1990	1,609.0	28.0	1,039.0	24.1	570.0	39.6
1991	1,557.0	27.5	982.0	23.3	574.0	39.8
1992	1,528.9	29.6	943.5	22.9	585.4	40.5

Note: "—" indicates not available. "Percentage of pregnancies terminated by abortion" indicates the percentage of pregnancies resulting in live birth or abortion terminated by abortion. The number of abortions per 1,000 live births is from July 1 of the year shown to June 30 of the following year.

Sources: Reprinted with the permission of the Alan Guttmacher Institute from: 1973–1981: Stanley K. Henshaw and Ellen Blaine, *Abortion Services in the United States, Each State, and Metropolitan Area, 1981–1982* (New York: Alan Guttmacher Institute, 1985), 64; 1982–1983: Stanley K. Henshaw, "Characteristics of U.S. Women Having Abortions, 1982-1983," *Family Planning Perspectives* 19(1) (1987): 6–7; 1984–1986 (total): Stanley K. Henshaw and Jennifer Van Vort, "Abortion Services in the United States, 1987 and 1988," *Family Planning Perspectives,* 22(3) (1990): 103; 1984–1985 (white and nonwhite): Alan Guttmacher Institute, unpublished data; 1986 (white and nonwhite), 1987–1988: Stanley K. Henshaw, "Abortion Trends in 1987 and 1988: Age and Race," *Family Planning Perspectives,* 24(2) (1992): 86; 1989–1992: unpublished data, Alan Guttmacher Institute.

Table 10-18 Crime Rates, 1960–1995

377

Year	Violent crime					Property crime				Total
	Murder	Rape	Robbery	Aggravated assault	Total	Burglary	Larceny theft	Vehicle theft	Total	
1960	5.1	9.6	60	86	161	509	1,035	183	1,729	1,887
1965	5.1	12.1	72	111	200	663	1,329	257	2,249	2,249
1970	7.9	18.7	172	165	364	1,085	2,079	457	3,621	3,985
1975	9.6	26.3	218	227	482	1,526	2,805	469	4,800	5,282
1980	10.2	36.8	251	299	597	1,684	3,167	502	5,353	5,950
1983	8.3	33.7	217	279	538	1,338	2,869	431	4,637	5,175
1984	7.9	35.7	205	290	539	1,264	2,791	437	4,492	5,031
1985	7.9	36.7	209	303	556	1,287	2,901	462	4,651	5,207
1986	8.6	37.9	225	346	618	1,345	3,010	508	4,863	5,480
1987	8.3	37.4	213	351	610	1,330	3,081	529	4,940	5,550
1988	8.4	37.6	221	370	637	1,309	3,135	583	5,027	5,664
1989	8.7	38.1	233	383	663	1,276	3,171	630	5,077	5,740
1990	9.4	41.2	257	424	732	1,236	3,195	658	5,089	5,820
1991	9.8	42.3	273	433	758	1,252	3,229	659	5,140	5,898
1992	9.3	42.8	264	442	758	1,168	3,103	632	4,903	5,660
1993	9.5	41.1	256	440	747	1,099	3,032	606	4,738	5,484
1994	9.0	39.3	238	428	714	1,042	3,027	591	4,660	5,374
1995	8.2	37.1	221	418	685	988	3,045	561	4,593	5,278

Note: Figures are rates per 100,000 inhabitants. For definitions of crimes, see the sources. Data for additional years can be found in previous editions of *Vital Statistics on American Politics.*

Sources: 1960–1987: *Statistical Abstract of the United States, 1976* (Washington, D.C.: U.S. Government Printing Office, 1976), 153, *1987,* 155, *1989,* 166; 1988–1989: U.S. Department of Justice, Federal Bureau of Investigation, *Crime in the United States: Uniform Crime Reports 1989* (Washington, D.C.: U.S. Government Printing Office, 1990), 7–37; 1990–1991: *1991,* 5–49; 1992–1993: *1992–1993:* 5–49, 1994–1995: *1994–1995: 1994–1995:* 5, 10, 13, 23, 26, 31, 35, 38, 43, 49.

Table 10-19 States with the Death Penalty, Number of Executions (1930–1996), and Number on Death Row (1996)

State	Method[a]	Number executed							Number awaiting execution[c]
		1930s	1940s	1950s	1960s	1970s	1980s	1990s[b]	
Alabama	electrocution	60	50	20	5	0	7	6	151
Alaska	none	0	0	0	0	0	0	0	0
Arizona	gas chamber	17	9	8	4	0	0	5	122
Arkansas	lethal injection	53	8	18	9	0	0	11	42
California	gas chamber or lethal injection	108	80	74	30	0	0	4	444
Colorado	lethal injection	25	13	3	6	0	0	0	4
Connecticut	lethal injection	5	10	5	1	0	0	0	5
Delaware	lethal injection	8	4	0	0	0	0	8	11
District of Columbia	none	20	16	4	0	0	0	0	0
Florida	electrocution	44	65	49	12	1	20	15	349
Georgia	electrocution	137	130	85	14	0	14	6	108
Hawaii	none	0	0	0	0	0	0	0	0
Idaho	lethal injection or firing squad	0	0	3	0	0	0	1	19
Illinois	lethal injection	61	18	9	2	0	0	7	172
Indiana	lethal injection	31	7	2	1	0	2	2	49
Iowa	none	8	7	1	2	0	0	0	0
Kansas	none	0	5	5	5	0	0	0	0
Kentucky	electrocution	52	34	16	1	0	0	0	28
Louisiana	lethal injection	58	47	27	1	0	18	5	58
Maine	none	0	0	0	0	0	0	0	0
Maryland	lethal injection	16	45	6	1	0	0	1	17
Massachusetts	none	18	9	0	0	0	0	0	0
Michigan	none	0	0	0	0	0	0	0	0

State	Method								
Minnesota	none	0	0	0	0	0	0	0	0
Mississippi	lethal injection	48	60	36	10	0	4	0	53
Missouri	lethal injection	36	15	7	4	0	1	19	94
Montana	lethal injection or hanging	5	1	0	0	0	0	1	6
Nebraska	electrocution	0	2	2	0	0	0	2	9
Nevada	lethal injection	8	0	9	2	1	3	2	81
New Hampshire	lethal injection	1	0	0	0	0	0	0	0
New Jersey	lethal injection	40	14	17	3	0	0	0	16
New Mexico	lethal injection	2	2	3	1	0	0	0	3
New York	lethal injection	153	114	52	10	0	0	0	0
North Carolina	gas chamber or lethal injection	131	12	19	1	0	3	5	154
North Dakota	none	0	0	0	0	0	0	0	0
Ohio	electrocution or lethal injection	82	1	32	7	0	0	0	150
Oklahoma	lethal injection	34	13	7	6	0	0	7	124
Oregon	lethal injection	2	12	4	1	0	0	0	22
Pennsylvania	lethal injection	82	6	31	3	0	0	2	201
Rhode Island	none	0	0	0	0	0	0	0	0
South Carolina	electrocution	67	61	26	8	0	2	4	71
South Dakota	lethal injection	0	1	0	0	0	0	0	2
Tennessee	electrocution	47	37	8	1	0	0	0	102
Texas	lethal injection	120	74	74	29	0	33	73	394
Utah	firing squad or lethal injection	2	4	6	1	1	2	2	10
Vermont	none	1	1	2	0	0	0	0	0
Virginia	electrocution or lethal injection	28	35	23	6	0	8	24	53
Washington	lethal injection or hanging	23	16	6	2	0	0	2	13

(Table continues)

Table 10-19 *(Continued)*

State	Method[a]	Number executed							Number awaiting execution[c]
		1930s	1940s	1950s	1960s	1970s	1980s	1990s[b]	
West Virginia	none	20	11	9	0	0	0	0	0
Wisconsin	none	0	0	0	0	0	0	0	0
Wyoming	lethal injection	4	2	0	1	0	0	1	0
U.S. government	lethal injection	10[d]	13[d]	9[d]	1[d]	0[d]	0[d]	0	10
U.S. military	lethal injection							0	9
Total[e]		1,667	1,284	717	191	3	117	215	3,153[f]

[a] In some states, method depends on when sentenced. For details, see source.
[b] Through July 31, 1996.
[c] As of July 31, 1996.
[d] One hundred and sixty executions have been carried out under military authority since 1930.
[e] The national total counts multiple death-sentence inmates once. However, they are included in the state total for each state where they are sentenced to death.
[f] Number of inmates; some are multiple-sentenced and are listed in each state.

Sources: Number executed in 1930s–1970s: U.S. Department of Justice, Bureau of Justice Statistics, *Sourcebook of Criminal Justice Statistics-1989* (Washington, D.C.: U.S. Government Printing Office, 1990), 631; method, number executed in 1980–1996, number awaiting execution: NAACP Legal Defense and Educational Fund, *Death Row, U.S.A.*, Summer 1996.

Table 10-20   Number of Federal and State Prisoners, 1925–1995, and Cost
per Prisoner per Year, 1980–1995

Year	Number of prisoners	Rate (per 100,000 population)	Cost per prisoner per year
1925	91,669	79	—
1930	129,453	104	—
1935	144,180	113	—
1940	173,706	131	—
1945	133,649	98	—
1950	166,123	109	—
1955	185,780	112	—
1960	212,953	117	—
1965	210,895	108	—
1970	196,429	96	—
1973	204,211	96	—
1974	218,466	102	—
1975	240,593	111	—
1976	262,833	120	—
1977	285,456	129	—
1978	294,396	132	—
1979	301,470	133	—
1980	315,974	139	$10,350
1981	353,167	154	13,570
1982	394,374	171	15,830
1983	419,820	179	16,250
1984	443,398	188	17,320
1985	480,568	202	14,590
1986	522,084	217	15,220
1987	560,812	231	15,890
1988	603,732	247	16,320
1989	680,907	276	16,950
1990	739,980	297	17,550
1991	789,610	313	17,706
1992	846,277	332	18,330
1993	932,074	359	19,119
1994	1,016,760	389	19,433
1995	1,080,728	409	19,655

Note: "—" indicates not available. Definition of prisoners has varied somewhat over the years. See sources for details. Costs are in current dollars and are the averages for federal and state agencies. Costs are approximate due to variations in reporting practices. Data for additional years can be found in earlier editions of *Vital Statistics on American Politics.*

Sources: Number of prisoners and rate, 1925–1994: U.S. Department of Justice, Bureau of Justice Statistics, *Sourcebook of Criminal Justice Statistics, 1995* (Washington, D.C.: U.S. Government Printing Office, 1994), 600; 1995: U.S. Department of Justice, Bureau of Justice Statistics Bulletin, *Prisoners and Jail Inmates, 1995* (Washington, D.C.: U.S. Government Printing Office, 1996), 3; cost per prisoner: Criminal Justice Institute, *The Corrections Yearbook* (South Salem, N.Y.: Criminal Justice Institute), annual volumes, 1981–1996.

11

Economic Policy

- **Gross Domestic Product (GDP)**
- **Consumer Price Index (CPI)**
- **Federal Budget**
- **National Debt**
- **Tax Breaks**
- **Labor Unions**
- **Unemployment**

Economic policy makers labor under the burden of an overabundance of numbers. Statistics recording various aspects of the economy's performance appear regularly—often monthly. These statistics are important, not simply because of the conditions they report, but for the way they filter into economic calculations: expectations and reactions to indicators of past performance are critical determinants of how the economy performs in the future. Moreover, there is a direct link to politics because the public's perceptions of economic performance help shape choices in the voting booth: properly or not, presidents often get blamed when the economy turns down and (less often) praised when it recovers. President Ronald Reagan's public approval ratings plummeted as an economic downturn continued through 1982, as did President George Bush's ratings in 1992 as candidate Bill Clinton stressed economic problems (Figure 3-5). Subsequent economic recoveries played a substantial role in shaping the mood of the voters to secure Reagan's 1984 reelection in a landslide and President Clinton's reelection in 1996.

When one turns to even simple economic matters, fundamental issues and terms arise that distinguish the discourse from that in other areas of politics. One is the overall size of the economy, usually measured by the gross domestic product, or GDP (Table 11-1).[1] Knowing what the GDP is and what it means is important even to a minimal understanding of economic statistics and policy. Without some sense of the size of the economy, it is impossible to make informed judgments about economic matters. For example, a trillion-dollar national debt is unquestionably large, but many argue that it is not overburdening because it in fact represents the same proportion of the total economy as numerically smaller deficits did in earlier years (Figure 11-2). Another case in point is the relative size of federal outlays (Figure 11-1).

A second key concept is that of constant dollars, which is explained in the introduction to Chapter 9 in connection with defense spending. A few additional points are appropriate here. Note that the basis for many constant dollar calculations is the Consumer Price Index, or CPI (Table 11-2). One can see from this index that a market basket of goods that cost $100 in 1982–1984 would have cost $29.60 in 1960. Unfortunately, while 1982–1984 is the base period in Table 11-2, other tabulations, such as those in Table 11-1, use a different base. This makes it more difficult to compare the data. However, the concept of a constant dollar is unchanged by which year is used as the base. (However, the CPI is not always used as the basis for such adjustments, and here it is not possible to move precisely from the figures in Table 11-2 to those in 11-1.)

During Reagan's and Bush's presidencies, as well as during the first Clinton administration, economic news was dominated by the annual deficit and the accumulating national debt. The growth in the federal debt (Table 11-6) helped focus public attention on government spending and taxing, as politicians and economists alike tried to assess ways of reducing the gap between income and expenditures. Economic growth could provide the basis for greater tax revenues to balance the budget and reduce the deficit ("Grow our way out," as Reagan insisted). But as the national debt continued to mount in relation to GDP (Figure 11-2), political and economic demands for reduction of the debt constrained government spending and compelled consideration of additional revenue sources. While as of 1997 the annual deficit has been reduced and the accumulated debt (as a percentage of GDP) has declined slightly (Figure 11-2), further changes may be necessary. Tax increases are one means of attacking the problem. Table 11-7 displays the revenue loss to the federal government from selected tax breaks, some of which have already been curtailed to raise revenue.

Cutting spending is another means of deficit reduction. Although federal budget outlays (Tables 11-3 and 11-4) may give the impression of vast sums and a variety of programs suitable for cuts, the data in Table 11-5 show that mandatory programs account for half of federal budget outlays. An increasing proportion of the federal budget has become relatively uncontrollable from the president's standpoint. Reducing spending in the mandatory category would require that Congress rewrite laws affecting payments to which beneficiaries are entitled on the basis of past commitments. Programs that fall under this heading, such as Social Security, are referred to as *entitlement programs*.

Labor union membership, unemployment, and inflation are three other noteworthy features of the economic landscape that merit inclusion when considering politics. The long slide in the percentage of the work force belonging to unions (Table 11-8), the large-scale entry of women into the labor force since World War II (Table 11-9), the fluctuations in the annual unemployment rate since 1929 (Table 11-10), and the relatively high unemployment rates among black teenagers (Table 11-11) document critical economic trends with political ramifications.

Because economic issues are an important aspect of political policy making and because economic conditions affect voter choices, economic data rank among the most vital of vital statistics on American politics

Note

1. In 1991, the Bureau of Economic Analysis began using gross domestic product (GDP), rather than gross national product (GNP), as the primary measure of U.S. production. Other government agencies subsequently switched to GDP. Consequently, most of the tables in this volume use the GDP base. So that readers can have some sense of the magnitude of this change, which is generally small, both GDP and GNP are presented in Table 13-1. A detailed accounting of the meaning of, and difference between, the two measures is U.S. Department of Commerce, *National Income and Product Accounts of the United States* (Washington, D.C.: U.S. Government Printing Office, 1993), volume 1, M-5.

Table 11-1 Gross National and Gross Domestic Products, 1929–1996 (billions)

Year	Current dollars		Annual percentage change		Constant (1992) dollars		Annual percentage change	
	GNP	GDP	GNP	GDP	GNP	GDP	GNP	GDP
1929	$104.6	$103.8	—	—	796.8	$790.9	—	—
1930	91.8	91.1	-12.2	-12.3	725.4	719.7	-9.0	-9.0
1931	76.9	76.4	-16.2	-16.1	678.5	674.0	-6.5	-6.4
1932	58.9	58.6	-23.4	-23.4	588.0	584.3	-13.3	-13.3
1933	56.5	56.2	-4.1	-4.0	580.3	577.3	-1.3	-1.2
1934	66.1	65.9	17.0	17.1	643.7	641.1	10.9	11.0
1935	73.5	73.1	11.2	11.0	701.4	698.4	9.0	8.9
1936	83.9	83.6	14.1	14.3	792.4	790.0	13.0	13.1
1937	92.2	91.8	9.9	9.7	835.0	831.5	5.4	5.2
1938	86.3	85.9	-6.4	-6.4	804.9	801.2	-3.6	-3.6
1939	92.3	91.9	7.0	7.0	870.3	866.5	8.1	8.1
1940	101.6	101.2	10.1	10.1	944.2	941.2	8.5	8.6
1941	127.2	126.7	25.2	25.2	1,105.9	1,101.8	17.1	17.1
1942	162.1	161.6	27.4	27.6	1,312.7	1,308.9	18.7	18.8
1943	198.7	198.3	22.6	22.7	1,526.3	1,523.0	16.3	16.3
1944	220.2	219.7	10.8	10.8	1,648.2	1,644.7	8.0	8.0
1945	223.5	223.2	1.5	1.6	1,629.3	1,626.7	-1.1	-1.1
1946	223.3	222.6	-0.1	-0.3	1,452.0	1,447.7	-10.9	-11.0
1947	245.8	244.6	10.1	9.9	1,437.0	1,430.7	-1.0	-1.2
1948	271.2	269.7	10.3	10.3	1,498.8	1,491.0	4.3	4.2
1949	269.1	267.8	-0.8	-0.7	1,486.8	1,479.8	-.8	-0.8
1950	296.1	294.6	10.0	10.0	1,619.1	1,611.3	8.9	8.9
1951	341.7	339.7	15.4	15.3	1,743.7	1,734.0	7.7	7.6
1952	360.7	358.6	5.6	5.5	1,809.0	1,798.7	3.7	3.7
1953	381.7	379.7	5.8	5.9	1,891.0	1,881.4	4.5	4.6

(Table continues)

Table 11-1 *(Continued)*

Year	Current dollars		Annual percentage change		Constant (1992) dollars		Annual percentage change	
	GNP	GDP	GNP	GDP	GNP	GDP	GNP	GDP
1954	383.4	381.3	0.4	0.4	1,878.6	1,868.2	-0.7	-0.7
1955	417.7	415.1	8.9	8.9	2,012.9	2,001.1	7.1	7.1
1956	440.9	438.0	5.6	5.5	2,053.2	2,040.2	2.0	2.0
1957	464.2	461.0	5.3	5.3	2,092.4	2,078.5	1.9	1.9
1958	470.1	467.3	1.3	1.4	2,069.2	2,057.5	-1.1	-1.0
1959	510.1	507.2	8.5	8.5	2,222.0	2,210.2	7.4	7.4
1960	529.3	526.6	3.9	3.8	2,276.0	2,262.9	2.4	2.4
1961	548.4	544.8	3.5	3.5	2,329.1	2,314.3	2.3	2.3
1962	589.4	585.2	7.5	7.4	2,471.5	2,454.8	6.1	6.1
1963	621.9	617.4	5.5	5.5	2,577.3	2,559.4	4.3	4.3
1964	668.0	663.0	7.4	7.4	2,727.8	2,708.4	5.8	5.8
1965	724.5	719.1	8.5	8.5	2,901.4	2,881.1	6.4	6.4
1966	793.0	787.8	9.5	9.5	3,087.8	3,069.2	6.4	6.5
1967	839.1	833.6	5.8	5.8	3,166.4	3,147.2	2.5	2.5
1968	916.7	910.6	9.2	9.2	3,314.5	3,293.9	4.7	4.7
1969	988.4	982.2	7.8	7.9	3,413.3	3,393.6	3.0	3.0
1970	1,042.0	1,035.6	5.4	5.4	3,417.1	3,397.6	0.1	0.1
1971	1,133.1	1,125.4	8.7	8.7	3,532.1	3,510.0	3.4	3.3
1972	1,246.0	1,237.3	10.0	9.9	3,726.3	3,702.3	5.5	5.5
1973	1,395.4	1,382.6	12.0	11.7	3,950.1	3,916.3	6.0	5.8
1974	1,512.6	1,496.9	8.4	8.3	3,930.2	3,891.2	-0.1	-0.6
1975	1,643.9	1,630.6	8.7	8.9	3,903.3	3,873.9	-0.7	-0.4
1976	1,836.1	1,819.0	11.7	11.5	4,118.8	4,082.9	5.5	5.4
1977	2,047.5	2,026.9	11.5	11.4	4,314.5	4,273.6	4.8	4.7
1978	2,313.5	2,291.4	13.0	13.0	4,543.7	4,503.0	5.3	5.4
1979	2,590.4	2,557.5	12.0	11.6	4,687.4	4,630.6	3.2	2.8

387

Year								
1980	2,819.5	2,784.2	8.8	8.9	4,670.8	4,615.0	-0.0	-0.3
1981	3,150.6	3,115.9	11.7	11.9	4,769.9	4,720.7	2.1	2.3
1982	3,273.2	3,242.1	3.9	4.1	4,662.0	4,620.3	-2.3	-2.1
1983	3,546.5	3,514.5	8.3	8.4	4,844.8	4,803.7	3.9	4.0
1984	3,933.5	3,902.4	10.9	11.0	5,178.0	5,140.1	6.9	7.0
1985	4,201.0	4,180.7	6.8	7.1	5,346.7	5,323.5	3.3	3.6
1986	4,435.1	4,422.2	5.6	5.8	5,501.2	5,487.7	2.9	3.1
1987	4,701.3	4,692.3	6.0	6.1	5,658.2	5,649.5	2.9	2.9
1988	5,062.6	5,049.6	7.7	7.6	5,878.5	5,865.2	3.9	3.8
1989	5,452.8	5,438.7	7.7	7.7	6,075.7	6,062.0	3.4	3.4
1990	5,764.9	5,743.8	5.7	5.6	6,157.0	6,136.3	1.3	1.2
1991	5,932.4	5,916.7	2.9	3.0	6,094.9	6,079.4	-1.0	-0.9
1992	6,255.5	6,244.4	5.4	5.5	6,255.5	6,244.4	2.6	2.7
1993	6,563.5	6,553.0	4.9	4.9	6,396.8	6,386.1	2.3	2.3
1994	6,931.8	6,935.7	5.6	5.8	6,605.6	6,608.4	3.3	3.5
1995	7,246.7	7,253.8	4.5	4.6	6,736.4	6,742.2	2.0	2.0
1996	7,567.1	7,576.1	4.4	4.4	6,899.7	6,906.8	2.4	2.4

Note: "——" indicates data not available.

Sources: U.S. Department of Commerce, *Survey of Current Business* (Washington, D.C.: U.S. Government Printing Office, May 1997), 10, 14.

388

Table 11-2 Consumer Price Index, 1950–1996

Year	All items	Food	Shelter	Fuel, oil, and other household fuel commodities	Gas and electricity	Apparel and upkeep	Transportation Private[a]	Transportation Public	Medical care	All commodities	All services
1950	24.1	25.4	—	11.3	19.2	40.3	24.5	13.4	15.1	29.0	16.9
1955	26.8	27.8	22.7	12.7	20.7	42.9	26.7	18.5	18.2	31.3	20.4
1960	29.6	30.0	25.2	13.8	23.3	45.7	30.6	22.2	22.3	33.6	24.1
1961	29.9	30.4	25.4	14.1	23.5	46.1	30.8	23.2	22.9	33.8	24.5
1962	30.2	30.6	25.8	14.2	23.5	46.3	31.4	24.0	23.5	34.1	25.0
1963	30.6	31.1	26.1	14.4	23.5	46.9	31.6	24.3	24.1	34.4	25.5
1964	31.0	31.5	26.5	14.4	23.5	47.3	32.0	24.7	24.6	34.8	26.0
1965	31.5	32.2	27.0	14.6	23.5	47.8	32.5	25.2	25.2	35.2	26.6
1966	32.4	33.8	27.8	15.0	23.6	49.0	32.9	26.1	26.3	36.1	27.6
1967	33.4	34.1	28.8	15.5	23.7	51.0	33.8	27.4	28.2	36.8	28.8
1968	34.8	35.3	30.1	16.0	23.9	53.7	34.8	28.7	29.9	38.1	30.3
1969	36.7	37.1	32.6	16.3	24.3	56.8	36.0	30.9	31.9	39.9	32.4
1970	38.8	39.2	35.5	17.0	25.4	59.2	37.5	35.2	34.0	41.7	35.0
1971	40.5	40.4	37.0	18.2	27.1	61.1	39.4	37.8	36.1	43.2	37.0
1972	41.8	42.1	38.7	18.3	28.5	62.3	39.7	39.3	37.3	44.5	38.4
1973	44.4	48.2	40.5	21.1	29.9	64.6	41.0	39.7	38.8	47.8	40.1
1974	49.3	55.1	44.4	33.2	34.5	69.4	46.2	40.6	42.4	53.5	43.8
1975	53.8	59.8	48.8	36.4	40.1	72.5	50.6	43.5	47.5	58.2	48.0
1976	56.9	61.6	51.5	38.8	44.7	75.2	55.6	47.8	52.0	60.7	52.0
1977	60.6	65.6	54.9	43.9	50.5	78.6	59.7	50.0	57.0	64.2	56.0
1978	65.2	72.0	60.5	46.2	55.0	81.4	62.5	51.5	61.8	68.8	60.8
1979	72.6	79.9	68.9	62.4	61.0	84.9	71.7	54.9	67.5	76.6	67.5
1980	82.4	86.8	81.0	86.1	71.4	90.9	84.2	69.0	74.9	86.0	77.9
1981	90.9	93.6	90.5	104.6	81.9	95.3	93.8	85.6	82.9	93.2	88.1

Year											
1982	96.5	97.4	96.9	103.4	93.2	97.8	97.1	94.9	92.5	97.0	96.0
1983	99.6	99.4	99.1	97.2	101.5	100.2	99.3	99.5	100.6	99.8	99.4
1984	103.9	103.2	104.0	99.4	105.4	102.1	103.6	105.7	106.8	103.2	104.6
1985	107.6	105.6	109.8	95.9	107.1	105.0	106.2	110.5	113.5	105.4	109.9
1986	109.6	109.0	115.8	77.6	105.7	105.9	101.2	117.0	122.0	104.4	115.4
1987	113.6	113.5	121.3	77.9	103.8	110.6	104.2	121.1	130.1	107.7	120.2
1988	118.3	118.2	127.1	78.1	104.6	115.4	107.6	123.3	138.6	111.5	125.7
1989	124.0	125.1	132.8	81.7	107.5	118.6	112.9	129.5	149.3	116.7	131.9
1990	130.7	132.4	140.0	99.3	109.3	124.1	118.8	142.6	162.8	122.8	139.2
1991	136.2	136.3	146.3	94.6	112.6	128.7	121.9	148.9	177.0	126.6	146.3
1992	140.3	137.9	151.2	90.7	114.8	131.9	124.6	151.4	190.1	129.1	152.0
1993	144.5	140.9	155.7	90.3	118.5	133.7	127.5	167.0	201.4	131.5	157.9
1994	148.2	144.3	160.5	88.8	119.2	133.4	131.4	172.0	211.0	133.8	163.1
1995	152.4	148.4	165.7	88.1	119.2	132.0	136.3	175.9	220.5	136.4	168.7
1996	156.9	153.3	171.0	99.2	122.1	131.7	140.0	181.9	228.2	139.9	174.1

Note: "—" indicates not available. 1982–1984 equals 100. Data beginning in 1978 are for all urban consumers; earlier data are for urban wage earners and clerical workers. Data beginning 1983 incorporate a rental equivalence measure for homeowners' costs and therefore are not strictly comparable with earlier figures. Data for additional years can be found in previous editions of *Vital Statistics on American Politics*.

[a] Includes direct pricing of new trucks and motorcycles beginning September 1982.

Sources: U.S. President, *Economic Report of the President* (Washington, D.C.: U.S. Government Printing Office, 1997), Tables B-58, B-59, and B-60 from the online service of the U.S. Government Printing Office (*wais.access.gpo.gov*).

Table 11-3   Federal Budget: Total, Defense, and Nondefense Expenditures, 1940–2002 (billions)

	Current dollars			Constant (1992) dollars		
Year	National defense	Non-defense	Total	National defense	Non-defense	Total
1940	$1.7	$7.8	$9.5	$20.8	$88.3	$109.2
1941	6.4	7.2	13.7	69.5	80.6	150.2
1942	25.7	9.5	35.1	223.7	110.3	334.0
1943	66.7	11.9	78.6	525.2	143.9	669.1
1944	79.1	12.2	91.3	680.5	144.8	825.5
1945	83.0	9.7	92.7	765.4	97.8	862.4
1946	42.7	12.6	55.2	432.4	96.4	529.0
1947	12.8	21.7	34.5	122.0	154.1	276.2
1948	9.1	20.7	29.8	88.3	144.3	232.5
1949	13.2	25.7	38.8	123.4	178.6	302.0
1950	13.7	28.8	42.6	129.1	190.1	319.3
1951	23.6	21.9	45.5	215.8	134.9	350.6
1952	46.1	21.6	67.7	383.1	123.6	507.0
1953	52.8	23.3	76.1	396.7	131.9	528.5
1954	49.3	21.6	70.9	363.9	110.8	474.6
1955	42.7	25.7	68.4	311.9	139.1	450.9
1956	42.5	28.1	70.6	291.3	149.9	440.9
1957	45.4	31.1	76.6	291.0	159.0	449.9
1958	46.8	35.6	82.4	286.2	171.9	458.1
1959	49.0	43.1	92.1	272.5	208.0	480.4
1960	48.1	44.1	92.2	257.2	200.9	458.2
1961	49.6	48.1	97.7	258.6	215.4	473.9
1962	52.3	54.5	106.8	267.2	244.7	511.8
1963	53.4	57.9	111.3	261.9	252.5	514.4
1964	54.8	63.8	118.5	265.7	273.5	539.0
1965	50.6	67.6	118.2	245.6	285.1	530.9
1966	58.1	76.4	134.5	270.8	315.4	586.2
1967	71.4	86.0	157.5	320.0	345.0	665.0
1968	81.9	96.2	178.1	349.2	372.3	721.5
1969	82.5	101.1	183.6	333.5	371.2	704.7
1970	81.7	114.0	195.6	310.7	396.9	707.6
1971	78.9	131.3	210.2	283.0	432.2	715.1
1972	79.2	151.5	230.7	262.3	476.3	738.7
1973	76.7	169.0	245.7	239.6	509.6	749.1
1974	79.3	190.0	269.4	228.3	531.2	759.4
1975	86.5	245.8	332.3	224.1	623.6	847.6
1976	89.6	282.2	371.8	216.8	668.7	885.4
TQ[a]	22.3	73.7	96.0	52.1	168.9	221.0
1977	97.2	312.0	409.2	216.4	685.1	901.4
1978	104.5	354.3	458.7	217.4	727.1	944.5
1979	116.3	387.7	504.0	221.8	735.1	957.0
1980	134.0	457.0	590.9	229.3	786.2	1,015.5
1981	157.5	520.7	678.2	241.8	814.4	1,056.3
1982	185.3	560.4	745.8	263.7	822.6	1,086.3

Table 11-3   *(Continued)*

Year	Current dollars			Constant (1992) dollars		
	National defense	Non-defense	Total	National defense	Non-defense	Total
1983	209.9	598.5	808.4	284.0	839.5	1,123.5
1984	227.4	624.5	851.9	287.4	841.6	1,129.1
1985	252.7	693.8	946.5	306.2	902.7	1,209.0
1986	273.4	717.1	990.5	324.8	905.7	1,230.4
1987	282.0	722.2	1,004.2	330.0	883.8	1,213.8
1988	290.4	774.1	1,064.5	333.9	911.7	1,245.6
1989	303.6	840.1	1,143.7	338.3	946.4	1,284.7
1990	299.3	953.8	1,253.2	324.6	1,029.1	1,353.7
1991	273.3	1,051.1	1,324.4	283.3	1,082.8	1,366.1
1992	298.4	1,083.3	1,381.7	298.4	1,083.3	1,381.7
1993	291.1	1,118.3	1,409.4	286.2	1,088.5	1,374.8
1994	281.6	1,180.1	1,461.7	270.9	1,122.4	1,393.2
1995	272.1	1,243.7	1,515.7	255.5	1,155.2	1,410.6
1996	265.7	1,294.6	1,561.3	242.1	1,177.5	1,419.6
1997 est.	267.2	1,363.8	1,631.0	237.4	1,208.1	1,445.6
1998 est.	259.4	1,428.1	1,687.5	224.7	1,231.4	1,456.1
1999 est.	261.4	1,499.3	1,760.7	220.7	1,258.9	1,479.6
2000 est.	267.2	1,547.2	1,814.4	219.9	1,264.6	1,484.6
2001 est.	268.0	1,576.4	1,844.5	215.0	1,255.5	1,470.4
2002 est.	273.2	1,606.5	1,879.7	213.5	1,247.8	1,461.3

[a] Transitional quarter when fiscal year start was shifted from July 1 to October 1.

Source: Office of Management and Budget, *Budget of the United States Government, Fiscal Year 1998, Historical Tables* (Washington, D.C.: U.S. Government Printing Office, 1997), 95–103.

Table 11-4 Federal Budget Outlays, by Function, 1970–1997 (billions)

Function	1970	1975	1980	1985	1990	1993	1994	1995	1996	1997 (est.)
National defense	$81.7	$86.5	$134.0	$252.7	$299.3	$291.1	$281.6	$272.1	$265.7	$267.2
Human resources	75.3	173.2	313.4	471.8	619.3	827.5	869.4	923.8	958.3	1,019.4
Education, training, employment, and social services	8.6	16.0	31.8	29.3	38.8	50.0	46.3	54.3	52.0	51.3
Health	5.9	12.9	23.2	33.5	57.7	99.4	107.1	115.4	119.4	127.6
Income security	15.6	50.2	86.6	128.2	147.1	207.3	214.1	220.5	226.0	238.9
Social Security and Medicare[a]	36.5	77.5	150.6	254.4	346.7	435.1	464.3	495.7	523.9	562.0
Veterans' benefits and services	8.7	16.6	21.2	26.3	29.1	35.7	37.6	37.9	37.0	39.7
Physical resources	15.6	35.4	66.0	56.9	126.0	46.8	70.6	59.2	64.1	68.0
Commerce and housing credit[a]	2.1	9.9	9.4	4.3	67.6	-21.9	-4.2	-17.8	-10.6	-8.8
Community, regional development	2.4	4.3	11.3	7.7	8.5	9.1	10.5	10.6	10.7	12.8
Energy	1.0	2.9	10.2	5.7	3.3	4.3	5.2	4.9	2.8	2.1
Natural resources and environment	3.1	7.3	13.9	13.4	17.1	20.2	21.1	22.1	21.6	22.8
Transportation	7.0	10.9	21.3	25.8	29.5	35.0	38.1	39.4	39.6	39.3
Net interest[a]	14.4	23.2	52.5	129.5	184.2	198.8	203.0	232.2	241.1	247.4
Other functions[b]	17.3	27.5	45.0	68.2	60.9	82.6	74.9	73.0	68.8	75.5
Administration of justice	1.0	3.0	4.6	6.3	10.1	15.0	15.3	16.2	17.5	20.8
Agriculture	5.2	3.0	8.8	25.6	12.0	20.4	15.0	9.8	9.2	10.3
General government	2.3	10.4	13.0	11.6	10.7	13.0	11.3	13.8	11.9	13.1
General science, space, technology	4.5	4.0	5.8	8.6	14.4	17.0	16.2	16.7	16.7	16.6
International affairs	4.3	7.1	12.7	16.2	13.8	17.2	17.1	16.4	13.5	14.8
Undistributed offsetting receipts[a]	-8.6	-13.6	-19.9	-32.7	-36.6	-37.4	-37.8	-44.5	-37.6	-46.5
Total outlays[a]	195.6	332.3	590.9	946.5	1,253.2	1,409.4	1,461.7	1,515.7	1,560.3	1,631.0

Note: Amounts in current dollars. For 1940–1975, ending June 30. Beginning 1980, ending September 30. Data for earlier years can be found in previous editions of *Vital Statistics on American Politics.*

[a] Includes both on- and off-budget amounts.
[b] Includes other outlays not shown separately.

Sources: Office of Management and Budget, *Budget of the U.S. Government, Fiscal Year 1998, Historical Tables* (Washington, D.C.: U.S. Government Printing Office, 1997), 42–49.

Figure 11-1   Federal Outlays as a Percentage of GNP/GDP, 1869–2002

Percent of GNP/GDP

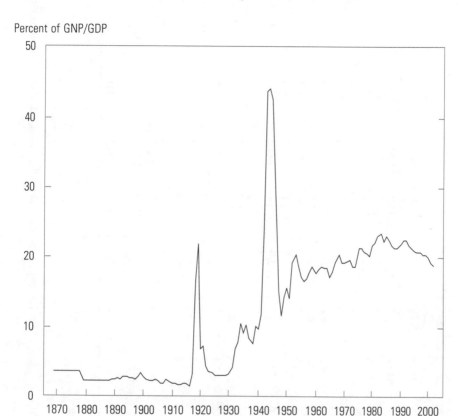

Note: Averaged by decade for 1869–1888. Percentage of GNP is shown through 1929, percentage of GDP thereafter. Figures for 1997–2002 are estimates.

Sources: 1869–1929: U.S. Bureau of the Census, *Historical Statistics of the United States* (Washington, D.C.: U.S. Government Printing Office, 1975), 224, 1,114; 1933–2002: Office of Management and Budget, *Budget of the United States Government, Fiscal Year 1998, Historical Tables* (Washington, D.C.: U.S. Government Printing Office, 1997), 21–22.

Table 11-5 Mandatory and Discretionary Federal Budget Outlays, 1962–1997

Outlays	1962	1965	1970	1975	1980	1985	1990	1995	1997 (est.)
Mandatory and related programs outlays, total[a]	$34.7	$40.4	$75.5	$174.5	$314.9	$530.8	$752.7	$970.1	$1,081.0
Health	0.1	0.3	2.8	7.1	14.7	23.9	42.9	93.4	103.6
Income security	8.7[b]	8.9[b]	14.7	46.7	75.8	109.1	123.6	181.3	198.0
Medicare			5.8	12.2	31.0	64.1	95.8	156.9	191.6
Social Security	14.0	17.1	29.6	63.6	117.1	186.4	246.5	333.3	364.2
Veterans' benefits and services	4.4	4.3	6.6	12.5	14.0	15.9	15.9	19.9	20.6
Net interest[c]	6.9	8.6	14.4	23.2	52.5	129.4	184.2	232.2	247.4
Undistributed offsetting receipt[c]	-5.3	-5.9	-8.6	-13.6	-19.9	-32.7	-36.6	-44.5	-46.5
Discretionary programs outlays, total[a]	72.1	77.8	120.2	157.8	276.1	415.7	500.4	545.6	550.0
Domestic, total[a]	14.0	22.1	34.3	62.0	128.7	145.2	181.2	252.0	262.5
Education, training, employment, and social services	0.9	1.8	7.3	12.9	25.6	21.7	27.6	38.6	41.1
General science, space, and technology	1.7	5.8	4.5	4.0	5.8	8.6	14.4	16.7	16.5
Health	1.1	1.5	3.1	5.8	8.5	9.6	14.9	22.0	24.0
Income security	0.5	0.5	1.0	3.5	10.8	19.2	23.5	39.2	40.9
Natural resources and environment	2.3	2.8	3.5	8.1	15.5	15.1	17.8	21.9	21.7
Transportation	1.4	1.6	2.6	5.9	20.7	24.8	27.9	37.1	36.8
International affairs	5.5	4.7	4.0	8.2	12.8	17.4	19.1	20.1	19.6
National defense	52.6	51.0	81.9	87.6	134.6	253.1	300.1	273.6	268.0
Total outlays	106.8	118.2	195.7	332.3	591.0	946.5	1,253.1	1,515.7	1,631.0
Mandatory program outlays as a percentage of total outlays	32.5	34.2	38.6	52.5	53.3	56.1	60.1	64.0	66.3

Note: Amounts in billions of current dollars.

[a] Includes other outlays not shown separately.

[b] Medicare outlays began in fiscal year 1967.

[c] Includes both on- and off-budget amounts.

Source: Office of Management and Budget, *Budget of the U.S. Government, Fiscal Year 1998, Historical Tables* (Washington, D.C.: U.S. Government Printing Office, 1997), 113–127.

Table 11-6   The National Debt, 1940–2002

Year	Debt held by the public (millions)	As a percentage of GDP	Year	Debt held by the public (millions)	As a percentage of GDP
1940	$42,772	43.7	1972	322,377	27.4
1941	48,223	41.8	1973	340,910	26.1
1942	67,753	46.6	1974	343,699	23.9
1943	127,766	71.1	1975	394,700	25.4
1944	184,796	89.4	1976	477,404	27.6
1945	235,182	108.2	TQ[a]	495,509	27.2
1946	241,861	111.0	1977	549,103	27.9
1947	224,339	98.2	1978	607,125	27.4
1948	216,270	85.3	1979	640,308	25.7
1949	214,322	79.5	1980	709,838	26.1
1950	219,023	80.3	1981	785,338	25.8
1951	214,326	66.8	1982	919,785	28.6
1952	214,758	61.5	1983	1,131,596	33.1
1953	218,383	58.6	1984	1,300,498	34.1
1954	224,499	59.5	1985	1,499,908	36.6
1955	226,616	57.3	1986	1,736,709	39.7
1956	222,156	52.1	1987	1,888,680	41.0
1957	219,320	48.7	1988	2,050,799	41.4
1958	226,336	49.3	1989	2,189,882	40.9
1959	234,701	47.9	1990	2,410,722	42.4
1960	236,840	45.7	1991	2,688,137	45.9
1961	238,357	44.9	1992	2,998,834	48.8
1962	248,010	43.7	1993	3,247,471	50.2
1963	253,978	42.4	1994	3,432,117	50.2
1964	256,849	40.1	1995	3,603,373	50.1
1965	260,778	38.0	1996	3,732,964	49.9
1966	263,714	35.0	1997 est.	3,875,775	49.3
1967	266,626	32.8	1998 est.	4,021,358	48.9
1968	289,545	33.4	1999 est.	4,159,413	48.3
1969	278,108	29.3	2000 est.	4,268,984	47.2
1970	283,198	28.1	2001 est.	4,327,965	45.6
1971	303,037	28.1	2002 est.	4,333,122	43.5

Note: Amounts in current dollars.

[a] Transitional quarter when fiscal year start was shifted from July 1 to October 1.

Source: Office of Management and Budget, *Budget of the U.S. Government, Fiscal Year 1998, Historical Tables* (Washington, D.C.: U.S. Government Printing Office, 1997), 102–103.

Figure 11-2   The National Debt as a Percentage of GDP, 1940–2002

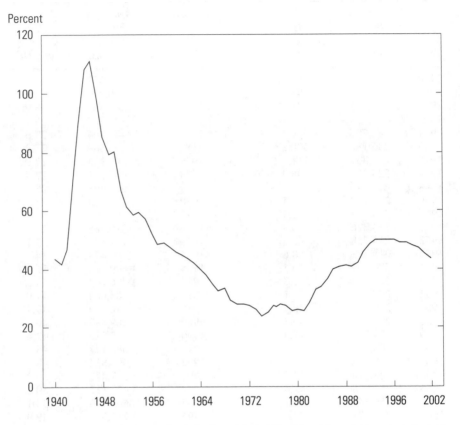

Note: Amounts in current dollars. Figures reflect debt held by the public and do not include debt held by federal government accounts. Transitional quarter when fiscal year start was shifted from July 1 to October 1 in 1976. 1997–2002 percentages are estimates.

Source: Office of Management and Budget, *Budget of the U.S. Government, Fiscal Year 1998, Historical Tables* (Washington, D.C.: U.S. Government Printing Office, 1997), 102–103.

Table 11-7 Cost of Selected Tax Breaks: Revenue Loss Estimates for Selected Tax Expenditures, 1980–2002 (millions)

Type of tax expenditure	1980	1985	1990	1995	1996	1998	2000	2002
Commerce and housing credit								
Exclusion of interest on life insurance savings	$3,490	$2,175	$7,265	$10,075	$10,200	$11,570	$13,120	$14,885
Deductibility of interest on consumer credit	4,745	15,530	1,525	0	0	0	0	0
Deductibility of mortgage interest on owner-occupied homes	15,615	24,785	37,580	51,270	47,525	52,115	56,830	62,060
Deductibility of property tax on owner-occupied homes	7,310	9,315	9,520	14,845	15,900	17,435	19,015	20,765
Deferral of capital gains on home sales	1,010	1,775	12,635	17,140	14,410	15,290	16,220	17,205
Exclusion of capital gains on home sales for persons age 55 and over	535	830	3,230	4,820	5,225	5,095	5,295	5,495
Investment credit, other than ESOP's, rehabilitation of structures, energy property, and reforestation expenditures	18,250	24,445	0	0	0	0	0	0
Accelerated depreciation of machinery and equipment	—	20,145	18,655	16,120	2,020	1,400	690	285
Education, training, employment, and social services								
Deductibility of charitable contributions (education)	1,090	1,345	1,195	1,535	1,685	1,860	2,050	2,260
Credit for child and dependent care expenses	885	2,700	3,895	2,900	2,580	2,840	3,130	3,455
Deductibility of charitable contributions, other than education and health	6,270	10,175	10,870	14,015	15,375	16,950	18,690	20,605
Health								
Exclusion of employer contributions for medical insurance premiums and medical care	12,075	21,095	26,360	60,670	64,450	75,750	86,900	98,995
Deductibility of medical expenses	3,150	3,620	2,860	3,660	3,675	4,535	5,270	6,100
Exclusion of interest on state and local debt for private nonprofit health facilities	425	1,405	2,765	895	1,285	1,210	1,120	1,050

(Table continues)

Table 11-7 *(Continued)*

Type of tax expenditure	1980	1985	1990	1995	1996	1998	2000	2002
Social Security and Medicare								
Exclusion of Social Security benefits								
Disability insurance benefits	690	1,170	1,210	1,895	2,090	2,615	3,045	3,545
OASI benefits for retired workers	6,890	12,955	16,040	16,875	17,005	18,495	20,190	21,495
Benefits for dependents and survivors	1,015	3,755	2,995	3,610	3,795	4,175	4,530	4,895
Income security								
Exclusion of workmen's compensation benefits	2,200	2,225	2,735	4,475	4,695	5,305	5,855	6,660
Net exclusion of pension contributions and earnings								
Employer plans	19,785	48,525	45,385	55,540	55,410	56,245	57,085	57,940
Individual Retirement Accounts	—	12,695	6,620	6,245	8,025	8,600	9,125	9,520
Keoghs	1,925	1,960	1,460	4,435	3,030	3,325	3,680	4,080
Veterans benefits and services								
Exclusion of veterans disability compensation	1,065	1,695	1,580	1,985	2,615	2,930	3,280	3,675
General purpose fiscal assistance								
Deductibility of nonbusiness state and local taxes other than on owner-occupied homes	14,690	21,455	18,875	27,250	28,265	30,995	33,800	36,910

Note: "—" indicates not available. Amounts in current dollars. Fiscal year basis. Tax expenditures are defined as revenue losses attributable to provisions of the federal tax laws which allow a special exclusion, exemption, or deduction from gross income or which provide a special credit, a preferential rate of tax, or a deferral of liability. The Internal Revenue Service collected slightly under $500 billion in 1987 through individual and corporate income taxes. Data for additional years can be found in previous editions of *Vital Statistics on American Politics.*

Sources: 1980–1991: Office of Management and Budget, *Budget of the U.S. Government* (Washington, D.C.: U.S. Government Printing Office), annual; 1995: Office of Management and Budget, *Budget of the U.S. Government, 1996, Analytical Perspectives* (Washington, D.C.: U.S. Government Printing Office, 1995), 43–46; 1996–2002: *1998:* 76–78.

Table 11-8 Membership in Labor Unions, 1900–1996

Year	Membership (in thousands)	Percent in unions	
		Nonagricultural employment	Labor force
1900	932.4	6.5	3.3
1905	1,947.1	10.8	6.0
1910	2,168.5	10.3	5.9
1915	2,597.6	11.5	6.6
1920	4,823.3	17.6	11.7
1925	3,685.1	12.8	8.2
1930	3,749.6	12.7	7.5
1935	3,649.6	13.5	6.9
1940	7,296.7	22.5	13.1
1945	12,254.2	30.4	22.8
1950	14,294.2	31.6	23.0
1955	16,126.9	31.8	24.8
1960	15,516.1	28.6	22.3
1965	18,268.9	30.1	24.5
1970	20,990.3	29.6	25.4
1971	20,711.1	29.1	24.5
1972	21,205.8	28.8	24.4
1973	21,881.3	28.5	24.5
1974	22,165.4	28.3	24.1
1975	22,207.0	28.9	23.7
1976	22,153.0	27.9	23.0
1977	21,632.1	26.2	21.8
1978	21,756.5	25.1	21.3
1979	22,025.4	24.5	21.0
1980	20,968.2	23.2	19.6
1981	20,646.8	22.6	19.0
1982	19,571.4	21.9	17.8
1983	18,633.6	20.7	16.6
1984	18,306.0	19.4	16.1
1985	16,996.0	18.0	14.7
1986	16,975.0	17.5	14.4
1987	16,913.0	17.0	14.1
1988	17,002.0	16.8	14.0
1989	16,960.0	16.4	13.7
1990	16,740.0	16.1	13.3
1991	16,568.0	16.1	13.1
1992	16,390.0	15.8	12.8
1993	16,389.0	15.8	12.7
1994	16,748.0	15.5	12.8
1995	16,360.0	14.9	12.4
1996	16,269.0	14.5	12.1

Note: Comparisons of two years in which both sources reported union membership show that the counts by Troy and Sheflin are about one million members higher per year than the counts based on the Current Population Surveys reported by the Bureau of Labor Statistics in *Employment and Earnings.* In 1985–1993, self-employed workers whose businesses are incorporated are excluded from calculations for the percent in unions in nonagricultural employment.

Sources: 1900–1984: Leo Troy and Neil Sheflin, *U.S. Union Sourcebook* (West Orange, N.J.: Industrial Relations Data and Information Services, 1985), A-1, A-2, 3–10; 1985–1996: U.S. Department of Labor, Bureau of Labor Statistics, *Employment and Earnings,* January 1987 (Washington, D.C.: U.S. Government Printing Office, 1987), 219; (1988), 222; (1990), 232; (1992), 228; (1994), 248; (1996), 214; (1997), 211; size of the labor force from *Employment and Earnings,* January 1997, 158.

Table 11-9   Civilian Labor Force Participation Rate, Overall and by Sex and Race, 1948–1996 (percent)

Year	Total	Male	Female	White	Black and other nonwhite
1948	58.8	86.6	32.7	—	—
1950	59.2	86.4	33.9	—	—
1955	59.3	85.4	35.7	58.7	64.2
1956	60.0	85.5	36.9	59.4	64.9
1957	59.6	84.8	36.9	59.1	64.4
1958	59.5	84.2	37.1	58.9	64.8
1959	59.3	83.7	37.1	58.7	64.3
1960	59.4	83.3	37.7	58.8	64.5
1961	59.3	82.9	38.1	58.8	64.1
1962	58.8	82.0	37.9	58.3	63.2
1963	58.7	81.4	38.3	58.2	63.0
1964	58.7	81.0	38.7	58.2	63.1
1965	58.9	80.7	39.3	58.4	62.9
1966	59.2	80.4	40.3	58.7	63.0
1967	59.6	80.4	41.1	59.2	62.8
1968	59.6	80.1	41.6	59.3	62.2
1969	60.1	79.8	42.7	59.9	62.1
1970	60.4	79.7	43.3	60.2	61.8
1971	60.2	79.1	43.4	60.1	60.9
1972	60.4	78.9	43.9	60.4	60.2
1973	60.8	78.8	44.7	60.8	60.5
1974	61.3	78.7	45.7	61.4	60.3
1975	61.2	77.9	46.3	61.5	59.6
1976	61.6	77.5	47.3	61.8	59.8
1977	62.3	77.7	48.4	62.5	60.4
1978	63.2	77.9	50.0	63.3	62.2
1979	63.7	77.8	50.9	63.9	62.2
1980	63.8	77.4	51.5	64.1	61.7
1981	63.9	77.0	52.1	64.3	61.3
1982	64.0	76.6	52.6	64.3	61.6
1983	64.0	76.4	52.9	64.3	62.1
1984	64.4	76.4	53.6	64.6	62.6
1985	64.8	76.3	54.5	65.0	63.3
1986	65.3	76.3	55.3	65.5	63.7
1987	65.6	76.2	56.0	65.8	64.3
1988	65.9	76.2	56.6	66.2	64.0
1989	66.5	76.4	57.4	66.7	64.7
1990	66.5	76.4	57.5	66.9	64.4
1991	66.2	75.8	57.4	66.6	63.8
1992	66.4	75.8	57.8	66.8	64.6
1993	66.3	75.4	57.9	66.8	63.8
1994	66.6	75.1	58.8	67.1	63.9
1995	66.6	75.0	58.9	67.1	64.3
1996	66.8	74.9	59.3	67.2	64.6

Note: "—" indicates not available. Figures are for persons sixteen years of age and over. The participation rate is the percentage of adults considered to be in the labor force. It is roughly those persons who are working, temporarily laid off, or looking for work. For details, see U.S. Bureau of the Census, *Statistical Abstract of the United States, 1992* (Washington, D.C.: Government Printing Office, 1992), 378.

Source: U.S. President, *Economic Report of the President* (Washington, D.C.: U.S. Government Printing Office, 1997), Table B-37 from the online service of the U.S. Government Printing Office *(wais.access.gpo.gov)*.

Table 11-10   Unemployment Rate Overall, 1929–1996, and by Sex and
Race, 1948–1996 (percent)

Year	Civilian workers	Male	Female	White	Nonwhite
1929	3.2	—	—	—	—
1933	24.9	—	—	—	—
1939	17.2	—	—	—	—
1940	14.6	—	—	—	—
1941	9.9	—	—	—	—
1942	4.7	—	—	—	—
1943	1.9	—	—	—	—
1944	1.2	—	—	—	—
1945	1.9	—	—	—	—
1946	3.9	—	—	—	—
1947	3.9	—	—	—	—
1948	3.8	3.6	4.1	3.5	5.9
1949	5.9	5.9	6.0	5.6	8.9
1950	5.3	5.1	5.7	4.9	9.0
1951	3.3	2.8	4.4	3.1	5.3
1952	3.0	2.8	3.6	2.8	5.4
1953	2.9	2.8	3.3	2.7	4.5
1954	5.5	5.3	6.0	5.0	9.9
1955	4.4	4.2	4.9	3.9	8.7
1956	4.1	3.8	4.8	3.6	8.3
1957	4.3	4.1	4.7	3.8	7.9
1958	6.8	6.8	6.8	6.1	12.6
1959	5.5	5.2	5.9	4.8	10.7
1960	5.5	5.4	5.9	5.0	10.2
1961	6.7	6.4	7.2	6.0	12.4
1962	5.5	5.2	6.2	4.9	10.9
1963	5.7	5.2	6.5	5.0	10.8
1964	5.2	4.6	6.2	4.6	9.6
1965	4.5	4.0	5.5	4.1	8.1
1966	3.8	3.2	4.8	3.4	7.3
1967	3.8	3.1	5.2	3.4	7.4
1968	3.6	2.9	4.8	3.2	6.7
1969	3.5	2.8	4.7	3.1	6.4
1970	4.9	4.4	5.9	4.5	8.2
1971	5.9	5.3	6.9	5.4	9.9
1972	5.6	5.0	6.6	5.1	10.0
1973	4.9	4.2	6.0	4.3	9.0
1974	5.6	4.9	6.7	5.0	9.9
1975	8.5	7.9	9.3	7.8	13.8
1976	7.7	7.1	8.6	7.0	13.1
1977	7.1	6.3	8.2	6.2	13.1
1978	6.1	5.3	7.2	5.2	11.9
1979	5.8	5.1	6.8	5.1	11.3
1980	7.1	6.9	7.4	6.3	13.1
1981	7.6	7.4	7.9	6.7	14.2
1982	9.7	9.9	9.4	8.6	17.3

(Table continues)

Table 11-10   *(Continued)*

Year	Civilian workers	Male	Female	White	Nonwhite
1983	9.6	9.9	9.2	8.4	17.8
1984	7.5	7.4	7.6	6.5	14.4
1985	7.2	7.0	7.4	6.2	13.7
1986	7.0	6.9	7.1	6.0	13.1
1987	6.2	6.2	6.2	5.3	11.6
1988	5.5	5.5	5.6	4.7	10.4
1989	5.3	5.2	5.4	4.5	10.0
1990	5.6	5.7	5.5	4.8	10.1
1991	6.8	7.2	6.4	6.1	11.1
1992	7.5	7.9	7.0	6.6	12.7
1993	6.9	7.2	6.6	6.1	11.7
1994	6.1	6.2	6.0	5.3	10.5
1995	5.6	5.6	5.6	4.9	9.6
1996	5.4	5.4	5.4	4.7	9.3

Note: "—" indicates not available. 1929–1947 figures are for persons fourteen years of age and over. 1948–1992 figures are for persons sixteen years of age and over.

Source: U.S. President, *Economic Report of the President* (Washington, D.C.: U.S. Government Printing Office, 1997), Tables B-33 and B-40 from the online service of the U.S. Government Printing Office (*wais.access.gpo.gov*).

Table 11-11   Unemployment, by Race, Sex, and Age, 1955–1996 (percent)

	White				Black[a]			
	Male		Female		Male		Female	
Year	16–19	20 and over	16–19	20 and over	16–19	20 and over	16–19	20 and over
1955	11.3	3.3	9.1	3.9	13.4	8.4	19.2	7.7
1960	14.0	4.2	12.7	4.6	24.0	9.6	24.8	8.3
1965	12.9	2.9	14.0	4.0	23.3	6.0	31.7	7.5
1970	13.7	3.2	13.4	4.4	25.0	5.6	34.5	6.9
1972	14.2	3.6	14.2	4.9	31.7	7.0	40.5	9.0
1973	12.3	3.0	13.0	4.3	27.8	6.0	36.1	8.6
1974	13.5	3.5	14.5	5.1	33.1	7.4	37.4	8.8
1975	18.3	6.2	17.4	7.5	38.1	12.5	41.0	12.2
1976	17.3	5.4	16.4	6.8	37.5	11.4	41.6	11.7
1977	15.0	4.7	15.9	6.2	39.2	10.7	43.4	12.3
1978	13.5	3.7	14.4	5.2	36.7	9.3	40.8	11.2
1979	13.9	3.6	14.0	5.0	34.2	9.3	39.1	10.9
1980	16.2	5.3	14.8	5.6	37.5	12.4	39.8	11.9
1981	17.9	5.6	16.6	5.9	40.7	13.5	42.2	13.4
1982	21.7	7.8	19.0	7.3	48.9	17.8	47.1	15.4
1983	20.2	7.9	18.3	6.9	48.8	18.1	48.2	16.5
1984	16.8	5.7	15.2	5.8	42.7	14.3	42.6	13.5
1985	16.5	5.4	14.8	5.7	41.0	13.2	39.2	13.1
1986	16.3	5.3	14.9	5.4	39.3	12.9	39.2	12.4
1987	15.5	4.8	13.4	4.6	34.4	11.1	34.9	11.6
1988	13.9	4.1	12.3	4.1	32.7	10.1	32.0	10.4
1989	13.7	3.9	11.5	4.0	31.9	10.0	33.0	9.8
1990	14.2	4.3	12.6	4.1	32.1	10.4	30.0	9.6
1991	17.5	5.7	15.2	4.9	36.5	11.5	36.1	10.5
1992	18.4	6.3	15.7	5.4	42.0	13.4	37.2	11.7
1993	17.6	5.6	14.6	5.1	40.1	12.1	37.5	10.6
1994	16.3	4.8	13.8	4.6	37.6	10.3	32.6	9.8
1995	15.6	4.3	13.4	4.3	37.1	8.8	34.3	8.6
1996	15.5	4.1	12.9	4.1	36.9	9.4	30.3	8.7

[a] Black and other prior to 1972.

Source: U.S. President, *Economic Report of the President* (Washington, D.C.: U.S. Government Printing Office, 1997), Table B-41 from the online service of the U.S. Government Printing Office *(wais.access.gpo.gov)*.

Appendix

Table A-1 Regions as Defined by the U.S. Census Bureau

Northeast	Midwest	South	West
New England	East north central	South Atlantic	Mountain
Connecticut	Illinois	Delaware	Arizona
New Hampshire	Indiana	District of	Colorado
Maine	Michigan	Columbia	Idaho
Massachusetts	Ohio	Florida	Montana
Rhode Island	Wisconsin	Georgia	Nevada
Vermont	West north central	Maryland	New Mexico
Middle Atlantic	Iowa	North Carolina	Utah
New Jersey	Kansas	South Carolina	Wyoming
New York	Minnesota	Virginia	Pacific
Pennsylvania	Missouri	West Virginia	Alaska
	Nebraska	East south central	California
	North Dakota	Alabama	Hawaii
	South Dakota	Kentucky	Oregon
		Mississippi	Washington
		Tennessee	
		West south central	
		Arkansas	
		Louisiana	
		Oklahoma	
		Texas	

Source: U.S. Bureau of the Census, *Statistical Abstract of the United States, 1992* (Washington, D.C.: U.S. Government Printing Office, 1992), Figure 1.

Table A-2   Regions as Defined by Congressional Quarterly, Gallup Poll, *New York Times*/CBS News Poll, and Voter Research & Surveys

East	Midwest	South	West
Connecticut	Illinois	Alabama	Alaska
Delaware	Indiana	Arkansas	Arizona
District of Columbia	Iowa	Florida	California
Maine	Kansas	Georgia	Colorado
Maryland	Michigan	Kentucky	Hawaii
Massachusetts	Minnesota	Louisiana	Idaho
New Hampshire	Missouri	Mississippi	Montana
New Jersey	Nebraska	North Carolina	Nevada
New York	North Dakota	Oklahoma	New Mexico
Pennsylvania	Ohio	South Carolina	Oregon
Rhode Island	South Dakota	Tennessee	Utah
Vermont	Wisconsin	Texas	Washington
West Virginia		Virginia	Wyoming

Sources: The Gallup Organization; Congressional Quarterly.

Table A-3   Regions for Partisan Competition Table (Table 1-3)

New England	Middle Atlantic	Midwest	Plains
Connecticut	Delaware	Illinois	Iowa
Maine	New Jersey	Indiana	Kansas
Massachusetts	New York	Michigan	Minnesota
New Hampshire	Pennsylvania	Ohio	Nebraska
Rhode Island		Wisconsin	North Dakota
Vermont			South Dakota

South	Border	Rocky Mountain	Pacfic Coast
Alabama	District of	Arizona	Alaska
Arkansas	Columbia	Colorado	California
Florida	Kentucky	Idaho	Hawaii
Georgia	Maryland	Montana	Oregon
Louisiana	Missouri	Nevada	Washington
Mississippi	Oklahoma	New Mexico	
North Carolina	West Virginia	Utah	
South Carolina		Wyoming	
Tennesse			
Texas			
Virginia			

Table A-4   Regions for School Desegregation Table (Table 10-14)

South	Border	Northeast	Midwest	West	Excluded
Alabama	Delaware	Connecticut	Illinois	Arizona	Alaska
Arkansas	District of	Maine	Indiana	California	Hawaii
Florida	Columbia	Massachusetts	Iowa	Colorado	
Georgia	Kentucky	New Hamp-	Kansas	Idaho	
Louisiana	Maryland	shire	Michigan	Montana	
Mississippi	Missouri	New Jersey	Minnesota	Nevada	
North	Oklahoma	New York	Nebraska	New Mexico	
Carolina	West Virginia	Pennsylvania	North	Oregon	
South		Rhode Island	Dakota	Utah	
Carolina		Vermont	Ohio	Washington	
Tennessee			South	Wyoming	
Texas			Dakota		
Virginia			Wisconsin		

Source: Gary Orfield and Franklin Monfort, "Status of School Desegregation: The Next Generation" (Alexandria, Va.: National School Boards Association, 1992), 2.

Guide to References for Political Statistics

The Internet and the World Wide Web

Electronic sites are fast becoming an important source for all kinds of information, especially about current people and events. It is also becoming easier to access this information because of powerful search engines and because many web sites provide links to related sites.

It would be impossible, as well as pointless, for us to try to provide anything like a comprehensive list of relevant sites. Nevertheless, we have listed a number of significant sites for finding information about U.S. government and politics. Even this small selection of sites, together with their links to related sites, is enough to keep even the most dedicated political and data junkies busy.

Many web sites are immediately identifiable from their URL addresses. We separately identify only those that are not obvious.

Campaign finances

http://www.fec.gov/ (Federal Election Commission)
> Has Census Bureau data and data from other government departments and agencies

http://www.census.gov/
> Has links to federal government agencies and state data centers

Congress

http://thomas.loc.gov/
http://www.house.gov/
http://www.senate.gov/

Courts

http://www.uscourts.gov/

Elections

http://www.fec.gov/ (Federal Election Commission)
http://www.lsu.edu/guests/poli/public_html/1996camp.html
    Has 1996 elections materials

Library of Congress

http://lcweb.loc.gov/
http://lcweb2.loc.gov/glin/lawhome.html (Law Library of Congress)

Media

http://www.nytimes.com/
http://www.washingtonpost.com/
http://www.abcnews.com/
http://www.nbc.com/
http://www.cbs.com/
http://www.c-span.org/
http://www.people-press.org/ (Pew Research Center for the People and the Press)

Political parties

http://www.rnc.org/ Republican National Committee
http://www.massgop.com/national.htm (National Republican Party)
    Has links to numerous sites relating to the Republican party
http://www.democrats.org/ (Democratic National Committee)
    Has links to numerous sites relating to the Democratic party

President

http://www.whitehouse.gov/

Public opinion

http://www.gallup.com/ (The Gallup Poll)
http://www.icpsr.umich.edu/ (The Inter-University Consortium for Political and Social Research)

State and local governments (see also Census site, above)

http://www.ncsl.org/ (National Conference of State Legislatures)
    Has links to sites of individual state legislatures
http://www.csg.org/ (Council of State Governments)
http://www.loc.gov/global/state/stategov.html (Library of Congress)

General

Alonso, William, and Paul Starr, eds. *The Politics of Numbers.* New York: Russell Sage, 1987.
> Excellent analysis of issues relating to the collection and publication of statistics, especially the U.S. census.

Austin, Erik W., and Jerome M. Clubb. *Political Facts of the United States Since 1789.* New York: Columbia University Press, 1986.
> Convenient one-volume compilation of otherwise all-too-often elusive data on politics in the nation; one strength is the long time series.

Congressional Information Service. *American Statistics Index: A Comprehensive Guide and Index to the Statistical Publications of the U.S. Government.* Washington, D.C.: Congressional Information Service, 1973–. Annual, with monthly supplements.
> Definitive guide, multiply indexed, to statistics "of probable research significance" in government publications; 1974 "Annual and Retrospective Edition" includes not only items in print but also significant items published over the preceding decade.

———. *Statistical Reference Index: A Selective Guide to American Statistical Publications from Sources Other than the U.S. Government.* Washington, D.C.: Congressional Information Service, 1980–. Annual, with bimonthly supplements.
> A complement to *American Statistics Index,* indexes statistics from private and public sources other than the U.S. federal government.

Congressional Quarterly Weekly Report. Washington, D.C.: Congressional Quarterly, 1945–. Weekly.
> Newsweekly covering political developments in Congress, the presidency, the Supreme Court, and national politics; individual voting records on all roll-call votes in the House and Senate; texts of presidential press conferences and major statements.

Congressional Research Service. *The Constitution of the United States: Analysis and Interpretation.* Washington, D.C.: U.S. Government Printing Office, 1987. 99th Cong., 1st sess., S.Doc. 99-16. Supplement issued 100th Cong., 1st sess., S.Doc. 100-9.
> Not statistics laden, but an essential document with commentary and annotations of Supreme Court decisions and tables on proposed constitutional amendments pending and unratified, laws (congressional, state, or local) held unconstitutional by the Supreme Court, and Supreme Court decisions overruled by subsequent decisions. U.S. law requires a new edition every ten years with biennial supplements between editions to keep this work current.

Maier, Mark H. *The Data Game: Controversies in Social Science Statistics,* 2d ed. Armonk, N.Y.: Sharpe, 1995.
> Discussion of statistical source material, with an emphasis on inaccuracies, ambiguities, misinterpretations, and unavailability as well as on the relationship between statistics and important social questions.

National Journal. Washington, D.C.: National Journal, Inc., 1969–. Weekly.
>   Newsweekly about government; reviews recent actions and features analyses of policy and political issues.

U.S. Bureau of the Census. *Historical Statistics of the United States, Colonial Times to 1970.* Bicentennial edition. Washington, D.C.: U.S. Government Printing Office, 1975.
>   Invaluable, broad-ranging collection of more than 12,000 time series covering the nation's history; often the series can be updated by the annual *Statistical Abstract of the United States* (see below).

————. *Statistical Abstract of the United States.* Washington, D.C.: U.S. Government Printing Office, 1879–. Annual.
>   Strong, indispensable collection of nationally significant statistics from public and private sources on economics, politics, and society; generally worth checking first; also a useful guide to sources for additional statistics; indicates which time series update those in *Historical Statistics of the United States* (see above).

U.S. Congress. House. *Constitution, Jefferson's Manual, and Rules of the House of Representatives of the United States.* Washington, D.C.: U.S. Government Printing Office. Biennial.
>   Solid reference on the Constitution with full notes on all ratifications; indexed.

Elections

Barone, Michael, with William Lilley III and Laurence J. DeFranco. *State Legislative Elections: Voting Patterns and Demographics.* Washington, D.C.: Congressional Quarterly, 1997.
>   Political analysis of state legislative elections in all 50 states, plus population and demographic information.

Bartley, Numan V., and Hugh D. Graham. *Southern Elections: County and Precinct Data, 1950–1972.* Baton Rouge, La.: Louisiana State University Press, 1978.
>   Gubernatorial and senatorial contests, primaries, and referenda in southern states; some socioeconomic and geographic analysis of the elections.

Brace, Kim, et al. *The Election Data Book.* Lanham, Md.: Bernan Press, 1993.
>   Extensive compilation of general election and primary vote totals, by state and county, for president, governor, and U.S. senator and representative. Voter registration and turnout figures by state since 1948; by country for most recent election. Information on voting precincts, registration methods, and voting equipment. State maps with county and congressional districts boundaries.

Congressional Quarterly. *Congressional Quarterly's Guide to U.S. Elections.* 3d ed. Washington, D.C.: Congressional Quarterly, 1994.
>   Superb collection of vote returns for presidential, gubernatorial, and House elections since 1824, electoral college votes since 1789, senatorial elections since 1913, presidential primaries since 1912, and primaries for governor and senator since 1956 (in southern states since 1919); general and candidate indexes; biographies of presidential and vice-presidential candidates; lists of governors

and senators since 1789; discussions of and data on political parties and presidential nominating conventions throughout the nation's history.

Cook, Rhodes, and Alice V. McGillivray. *U.S. Primary Elections: President, Congress, Governors: 1995–1996.* Washington, D.C.: Congressional Quarterly, 1997.
> Includes county-by-county results of all presidential primaries plus data on caucuses. Official results of 1995 and 1996 gubernatorial, senatorial, and House primaries. Updates a series that began in 1993 (under various titles).

Glashan, Roy R. *American Governors and Gubernatorial Elections, 1775–1978.* Westport, Conn.: Meckler, 1979.
> Details about state governors (such as birthdates, party affiliations, principal occupations, terms of office) and election data.

Kallenbach, Joseph E., and Jessamine S. Kallenbach. *American State Governors, 1776–1976.* Dobbs Ferry, N.Y.: Oceana Publications, 1977–1982.
> Election results and biographical data on governors.

Ladd, Everett Carll and staff and associates of the Roper Center for Public Opinion Research. *America at the Polls: A Roper Center Databook.* University of Connecticut: Roper Center, 1995–.
> Resource combining survey and aggregate vote data after each national election.

McGillivray, Alice V. *Congressional and Gubernatorial Primaries: 1991–1992.* Washington, D.C.: Congressional Quarterly, 1993.
> County-by-county primary results for governors and U.S. senators and representatives.

———. *Presidential Primaries and Caucuses: 1992.* Washington, D.C.: Congressional Quarterly, 1992.
> County-by-county results for presidential primaries in 1992. Voter registration figures by county.

McGillivray, Alice V., and Richard M. Scammon, eds. *America at the Polls: A Handbook of Presidential Election Statistics.* Washington, D.C.: Congressional Quarterly, 1994.
> Two volumes span 1920–1992, providing popular votes (state and county) for president as well as state presidential primary results. Available on disk.

Mullaney, Marie. *American Governors and Gubernatorial Elections, 1979–1987.* Westport, Conn.: Meckler, 1988.
> Details about state governors (such as birthdates, party affiliations, principal occupations, terms of office) and election data.

Nomination and Election of the President and Vice President of the United States. Washington, D.C.: U.S. Government Printing Office, 1960–. Quadrennial.
> Compilation of federal and state laws and party rules governing nomination and election of the president.

Reapportionment Law: The 1990s. Denver: National Conference of State Legislatures, 1989.
> Detailed discussion of law relating to redistricting.

Redistricting Provisions: 50 State Profiles. Denver: National Conference of State Legislatures, 1989.

Compilation of state constitutional and statutory requirements regarding congressional and state legislative districting.

Republican National Committee. *The (Year) Republican Almanac: State Political Profiles.* Washington, D.C.: Republican National Committee, 1973–. Biennial.

In its most recent edition, a voluminous statistical report of political, especially election, data about each state of the nation.

Runyon, John H., Jennefer Verdini, and Sally S. Runyan, eds. *Source Book of American Presidential Campaign and Election Statistics, 1948–1968.* New York: Frederick Ungar, 1971.

Information on presidential campaign staffs, candidate itineraries, media exposure, campaign costs, and public opinion polls.

Scammon, Richard M., Alice V. McGillivray, and Rhodes Cook, eds. *America Votes: A Handbook of Contemporary American Election Statistics.* Washington, D.C.: Congressional Quarterly, Elections Research Center, 1956–. Biennial.

Convenient compilation of vote totals and statistics by state for general elections and primaries for president, governor, and senator, principally since 1945 (comparable district-level data for members of Congress); county-level totals and statistics for most recent general election for president, governor, and senator; state maps with county and congressional districts boundaries.

U.S. Bureau of the Census. Current Population Reports. Population Characteristics, Series P-20. *Voting and Registration in the Election of November (Year).* Washington, D.C.: U.S. Government Printing Office, 1964–. Biennial.

Survey results on voter registration and turnout in presidential and midterm general elections for the nation and regions (and sometimes states and metropolitan areas) for various groups.

Political Parties

Appleton, Andrew M., and Daniel S. Ward. *State Party Profiles: A 50-State Guide to Development, Organization, and Resources.* Washington, D.C.: Congressional Quarterly, 1997.

Brief descriptions of party histories, organizational development, current party organizations, a resource guide, and references, for all fifty states.

Bain, Richard C., and Judith H. Parris. *Convention Decisions and Voting Records.* 2d ed. Washington, D.C.: Brookings, 1973.

Data on convention actions through 1972.

Congressional Quarterly. *National Party Conventions, 1831–1996.* 7th ed. Washington, D.C.: Congressional Quarterly, 1997.

Summarizes conventions, with results of ballots, nominees, and party profiles.

Cotter, Cornelius P., James L. Gibson, John F. Bibby, and Robert J. Huckshorn. *Party Organizations in American Politics.* New York: Praeger, 1984.
Contains information on the characteristics of state parties and assessments of their organizational strength as of the late 1970s. Also rates states on support for and regulation of political parties.

David, Paul T. *Party Strength in the United States, 1872–1970.* Charlottesville, Va.: University Press of America, 1972. Updated for 1972 in *Journal of Politics* 36 (1972): 785–796; for 1974 in *Journal of Politics* 38 (1974): 416–425; for 1976 in *Journal of Politics* 40 (1976): 770–780.
Measures of party competition in the states covering several offices and an admirably lengthy historical span.

Miller, Warren E., and M. Kent Jennings. *Parties in Transition.* New York: Russell Sage, 1986.
Descriptions and analyses of delegates to the 1972–1980 Republican and Democratic national conventions.

Schapsmeier, Edward L., and Frederick H. Schapsmeier. *Political Parties and Civic Action Groups.* Westport, Conn.: Greenwood Press, 1981.
Brief descriptions of political organizations, current and past. Includes political parties, civic organizations, and all types of special interest groups.

Campaign Finance and Political Action Committees (PACs)

Alexander, Herbert E., and Anthony Corrado. *Financing the 1992 Election.* Armonk, N.Y.: M.E. Sharpe, 1995.
Detailed statistical coverage of fund-raising and spending in all phases of the presidential campaign; continues a series of books by Alexander on financing presidential campaigns since 1960.

Federal Election Commission. *Annual Report.* Washington, D.C.: U.S. Government Printing Office, 1976–.
Cumulative figures since the mid-1970s on contributions and spending in federal election campaigns; also information on political action committee (PAC) growth and activities.

———. *Reports on Financial Activity.* Washington, D.C.: U.S. Government Printing Office, 1980–.
Multivolume work reporting revenues and spending in congressional and presidential campaigns by candidates, party, and nonparty political committees (PACs); reports typically cover a two-year campaign cycle (for example, 1987–1988).

Heard, Alexander E. *The Costs of Democracy.* Chapel Hill, N.C.: University of North Carolina Press, 1960.
A classic work—published in 1960, when hard data on campaign contributions and spending were hard to secure.

Makinson, Larry. *Open Secrets: The Encyclopedia of Congressional Money and Politics.* 3d ed. Washington, D.C.: Congressional Quarterly, 1994.

Summary information about individual and PAC contributions, plus a listing of members of Congress and their sources of PAC money.

———. *The Price of Admission: Campaign Spending in the 1994 Election.* Washington, D.C.: Center for Responsive Politics, 1995.
Convenient compilation of total and PAC receipts for winners, total spending for winners and losers. One of a series of books since 1988.

Malbin, Michael J. *Parties, Interest Groups, and Campaign Finance Laws.* Washington, D.C.: American Enterprise Institute for Public Policy Research, 1980.
Early (1980) collection pulling together analyses in an increasingly investigated area.

Public Opinion

The American Enterprise. Washington, D.C.: American Enterprise Institute for Public Policy Research, 1990–. Bimonthly.
Regular "Public Opinion and Demographic Report" section presents poll data from several sources on selected topics; a more limited continuation of *Public Opinion,* previously published (1978–1989) by the same organization.

Converse, Philip E., Jean D. Dotson, Wendy J. Hoag, and William H. McGee III. *American Social Attitudes Data Sourcebook, 1947–1978.* Cambridge, Mass.: Harvard University Press, 1980.
Compendium of national polling data from the Survey Research Center at the University of Michigan, ranging across major social issues.

Dey, E. L., A. W. Astin, and W. F. Korn. *The American Freshman: Twenty-five Year Trends. Los Angeles: Higher Education Research Institute, University of California, Los Angeles, 1991.* National Norms for Fall, 1991–. Annual.
Reports of national surveys of college freshmen, including attitudes toward jobs, subject interests, and liberalism/conservatism.

The Gallup Poll: Public Opinion 1935–71. 3 vols. New York: Random House, 1972. Wilmington, Del.: Scholarly Resources, Inc., 1972–. Annual. Years 1972–1977 contained in 2 vols.
Poll data from thousands of Gallup surveys since 1935 on then-current topics, presented chronologically.

The Gallup Report: Political, Social and Economic Trends. Princeton, N.J.: American Institute of Public Opinion, 1965–. Monthly. Previously titled *Gallup Opinion Index* and *The Gallup Political Report.*
Compilation of recent Gallup public opinion data on political and social issues, often presented with historical trends.

Miller, Warren E., and Santa Traugott. *American National Election Studies Data Sourcebook, 1952–1986.* Cambridge, Mass.: Harvard University Press, 1989.
Compendium of polling data from the National Election Studies covering presidential and congressional election years.

Niemi, Richard G., John E. Mueller, and Tom W. Smith. *Trends in Public Opinion.* Westport, Conn.: Greenwood Press, 1989.
> Public opinion polls on numerous political and other topics; based primarily on the General Social Survey. Provides time series, often quite long, of identically worded questions.

Opinion Research Service. *American Public Opinion Index.* Louisville, Ky.: Opinion Research Service, 1981–. Annual.
> Indexes scientifically drawn samples of national, state, and local universes.

POLL (The Public Opinion Location Library). Storrs, Ct.: Roper Center for Public Opinion Research.
> A computer-based information retrieval system for public opinion survey data. Extensive coverage for 1955 to the present; some coverage of earlier years.

Public Opinion Quarterly. Chicago: University of Chicago Press, 1937–. Quarterly.
> Analysis of the mechanics and findings of survey research; regular thematic presentation of poll results.

The Public Perspective: A Roper Center Review of Public Opinion and Polling. Storrs, Ct.: The Roper Center for Public Opinion Research, 1989–. Bimonthly.
> Poll results and articles on public opinion and polling.

Wood, Floris W., ed. *An American Profile—Opinions and Behavior, 1972–1989.* Detroit: Gale, 1990.
> Poll results of the General Social Survey plus a chronology of world events.

Media

ADI Book. Beltsville, Md.: Arbitron Television. Annual.
> Reports of television usage, including demographic and market analyses.

Broadcasting Publications. *Broadcasting Cablecasting Yearbook.* Washington, D.C.: Broadcasting Publications, 1982–. Annual. Continues *Broadcasting Cable Yearbook,* which combined *Broadcasting Yearbook* (1968–1979) and *Broadcasting Cable Sourcebook* (1973–1979).
> International directory of radio, television, and cable industries as well as related fields; presents some statistical overviews.

Cable and Station Coverage Atlas, 1986. Indianapolis, Ind.: Warren Publishing, 1986–. Annual.
> Data on television stations and the growing reach of cable systems.

Editor & Publisher—The Fourth Estate. New York: Editor & Publisher Co., 1884–. Weekly.
> Weekly periodical covering the media.

Magazine Index. Belmont, Calif.: Information Access Co., 1977–.
> Indexes a long list of magazines, including a number of political news magazines.

Multimedia Audiences: Television Audiences. New York: Mediamark Research, Inc., 1979–. Semiannual.
Detailed reports of demographic and marketing segments of media audiences.

National Newspaper Index. Belmont, Calif.: Information Access Co., 1977–.
Indexes major national newspapers. The current list includes the *New York Times, Wall Street Journal, Christian Science Monitor, Los Angeles Times,* and the *Washington Post.* The *New York Times* has its own longstanding index.

Newsbank. New Canaan, Conn.: NewsBank, 1971–.
Microfiche collection of indexed articles from hundreds of American newspapers, from 1970 to the present, with newspapers from every state.

Nexus. Dayton, Ohio: Meade Data Central, Inc. On-line.
Full text of a number of newspapers and news, business, and medical magazines. Coverage varies, but is often since about 1980.

Nielsen Television Index. Northbrook, Ill.: A. C. Nielsen, 1955. Annual.
Overall and market section reports on television viewing and network program audiences.

Public Affairs Video Archives Catalogue. West Lafayette, Ind.: Public Affairs Video Archives, Purdue University, 1988–.
Archives of C-SPAN programming. Partial coverage 1987–September 1988, complete coverage since October 1988. Some other items, such as campaign commercials.

Sterling, Christopher H. *Electronic Media: A Guide to Trends in Broadcasting and Newer Technologies: 1920–1983.* New York: Praeger, 1984.
Data on growth, ownership, economics, employment and training, contents, audience and regulation of radio, television, and cable; strong on trends and time series.

Television Digest. *Television and Cable Factbook.* Washington, D.C.: Television Digest, 1946–. Annual.
Data on cable, television, and related industries; published in two volumes: "Stations" and "Cable and Services."

Television News Index and Abstracts. Nashville, Tenn.: Vanderbilt Television News Archives, Vanderbilt University, 1972–. Monthly.
Archives of nightly network news.

Congress

Bacon, Donald C., Roger H. Davidson, and Morton Keller, eds. *Encyclopedia of the United States Congress.* New York: Simon and Schuster, 1994.
Four volumes with more than 1,000 essays exploring the history, processes, and politics of Congress.

Balinski, Michel, and H. P. Young. *Fair Representation.* New Haven, Conn.: Yale University Press, 1982.
Analysis of methods of apportionment of representatives among the states.

Barone, Michael, and Grant Ujifusa. *The Almanac of American Politics.* Washington, D.C.: National Journal, 1972–. Biennial.

> Data-rich political analyses of each state, congressional district, representative, senator, and governor; current composition of committees; state maps with congressional district and county boundaries.

Congressional Quarterly. *American Leaders 1789–1994.* 3d ed. Washington, D.C.: Congressional Quarterly, 1994.

> Material on more than 11,000 members of Congress: age, religion, occupations, women, blacks, turnover, and shifts between chambers; data on congressional sessions, party composition, and leadership. Also includes biographical summaries of presidents, vice presidents, Supreme Court justices, and governors.

———. *Congress A to Z.* 2d ed. Washington, D.C.: Congressional Quarterly, 1993.

> Mostly essays but contains a number of useful listings of hard-to-find material such as treaties killed by the Senate, impeachment trials, women members of Congress, etc.

———. *Congress and the Nation.* Washington, D.C.: Congressional Quarterly, 1965–. Quadrennial. Years 1945–1964 contained in 1 vol.

> Akin to *Congressional Quarterly Almanac* (see below), but each volume now covers a presidential term.

———. *Congressional Districts in the 1990s.* Washington, D.C.: Congressional Quarterly, 1993.

> Profiles of each congressional district containing statistics on election returns, economic makeup, and demographics.

———. *Congressional Quarterly Almanac.* Washington, D.C.: Congressional Quarterly, 1945–. Annual.

> Each volume now covers legislation for a single session of Congress, appendices contain particularly useful data on Congress and politics.

——— ———. *Congressional Roll Call.* Washington, D.C.: Congressional Quarterly, 1974–. Annual.

> Compilation of every roll-call vote by every member of Congress and summary voting measures (ideology, party unity, presidential support, and voting participation).

———. *Congressional Yearbook.* Washington, D.C.: Congressinal Quarterly, 1994–. Annual.

> Summarizes each session of Congress.

———. *Guide to Congress.* 4th ed. Washington, D.C.: Congressional Quarterly, 1991.

> Massive, rich accounting of how Congress works and how it developed. Check here first for data covering all but the most recent years.

———. *Guide to 1990 Congressional Redistricting.* Parts I and II. Washington, D.C.: Congressional Quarterly, 1993.

> Descriptions and maps of 1990s districts. Contains a summary of the process by which districting plans were adopted.

———. *Landmark Legislation 1789–1994*. Washington, D.C., Congressional Quarterly, 1995.

Summary and historical and political background of major legislation and treaties.

———. *Politics in America*. Washington, D.C.: Congressional Quarterly, 1981–. Biennial.

Data-rich political analyses of each state, congressional district, representative, and senator; current composition of committees; state maps with congressional district and county boundaries.

(Year) Congressional Staff Directory. Mt. Vernon, Va.: Congressional Staff Directory, Ltd., 1959–. Biennial.

Names, addresses, phone numbers, and numerous biographies of senators' and representatives' personal staffs and the staffs of congressional committees and subcommittees.

CQ Staff Directories. Senate. *Biographical Directory of the American Congress, 1774–1996*. Washington, D.C.: Congressional Quarterly, 1997.

Biographies of U.S. senators and representatives to 1996.

Martis, Kenneth C. *The Historical Atlas of the United States Congressional Districts, 1789–1983*. New York: Free Press, 1983.

———. *Historical Atlas of Political Parties in the United States Congress, 1789–1989*. New York: Macmillan, 1989.

Congressional-based perspective on the surge and decline of political parties.

Martis, Kenneth C., and Gregory A. Elmes. *The Historical Atlas of State Power in Congress, 1790–1990*. Washington.: Congressional Quarterly, 1993.

Maps, tables, and text describing changes in apportionment among the states.

Nelson, Garrison, ed. *Committees in the U.S. Congress 1947–1992*. Washington, D.C.: Congressional Quarterly, 1993.

Two volumes giving definitive data on individual congressional committee membership.

Ornstein, Norman J., Thomas E. Mann, and Michael J. Malbin, eds. *Vital Statistics on Congress*. Washington, D.C.: Congressional Quarterly, 1980–. Biennial.

Data on characteristics of members, elections, campaign finance, committees, staff, expenses, workload, budgeting, and voting alignments; most data series stretch back to World War II, some longer.

Parsons, Stanley B. *United States Congressional Districts, 1883–1913*. New York: Greenwood Press, 1990.

Demographic and geographic data about American congressional districts between 1883 and 1913, continues coverage of volumes listed below.

Parsons, Stanley B., William W. Beach, Dan Hermann, and Michael J. Dubin. *United States Congressional Districts and Data*. 2 vols. Westport, Conn.: Greenwood Press, 1978, 1986.

These two volumes cover 1789–1883.

Sharp, Michael. *The Directory of Congressional Voting Scores and Interest Group Ratings.* 2 vols, 2d ed. Washington, D.C.: Congressional Quarterly, 1996.

Contains voting scores (e.g., presidential support) and interest group ratings (eleven groups, as available) for all members of Congress from 1947 to 1995.

Silbey, Joel, ed. *Encyclopedia of the American Legislative System: Studies of the Principal Structures, Processes, and Policies of Congress and State Legislatures Since the Colonial Era.* New York: Scribner's, 1994–1996.

Three volumes covering state and national legislative levels.

U.S. Bureau of the Census. *Congressional District Atlas.* Washington, D.C.: U.S. Government Printing Office, 1960–. Frequency varies.

Detailed maps of congressional districts.

———. *Congressional District Data Book.* Washington, D.C.: U.S. Government Printing Office, 1961–. Frequency varies.

Census data by congressional district with maps.

U.S. Congress. Joint Committee on Printing. *Official Congressional Directory.* Washington, D.C.: U.S. Government Printing Office, 1809–. Biennial (in recent years).

Biographical data on current members and statistics on the sessions of Congress. Useful reference source on committees and subcommittees, foreign representatives and consular offices in the United States, press representatives, and state delegations.

Presidency and Executive Branch

Congressional Quarterly. *Congressional Quarterly's Guide to the Presidency.* 2d ed. Michael Nelson, ed. Washington, D.C.: Congressional Quarterly, 1996.

Detailed coverage of numerous aspects of presidents and administrations. Focus on the institution complements CQ's volumes on elections.

———. *Federal Regulatory Directory.* Washington, D.C.: Congressional Quarterly, 1979–. Frequency varies.

Descriptions and data provide extensive profiles of the major and minor regulatory agencies—more than 100 in all.

———. *Presidential Elections Since 1789.* 6th ed. Washington, D.C.: Congressional Quarterly, 1995.

Facts and figures on presidential elections; electoral college vote since 1789; primary returns since 1912; major-party candidate vote shares state-by-state; minor candidate vote totals; recent turnout and party support trends.

———. *Washington Information Directory.* Washington, D.C.: Congressional Quarterly, 1975–. Annual.

Names, addresses, phone numbers, and heads of thousands of federal government and private, nonprofit agencies in and about Washington, D.C.

DeGregorio, William A., and Connie Jo Dikerson. *The Complete Book of U.S. Presidents.* 5th ed. New York: Random House, 1997.
Biographies of presidents and cabinet members.

(Year) Federal Staff Directory. Mt. Vernon, Va.: Congressional Staff Directory, Ltd., 1982–. Biennial.
Names, addresses, phone numbers, and numerous biographies of key executives and assistants in the executive branch of the federal government.

Kane, Joseph Nathan. *Facts About the Presidents: A Compilation of Biographical and Historical Information.* 6th ed. New York: H. H. Wilson, 1993.
Chapter on each president and comparative statistics on all presidents.

Ragsdale, Lyn. *Vital Statistics on the Presidency.* Washington, D.C.: Congressional Quarterly, 1996.
Data on presidents—their careers, elections, speeches and appearances, approval ratings, and congressional relationships; focus is on postwar presidencies, with some longer time series.

U.S. Government Organization Manual. Washington, D.C.: U.S. Government Printing Office, 1935–. Annual.
Official federal government handbook detailing the organization, activities, and current officials in legislative, judicial, and executive governmental units.

Weekly Compilation of Presidential Documents. Washington, D.C.: U.S. Government Printing Office.
Highly useful collection of presidential activities; includes texts of proclamations, executive orders, speeches, and other presidential communications; supplements include acts gaining presidential approval, nominations submitted for Senate confirmation, and a list of White House press releases; indexed.

The Judiciary

The American Bench. Sacramento, Calif.: Reginald Bishop Forster & Associates, 1977–. Biennial.
Comprehensive listing of all judges in the United States, along with brief biographies of approximately 18,000 judges.

Biskupic, Joan, and Elder Witt. *Guide to the U.S. Supreme Court.* 3d ed. Washington, D.C.: Congressional Quarterly, 1996.
Solid, broad coverage of the Supreme Court and the development of the law; an excellent source that also refers readers to additional references.

The Corrections Yearbook. South Salem, N.Y.: Criminal Justice Institute, 1980–. Annual.
Inmate populations, budgets, facilities, staff, and other data for jails with average daily populations of 200 or more.

Curran, Barbara A., et al. *The Lawyer Statistical Report: The U.S. Legal Profession in the 1990s.* Chicago: American Bar Foundation, 1994.

A statistical profile of a changing profession, by age, gender, and place of employment; also profiles 1990 lawyer populations within states, metropolitan, and nonmetropolitan areas.

Cushman, Clare, ed. *The Supreme Court Justices.* Washington, D.C.: Congressional Quarterly, 1995.
Biographies of justices, including backgrounds, careers, and issues and cases on which they passed judgment.

Director of the Administrative Office of the United States Courts. *Annual Report.* Washington, D.C.: U.S. Government Printing Office, 1940–. Annual.
Numerous statistics about the kind, timing, and disposition of cases in the federal courts and about numbers and workloads of federal judges.

Dornette, W. Stuart, and Robert R. Cross. *Federal Judiciary Almanac.* New York: Wiley, 1987.
Data on various aspects of the federal judiciary.

Epstein, Lee, Jeffrey Segal, Harold J. Spaeth, and Thomas A. Walker. *Supreme Court Compendium,* 2d ed. Washington, D.C.: CQ Press, 1996.
Data on characteristics of justices, caseload, voting alignments, public opinion, and legal developments.

Friedman, Leon, and Fred L. Israel, eds. *The Justices of the United States Supreme Court.* New York: Chelsea House, 1995.
Biography on each justice including several typical opinions; tables showing acts of Congress held unconstitutional, decisions overruled by subsequent decisions, and summary biographical data.

Judges of the United States. 2d ed. Washington, D.C.: U.S. Government Printing Office, 1983.
Biographies of all federal judges through 1983.

(Year) Judicial Staff Directory. Mt. Vernon, Va.: Congressional Staff Directory, Ltd., 1986–. Annual.
Personnel listings for federal courts, maps of court jurisdictions, biographies of judges and staffs.

State Court Caseload Statistics: Annual Report. Williamsburg, Va.: Conference of State Court Administrators and the National Center for State Courts, 1976–. Annual.
Data on judicial workload in the state courts.

Widman, Iris J., and Mark J. Handler, comps. *Federal Judges and Justices: A Current Listing of Nominations, Confirmations, Elevations, Resignations, Retirements.* Littleton, Colo.: Rothman, 1987.
Useful compendium with revealing subtitle.

Federalism

Alexander, Herbert E., and Mike Eberts. *Public Financing of State Elections: A Data Book and Election Guide to Public Funding of Political Parties and Candidates in Twenty States.* Los Angeles: Citizens' Research Foundation, 1986.
  Important compendium for understanding and comparing state regulation of campaign finances.

Beyle, Thad, ed. *State Government.* Washington, D.C.: Congressional Quarterly, 1985–. Annual.
  Analysis of recent developments in state governments; reprints articles from a diverse set of state publications.

The Book of the States. Lexington, Ky.: Council of State Governments, 1935–. Biennial.
  Definitive reference to the current data on state government activities across the board.

Campaign Finance: Ethics and Lobby Law Blue Book. Lexington, Ky.: Council on Governmental Ethics Laws, Council of State Governments, 1990.
  Information about ethics laws, campaign finance reports and limits, personal disclosure requirements, and lobby laws in the states and in the Canadian provinces.

Campaign Finance Law. Washington, D.C.: D. T. Skelton Service Associates, Inc., Federal Election Commission's National Clearinghouse of Election Administration, 1981–. Annual.
  Rules and regulations for campaign financing in the states and nation.

Carpenter, Allan, and Carl Provorse. *Facts About the Cities.* 2d ed. New York: H. W. Wilson, 1996.
  Data on 300 cities, culled from federal sources. Includes limited political information (e.g., number of women in governing body).

The County Year Book. Washington, D.C.: National Association of Counties and International City Management Association, 1975–. Annual.
  Surveys issues and trends in county government and administration; a reliable source of data on county government.

Holli, Melvin G., and Peter Jones, eds. *Biographical Dictionary of American Mayors, 1820–1980.* Westport, Conn.: Greenwood Press, 1981.
  Covers 679 mayors in over a dozen cities; contains lists categorizing mayors by characteristics such as party, religion, and ethnicity.

Hornor, Edith R., ed. *Almanac of the 50 States: Basic Data Profiles with Comparative Tables.* Palo Alto, Calif.: Information Publications, 1985–. Annual.
  State-level summaries of data on government and elections, state expenditures, federal aid, population characteristics, crime, etc.

International City Management Association. *The Municipal Year Book.* New York: International City Management Association, 1934–. Annual.
  Reliable source for urban data and developments.

Lilley III, William, Laurence J. DeFranco, and William M. Diefenderfer III. *The Almanac of State Legislatures.* Washington, D.C., Congressional Quarterly, 1995.

Maps and statistical profiles of the geographic, economic, and political composition of state legislative districts.

———. *The State Atlas of Political and Cultural Diversity.* Washington, D.C.: Congressional Quarterly, 1996.

Racial and ancestral make-up of top state legislative districts. A diskette that is available contains data on all state legislative districts.

Marlin, John Tepper, and James S. Avery. *The Book of American City Rankings.* New York: Facts on File, 1983.

Nearly 300 thematic tables with data on the 100 largest U.S. cities.

Meltzer, Ellen. *The New Book of American Rankings.* 3d ed. New York: Facts on File, 1987.

State rankings and statistics on over 300 items. Some of the material is now dated.

National Directory of State Agencies. Bethesda, Md.: National Standards Association, 1976–. Annual since 1986.

Names of agency heads, addresses, and phone numbers of state agencies.

Significant Features of Fiscal Federalism. Washington, D.C.: U.S. Advisory Commission on Intergovernmental Relations, 1976–. Annual.

Convenient compilation of comparative state data on revenues, expenditures, and related matters; tables and figures present comparisons across states as well as state-by-state in-depth treatment.

State Administrative Officials Classified by Functions. Lexington, Ky.: Council of State Governments, 1977–. Biennial.

Lists state administrative officials by function; before 1977 issued as a supplement to *The Book of the States.*

State Elective Officials and the Legislatures. Lexington, Ky.: Council of State Governments, 1977–. Biennial.

Lists state elected officials and legislators; before 1977 issued as a supplement to *The Book of the States.*

State Information Book. Rockville, Md.: Infax, 1973–. Biennial.

Some statistics, but emphasizes names, addresses, phone numbers, and heads of departments and agencies, plus county seats and phone numbers.

State Legislative Sourcebook. Topeka, Kan.: Government Research Service, 1986–. Annual.

Tells how to find detailed information about state legislative activity, including offices, addresses, phone numbers, and price lists. State statistical abstracts. A list of state statistical abstracts (or near equivalents) can be found in recent editions of the *Statistical Abstract of the United States.* They are of widely varying quality.

Tax Foundation. *Facts and Figures on Government Finance.* Englewood Cliffs, N.J.: Prentice Hall, 1941–. Annual.

Data on government revenues, spending, and debt at the federal, state, and local levels.

The Transformation in American Politics: Implications for Federalism. Washington, D.C.: U.S. Advisory Commission on Intergovernmental Relations, 1986.

Wide-ranging treatment (much broader than the subtitle implies) of major recent trends in American politics with emphasis on relevant data.

U.S. Bureau of the Census. *Census of Governments.* Washington, D.C.: U.S. Government Printing Office, 1972–. Frequency varies.

Numbers and characteristics of governments, including special district governments dealing with subjects such as schools, parks and recreation, and sewage.

————. *City Government Finances; Government Finances; State Government Finances.* Washington, D.C.: U.S. Government Printing Office, 1909–; 1916–; 1965——. Annual.

These three series summarize government finances at city and state levels; great detail for states and the larger cities.

————. *County and City Data Book.* Washington, D.C.: U.S. Government Printing Office, 1952–. Frequency varies.

Demographic, economic, health, agricultural, and other information about counties, cities, and towns. Presidential voting by county.

————. *State and Metropolitan Area Data Book.* Washington, D.C.: U.S. Government Printing Office, 1979–. Frequency varies.

Demographic, economic, health, education, and other data about states and metropolitan statistical areas.

Foreign and Military Policy

Cochran, Thomas B., et al. *Nuclear Weapons Databook.* 2 vols. Cambridge, Mass.: Ballinger, 1987, 1990.

Descriptions, specifications, and deployments of American and Soviet nuclear weapons systems.

Joint Chiefs of Staff. *Military Posture for Fiscal Year (Year).* Washington, D.C.: U.S. Government Printing Office. Annual.

Brief review of all aspects of military preparedness of the U.S. and of the world military environment.

The Military Balance. London: International Institute of Strategic Studies, 1959–. Annual.

Statistical analysis of military forces and defense spending; figures given for countries and regional organizations such as NATO (North Atlantic Treaty Organization).

U.S. Arms Control and Disarmament Agency. *World Military Expenditures and Arms Transfers.* Washington, D.C.: U.S. Government Printing Office, 1965–. Annual (title varies).

Annual statistical accounts of military spending and the arms race.

U.S. Department of State. *Patterns of Global Terrorism.* Washington, D.C.: U.S. Department of State, 1983–. Annual.
Details on terrorist incidents around the world.

World Armaments and Disarmament: SIPRI Yearbook. Stockholm: Almqvist & Wiksell, New York: Oxford University Press, 1970–. Annual.
Overview of the arms race and efforts to promote disarmament; detailed data on world military spending.

Social Policy

Anderton, Douglas L., Richard E. Barrett, and Donald J. Bogue. *The Population of the United States.* 3d ed. New York: Free Press, 1997.
Extensive description of the nation's population characteristics, focusing on the years since 1960; topics include poverty, income, housing, educational attainment, ethnicity, migration, and so forth.

Black Elected Officials: A National Roster. Washington, D.C.: Joint Center for Political and Economic Studies, 1971–. Annual.
Lists black elected officials by office and address with summary tabulations on the historical trends and comparative state figures.

Center for the American Woman and Politics, National Information Bank on Women in Public Office. Eagleton Institute of Politics, Rutgers University.
Various reports provide data on women in public office, electoral turnout of women, and so forth. Both historical and contemporary information.

National Center for Health Statistics. *Monthly Vital Statistics Report.* Hyattsville, Md.: U.S. Department of Health and Human Services. 1952–.
Statistical reports and analyses of various aspects of health.

National Roster of Hispanic Elected Officials, (Year). Washington, D.C.: National Association of Latino Elected and Appointed Officials Education Fund, no date. Annual.
Lists Hispanic elected officials by office and state.

Schick, Frank L., and Renee Schick. *Statistical Handbook on U.S. Hispanics.* Phoenix: Oryx, 1991.
Numerous tables about social and political characteristics of U.S. Hispanics.

The State of Black America. New York: National Urban League, 1976–. Annual.
Yearly review assessing the conditions of blacks in the nation.

U.S. Department of Education. Center for Statistics. *Digest of Education Statistics.* Washington, D.C.: U.S. Government Printing Office, 1962–. Annual.
Current data on school enrollments, teachers, retention rates, educational attainment, finances, achievement, schools and school districts, federal education programs, and so forth.

U.S. Department of Education. Office of Educational Research and Improvement. *The Condition of Education: A Statistical Report.* Washington, D.C.: U.S. Government Printing Office, 1975–.

Data survey reviewing trends in elementary, secondary, and higher education; data portray student characteristics and performance as well as fiscal, material, and human resources deployed in education.

U.S. Department of Energy. Energy Information Administration. *Annual Energy Review.* Washington, D.C.: U.S. Government Printing Office, 1977–.

Data on energy supply and disposition, exploration, and reserves.

U.S. Department of Justice. Bureau of Criminal Justice Statistics. *Sourcebook of Criminal Justice Statistics.* Washington, D.C.: U.S. Government Printing Office, 1974–. Annual.

Brings together nationwide statistical data on the criminal justice system, public opinion, illegal activities, persons arrested, judicial proceedings, and persons under correctional supervision.

U.S. Department of Justice. Federal Bureau of Investigation. *Uniform Crime Reports for the United States.* Washington, D.C.: U.S. Government Printing Office, 1930–. Annual.

Variety of charts and tables on types and frequencies of crimes, persons arrested, and law enforcement personnel; several forty-year trends.

Economic Policy

Frumkin, Norman. *Guide to Economic Indicators.* 2d ed. Armonk, N.Y.: M. E. Sharpe, 1994.

Content, accuracy, relevance, and sources for fifty economic indicators.

(Year) Historical Chart Book. Washington, D.C.: Board of Governors of the Federal Reserve System, 1965–. Annual.

Long-range financial and business data, mostly from series maintained by the Federal Reserve Board.

Hoel, Arline Alchian, Kenneth W. Clarkson, and Roger LeRoy Miller. *Economics Sourcebook of Government Statistics.* Lexington, Mass.: Lexington Books, 1983.

Ranges across inflation, general business conditions, interest rates, employment and earnings, international finance and trade, and the budget; critical discussions of over fifty major statistical series produced by the federal government in these areas; also refers to primary and secondary sources containing the series.

Office of Management and Budget. *Budget of the United States Government.* Washington, D.C.: U.S. Government Printing Office. Annual.

Multivolume annual presentation of data on federal revenues and expenditures; while the details of the federal budget documents may be numbing to the uninitiated, even the novice can find two volumes particularly useful: *Historical Tables* and *The Budget in Brief,* both of which are designed for the general public.

O'Hara, Frederick M. *Handbook of United States Economic and Financial Indicators.* 2d ed. Westport, Conn.: Greenwood Press, 1997.
> Defines several hundred economic indicators culled from over fifty sources; provides information on publication schedules and historical trends.

Troy, Leo, and Neil Sheflin. *U.S. Union Sourcebook.* West Orange, N.J.: Industrial Relations Data and Information Services, 1985.
> Excellent source of statistical information on membership in American and Canadian unions; long historical coverage.

U.S. Bureau of Labor Statistics. *Employment and Earnings.* Washington, D.C.: U.S. Government Printing Office, 1961–. Annual.
> Various statistics on the nation's nonfarm workforce, including lengthy time series with data beginning in 1909.

———. *Handbook of Labor Statistics.* Washington, D.C.: U.S. Government Printing Office, 1927–. Frequency varies.
> Collection of data concerning employment, unemployment, earnings, school enrollment and educational attainment, productivity, prices, strikes, and so forth.

———. *Monthly Labor Review.* Washington, D.C.: U.S. Government Printing Office, 1915–.
> Covers most Bureau of Labor Statistics series, giving data concerning employment, hours, pay, strikes, prices and inflation, and so forth.

U.S. Council of Economic Advisers. *Economic Indicators.* Washington, D.C.: U.S. Government Printing Office, 1948–. Monthly.
> Data on total output, income, and spending; employment, unemployment, and wages; production and business activity; prices, currency, credit, and security markets; and federal finance.

U.S. Department of Agriculture. *Agricultural Statistics.* Washington, D.C.: U.S. Government Printing Office, 1937–. Annual.
> Vast array of agricultural data, including politically relevant displays, such as farm economic trends, price-support programs, and agricultural imports and exports.

U.S. Department of Commerce. *Survey of Current Business.* Washington, D.C.: U.S. Government Printing Office, 1921–. Monthly.
> Monthly publication with data on U.S. income and trade developments.

U.S. President. *The Economic Report of the President.* Washington, D.C.: U.S. Government Printing Office, 1947–. Annual.
> Reviews the national economic situation; presents a substantial appendix with long time series of critical economic data.

World Bank. *World Development Report.* New York: Oxford University Press, 1978–. Annual.
> Analysis of and data on worldwide capital and economic indicators, with an emphasis on development.

Miscellaneous

Some politically relevant information is found in general purpose almanacs. Such information is usually limited, but these sources have the advantage of being readily available.

Information Please Almanac: Atlas and Yearbook. Boston: Houghton Mifflin, 1947–. Annual.

Reader's Digest Almanac. Pleasantville, N.Y.: Reader's Digest, 1966–. Annual.

The World Almanac and Book of Facts. New York: Pharos Books, 1868–. Annual since 1886.

Index